THE FAITH WE LIVE BY

the FAITH we live by

By

A Team of Daughters of St. Paul

Second printing.

ST. PAUL EDITIONS

NIHIL OBSTAT:
ALBERT W. LOW
Diocesan Censor Deputatus

IMPRIMATUR:
✠ RICHARD CARDINAL CUSHING
Archbishop of Boston

October 10, 1969

ACKNOWLEDGMENTS

The Daughters of St. Paul express their deep gratitude to Rev. Peter Sullivan for his careful editing of this volume.

The quotation on pages 177-178 is reprinted from *The Risen Lord* by James Sullivan, by permission of the publishers GILL AND MACMILLAN.

Biblical quotations: THE CONFRATERNITY OF CHRISTIAN DOCTRINE EDITION. Addresses of Pope Paul VI: NC NEWS SERVICE TRANSLATION.

Library of Congress Catalog Card Number: 68—59044

—— Printed by the *Daughters of St. Paul*
50 St. Paul's Avenue, Jamaica Plain,
Boston, Mass. 02130

A LIVING FAITH, A FAITHFUL LIFE—is this not what we all desire? To iron out mediocrity, to rebel against hypocrisy in our lives—this is the negative approach to a living faith. What is its positive one? A union of life and faith.

Souls may be hesitant to accept Christ and His Church, because we do not mirror Him as He is. Let us forcefully take the step forward to double for Christ.

Life can be barren and useless or vitalizing and committed. For the fearless and the restless the fusion of faith with life is heroic idealism with lasting repercussions in our world.

Steep yourself in truth through the *Credo of the People of God* explained in these pages. Dwell at length on the living Christ—encounter Him—that He may permeate your activity. His grace will build on your nature a living witness to Himself. As Pope Paul once said, "Faith is the 'yes' which permits divine thought to enter ours. It pervades the whole personality of the believer and engages his entire manner of living. Faith is the step by which he crosses the threshold of God's kingdom and enters upon the path of his eternal destiny."

CONTENTS

13

1

FOR PEACE OF MIND AND ETERNAL HAPPINESS

"Let no one deceive himself by believing that he has known God, if he confesses Him with a dead faith, that is, a faith without good works.... Belief in God is to love Him by believing, to observe His law, to go to Him and, believing, to incorporate oneself in Him. This is the faith God requires of us" (St. Augustine).

Already we are approaching the end of the twentieth century, an era astounding for change and progress, especially since the end of World War II. So breathtaking has been our technological development that man now goes to the moon, circles it many times, lands, stays there for hours, and then returns safely to earth.[1] However, scientific feats have not been matched by a corresponding improvement in morality. The world today is in a greater state of religious confusion than perhaps at any other period of its history. Strangely enough, increased knowledge, leading to extensive engineering achievement, is one of the root causes of the trouble. Another, and the most important, is the fact that multitudes of men have lost their religious bearings. The great truths of faith no longer influence the mind or will. That is why ours is an era forever tormented by doubts and fears. How easy it is to give way to despair, to resort to drugs, alcohol, sensual pleasure, violence even, in order to relieve the tension!

No wonder we are confused when we read the printed word, listen to the radio, go to the movies and watch television. Many have slipped their moorings and are drifting rudderless in uncharted and highly dangerous seas.

What the modern world must do is adjust its sights properly. When you look through a pair of binoculars at an

---

1. During their almost three hours of extra-vehicular activity on the moon's surface on the night of Sunday, July 20, 1969, America's two astronauts, Commanders Armstrong and Aldrin planted the United States flag, fixed a solar wind gauge, placed a gnomen to measure shadows cast by the sun, set up a seismometer to detect possible lunar quakes, drove into the ground a long tube to collect soil samples and positioned a bank of one-hundred small reflectors to trap laser beams flashed upon them from earth. They also collected many pounds of rock samples for future geological analysis.

object, or train a telescope on a planet, you keep manipulating
the instrument until everything is in proper focus. Then the
picture becomes crisp and clear. If we are to have peace of
mind in this world, and eternal happiness in the next, we
must address ourselves immediately to the task of reassessing
our values, of putting essential truths first. Otherwise, we run
the risk of being caught up by every passing fad that poses as
a solution for human ills. Christ Himself has warned us against
this.

"For many will come in my name, saying, 'I am the
Christ,' and they will lead many astray. For you shall hear of
wars and rumors of wars. Take care that you do not be alarmed,
for these things must come to pass, but the end is not yet.
For nation will rise against nation, and kingdom against kingdom; and there will be pestilences and famines and earthquakes in various places. But all these things are the beginning of sorrows.

"Then they will deliver you up to tribulation, and will
put you to death; and you will be hated by all nations for my
name's sake. And then many will fall away, and will betray
one another, and will hate one another. And many false
prophets will arise, and will lead many astray. And because
iniquity will abound, the charity of the many will grow cold.
But whoever perseveres to the end, he shall be saved" (Mt.
24:4-13).

We said that if man is to save himself he must properly
adjust his sights. How is this to be done? In one way only—
he must look at things through the eyes of Christ. Since Jesus
is God—a truth we will deal with later in these pages—it
follows that He has all the answers, certainly those to our
spiritual problems. Solutions will be found, not only in the
doctrine He taught, but likewise in His very Person and life:
for true religion, as we are beginning to find out more and
more, is a dynamic, personal encounter with the God-Man,
Jesus of Nazareth. When we meet Him face to face, all misgivings vanish.

Search the Scriptures and find this out for yourself. In
the first chapter of St. John's Gospel we read how after hearing one of His sermons, two disciples followed Him. Our
Lord asked them: "What do you seek?" They replied: "Where
do you live?" Jesus said to them: "Come and see." St. John
continues: "They came and saw where he was staying and
they stayed with him that day."

Here indeed is a remarkable event. Up until then they had been ignorant of His very existence. Yet, on becoming better acquainted with Him, so magnetic was His personality, so sure were they that they could rely on Him, that they had finally found the Messiah, that they could not tear themselves away from Him and later went out looking for others to bring to Him

Then there was Nicodemus, a Pharisee, an influential man in the Jewish community. He came secretly to Jesus by night and listened fascinated while the Master solved his difficulties and traced the road to eternal life.

The Samaritan woman drawing water at the well and who was in deep spiritual trouble—she had had five husbands and the one with whom she was then living was not her lawful spouse—was astounded to find He could read her very mind! Then unable to contain herself any longer, she ran and brought back all the townspeople to greet Him!

Also there was Mary of Bethany, the sister of Lazarus. On one occasion Jesus visited her and her sister Martha at their home. Martha busied herself preparing the meal, while Mary sat at the feet of Christ, treasuring every word that fell from His lips. Realizing that she was doing all the work and that Mary was contributing nothing, woman-like Martha complained to Jesus: "Lord, is it no concern of yours that my sister has left me to serve alone? Tell her therefore to help me." What was Christ's answer? Ponder it deeply, for here again you will see Him once more in His role of Master and Teacher, always ready with the right answer to every problem. "Martha, Martha, you are anxious and troubled about many things; and yet only one thing is needful. Mary has chosen the better part, and it will not be taken away from her."

On one occasion, the rulers wanted to arrest Christ and sent policemen to seize Him. But they returned empty-handed. "Why have you not brought him?" inquired the authorities and received the answer: "Never did man speak as this man."

Finally, there is that magnificent episode when after the resurrection He appeared to two disciples on their way to Emmaus. So captivating was this Stranger that they too were loath to let Him go! "Stay with us," they pleaded, "for it is getting toward evening and the day is now far spent." Then during the evening meal He revealed Himself to them in the breaking of bread, and at once they knew the secret of His influence. "Was not our heart burning within us while he was speaking on the road and explaining to us the Scriptures?" they kept telling one another. "Explain to us the Scriptures!" Yes, indeed! The omniscient Teacher had solved all their difficulties.

Jesus Christ strides through the pages of the Gospel, absolutely certain of Himself. What other religious leader in any age has been so sure as He has been? Listen to the words in which He describes Himself and His mission.

"If anyone thirst, let him come to me and drink" (Jn. 7:37).

"If you abide in my word, you shall be my disciples indeed, and you shall know the truth and the truth shall make you free" (Jn. 8:31-32).

"You call me Master and Lord and you say well, for so I am" (Jn. 13:13).

"I am the way and the truth and the life. No one comes to the Father but through me" (Jn. 14:5-6).

"One only is your Master: the Christ" (Mt. 23:10).

"He that shall drink of the water that I will give him shall not thirst for ever. But the water that I will give him shall become in him a fountain of water, springing up into life everlasting" (Jn. 4:13-14).

No wonder Peter cried out: "Lord, to whom shall we go? You have the words of eternal life. And we have come to believe and to know that you are the Christ, the Son of God" (Jn. 6:69-70).

CHALLENGE

To follow Christ is to surrender oneself to Him, to enter wholeheartedly on His way. It takes heroism — in fact, the *habit of heroism*. It calls for our service and rejects selfishness.

By this kind of love a man is saved. He who lives for himself never finds the happiness he is looking for.

Live for Christ! Glory in Him!

Profession of Faith

The teachings and actions of Jesus Christ are to be found in the four Gospels, but since they were written nearly two thousand years ago much has happened in the Church. Nothing new has been added to the original deposit of faith. But there has been a development. Dogmas have been proclaimed in various centuries, so that today the Catholic Church offers for our belief a body of truths that it has taken centuries to clarify. Viewing the sad state of mankind today, Pope Paul VI considered it necessary to proclaim formally this body of truth once again in the profession of faith called "The Credo of the People of God." By doing so, he hoped that it would prove a beacon light to those who are searching for the answers to those complex problems that gnaw at the souls of men. The pages that follow will analyze in detail this profession of faith of Christ's Vicar on earth.

We now give in full the "Credo" of Pope Paul VI. The reader should ponder it carefully, so that it will sink into the mind and remain there to influence his whole life. As he goes from chapter to chapter in this present work he should refer back to it constantly, for in that way, the Credo will appear to him as one whole and he will reap the greatest possible benefit from it. Here now is the "Credo" of Pope Paul VI.

The "Credo" of the People of God

We believe in one only God, Father, Son and Holy Spirit, creator of things visible such as this world in which our transient life passes, of things invisible such as the pure spirits which are also called angels,[1] and creator in each man of his spiritual and immortal soul.

We believe that this only God is absolutely one in His infinitely holy essence as also in all His perfections, in His omnipotence, His infinite knowledge, His providence, His will and His love. He is "He who is," as He revealed to Moses;[2] and He is "love," as the apostle John teaches us:[3] so that these two names, being and love, express ineffably the same divine reality of Him who has wished to make Himself known to us, and who, "dwelling in light inaccessible,"[4] is in Himself above every name, above every thing and above every created intellect. God alone can give us right and full knowledge of this reality by revealing Himself as Father, Son and Holy Spirit, in whose eternal life we are by grace called to share, here below in the obscurity of faith and after death in eternal light. The mutual bonds which eternally constitute the Three Persons, who are each one and the same divine being, are the blessed inmost life of God thrice holy, infinitely beyond all that we can conceive in human measure.[5]

He
that shall
drink
of the
water
that I will
give him
shall not
thirst
forever
John 4

We give thanks, however, to the divine goodness that very many believers can testify with us before men to the unity of God, even though they know not the mystery of the most holy Trinity.

We believe then in the Father who eternally begets the Son; in the Son, the Word of God, who is eternally begotten; in the Holy Spirit, the uncreated Person who proceeds from the Father and the Son as their eternal love. Thus in the Three Divine Persons, coeternal and coequal with one another, [6] the life and beatitude of God perfectly one superabound and are consummated in the supreme excellence and glory proper to uncreated being, and always "there should be venerated unity in the Trinity and Trinity in the unity." [7]

We believe in our Lord Jesus Christ, who is the Son of God. He is the Eternal Word, born of the Father before time began, and one in substance with the Father, [8] and through Him all things were made. He was incarnate of the Virgin Mary by the power of the Holy Spirit, and was made man; equal therefore to the Father according to His divinity, and inferior to the Father according to His humanity; [9] and Himself one, not by some impossible confusion of His natures, but by the unity of His person. [10]

He dwelt among us, full of grace and truth. He proclaimed and established the Kingdom of God and made us know in Himself the Father. He gave us His new commandment to love one another as He loved us. He taught us the way of the beatitudes of the Gospel: poverty in spirit, meekness, suffering borne with patience, thirst after justice, mercy, purity of heart, will for peace, persecution suffered for justice sake. Under Pontius Pilate He suffered — the Lamb of God bearing on Himself the sins of the world, and He died for us on the cross, saving us by His redeeming blood. He was buried, and, of His own power, rose on the third day, raising us by His resurrection to that sharing in the divine life which is the life of grace. He ascended to heaven, and He will come again, this time in glory, to judge the living and the dead: each according to his merits — those who have responded to the love and piety of God going to eternal life, those who have refused them to the end going to the fire that is not extinguished.

And His Kingdom will have no end.

We believe in the Holy Spirit, who is Lord, and Giver of life, who is adored and glorified together with the Father and the Son. He spoke to us by the prophets; He was sent by Christ after His resurrection and His ascension to the Father; He illuminates, vivifies, protects and guides the Church; He purifies the Church's members if they do not shun His grace. His action, which penetrates to the inmost of the soul, enables man to respond to the call of Jesus: Be perfect as your Heavenly Father is perfect (Mt. 5:48).

We believe that Mary is the Mother, who remained ever a Virgin, of the Incarnate Word, our God and Savior Jesus Christ,[11] and that by reason of this singular election, she was, in consideration of the merits of her Son, redeemed in a more eminent manner,[12] preserved from all stain of original sin[13] and filled with the gift of grace more than all other creatures.[14]

Joined by a close and indissoluble bond to the Mysteries of the Incarnation and Redemption,[15] the Blessed Virgin, the Immaculate, was at the end of her earthly life raised body and soul to heavenly glory[16] and likened to her risen Son in anticipation of the future lot of all the just; and we believe that the Blessed Mother of God, the New Eve, Mother of the Church,[17] continues in heaven her maternal role with regard to Christ's members, cooperating with the birth and growth of divine life in the souls of the redeemed.[18]

We believe that in Adam all have sinned, which means that the original offense committed by him caused human nature, common to all men, to fall to a state in which it bears the consequences of that offense, and which is not the state in which it was at first in our first parents — established as they were in holiness and justice, and in which man knew neither evil nor death. It is human nature so fallen, stripped of the grace that clothed it, injured in its own natural powers and subjected to the dominion of death, that is transmitted to all men, and it is in this sense that every man is born in sin. We therefore hold, with the Council of Trent, that original sin, is transmitted with human nature, "not by imitation, but by propagation" and that it is thus "proper to everyone." [19]

We believe that Our Lord Jesus Christ, by the sacrifice of the cross redeemed us from original sin and all the personal sins committed by each one of us, so that, in accordance with the word of the apostle, "where sin abounded, grace did more abound." [20]

We believe in one Baptism instituted by our Lord Jesus Christ for the remission of sins. Baptism should be administered even to little children who have not yet been able to be guilty of any personal sin, in order that, though born deprived of supernatural grace, they may be reborn "of water and the Holy Spirit" to the divine life in Christ Jesus. [21]

We believe in one, holy, catholic, and apostolic Church, built by Jesus Christ on that rock which is Peter. She is the Mystical Body of Christ; at the same time a visible society instituted with hierarchical organs, and a spiritual community; the Church on earth, the pilgrim People of God here below, and the Church filled with heavenly blessings; the germ and the first fruits of the Kingdom of God, through which the work and the sufferings of Redemption are continued throughout human history, and which looks for its perfect accomplishment beyond time in glory. [22] In the course of time, the Lord Jesus forms His Church by means of the sacraments emanating from His plenitude. [23] By these she makes her members participants in the Mystery of the Death and Resurrection of Christ, in the grace of the Holy Spirit who gives her life and movement. [24] She is therefore holy, though she has sinners in her bosom, because she herself has no other life but that of grace: it is by living by her life that her members are sanctified; it is by removing themselves from her life that they fall into sins and disorders that prevent the radiation of her sanctity. This is why she suffers and does penance for these offenses, of which she has the power to heal her children through the blood of Christ and the gift of the Holy Spirit.

Heiress of the divine promises and daughter of Abraham according to the Spirit, through that Israel whose scriptures she lovingly guards, and whose patriarchs and prophets she venerates; founded upon the apostles and handing on from century to century their ever-living word and their powers as pastors in the successor of Peter and the bishops in communion with him; perpetually assisted by the Holy Spirit, she has the charge of guarding, teaching, explaining and spreading the Truth which God revealed in a then veiled manner by the prophets, and fully by the Lord Jesus. We believe all that is contained in the word of God written or handed down, and that the Church proposes for belief as divinely revealed, whether by a solemn judgment or by the ordinary and universal magisterium.[25] We believe in the infallibility enjoyed by the successor of Peter when he teaches ex cathedra as pastor and teacher of all the faithful,[26] and which is assured also to the episcopal body when it exercises with him the supreme magisterium.[27]

We believe that the Church founded by Jesus Christ and for which He prayed is indefectibly one in faith, worship and the bond of hierarchical communion. In the bosom of this Church, the rich variety of liturgical rites and the legitimate diversity of theological and spiritual heritages and special disciplines, far from injuring her unity, make it more manifest.[28]

Recognizing also the existence, outside the organism of the Church of Christ, of numerous elements of truth and sanctification which belong to her as her own and tend to Catholic unity,[29] and believing in the action of the Holy Spirit who stirs up in the heart of the disciples of Christ love of this unity,[30] we entertain the hope that the Christians who are not yet in the full communion of the one only Church will one day be reunited in one flock with one only shepherd.

We believe that the Church is necessary for salvation, because Christ, who is the sole mediator and way of salvation, renders Himself present for us in His body which is the Church.[31] But the divine design of salvation embraces all men; and those who without fault on their part do not know the Gospel of Christ and His Church, but seek God sincerely, and under the influence of grace endeavor to do His will as recognized through the promptings of their conscience, they, in a number known only to God, can obtain salvation.[32]

We believe that the Mass, celebrated by the priest representing the person of Christ by virtue of the power received through the sacrament of Orders, and offered by him in the name of Christ and the members of His Mystical Body, is the sacrifice of Calvary rendered sacramentally present on our altars. We believe that as the bread and wine consecrated by the Lord at the Last Supper were changed into His body and His blood which were to be offered for us on the cross, likewise the bread and wine consecrated by the priest are changed into the body and blood of Christ enthroned gloriously in heaven, and we believe that the mysterious presence of the Lord, under what continues to appear to our senses as before, is a true, real and substantial presence.[33]

Christ cannot be thus present in this sacrament except by the change into His body of the reality itself of the bread and the change into His blood of the reality itself of the wine, leaving unchanged only the properties of the bread and wine which our senses perceive. This mysterious change is very appropriately called by the Church "transubstantiation." Every theological explanation which seeks some understanding of this mystery must, in order to be in accord with Catholic faith, maintain that in the reality itself, independently of our mind, the bread and wine have ceased to exist after the Consecration, so that it is the adorable body and blood of the Lord Jesus that from then on are really before us under the sacramental species of bread and wine,[34] as the Lord willed it, in order to give Himself to us as food and to associate us with the unity of His Mystical Body.[35]

The unique and indivisible existence of the Lord glorious in heaven is not multiplied, but is rendered present by the sacrament in the many places on earth where Mass is celebrated. And this existence remains present, after the sacrifice, in the Blessed Sacrament which is, in the tabernacle, the living heart of each of our churches. And it is our very sweet duty to honor and adore in the blessed Host which our eyes see, the Incarnate Word whom they cannot see, and who, without leaving heaven, is made present before us.

We confess that the Kingdom of God begun here below in the Church of Christ is not of this world whose form is passing, and that its proper growth cannot be confounded with the progress of civilization, of science or of human technology, but that it consists in an ever more profound knowledge of the unfathomable riches of Christ, an ever stronger hope in eternal blessings, an ever more ardent response to the love of God, and an ever more generous bestowal of grace and holiness among men. But it is this same love which induces the Church to concern herself constantly about the true temporal welfare of men. Without ceasing to recall to her children that they have not here a lasting dwelling, she also urges them to contribute, each according to his vocation and his means, to the welfare of their earthly city, to promote justice, peace and brotherhood among men, to give their aid freely to their brothers, especially to the poorest and most unfortunate. The deep solicitude of the Church, the Spouse of Christ, for the needs of men, for their joys and hopes, their griefs and efforts, is therefore nothing other than her great desire to be present to them, in order to illuminate them with the light of Christ and to gather them all in Him, their only Savior. This solicitude can never mean that the Church conform herself to the things of this world, or that she lessen the ardor of her expectation of her Lord and of the eternal Kingdom.

We believe in the life eternal. We believe that the souls of all those who die in the grace of Christ—whether they must still be purified in purgatory, or whether from the moment they leave their bodies Jesus takes them to paradise as He did for the Good Thief—are the People of God in the eternity beyond death, which will be finally conquered on the day of the Resurrection when these souls will be reunited with their bodies.

We believe that the multitude of those gathered around Jesus and Mary in paradise forms the Church of Heaven, where in eternal beatitude they see God as He is,[36] and where they also, in different degrees, are associated with the holy angels in the divine rule exercised by Christ in glory interceding for us and helping our weakness by their brotherly care.[37]

We believe in the communion of all the faithful of Christ, those who are pilgrims on earth, the dead who are attaining their purification, and the blessed in heaven, all together forming one Church; and we believe that in this communion the merciful love of God and His saints is ever listening to our prayers, as Jesus told us: Ask and you will receive.[38]

Thus it is with faith and in hope that we look forward to the resurrection of the dead, and the life of the world to come. Blessed be God Thrice Holy. Amen.

1. Cf. Dz.-Sch. 3002.
2. Cf. Ex. 3:14.
3. Cf. 1 Jn. 4:8.
4. Cf. 1 Tim. 6:16.
5. Cf. Dz.-Sch. 804.
6. Cf. Dz.-Sch. 75.
7. Cf. *ibid.*
8. Cf. Dz.-Sch. 150.
9. Cf. Dz.-Sch. 76.
10. Cf. *Ibid.*
11. Cf. Dz.-Sch. 251-252.
12. Cf. Lumen Gentium, 53.
13. Cf. Dz.-Sch. 2803.
14. Cf. Lumen Gentium, 53.
15. Cf. Lumen Gentium, 53, 58, 61.
16. Cf. Dz.-Sch. 3903.
17. Cf. Lumen Gentium, 53, 56, 61, 63; cf. Paul VI, Alloc. for the Closing of the Third Session of the Second Vatican Council: AAS LVI [1964] 1016; cf. Exhort. Apost. Signum Magnum, Introd.
18. Cf. Lumen Gentium, 62; cf. Paul VI, Exhort. Apost. Signum Magnum, p. 1, n. 1.
19. Cf. Dz-Sch. 1513.
20. Cf. Rom. 5:20
21. Cf. Dz.-Sch. 1514.
22. Cf. Lumen Gentium, 8, 5.
23. Cf. Lumen Gentium, 7, 11.
24. Cf. Sacrosanctum Concilium, 5, 6; cf. Lumen Gentium, 7, 12, 50.
25. Cf. Dz.-Sch. 3011.
26. Cf. Dz.-Sch. 3074.
27. Cf. Lumen Gentium, 25.
28. Cf. Lumen Gentium, 23; cf. Orientalium Ecclesiarum, 2, 3, 5, 6.
29. Cf. Lumen Gentium, 8.
30. Cf. Lumen Gentium, 15.
31. Cf. Lumen Gentium, 14.
32. Cf. Lumen Gentium, 16.
33. Cf. Dz.-Sch. 1651.
34. Cf. Dz.-Sch. 1642, 1651-1654; Paul VI, Enc. Mysterium Fidei.
35. Cf. S. Th., III, 73, 3.
36. Cf. 1 Jn. 3:2; Dz.-Sch. 1000.
37. Cf. Lumen Gentium, 49.
38. Cf. Lk. 10:9-10; Jn. 16:24.

Here also are the texts of the Apostles' Creed and the Nicene Creed, upon which Pope Paul's *Credo* is based and of which it is an amplification:

The Apostles' Creed

I believe in God, the Father Almighty,
Creator of heaven and earth;
and in Jesus Christ, His only Son, our Lord;
who was conceived by the Holy Spirit,
born of the Virgin Mary,
suffered under Pontius Pilate,
was crucified, died and was buried.
He descended into hell;
the third day He arose again from the dead;
He ascended into heaven, sits at the
right hand of God, the Father Almighty;
from thence He shall come to judge
the living and the dead.
I believe in the Holy Spirit, the holy Catholic Church,
the communion of saints,
the forgiveness of sins,
the resurrection of the body
and life everlasting. Amen.

The Nicene Creed

I believe in one God.
The Father almighty,
maker of heaven and earth,
and of all things visible and invisible.
And I believe in one Lord, Jesus Christ,
 the only-begotten Son of God.
 Born of the Father before all ages.
God of God, Light of Light, true God of true God.
Begotten, not made,
 of one substance with the Father.
By whom all things were made.

Who for us men and for our salvation
    came down from heaven.
And he became flesh by the Holy Spirit
    of the Virgin Mary: and was made man.
He was also crucified for us, suffered under
    Pontius Pilate, and was buried.
And on the third day he rose again,
    according to the Scriptures.
He ascended into heaven
    and sits at the right hand of the Father.
He will come again in glory
    to judge the living and the dead.
And of his kingdom there will be no end.
And I believe in the Holy Spirit,
    the Lord and Giver of life,
    who proceeds from the Father and the Son.
Who together with the Father and the Son
    is adored and glorified,
    and who spoke through the prophets.
And one holy, catholic, and apostolic Church.
I confess one baptism for the forgiveness of sins.
And I await the resurrection of the dead.
And the life of the world to come. Amen.

2

GOD

We believe in one only God, Father, Son and Holy Spirit...

...who, "dwelling in light inaccessible," is in Himself above every name, above every thing and above every created intellect."

THE CREDO

Pope Paul opens his Creed with a clear declaration of belief in God's existence. This latter is the source truth from which all others flow.

Atheism

Incredibly, there are many people who do not believe that there is a God.

"Ignorance of religious matters is God's worst enemy. Religion must be studied before being discussed or despised." This is the statement of one who had been a fervent Catholic until his fifteenth year. Misled by youthful passions and materialistic reading, he became an atheist and remained one for fifteen years. He admitted religious ignorance as a notable factor contributing to his atheistic tenets: "I can assure you that I have been reformed by a book that I had completely ignored until I was thirty-one years old—the *Gospel.*"

Atheism takes on many forms. The word itself means "without God" but it also signifies being "against God."
Some atheists claim, "There is no God, because if He existed He would not permit injustice and evil in the world." To this we can reply that God created man free. If man chooses to abuse his freedom, God will not frustrate his will. He will permit the evil, but somehow He will draw from it a greater good. In addition, He always gives grace to those who seek His help.

Others falsely reason: "If there is a God, He is so mysterious that we could never understand Him." But God has revealed Himself through the patriarchs and prophets, finally sending us His only-begotten Son, the Master, who is with us all days through the Church He established.

There are atheists who say they believe in God but then act as if He did not exist, following their selfish inclinations. This type of atheism is very widespread, and its proponents, not following the dictates of their consciences, burden themselves with a heavy responsibility.

The atheist who affirms that science explains all things — origin of the world and man — adds, "God is not necessary." Yet, if God did not exist, nothing would *be,* as we will see later in this chapter. He is our Creator and Provident Father who created man and all things and keeps us in continual existence.

The freedom of man is exaggerated out of proportion by the atheist who denies our dependence on God. For him, man is the sole fashioner of his own history. The truth is that God creates man free but not independent of Him. God is the only independent Being. He exists by His own power alone. We, however, exist and continue to exist on His power alone. We are, therefore, by nature dependent beings.

Although the Fathers of the Council did not issue a special document about atheism, still there were many references to it in the *Pastoral Constitution on the Church in the Modern World.* After describing various types of atheism, the Council said:

In her loyal devotion to God and men, the Church has already repudiated and cannot cease repudiating sorrowfully but as firmly as possible, those poisonous doctrines and actions which contradict reason and the common experience of humanity, and dethrone man from his native excellence.

Still, she strives to detect in the atheistic mind the hidden causes for the denial of God; conscious of how weighty are the questions which atheism raises, and motivated by love for all men, she believes these questions ought to be examined seriously and more profoundly (nn. 20, 21).

Some new viewpoints emerged from the council discussions. First, the Council Fathers ignored the traditional idea that a normally intelligent person could not be a positive atheist over a more or less protracted period without moral guilt. Instead of this, they implied that it *is possible* for a normal adult to accept explicit atheism for a longer period without any question of moral guilt on the part of the unbeliever. This is not stated in so many direct words, but it can be inferred from the general tenor of the documents.

There was another departure from the traditional view of looking at atheism, when the Fathers asserted that an atheist is not necessarily excluded from salvation, provided that his atheism has not made him act against his moral conscience.

(Of course, this does not excuse us from laboring and praying for the conversion of non-believers. Nor should we assume that salvation is easy for a heretic or an atheist.)

The *Dogmatic Constitution on the Church* reads:

Those can attain to salvation who through no fault of their own do not know the Gospel of Christ or His Church, yet sincerely seek God and moved by grace strive by their deeds to do His will as it is known to them through the dictates of conscience. *Nor does Divine Providence deny the helps necessary for salvation to those who, without blame on their part, have not yet arrived at an explicit knowledge of God and with His grace strive to live a good life. Whatever good or truth is found among them is looked upon by the Church as a preparation for the Gospel (n. 16).*

The Vatican Secretariat for Non-Christians in a document entitled, *Toward the Meeting of Religions,* issued September 21, 1967, reaffirms the above:

A regime of personal graces therefore undoubtedly exists outside the Church and has existed prior to the Church. *"God has other ways of saving souls outside the cone of light which is the revelation of salvation"* (Paul VI, *Osservatore Romano,* May 15, 1965) despite the uncertitude and the arguments carried on by theologians as to the channels by which this grace can reach individual souls, and on the nature of this grace. What is certain is the fact that God's action reaches men in the very experiences of life and of their conscience, that all divine grace is *grace of Christ through the Church* and that it ordains these men to take their part at the end of time among the People of God. "Then, as may be read in the holy Fathers, all just men from the time of Adam, 'from Abel, the just one, to the last of the elect,' will be gathered together with the Father in the Universal Church" (cf. Dogmatic Constitution on the Church, n. 2).

In dealing with atheism Pope Paul has stressed the necessity for proper thinking in order to arrive at the truth. He said:

In order to reach the certainty of that ineffable and sovereign existence, it is sufficient, we were saying, to think well. A guarantee of this is given to us by the explicit teachings of the First Vatican Council which, in summarizing the centuries-old doctrine of the Church and — we may add — of human philosophy, states that "God, the beginning and end of all things, can be known with certainty by the natural light of reason through things created."

Why is it then, that many men, even scholars, express the contrary? We answer, because they are not making use of their minds in accordance with the authentic laws of thought, in search of truth.

We are aware of saying something grave. Nevertheless it is so.

God is

Apart from organized religion, we can establish the fact of God's existence by reason alone.

There are five main philosophical proofs for the existence of God, all most clear and convincing. They are based upon the fact of *motion* or change in all its forms; upon the concept of *causation;* upon the idea of *contingency,* i.e., objects may or may not be; upon the presence of *perfection in beings* and lastly from the observation of *order* in the operations of the cosmos.

We will treat all of these proofs in detail.

Motion

Motion, by which we mean change in its widest sense, is obvious all around us. Father Peter Sullivan writes in his book *Christ the Answer* (Boston: St. Paul Editions, 1964):

By motion we mean change in its widest sense. Now there are many kinds of change. Movements of mind and will comprise spiritual changes. Birth and death are examples of substantial change. Qualitative change occurs when a person becomes sick or recuperates. Quantitative change takes place when one thing is added to or subtracted from another. Then there is local motion or movement from place to place. Indeed, when we speak of "motion," perhaps it is this latter which springs most readily to the mind of the average person, since it is the one with which he is most familiar.

The existence of motion presupposes that the motion shall have been initiated by an outside agent. This is a necessary and universal law, for motion cannot be its own originator. Were it otherwise, the same object would be in two diametrically opposed states at the same time and under the same conditions. Obviously this is nonsense.

From your presence where can I flee?

Psalm 138

Nor in seeking an explanation can we go back to infinity by a series of secondary movers. For unless we admit a prime or *first* mover, itself unmoved, then any kind of motion is out of the question. An automobile requires someone to turn the key in the ignition. A clock will not tick without a spring. A television set does not operate until the knob is twirled. Thus reason forces upon us the conclusion that there must be a prime mover, unmoved by anything. This Prime Mover we call God.

The Maker

Nothing ever makes itself! This tremendous universe, whose very immensity overwhelms all human thought, had a beginning! Science and reason unquestionably affirm that. Someday it must have an end. Science and reason agree to that also.

If there had ever been a moment when nothing existed, nothing could ever have existed. Therefore, since these things exist, we know that someone who made them exists, someone who always was, someone who created all these things out of nothingness. This Someone we call God.

In other words, every effect must have a cause and that cause was itself caused, and so on. Eventually, we must reach a first cause, *itself uncaused,* which is self-existing, and without which nothing could exist or continue to exist. This First Cause we call God.

Once a European scholar was crossing the Sahara desert with a band of Arabs. One evening, near sunset, the Arab leader knelt on the ground and began to pray.

"What are you doing?" the scholar asked.

"I'm praying," the Arab replied calmly.

"Praying? To whom?"

"To God."

Then the scholar smiled as if he knew much more than the poor Arab. "But have you ever seen your God? Have you ever touched Him?"

"No, sir."

"Then you are mistaken," said the scholar. "You can't believe in a God whom you cannot see, hear or touch."

The Arab did not argue with the scholar, but the next morning he found a fine chance to answer him. The scholar got up just as the sky was beginning to grow light. "There was a camel here during the night," he remarked.

"Why do you say that?" replied the Arab. "Did you see or feel one?"

"No, no, of course not," replied the scholar.

"Then you must be mistaken. You can't believe in a camel which you did not see or touch."

"Of course I can," retorted the scholar. "Maybe you don't believe that one was here, but I can't help but believe it. He made tracks here in the sand."

Just then the sun rose round and red over the eastern horizon. Pointing to that great glowing star, the Arab declared, "Look at that! The sun, too, is a sign—a clear sign that its Maker exists!"

Utter dependence

Our third proof for the existence of God depends upon the *contingency* of created being. Contingency means that a thing may be or may not be; there is no necessity for its existence. Reflection upon ourselves and every object in creation will soon convince us that each and all are contingent. There was a time when we did not exist. We had nothing to say about it.

Now, since we and all contingent beings do not possess within ourselves the reason for our existence, it must be looked for elsewhere. Could numberless contingent beings all together be the answer? No, because just multiplying the number of contingent, dependent beings does not change their nature. All of them together will still be contingent and will have to depend on some outside source for their being.

Thus, it must be concluded that contingent beings presuppose a necessary Being, that is, a Being to whose nature existence belongs. This necessary, self-existing Being, who holds within Himself the source of His own existence, we call God.

Perfection does exist

The fourth argument is based on the various kinds of perfection found in creatures. For example, let us take the perfection of beauty and goodness. A flower, a horse, a scientist, a saint all possess beauty and goodness, but in varying degrees. No creature possesses any perfection in the fullest possible degree: no creature, for example, is beauty or goodness itself. Every creature has some perfection, but others have something it does not have, and no creature has all perfection possible.

Now, where do the perfections in creatures originate? Their perfection could not possibly have come from themselves since they did not even exist by their own power, as we have seen from the above proof concerning contingency. (Besides, if creatures could give themselves perfections, they would give them in the fullest degree, not just partially!)

Therefore we must look outside them for the source of their perfections. And as we have seen from previous proofs, an infinite number of causes is absurd.

There must be One who has in the fullest degree possible all the perfections which creatures possess only in part. Since no one can give what he does not have, there must be One who is Perfection itself and who gives perfection to creatures. This all-perfect Being we call God.

Harmony has an author

Our fifth argument is based upon the fact of *universal order*. In his book, *Christ the Answer*, Father Peter Sullivan speaks of this thus:

Perhaps the best known and most interesting of the five metaphysical proofs for the existence of God is the one drawn from the design displayed in the construction of the universe — from atoms to galaxies — and the laws which regulate its movements....

The human body is a marvel of medical science. A model of efficiency, it may be compared to a well-organized state. For defense purposes it levies a standing army of blood cells. It has a sanitary scheme eliminating waste products in a most thorough manner, and it maintains a transport system carrying food to the various organs. The brain is the capital and seat of government, ruling the other faculties, while at the same time serving as a communications station, receiving and transmitting messages along the nerves. Here without doubt is order, but upon inquiry elsewhere we find that methodical action is not confined merely to insects, birds and the organs of man. It characterizes all nature, from the minutest particle in the atomic nucleus to the stupendous solar system....

Physicists are of the opinion that the atom has a form similar to the solar system, the electrons spinning around the nucleus as the planets revolve around the sun. This analogy is not completely satisfactory, nor does it explain the role of the subatomic particles. But as far as it goes, it is a workable hypothesis and serves to explain all chemical and physical phenomena associated with movements inside the atom — conduction, ionization, spectroscopic peculiarities, valence, etc. Speaking generally, therefore, two primal physical laws operate within the atom — one the law of attraction, by which the electrons are drawn towards the nucleus, the other the law of repulsion, by which they tend to fly away from it. The mutual interaction of both these laws begets harmony and stability within the atom.

Now the same thing holds true for those colossal worlds scattered so profusely through the vastness of space. The sun is the center of our system, and the planets circle round it, but in their motion are subject to the same regulations as we saw illustrated in the case of the atom, being attracted towards, though at the same time urged away from the sun. Study the position for a second! Here as before there is an equilibrium between opposite forces, a balance so scrupulously adjusted that the celestial spheres whirl noiselessly with their immense bulk through the vast solitudes of space with perfect precision and nought ever goes amiss! Yet scientists inform us that a split-second miscalculation would precipitate a cataclysm!

What is the meaning of it all? How is it that plants, insects and animals pursue their end with predetermined purpose? Why is the human machine so perfect? How explain the atom's construction and the rhythm of the star-spangled heavens? Only two answers are possible — either it is all the work of chance, or else an infinitely intelligent and powerful Being has caused it. Let us examine the first of these suppositions and see how it works.

Now if chance governs nature, how is it that astronomers can foretell with unerring accuracy not only the day and hour, but even the very second of an eclipse due one hundred years later? Again, suppose you had four rods of equal length, joined loosely at the ends to form a four-sided figure. By throwing this framework, how often do you think you could make a perfect square? You don't know. You don't even have a mathematical probability to go on. You might on the first occasion, but on the other hand you might try for an eternity and never succeed at all. And why? Simply because chance is erratic, not subject to law. Could chance construct a color television set with all its intricate mechanism or a jet airliner with its multiplicity of bewildering gadgets or a streamlined ocean greyhound or an atomic-powered submarine or a space-capsule? Obviously, the answer is in the negative.

Now, if chance cannot cause these, how much more is it incapable of producing the infinite complexities of nature and the universe! Intelligence must have produced them — infinite intelligence, for the magnitude of creation demands it. Infinite Wisdom rules the stars, and this infinite Wisdom we call GOD.

It was a consideration of all these various factors that made Albert Einstein, author of the theory of relativity and greatest physicist of all time, write: "I believe that God does not play dice with the universe."

And John Glenn, after orbiting the earth, pointed to the order in the universe as a proof of the existence of God: "...Galaxies, millions of light years across, all traveling in prescribed orbits in relation to one another! Could all of this have just happened? Was this an accident that someone tossed up a bunch of flotsam and jetsam, and it suddenly started making these orbits of its own accord? I can't believe that's really true.

"I think this was a definite plan. This is one big thing in space that shows me there is a God, some Power that put all this into orbit and keeps it there. It wasn't just an accident."

We find the same thought in the following words of the Second Vatican Council's *Constitution on Divine Revelation:*

"God gives men an enduring witness to Himself in created realities....

"God, the beginning and end of all things, can be known with certainty from created reality by light of human reason" (nn. 3, 6).

The existence of order in nature likewise had an over-powering effect on the mind of Nils Stensen, rated as a genius of the first rank on account of his original discoveries in the fields of anatomy, embryology and physiology, findings that have profoundly affected modern research in crystallography, geology and palaeontology. Speaking of the human body, Stensen made this comparison:

"Just as you ask for the artist and master whenever you are looking at a statue or a picture, much more must you do so when examining the structure of the human body.... In true anatomy, God first leads us by the hand of the anatomist to the understanding of the body and then to the knowledge of Himself."

Stensen was a profoundly religious man and penned the following words, professing his belief in the workings of Divine Providence:

"You without whose beckoning
no hair falls from the head,
no leaf from the tree,
no bird from the air,
without whom no thought proceeds from the soul,
no word from the mouth,
no action from the hand—
You have previously led me by unknown paths:
lead me now, blind or seeing, by the paths of grace.
It is easier for You to lead me where You will
than for me to follow
the way my own desires would draw me."

The book, *The Evidence of God in an Expanding Universe,* compiled by John Clover Monsma, brings together the views of forty American scientists about God and religion. These contributors represent practically the entire range of the physical sciences. They unanimously testify that in whatever field their specialty lies, be it scanning the vast heavens or studying the tiniest forms of life, they have encountered undeniable evidence of the existence of God.

The echo

In addition to the five proofs mentioned above, theologians also use another. It is based upon the fact of *conscience,* the capacity we have within ourselves for knowing what is right and wrong. Cardinal Newman once wrote a novel entitled, "Callista," the plot of which is laid in the early ages of Christianity. In chapter 27 he puts into the mouth of Callista, the heroine, these words which so beautifully tell us that God is there:

Whereas I...feel that God within my heart. I feel myself in His presence! He says to me: "Do this; don't do that." You may tell me that this dictate is a mere law of my nature, as to joy or grieve. I cannot understand this. *No, it is the echo of a person speaking to me.* Nothing shall persuade me that it does not ultimately proceed from a person external to me. It carries with it its proof of its divine origin. My nature feels towards it as toward a person. When I obey it, I feel a satisfaction; when I disobey, a sadness—just like that which I feel in pleasing or offending some reverend friend. So you see, Polemon, I believe in what is more than a mere "something." I believe in what is more real to me than sun, moon, stars, and the fair earth, and the voice of friends. You will say: "Who is he? Has he ever told you anything about himself?" Alas! no!—the more's the pity! But I will not give up what I have because I have not more. An echo implies a voice; a voice, a speaker. That speaker I love and I fear.

The fact that God can be known by reason played an important part in the conversion of St. Hilary. He was born a pagan and reared in idolatry. Still, as he thought about things, it became clear to him that man was free and had been placed in the world to practice virtue, for which he would be rewarded in the hereafter. Gradually he arrived at the idea of the one true God, creator of all things. He read the Old Testament and was deeply impressed by the words God used of Himself in addressing Moses: "I am who am." Then he read the New Testament and learned from the Gospel of St. John that Jesus Christ was God, consubstantial with the Father. God gave him the gift of faith and though somewhat advanced in age, he was baptized. Later he became bishop of Poitiers in France and today is venerated as a Doctor of the Church.

The great St. Augustine proclaims thus his faith in the existence of God: "Not without doubting, but with assured conscience do I love You, Lord! You have stricken my heart with Your word and I loved You.... Too late have I loved You, O Beauty so ancient and so new! Too late have I loved You! You were with me, and I was not with You! I was abroad, running after those beauties which You have made. Those things, which could have no being but in You, kept me far from You. You have called, You have cried out and at last pierced my deafness. You have enlightened, You have shone forth and my blindness is dispelled. I have tasted You and am hungry for You. You have touched me and I am afire with the desire of Your embraces....

"You have made us for Yourself, O Lord, and our hearts shall never rest until they rest in You."

St. Columban, the noted Irish missionary, once asked Discolus his disciple: "Discolus, why are you always smiling?" In his simplicity Discolus replied: "Because no one can take God from me."

St. Felix of Cantalice in Italy used to say: "All earthly creatures can lift us up to God if we know how to look upon them with an eye that is pure."

God, the Holy One

He is HE WHO IS as He revealed to Moses....

We believe that this only God is absolutely one in His infinitely holy essence as also in His perfections, in His omnipotence, His infinite knowledge....

THE CREDO

Following his statement of belief in God's existence, Paul VI proceeds to describe the Almighty's attributes. The latter word is used in theology to signify the perfections that belong to God alone. Again, by reasoning and apart from revealed religion, we can deduce the principal characteristics of the Supreme Being. The first of these, and root of all the others, is the truth that God exists *from Himself.* He did not create Himself, for in order to do this He would have to exist prior to Himself, an obvious contradiction in terms. Nor was He created by anyone else for this leads to an infinity of causes which fails to satisfy the inquiring mind.

Theologians have coined a special word for this basic attribute of God. They call it *aseity*. This word comes from two Latin ones: "a" meaning *from* and "se" meaning *himself*. The two words put together give "Ase" while the three other letters "ity" suffixed give the abstract English noun *aseity*, meaning *from Himself*.

The other attributes of God are: *simplicity*, i.e., He is wholly and entirely a spiritual substance with no material composition and not extended in space as are we; *immutability* or changelessness; *eternity*, which means that He had no beginning and will have no end; *unicity*, or *unity*, which means that there is but *one* God; *infinity*, indicating that He possesses every perfection, *sanctity* or holiness; and *immensity* or, that He is in all space and all possible space and this by reason of His presence, His essence and His power. Hence, St. Augustine says to the sinner: "If you desire to commit sin, seek a place where God will not see you, and then do what you want." But where can we find this place, if God is everywhere? "Hence we must fear God in public and in private. Are you walking? He sees you. Is the light shining? He sees you. Is it dark? He sees you. You enter a room? He sees you. Oh! Let us fear Him who has care to always keep His eye on us, and fearing Him, let us try not to offend Him."

"God," continues the saint, "is an incomprehensible, incorporeal, immutable spirit, whole and entire in all places, indivisible, present everywhere, who penetrates all, knows all, contains all, sees all, governs all, infinitely perfect, whole and entire in heaven, on earth and everywhere. He is beyond all human understanding and language and calculation. If you seek to know His greatness, it is immense; His beauty, it is inexpressible; His sweetness, it is infinite; His splendor, His strength, His goodness are incomparable."

Theology also teaches that God is *omniscient*, or that He knows not merely *all* things, but all possible things, and that He is *omnipotent*, indicating that He can do everything that does not involve a contradiction. We can explain this latter best by examples. Often we hear irreligious people ask: "Could God make a stone that He couldn't lift?" or "Could God make a square circle?" These questions, and others like them are senseless because they involve contradictions — in other words, they deny the very thing that they assert.

The Bible is filled with references to the attributes of God. Let us see what it has to say about each one in particular:

I am who am

Moses said to God, "If they ask me 'What is his name?' what am I to tell them?" God replied, "I Am Who Am." Then he added, "This is what you shall tell the Israelites: "I Am *sent me to you." (Ex. 3)*

We have seen how St. Hilary was led to a belief in God's existence by the use of his reason. This same faculty also convinced him of God's aseity, as we see from the following which he himself wrote:

"I found the testimony of God the Creator about Himself expressed in the following manner: '*I Am Who Am*' and again: 'Thus shall you say to the children of Israel: *He who is* has sent me to you.' I was filled with admiration at such a clear definition of God, which spoke of the incomprehensible nature in language most suitable to our human understanding.

"It is known that there is nothing more characteristic of God than *to be,* because that itself which *is* does not belong to those things which will one day end or to those which had a beginning."

Simplicity

"God is a spirit and they who adore him should adore him in spirit and in truth" (Jn. 4:24).

"To whom can you liken God? With what equal can you confront him?" (Is. 40:18).

Immutability

"With whom there is no change or shadow of alteration" (Jas. 1:17).

The theologian James Alberione, S.S.P., puts it thus:

The sun rises and sets; time ticks on in fleeting hours; years and seasons pass without pausing. Only God is unchanging. For Him there is neither past nor future; He is always present in His eternity.

When we say that God is immutable, we do not mean to imply that He does not possess free will. He does, and this is a Catholic dogma. But just how He can be changeless and free simultaneously is a mystery which no human being will ever solve.

Eternity

"I am the Alpha and the Omega, the beginning and the end; he who is and who was and who is to come" (Apoc. 1:8).

Psalm 101 describes in poetic fashion the eternity of God:

I say:
O my God,
through all generations your years endure
Of old you established the earth
and the heavens are the work of your hands.
They shall perish,
but you remain
though all of them grow old like a garment.
Like clothing you change them,
and they are changed,
but you are the same
and your years have no end.

Immensity

Psalm 138:7-12:

Where can I go from your spirit?
from your presence where can I flee?
If I go up to the heavens, you are there;
if I sink to the nether world, you are present there.
If I take the wings of the dawn,
if I settle at the farthest limits of the sea,
Even there your hand shall guide me,
and your right hand shall hold me fast.
If I say, "Surely the darkness shall hide me,
and the night shall be my light"—
For you darkness itself is not dark,
and night shines as the day.
(Darkness and light are the same.)

Infinity

"Great is the Lord and highly to be praised: His greatness is unsearchable" (Ps. 144:3).

"Behold, the nations count as a drop of the bucket, as dust on the scales; the coastlands weigh no more than powder.... Before him all the nations are as nought, as nothing and void he accounts them" (Is. 40:15-17).

"God is in everything, outside of everything, before everything, above everything, and below everything," exclaims St. Gregory the Great. "He is above everything because of His omnipotence; before everything because He always was; below everything because He sustains them;

outside of everything because of His immensity; in all because of His spirituality and faculty of penetration... He is in all places and not enclosed in any; He is everywhere and not restricted to any one place; He is seen everywhere in His creatures, without ever being seen what He is in reality. O abyss of greatness! Who, then, is God?... Let us adore Him and remain silent!..."

Unicity or unity

"The Lord your God is one God" (Dt. 6:4).

In China today many Catholics are confessing their belief in the one true God, even though it may mean death. A newspaper reported that at the Ward Road, a jail in Shanghai, young Mathias Ma, a boy of eighteen years, was tortured by the Reds. Scorching his eyes with bright lights and tightening steel chains about his wrists, they shouted repeatedly into his ears, "Say there is no God!" *"But one,"* replied the young man. As he slipped into unconsciousness he repeated his profession of faith, "There is no God *but one."* Mathias Ma knew that God said, "I am the Lord your God; you shall not have strange gods before Me." He had not studied his religion simply to pass the examinations; he studied to learn how to plan his life according to the eternal truths.

Sanctity

"For I, the Lord am your God; and you shall make and keep yourselves holy, because I am holy..." (Lev. 11:44).

Omniscience

"Oh the depths of the riches of the wisdom and of the knowledge of God! How incomprehensible are his ways! For 'who has known the mind of the Lord, or who has been his counsellor? Or who has first given to him, that recompense should be made him?' For from him and through him and unto him are all things" (Rom. 11:33-36).

Omnipotence

"All that the Lord wills he does in heaven and on earth, in the seas and in all the deeps" (Ps. 134:6).

"Who is this God of mine?" asks St. Bernard.

This is his answer: "He is an omnipotent will, an immense virtue, an eternal light, an incommutable reason, supreme happiness. He creates men so that they may partake of Him, He makes men holy in order to possess them, He inflames them in order to glorify them, He directs them in their ways, He creates them out of love, He imposes a rule upon them in order to render them wise, He fortifies them to make them practice virtue, He visits them in order to comfort them, He illuminates them so that they may know Him, He destines them to immortality, He fills them with graces in order to lead them to happiness. He protects them in order to keep them safe from all dangers."

Some say God is dead. Answering with the words of Pope Paul, we reply:

"It is not the Sun that has been extinguished, it is the eye of man that is clouded over. Secularization is admitted by many as a process of thought which finds in itself and in a knowledge of things an autonomy which dispense from reference to a higher and transcendent principle which is called God.... Knowledge of God, it is maintained, is impossible....

"We must remember an elementary and basic truth: God is hidden. Many are the signs, many are the ways, many are the voices, many are the stimulations that speak to us and lead us to the threshold of His ineffable reality.... The rational knowledge we may have of God is by means of demonstration, which requires a simple discipline, though a rigorous one.... Therefore, we are confronted with a first duty, that of enjoying the knowledge which we already have of God and a second duty, that of seeking Him – of seeking Him ardently where, how and when He allows Himself to be met...."

CHALLENGE

When we contemplate the awesome attributes of God, when we realize our nothingness and hopelessness before Him, when we understand that this God whom words fail to describe, wants us to serve Him and to love Him, our response is immediate, unqualified and persevering. Our entire relation with the Creator who is our Father and who loves us with an unsurpassable love is well brought out by the following simple though profound poem:

No Father so tender, so grateful,
No one worth serving but God,
No Friend so unchanging, so faithful,
No one worth trusting but God.

No heart holds this wealth of affection,
No one worth loving but God,
In His exquisite, endless perfection,
No one worth seeking but God.

3

GOD
ONE
AND
TRIUNE

God alone can give us right and full knowledge of this reality by revealing himself as Father, Son and Holy Spirit, in whose eternal life we are by grace called to share, here below in the obscurity of faith and after death in eternal light.

The mutual bonds which eternally constitute the THREE PERSONS WHO ARE EACH ONE AND THE SAME DIVINE BEING, are the blessed inmost life of God thrice holy, infinitely beyond all that we can conceive in human measure.

We give thanks, however, to the divine goodness that very many believers can testify with us before men to the unity of God, even though they know not the mystery of the holy Trinity....

Thus in the three divine persons, "Coaeternae sibi et coaequales" (coeternal and coequal with one another), the life and beatitude of God perfectly one superabound and are consummated in the supreme excellence and glory proper to uncreated being, and always "there should be venerated unity in the Trinity and Trinity in the unity."

Blessed be God Thrice Holy. Amen.

THE CREDO

In the Old Testament God revealed Himself to the Chosen People as the One and Only God.

The Lord your God is one God. (Dt. 6:4)

The cult or worship of the one God was unique to the Jews before the coming of Christ, while, instead, the pagans around Israel worshiped many gods.

God gave His People ten commandments, three of which pertained to their relationship with God.

I, the Lord, am your God, who brought you out of the land of Egypt, that place of slavery. You shall not have other gods besides me. You shall not carve idols for yourselves in the shape of anything in the sky above or the earth below or in the waters beneath the earth; you shall not bow down before them or worship them. For I, the Lord, your God, am a jealous God. (Ex. 20:2-5)

You shall not take the name of the Lord, your God in vain. (Ex. 20:7)

Remember to keep holy the Sabbath day. (Ex. 20:8)

These commands were, in reality, bonds of love uniting Creator and creature. They prepared the way for a new dispensation of love in which God would reveal to all men the mystery of His innermost life. Through Christ man came to know of the Blessed Trinity — one God in three divine Persons.

Christianity rests on the final mandate of Christ to His apostles: "Go, therefore, and make disciples of all nations, baptizing them in the name of the *Father*, and of the *Son*, and of the *Holy Spirit*" (Mt. 28:19).

Baptizing them in *the Name* of the Father...: All three Persons of the Blessed Trinity are named, so that there may be but one and the same grace, as there is but one and the same divinity among Them, because the Name of Trinity signifies one sole God but three Persons (St. Jerome).

Vatican II in the *Constitution on the Church* states the mission of the three divine Persons:

"The *eternal Father,* by a free and hidden plan of His own wisdom and goodness, created the whole world. His plan was to raise men to a participation of the divine life. All the elect, before time began, the Father foreknew and predestined to become conformed to the image of His Son, that he should be the firstborn among many brethren. He planned to assemble in the holy Church all those who would believe in Christ. Already from the beginning of the world the foreshadowing of the Church took place. It was prepared in a remarkable way throughout the history of the people of Israel and by means of the Old Covenant. In the present era of time the Church was constituted and, by the outpouring of the Spirit, was made manifest....

"The *Son*, therefore, came, sent by the Father. It was in Him, before the foundation of the world, that the Father chose us and predestined us to become adopted sons, for in Him it pleased the Father to re-establish all things. To carry out the will of the Father, Christ inaugurated the kingdom of heaven on earth and revealed to us the mystery of that kingdom....

"When the work which the Father gave the Son to do on earth was accomplished the *Holy Spirit* was sent on the day of Pentecost in order that He might continually sanctify the Church, and thus, all those who believe would have access through Christ in one Spirit to the Father. To men, dead in sin, the Father gives life through Him, until, in Christ, He brings to life their mortal bodies. The Spirit dwells in the Church and in the hearts of the faithful, as in a temple. In them He prays on their behalf and bears witness to the fact that they are adopted sons.

"The Church both prays and labors in order that the entire world may become the People of God, the Body of the Lord and the Temple of the Holy Spirit, and that in Christ, the Head of all, all honor and glory may be rendered to the Creator and Father of the universe" (n. 17).

The mystery of Three

The entire doctrine of the Trinity is present in St. Matthew's account of the baptism of Christ (cf. 3:16-17).

In the ancient profession of faith, called "The Athanasian Creed," the doctrine of the Blessed Trinity is expressed in these terms:

"We venerate one God in the Trinity, and the Trinity in oneness; neither confounding the persons, nor dividing the substance; for there is one person of the Father, another of the Son, and another of the Holy Spirit; but the divine nature of the Father and of the Son and of the Holy Spirit is one, their glory is equal, their majesty is coeternal.

"Of such a nature as the Father is, so is the Son, so is the Holy Spirit; the Father is uncreated, the Son is uncreated, the Holy Spirit is uncreated...the Father is eternal, the Son is eternal, the Holy Spirit is eternal: and nevertheless there are not three eternals, but one eternal,...thus the Father is God, the Son is God, the Holy Spirit is God.

"The Father was not created nor begotten by anyone. The Son is from the Father alone, not made or created, but begotten. The Holy Spirit is from the Father and the Son, not created nor begotten, but proceeding.

"In this Trinity there is nothing first or later, nothing greater or less, but all three Persons are coeternal and coequal with one another."

The Fathers of the Second Vatican Council repeated the same profession of faith thus: "Before the whole world, let all Christians confess their faith in the triune God, one and three" (Decree on Ecumenism, n. 12).

From the beginning of the Church until now, Christian thinkers have deeply pondered this mystery. They know it is incomprehensible, but their efforts are directed mainly at showing that it involves no contradiction, rather than at unravelling it. In the process they have managed to throw more light on it from different angles. Father Wilfred Hurley, C.S.P., in his book, *The Creed of a Catholic* (Boston: St. Paul Editions, 1965) strives to make the doctrine less difficult:

However, we can more or less try to understand it [the mystery of the Trinity] although in a most limited way, by considering our own beings. For in each and every one of us there is a sort of triple unity which we find it very hard to explain, although the fact is obvious enough.

For example, I can consider my own being.

I exist. I think a thought. It is a spiritual thought, yet it is real. Since it was not in the outside world, it must have been produced by the mind itself. Thus I have given birth to a thought. Not with the physical birth by which man produces man, but in a spiritual birth, through which I have produced an idea.

Hence I exist and my thought exists. In a sense, my thought and myself are distinct, for I can exist without thinking, as in a coma. On the other hand, my thought may be written down and may continue to exist long after I am gone, and so it has an existence of its own.

But I have another existence. I have a will as well as an intellect and thus besides existing and thinking, I can love or hate. And I can think without loving or hating as in a moment of idle daydreaming.

But while myself, my mind, and my will are distinct, yet they are all one. It is the same myself—who is, who thinks, and who wills. Over this simple mystery, this mystery within my own being, the philosophies of the world have pondered for ages. Yet, could I explain to myself this mystery within myself, I might perhaps better understand the mystery of the divine Trinity.

Now to apply this analogy to God. God thinks a thought. But while my thought is a puny, imperfect representation, God's thought has the length and breadth and depth of eternity itself. Again, my thoughts are many, for they come and go. God's thought is infinitely different. God does not think one thought one minute and another the next, because all is present to God at once. God being an Infinite Unity has but one thought as eternal as Himself. Into this thought God puts Himself, so entirely, that it is as living as He is. Infinite as He is. Perfect as He is.

Again, when a thought is expressed, it is expressed in words. Thus I put an idea in words. I may even put these words into a book.

The book thus written, to which I have given birth, I may even refer to as my brain-child.

Thus it can be said also with God's thought. It is His thought, His Word, His Son. Either Word or Son, it is the one and the same, except from different points of view.

Hence, we understand more fully St. John's awe-inspiring words, as putting his pen to the paper of his Gospel, he starts to write: "In the beginning was the Word, and the Word was with God, and the Word was God.... And the Word was made flesh and dwelt among us." The "Word" is Jesus Christ, the Second Person of the Blessed Trinity.

Moreover, while I have good and evil thoughts, this one Infinite Thought of God's is a thought of Infinite Goodness. Thus God the Father loves God the Son as the Image of His perfection. And the Son loves the Father. It is an infinite, absolute, perfect love between Them. And this infinite perfect love is the Third Person of the Blessed Trinity which we call the "Holy Spirit."

And thus God exists. One God, three Persons, the Father, the Son, and the Holy Spirit. Just as I exist, I think and I love, and yet I am one.

This analogy is not new. It was first intimated by St. Augustine fifteen hundred years ago. It does not pretend to explain in full, or to explain away, the mystery of the Trinity. Yet it does help somewhat to make the mystery a little more understandable to us. And perhaps it gives us a deeper meaning to God's own words: "...Let us make man to our image and likeness...."

In His divine revelation to man God reveals that while there is but one God, yet there are three persons in God: the Father, the Son and the Holy Spirit!

However, remember in speaking of the "persons" in God, we do not use the term in exactly the same way we use it when speaking of people. We use it only for the lack of another term to show our meaning better.

Usually in speaking of someone as a "person" we mean some intelligent being who thinks, says and does things by itself. And hence this one being is responsible for everything that is done, thought or said. Certainly not a part of this person, such as the mind or tongue, or hand, but the whole of this being is responsible. But when we speak of the three Persons in God, it is because to each belongs something we cannot attribute to the other.

For instance, there is their distinct origin! *The Father is unbegotten. The Son is begotten of the Father. And from the Father and the Son proceeds the Holy Spirit, who comes from Them as from one source. Hence the three divine Persons are really distinct from one another.*

But yet there is no contradiction. For God is only one in nature; while He is three under the different aspect of person. "Person" determines what an individual "is", while "nature" determines what an "individual" can do.

Hence, the "Holy Trinity" does not mean that there are three Gods in one God, nor that the three divine Persons are but one Person. We only say that there are three Persons in one God. Three Persons, but only one God in nature or essence.

Somewhat similar, as a soul has will, understanding, and memory; yet it is but one soul.

While the writers try to make the teaching on the Trinity less obscure by words, the saints endeavor to explain it by symbols. Perhaps the best known incident of this kind is connected with St. Patrick who converted Ireland to the true faith. During his mission journeys he once found himself in the western province of Connacht where he instructed the two daughters — Eithne (the fair) and Fidelma (the ruddy) — of King Laoghaire in Christian doctrine. Tradition says that he used a shamrock to illustrate the truth of the Trinity, and that is why, to this very day, Irish people wear the shamrock on March 17th, the feast of St. Patrick!

In 1917 the Blessed Virgin appeared to three shepherd children — two girls and a boy — on five successive occasions at Fatima. Prior to the actual visitations of the Mother of God, however, they saw an angel three different times. The third time he recited this beautiful prayer to the Blessed Trinity, which we should learn by heart and repeat often:

"Most holy Trinity, Father, Son and Holy Spirit, I adore You profoundly and I offer You the most precious body and blood, soul and divinity of Jesus Christ, present in all the tabernacles of the world, in reparation for the outrages, sacrileges and indifference by which He is offended. And by the infinite merits of His most Sacred Heart, and through the Immaculate Heart of Mary, I beg the conversion of poor sinners."

Then he communicated miraculously the body and blood of Christ to the children, after which he repeated the above prayer three times, obviously in honor of each Person of the Trinity.

O most Blessed Trinity, You are really our honor, our joy, our all! Glory be now and forever to the Father who created us, to the Son who redeemed us, and to the Holy Spirit who sanctifies us. The most Blessed Trinity: Father, Son and Holy Spirit, is found in the man who lives in the state of grace. Blessed is the soul who participates in the life of the most

Blessed Trinity, lives in It, with It, for It and prepares himself to enter and remain in the joy of his God, One and Triune, for all eternity.

the Persons of the Trinity

God the Father

We believe in the FATHER who eternally begets the Son...
THE CREDO

Father: this is the rightful name of the First Person of the Blessed Trinity because it is from Him as Principle — although He Himself has no principle — that the Son is begotten by intellective generation. From Them Both proceeds the third Person and all this without priority or causality. This paternity of the Father in regard to the Son is to be understood in the strict sense.

In a figurative way, the First Person is also called "Father of the Universe" because He created it.

In a third and more important manner He is termed the Father of men, especially through sanctifying grace by which we are made the sons of God and share in a most mysterious way in His divine life.

It is from Christ Himself that we learn to speak of the Father in this fashion. Did He not teach us the Lord's prayer beginning: "Our Father who art in heaven" during the Sermon on the Mount?

Our attitude toward God our Father in the supernatural order should be modeled upon that which characterizes the relation between parent and child in the natural one. The child admires, loves, confides in and asks its father for everything. So should we be likewise in our dealings with God, our Father. In His preaching during the public ministry, Christ tried to impress this truth upon His hearers — and, of course, upon us — time and time again. This particular teaching deeply impressed St. Paul, so much so, in fact, that he wrote in his epistle to the Ephesians (3:8-9, 14-15):

"Yes to me, there has been given this grace to announce... the mystery which has been hidden from eternity in God.... For this reason I bend my knees to the Father of our Lord Jesus Christ, from whom all fatherhood in heaven and on earth receives its name."

Your Majesty Co-Eternal

My God,
words are so poor and feeble
when confronted with Your majesty.
Your greatness infinitely surpasses
the power of human speech.
But, my God,
You reveal to me,
small as I am,
the very life of the Divine Family.
You are Father
You are Son
You are Holy Spirit.
And yet You are One – the only One.
Even if I cannot always understand
       what You reveal to me.
I always believe!
For You are the Infinite God
and I am Your finite creature....

God the Son or the Word

...in the SON, the WORD OF GOD, who is eternally begotten...
THE CREDO

The fact that the Word is the Second Person of the Blessed Trinity is revealed to us in the first chapter of St. John's Gospel: "In the beginning was the Word and the Word was with God and the Word was God.... All things were made through him, and without him was made nothing that has been made" (1:1-3).

The following quotation from St. John Chrysostom will serve to clarify this point a little further:

The Word is a distinct Person, proceeding from the Father Himself without alteration. Just as the expression "In the beginning was the Word" reveals His eternity, so "He was in the beginning *with* God" has revealed to us His co-eternity. For the Father was never without the Word, but always God was with God though each in His own Person.

Christ, the Son of God is called the Word because He proceeds from the Father by way of knowledge. The Father knows Himself; His act of knowing Himself produces an Idea – a Word; and this Idea, this Word that the Father generates, is infinite, eternal, living – a Person – the second Person of the Blessed Trinity, equal in all things to the Father.

God the Holy Spirit,
Paraclete, Sanctifier and Comforter

...in the HOLY SPIRIT, the uncreated Person who proceeds from the Father and the Son as Their eternal love...

We believe in the Holy Spirit, who is Lord, and Giver of life, who is adored and glorified together with the Father and the Son.

THE CREDO

The distinct personality of the Holy Spirit is clearly indicated in Scripture. Thus we read in St. Paul's first epistle to the Corinthians (12:11): "But all these things are the work of one and the same Spirit, who allots to everyone according as he will."

St. Augustine clearly sums up the entire Catholic doctrine on the Holy Spirit in these words:

"Their [the Father's and the Son's] common Spirit, what does this mean? Is it their unity with each other, their holiness, their love? Their substantial and eternal communion? Their friendship and fellowship...? Yes, we say, it is their mutual charity, the love of the Father for the Son and the Son for the Father.

"It is by this reciprocal and essential gift that they preserve between them the unity in the bond of peace (Eph. 4:3). Thus we know that there be three: He who loves His offspring, He who loves His principle, and their love."

In the Blessed Trinity we find what are known as the "Divine Missions" or, to translate it in a free way, the active capacity for "sending" and the passive role of being "sent" as regards each Person. Thus the Father can "send" but not be "sent." Also, the Son, the Second Person can "send" along with the Father, and the Son can likewise be "sent." The Holy Spirit cannot "send" but can be "sent" by both Father and Son.

This truth has profound consequences for theology, since it influences God's entire relations with humanity. Thus the Redemption of the human race was accomplished by God the Son through the Incarnation, the Word being "sent" for this purpose by the Father. The mission or "sending" of the Holy Spirit is quite different. To Him is attributed the work of guiding the Church and sanctifying the individual soul.

That the Holy Spirit guards the Church we know from the words of Christ Himself: "I will ask the Father and he will give you another Advocate to dwell with you forever, the Spirit of truth.... You shall know him, because he will dwell with you, and be in you" (Jn. 14:16-17).

How this promise was fulfilled we read in the Acts of the Apostles (2:1-4): "And when the days of Pentecost were drawing to a close, they were all together in one place. And suddenly there came a sound from heaven, as of a violent wind blowing, and it filled the whole house where they were sitting. And there appeared to them parted tongues as of fire, which settled upon each of them. And they were all filled with the Holy Spirit and began to speak in foreign tongues, even as the Holy Spirit prompted them to speak."

That the presence of the Holy Spirit was experienced in the Church from the very beginning we learn again from the same source (8:14-17): "Now when the apostles in Jerusalem heard that Samaria had received the word of God, they sent to them Peter and John. On their arrival they prayed for them, that they might receive the Holy Spirit; for as yet he had not come upon any of them, but they had only been baptized in the name of the Lord Jesus. Then they laid their hands on them and they received the Holy Spirit."

Vatican II in the *Dogmatic Constitution on the Church* describes how the Holy Spirit assists the Church:

"In order that we may be unceasingly renewed in Him [Christ] (cf. Eph. 4:23), He has shared with us His Spirit, who, existing as one and the same being in the head and in the members, gives life to, unifies and moves through the whole body. This He does in such a way that His work could be compared by the holy fathers with the function which the principle of life, that is, the soul, fulfills, in the human body" (n. 7).

Pope Paul refers to all this in a general way in his *Credo* when he writes:

He was sent by Christ after His resurrection and His ascension to the Father; He illuminates, vivifies, protects and guides the Church.

The Holy Spirit is also called the "Sanctifier" because He makes holy the individual human soul. Pope Paul's *Credo* refers to this specific function in these words:

He purifies the Church's members if they do not shun His grace.

As we have already pointed out, God is present in all creatures in a threefold manner—by His presence, by His power and by His essence. However, His presence in us by grace is of a much higher and more intimate kind. Referring to this, St. John says (1:12): "He gave the power of becoming the sons of God; to those that believed in his name." This sonship is one in very truth: "that we should be called and should be the sons of God." By it we come into possession of the divine nature, not in a substantial way of course, yet in a true sense we are made "partakers of the divine nature" as we read in St. Peter's second epistle (1:4).

Thus, when we are in the state of grace, the most Blessed Trinity lives in our very soul. Our Lord Himself has said it: "If anyone love me, he will keep my word, and my Father will love him, and we will come to him and make our abode with him" (Jn. 14:23). As if this were not enough, we read again in the Apocalypse of St. John (3:20): "Behold, I stand at the door and knock. If any man listens to my voice and opens the door to me, I will come in to him and will sup with him, and he with me."

The saints were keenly aware of this beautiful teaching and put it into practice by being ever conscious of the presence of God. St. Margaret of Scotland, who died in 1093, was adept at this devotion, as were also St. Catherine of Siena, "the greatest woman of Christendom," and St. Teresa of Avila, who reformed the Carmelite Order. Many young people are restrained from sin by the thought of their parents. They would never do in private what they would be ashamed to do in public before their loved ones. If that be so for relatives, how much more is it true of God Himself, who is not only watching us but is present in our very selves by sanctifying grace. This thought then is a powerful brake against sinning. As St. Paul so forcibly puts it:

"Do you not know that you are the temple of God and that the Spirit of God dwells in you? If anyone destroys the temple of God, him will God destroy; for holy is the temple of God, and this temple you are" (1 Cor. 3:16).

All Three Divine Persons, moreover, inhabit the soul in the state of grace. Where One Person is, the Other Two must be.

Curiously enough, while most persons are conscious of the existence of God the Father and God the Son, still for some reason or other, certainly up until quite recent times, the Holy Spirit was relegated to the background. This so troubled Abbot Vonier, O.S.B., that in an effort to stimulate true devotion to the Holy Spirit he wrote a book entitled *The Forgotten Paraclete*. However, it must be noted, and with great satisfaction, that there has been renewed interest in the Holy Spirit as Sanctifier of the Church and the individual soul.

We should pray often for the gifts of the Holy Spirit— wisdom, understanding, knowledge, piety, counsel, fortitude and fear of the Lord. Beautiful prayers to the Holy Spirit are not difficult to find, and the feast of Pentecost, with the classic sequence of its Mass, can be easily made to play a very practical part in our lives.

Before he became a Catholic, Cardinal Newman went through a grave spiritual crisis. His health weakened and in order to recuperate, he took a vacation in Europe. On June 16, 1833, the ship on which he was traveling was stranded in the Mediterranean. It was then that he wrote the following beautiful hymn, "Lead Kindly Light."

> Lead kindly light amidst the encircling gloom,
> Lead Thou me on!
> The night is dark and I am far from home,
> Lead Thou me on!
> Keep Thou my feet, I do not ask to see,
> The distant scene, one step enough for me.
>
> I was not ever thus nor prayed that Thou
> Shouldst lead me on.
> I loved to choose and see my path, but now,
> Lead Thou me on!
> I loved the garish day and spite of fears
> Pride ruled my will, remember not past years!

CHALLENGE

God is fully glorified provided that men fully and consciously accept His work of salvation...that the whole human race might form one People of God and be built up into one temple of the Holy Spirit.... So at last there will be realized the plan of our Creator, who formed man to His own image and likeness, when all who share one human nature, regenerated in *Christ* through the *Holy Spirit* and beholding the glory of God, will be able to say with one accord: "Our Father."

DECREE ON THE MISSION ACTIVITY OF THE CHURCH

4

"WHO
CAN PROBE
HIS DEEDS?"

SIRACH 18:2

...CREATOR of things visible such as this world in which our transient life passes, of things invisible such as the pure spirits which are called angels. THE CREDO

The three divine Persons, in their indivisible unity, were infinitely happy. St. Thomas Aquinas says that "God enjoys a most excellent delight in Himself, as well as a universal joy in all things. For wealth He has the all-abundant self-sufficiency of all good things within Himself. For power He has His infinite strength. For honor, He has primacy and rule over all beings. For fame, He has the admiration of every intellect that knows Him however little. To Him, then, who is singularly blessed, be honor and glory unto the ages of ages." The three divine Persons needed nothing and no one.

But since God is love itself, He wished to share His bliss with others. Thus, God freely created the angels, the universe and finally man. We will treat each of these in detail.

The angels

Friends of God

The Catholic Church has always believed in the existence of angels. While of itself, reason alone could never prove this, still it can suggest very strong arguments as to why it should be so. The demonstration goes something as follows:

In the lowest form of creation we find the inanimate things such as rocks, the land and the sea. Then we have vegetative life—trees, plants and the like. Next we discover creatures which live and are guided by perception and instinct. Then comes man who possesses vegetable, animal and rational activity. It would be most reasonable then to suspect that our next discovery should be that of purely spiritual creatures. Otherwise reason would indicate that in the order of creatures from the lowest to the highest, if the angels did not exist, there would be an inordinate gap between mankind and God. Creation would be incomplete! Even imperfect! But since God does all things well, completely and perfectly, it is becoming that there should be pure spirits, or angels.

Whatever be the speculations of reason in this matter, certainly there is frequent positive mention of angels in both Old and New Testaments. Thus in the latter, an angel announces the birth of John the Baptist (cf. Lk. 1:5-25). St. Joseph is warned by an angel of the coming birth of the Child (cf. Mt. 1:18-25). Already an angel – Gabriel – had requested Mary's consent to be the Mother of God, a consent freely given (cf. Lk. 1:26-38). Again angels herald Christ's birth at Bethlehem (cf. Lk. 2:8-14), and once more an angel appears to Joseph in sleep, telling him to flee with the Child and His Mother into Egypt to escape Herod (cf. Mt. 2:13-15). When the time of danger is passed, there is another angelic appearance, and Joseph is told to return to Israel (cf. Mt. 2:19-23).

During His public life Christ Himself referred to the angels. At the start of His ministry He said to Nathanael: "Amen, amen, I say to you, you shall see heaven opened, and the angels of God ascending and descending upon the Son of Man" (Jn. 1:51). Addressing the multitudes Jesus once said: "But whoever disowns me before men will be disowned before the angels of God" (Lk. 12:9). In another discourse He said: "The Son of Man will send forth his angels, and they will gather out of his kingdom all scandals and those that work iniquity, and cast them into the furnace of fire, where there will be the weeping and the gnashing of teeth" (Mt. 13:41-42). "There will be joy among the angels of God over one sinner who repents," He has told us (Lk. 15:10).

When the apostles were ambitious for power, our Lord took a little child, set him in their midst and told them to become like him. Then He added: "See that you do not despise one of these little ones; for I tell you, their angels in heaven always behold the face of my Father in heaven" (Mt. 18:10).

Describing the resurrection of the dead to the apostles on Mount Olivet, just before His bitter passion and death, Jesus said: "And he will send forth his angels with a trumpet and a great sound, and they will gather together his elect from the four winds, from one end of the heavens to the other" (Mt. 24:31).

During His agony and bloody sweat in the garden Jesus is comforted by an angel: "And there appeared to him an angel from heaven to strengthen him" (Lk. 22:43). When Peter, rushing to defend His divine Master, lopped off the ear of Malchus, the servant of the high priest, our Lord said to him: "Put back your sword into its place; for all those who take the sword will perish by the sword. Or do you not suppose that I cannot entreat my Father, and he will even now furnish me with more than twelve legions of angels?" (Mt. 26:52-53).

All four evangelists who have recorded the resurrection tell us that: "An angel of the Lord came down from heaven, and drawing near rolled back the stone, and sat upon it. His countenance was like lightning, and his raiment like snow. And for fear of him the guards were terrified and became like dead men" (Mt. 28:2-4). Saints Matthew, Mark and Luke tell us that an angel announced the actual resurrection to the holy women upon their arrival at the sepulcher to anoint the body with sweet spices. Upon her arrival at the tomb alone, Mary Magdalene saw two angels in white, sitting, one at the head and one at the foot where the body of Jesus had been laid. They questioned her, "Woman, why are you weeping?" Just then our Lord appeared to Mary, who on recognizing Him cried out: "Rabboni! (Master!)" (cf. Jn. 20:13, 16).

Finally, after His ascension into heaven, two angels in white stood by the disciples and said: "Men of Galilee, why do you stand looking up to heaven? This Jesus who has been taken up from you into heaven, shall come in the same way as you have seen him going up to heaven" (Acts 1:11).

We have gone to some length in recording these events, for in today's secular world, there are many who view the existence of angels, not merely with suspicion, but with downright unbelief. The Fourth Lateran and Vatican I Councils declared that at the beginning of time God created from nothing both spiritual and corporal creation, that is, *angelic* and mundane. And Pope Pius XII in his encyclical letter, *Humani generis*, reproved those who questioned the personal character of the angels or the essential difference between spirit and matter.

The angels are pure spirits who adore, praise, glorify and serve God. They act as messengers between Him and man, revealing His divine will to creatures. This will be clear from the examples already given from the Gospels. They are, of course, vastly superior to man, both in intelligence and knowledge. By nature, they are the most excellent beings in God's creation and resemble Him the greatest. Being purely spiritual beings, they cannot be seen with human eyes. Sometimes God permits them to assume bodily form, and they then become visible. This happened in the case of the prophet Daniel and, of course, when Gabriel appeared to the Blessed Virgin.

In His love, God has appointed certain angels to guard, watch over, and aid us individually. These are called "our guardian angels." They help us by prayer, by protecting us from harm, and by inspiring us to do good. They look after each of us from birth until death, put good thoughts into the mind and move the will to do good. They offer our prayers and good works to God. Surely we should love, honor and venerate these glorious angelic creatures. If while here on earth we ask our friends to "pray for us," then in all confidence we should likewise ask these angels to do the same!

Also let us ask them to add their prayers to ours so that we may be more worthy of our eternal destiny. In the eternity which awaits us all, we will one day be with them in the realm of the blessed.

The prince of this world

It is Catholic doctrine that the angels were created with free will but did not enjoy the Beatific Vision, i.e., they did not enjoy the sight of God. This was to be their reward for passing some test, whose nature remains unknown to us. Some of the angels proved faithful to God. These are now happy with Him forever in heaven. Others failed and were condemned at once to hell, a place of eternal torments that was made for them simultaneously, where they will be excluded from the sight of God forever. We read in the second epistle of St. Peter (2:4): "For God did not spare the angels who fell into sin; he thrust them down to hell, chained them there in the abyss, to await their sentence in torment." Again we read in the epistle of St. Jude (1:6): "And the angels who did not preserve their original state, but forsook their abode, he has kept in everlasting chains under darkness for the judgment of the great day."

We have already seen that the four Gospels frequently mention the good angels. They also mention the bad ones, particularly Satan or Lucifer, their leader.

The latter is called the strong one (cf. Mt. 12:29; Mk. 3:27; Lk. 11:21). He is also called the evil one (cf. Mt. 13:19) and the prince of this world (cf. Jn. 12:31). He is a tempter who even tempts Jesus Christ, who is God Himself (cf. Mt. 4:1; Mk. 1:13; Lk. 4:2). His works are many and diverse. Thus, he takes the seed of the word from the mouths of those who receive it (cf. Mt. 13:19; Mk. 4:15; Lk. 8:12) and puts the betrayal of Christ into the mind of Judas (cf. Jn. 13:2). Finally he entered into Judas for the doing of the foul deed (cf. Lk. 22:3; Jn. 13:27). We also know from Christ Himself that Lucifer wished to have the disciples so that he could sift them like wheat (cf. Lk. 22:31) and is so malevolent that he sows cockle in God's wheat field (cf. Mt. 13:39). Satan went so far as to say that all the kingdoms of the world were in his power (cf. Lk. 4:6).

The devil does not respect anything; he tempts anyone: in fact, he preferably torments the most beautiful souls. Yet he cannot do all the evil he would like to do because he is like a tied dog; hence the Christian must live on guard but not have an unreasonable fear of him. "In your battle," says St. Cyprian, "God is He who begins the fight, it is He who fights, and it is He who triumphs, and to you He leaves the merit of the victory. Your war is God's war; your battle is Jesus Christ's battle. What do you fear? Why do you doubt as though you were to win through your own virtue? Take up the arms, go to war, fight as strong men, so that He who is never defeated may be with you."

Apart from the Gospels, there are numerous references to Satan and demons to be found throughout the Acts of the Apostles and the epistles of St. Paul and other books of the New Testament.

As in the case of the angels in general, so also the Fourth Lateran Council has clearly stated that God created Satan and the fallen angels good in themselves by nature, but that they became evil of their own free will. Thus, in the official view of the Church's magisterium, personal devils exist. No indications as to number are given, but it is clear from the statement of the Council that it envisages a great many demons.

In the life of St. John Mary Vianney, the author Henri Gheon entitles one of the chapters: "The Devil Comes in Person." As we turn the pages, we are astounded and terrified to find out what the devil did in his attempt to weaken the faith of this great servant of God. The unearthly harrassment continued for thirty-four years — from 1824 until 1858. These facts are incontestable and were sifted thoroughly before the humble parish priest was canonized. In the following words, written by the saint himself, we discover how he finally realized that he was being obsessed by the devil. We read as follows:

"I immediately opened my window and asked: 'Who is there?' But I saw nothing and went quietly to bed, recommending myself to God. I was not asleep when three more blows, struck this time not on the outer door but on the door on the stairs leading to my bedroom, made me jump. I got up and cried a second time: 'Who is there?' No one replied. When the noise began, I took it that it was thieves, with designs on the beautiful ornaments presented to the church by the Vicomte D'Ars, and I thought I had better take precautions. I asked two stout men to sleep at the presbytery to help in case of need. They came several nights running. They discovered nothing and remained convinced that the noise had another cause than the wickedness of men. I myself became certain of it, for one night in winter when much snow had fallen, three mighty blows were heard about midnight. I sprang instantly out of bed; I shot downstairs into the yard, thinking that this time I should catch the criminals in flight, intending to summon help. But to my great surprise, I heard nothing, and what is more, I saw no footprint in the snow. Then I no longer doubted that it was the devil who wanted to frighten me. I abandoned myself to God's will, praying to Him to be my protector and my guardian, to come near me with His angels when my enemy should again decide to torment me."

St. Paul warns: "Put you on the armor of God, that you may be able to stand against the deceits of the devil."

And St. Peter adds: "Be sober, be watchful! For your adversary the devil, as a roaring lion, goes about seeking someone to devour. Resist him, steadfast in the faith, knowing that the same suffering befalls your brethren all over the world."

Satan and his evil hordes tempt us to deprive God of our love. But we must remember always that although these evil angels can bring temptation, they cannot force us to sin, for we are the children of the living God, and nothing under heaven or on earth can harm us unless we give our consent. Moreover, for every temptation that they may bring to us, God gives us the grace and aid to overcome it.

One means at our disposal to ward off temptation is the use of sacramentals: making the sign of the cross with holy water, using blessed rosary beads, wearing a crucifix, medal or scapular. Recourse to St. Michael the Archangel "to defend us in battle against the snares of Satan" is also efficacious.

When we behold the heavens
Psalm 8

Not only did God create the angels, He also fashioned the universe. And out of nothing! There can be no other explanation, for the universe could not have created itself, nor was it made out of the spiritual substance of God. For again, it is an article of faith that the Almighty is absolutely and completely distinct from the objects and creatures He has produced.

The universe had a definite beginning in time — in other words, it was immediately created by God, out of nothing.

When we dealt with the attributes of God, we noted that among others, He possesses immensity, omnipotence and omniscience. Nowhere are these characteristics more manifest than in contemplating the vastness of the universe, the multitudes of bodies that inhabit it and the tremendous processes that go on within them. Let us take a quick look at each of these to see what we can find.

We get some faint idea of the illimitable reaches of the universe from the incredible discoveries of astronomy.

The latest of these are quasars, a contraction for "quasi-stellar radio sources." They are too massive to be stars and too compact to be galaxies, but they are the most powerful transmitters of radio waves so far detected in the universe. One of them is the farthest object ever seen in the heavens — perhaps from six to seven billion light years from the earth, and bounding away from it at the breathtaking speed of 76,000 miles per second, nearly half the speed of light. Far as this distance is, however, astronomers tell us that it is only half-way to the edge of the observable universe!

So much for the extent of the cosmos—what about the bodies that move in it? In order to learn something about them, let us map briefly the heavens. Our little earth—a mere speck of dust relatively speaking—with its smaller satellite, the moon, plus the other planets, Mercury, Venus, Mars, Jupiter, Saturn, Uranus, Neptune and Pluto belong to the solar system, their center being the sun. This entire solar system is located about two-thirds of the way from the center of the Milky Way, on one of the spiral arms of the nebula. On a cloudless night when there is no moon shining, scientists tell us that we can count about 8,000 stars with the naked eye. They all belong to our own galaxy which, shaped like a pocket watch, has a diameter from two to three hundred thousand light years at maximum. In addition to the stars that we can pick out with the naked eye, it contains, at a rough estimate, a hundred billion more!

On a clear, starry night, locate the constellation Andromeda. At midnight of December 31 of any year you can pick it out quite easily in the northeastern sky. Inspect this constellation closely and if conditions are favorable enough, you will notice a miniscule white smudge, just faintly visible to the naked eye. This is the next galaxy to ours and is at a distance of 2.2 million light years from us. Its central core or diameter is roughly 20,000 trillion miles across while the spiral arms occupy a distance of about 260,000 trillion miles and can be traced faintly over approximately twice this distance. This galaxy also contains hundreds of billions of stars! If instead of being on the earth within our own galaxy we were on the one in Andromeda, our *entire* galaxy would appear as hardly perceptible white smudge.

Besides the Milky Way galaxy, our own, and the one in Andromeda, there are billions of others in the universe, and there are billions of stars in each one! These colossal figures completely baffle the puny mind of man. He cannot cope with them. All he can do is stand in awe at the infinite power of their Maker—God!

"Twinkle, twinkle, little star: how I wonder what you are!" How often as children we heard this delightful nursery rhyme repeated to us. Today science can give us the answer as to what goes on in the stars—certainly in general terms. The

sun — really an insignificant star by cosmic standards — derives
its energy as the result of atomic fusion when helium is produced by various processes. The sun has been drawing on this
energy for at least two billion years. At its present rate, it will
continue to do so for another thirty billion years! What goes
on in the sun is typical of what transpires in the stellar population of the entire universe.

Such is the vastness of the universe! Such are the incal-
culable number of bodies that inhabit it! Such is the account
of what happens within them! Oh, the immensity of God,
His omnipotence, His omniscience!

On Christmas night, 1968, Commanders Borman, Lovell and
Anders, America's astronauts, circled the moon, at a distance of only
seventy miles from its surface. As they surveyed the lurrain [1] below, one could detect the awe in their voices. Then came that unforgettable moment in history, when these three courageous and religious men — the first men since the creation of the universe to ever
escape from the gravitational field of the earth and be captured
by that of another heavenly body — impressed by the fact of God as
they had never been impressed before in their lives, radioed back
to earth from the huge distance of 240,000 miles the account of creation as we read it in the first chapter of the book of Genesis:

"In the beginning God created the heavens and the earth; the
earth was waste and darkness covered the abyss, and the spirit of
God was stirring above the waters.

"God said, 'Let there be light, and there was light. God saw that
the light was good. God separated the light from the darkness, calling
the light Day and the darkness Night. And there was evening and
morning, the first day.

"And God said, 'Let there be a firmament in the midst of the
waters, to divide the waters.' And so it was. God made the firmament,
dividing the waters that were below the firmament from those that
were above it. God called the firmament Heaven. And there was
evening and morning, the second day.

"Then God said, 'Let the waters below the heavens be gathered
into one place and let the dry land appear.' And so it was. God called
the dry land Earth and the assembled waters Seas. And God saw that
it was good" (Gen. 1:1-8).

Seven months later, on July 20, 1969, during man's historic first landing on the moon, while on the lunar surface, Commanders Armstrong and Aldrin deposited messages from

---

1. A name for the surface of the moon.

heads of state and also the flags of various nations. Among the latter was one of Vatican State and along with the former was a Latin text of Psalm 8, personally selected by the Pope for the occasion and to which he added a dedicatory inscription, the latter penned in his own hand. The Psalm (English translation) and inscription now follow.

PSALM 8

O Lord, our Lord,
how glorious is your name over all the earth!
You have exalted your majesty above the heavens.
Out of the mouths of babes and sucklings
you have fashioned praise because of your foes,
to silence the hostile and the vengeful.
When I behold the heavens, the work of your fingers,
the moon and the stars which you set in place —
What is man that you should be mindful of him?
or the son of man that you should care for him?
You have made him little less than the angels,
and crowned him with glory and honor.
You have given him rule over the works of your hands,
putting all things under his feet:
All sheep and oxen,
yes, and the beasts of the field,
The birds of the air, the fishes of the sea,
and whatever swims the paths of the seas.
O Lord, our Lord,
how glorious is your name over all the earth!

THE PAPAL INSCRIPTION:
"For the glory of the name of God,
who gives men such power."

Four days prior to the historic moon flight, Pope Paul VI invited men to reflect on its significance:

"Let us just turn our gaze upwards, trying to peer into the depths of space; we are overcome with amazement, almost with giddiness, with a sense of mystery. The contrast between the dimensions of the space and time at our disposal and the infinite dimensions of the cosmos frightens us.

"This boundless reality, which envelops us and which we are now invited to consider, obliges us to take up again

"When I behold the heavens, the work of your fingers, the moon and the stars which you set in place — what is man, O God, that you should be mindful of him...?

Psalm 8

and confirm some fundamental thoughts, which are not so much scientific as philosophical. Two, among others. There exists a cosmos, there exists a universe; it exists independently of man, whom it preceded and whom it will outlive, of man who observes it, discovers it, studies it, explores it.

"Man is not the principle; man is not the cause of the world. Anyone who wishes to limit reality, the all, to the thought of man, is playing with the absurd. Our knowledge, our science, our truth does not produce things; it knows them, thinks them, forms images of them, makes them its own spiritually, but it does not create them. *Our science, though it is our greatness, is based on great humility.* Furthermore, if this cosmos exists, and shows itself to be on the one hand, so traversed by lines of a mysterious order (the sciences tell us so: mathematics, physics especially; the motions, energies, laws...found in it confirm this); and, on the other hand, one would say so charged with a thought not its own, but infused, reflected, operating, and able to be deciphered, known and also used, *it is a sign that this cosmos is derived from a transcendent principle, a creative mind, a secret and superior power.... That is: it is created."*

Only God really knows exactly *how* He made the universe, and this is why men of science can only formulate theories.

They also discuss the method that God used in creating *living things* and here, too, they give two chief theories, about plants and animals:

1) *The Theory of Changelessness.* The theory of changelessness, which means the theory of direct creation, holds that God created the first of each of the different kinds of plants and animals. He gave them power to reproduce others like themselves, and thus to fill the world with the wonder and beauty of many animals and plants. Notice that this theory states that God created the first of each type of nature's furniture — the first of the stately poplar trees, the first of the cobras, the first of the tigers, the first of the dandelions, and so forth. This theory of changelessness holds that the poplar tree produced seed from which grew poplars just like the first one. Through the ages since God first made poplars, they have reproduced poplars like themselves. Likewise, cobras have reproduced others like themselves ever since the good Lord saw a place for them among His earthly furnishings.

2) *The Theory of Evolution.* Evolution is another theory about the manner in which God created things. People who

hold to the theory of evolution have noticed certain likenesses among members of the plant kingdom, as well as likenesses among members of the animal kingdom. They observe that some plants are simple, that is, made up of very few parts. But they notice that other plants are more complex having many parts. They notice, too, that animal organisms range from the simple to the complex. The more complex the organism the more highly developed are the sensory powers.

The theory of evolution holds that God created a few different living things and gave them power to reproduce others, some of which would be like themselves, while others would be a little different. The ability of animals and plants to reproduce creatures slightly different from themselves would give the world its great variety of reptiles, fish, flowers and vegetables, land and air animals. It certainly is not beyond the power of almighty God to have created in such a manner.

Up to the present time, neither the theory of changelessness nor the theory of evolution has been definitely proved. As both theories are reasonable, the Church leaves you free to favor either theory.

Naturally we are not speaking here of evolutionary theories that leave no place for God the Creator.

The Church looks with favor upon those scientists who are trying to learn more and more about the laws of nature, as long as scientists bear in mind that the laws of nature come from God, and that they do not state as proved facts, ideas that are only theories.

"To our image and likeness"

Genesis 1

...and Creator in EACH MAN OF HIS SPIRITUAL AND IMMORTAL SOUL.

THE CREDO

Man, of course, like all else, owes his origin to God. We read in Genesis (1:26-27): "God said, 'Let us make mankind to our image and likeness; and let them have dominion over the fish of the sea, the birds of the air, the cattle, over all the wild animals and every creature that crawls upon the earth.' God created man in his image. In the image of God he created him. Male and female he created them. Then God blessed them and said to them, 'Be fruitful and multiply; fill the earth and subdue it. Have dominion over the fish of the sea, the birds of the air, the cattle and all the animals that crawl on the earth.'"

And again in Genesis (2:7) we read: "Then the Lord God formed man out of the dust of the ground and breathed into his nostrils the breath of life, and man became a living being."

Reason, considering the marvelous constitution of man, tells us that he could not have appeared by chance or through a blind and slow transformation of beings, as *absolute* evolutionism affirms.

On the creation of man, Sacred Scripture throws some rays of divine light. It says:

1) that man was created to the image and likeness of God;

2) that he is the noblest of all earthly creatures;

3) that in him there are two principles: one material (the body) and the other spiritual (the soul);

4) that the body was formed from already pre-existing matter;

5) that the soul was created immediately from nothing and infused into the body;

6) that all the human race derives from the first man, Adam, and from the first woman, Eve.

What, then, about the theory that the *body* of the first man evolved from the lower animals? Addressing theologians and scientists, Pope Paul VI said: "The theory of *evolutionism* favored today by many scientists and not a few theologians owing to its probability, will not seem acceptable to you where it is not decidedly in accord with the immediate creation of each and every human *soul* by God." Therefore, although we do not know with certainty the form of the pre-existing matter from which the body of the first man was formed, it is a certain fact that his soul (and the soul of every man) was created immediately from nothing by God.

"God formed man to be *imperishable; the image of his own nature* he made him" (Wis. 2:23).

"Every human being is a person," explains Pope John XXIII, "that is, his nature is endowed with intelligence and free will." The *Constitution on the Church in the Modern World* says that by his interior qualities man "outstrips the whole sum of mere things. He plunges into the depths of reality whenever he enters into his own heart; God, who probes the heart, awaits him there; there he discerns his proper destiny beneath the eyes of God. Thus, when he recognizes in himself *a spiritual and immortal soul,* he is not being mocked by a fantasy born only of physical or social influences, but is rather laying hold of the proper truth of the matter" (n. 14).

Is the soul of man truly spiritual?

Yes, the soul of man is spiritual. Reason itself tells us this. If the spiritual acts of man, such as understanding and willing, are independent of matter, their *causal-principle,* that is the soul, must also be independent. This is according to the well-known principle: "As the act is, so is the nature of the cause which produces it." It is sufficient to consider some of the acts which man performs, to be convinced that they do not come from matter, but from the spirit. We have concepts wholly immaterial and incorporeal, such as: God, virtue, vice, duty, etc. We have desires and resolutions superior to matter: we desire good, truth, honor; we hate vice, dishonesty, injustice.... We have abstract and universal concepts, such as: there is no effect without a cause; the whole is greater than a part, etc. We reflect on our acts and, while the body consumes itself with the years and work, the intellect perfects itself always more with age and practice.... All these things affirm in us a *principle* which does not in any way depend for its being on matter and which is entirely *spiritual:* the soul. Therefore, the doctrine which does not admit the existence of the spirit, that is, *materialism,* is repugnant to reason.

Is the soul of man truly immortal?

That the soul of man is truly immortal is a truth constantly admitted by the whole human race and by our own conscience. In fact:

1) Goodness, justice and wisdom exact reward for good and punishment for evil. This does not take place in the present life. A second life is therefore necessary.

2) The soul is, of its nature, simple and spiritual, hence it cannot break up into parts nor depend upon matter, or perish.

3) Human instinct invincibly desires a full and unending life with intuition of the infinite. We know that, to every natural instinct, there corresponds a law of nature. Therefore, the soul of man *is* immortal.

4) This certainty was perennial in all times and was universal for all religions and civilizations; even the most learned men, the best philosophers and thinkers of all ages have constantly professed such a doctrine. Thus the great

souls, the great benefactors, the lovers of justice and of goodness have believed.

The soul being immortal, man must order all the present life to the future, so as to win an immortal beatitude.

The present life is the time God grants to every man to prepare himself for his eternal happiness. Supreme happiness is possible, because it is absurd to think that God should have destined man to an unattainable end; man would be unhappy if he could not obtain that which forms his natural and supreme tendency.

Wealth, pleasure and power cannot make men perfectly happy. Not even wisdom, virtue, family joys or friendship can form the happiness of man, because even these are not unmixed with sorrows and are not eternal.

The object of our supreme happiness is only God, because He alone is the eternal good. He alone can satisfy fully and perpetually our intellect, desires, aspirations and all the spiritual and corporal faculties of man.

"One is the community of all peoples, one their origin, for God made the whole human race to live over the face of the earth. One also is their final goal, God" (Declaration on Relation of Church to Non-Christian Religions, n. 1).

The creative act of God by which He has produced the human race means that all men are equal in His sight. This doctrine has exceedingly important consequences for the modern world, as we shall see, when we come to treat the problem of racism. The Fathers of the Second Vatican Council realized this only too well and did not hesitate to put their convictions on paper. Thus we read in the *Pastoral Constitution on the Church in the Modern World:*

> Since all men possess a rational soul and are created
> in God's likeness, since they enjoy the same nature
> and origin...and the same divine calling and destiny,
> the basic equality of all must receive increasingly
> greater recognition. (n. 29)

CHALLENGE

In highlighting the value of our immortal soul, St. John Chrysostom writes: "You do not have another soul with which to ransom your soul. He who loses his money may substitute it with other things. So also, he who loses his ships, his property, his furniture and similar other things can still re-establish himself. But if you lose your soul, you will never be able to give something else which will replace it. Even if you were the king of the universe, you would not be able to buy another soul — not even one, even if you were to offer the whole world with all its treasures. Placing, therefore, everything else in the second order of importance, turn all your thoughts, all your cares, all your solicitude to procure the salvation of your soul."

His provident care

...His Providence...His Will... THE CREDO

Speaking of the creation, St. Augustine wrote: "Behold, the earth and sky exist, and they cry out: 'We are, because we were created, nor were we, before existing, able to make ourselves.' Now, this language of theirs is evidence itself. Hence, O Lord, You made these things; You who are beautiful, made them beautiful; You who are good, made them good; You who are Being, made them to be.

"Why did God deign to create all these things? In order to manifest His perfections by means of the goods given to creatures, and certainly not to acquire or add something to His own beatitude. Does God take care of all created things? Yes, in fact, He positively preserves them and upholds them — otherwise they would return to nothing — and He governs them so that nothing happens or could happen without God's will or permission. This care that God takes of created things is called divine Providence."

Divine Providence is never lacking; in fact, it is closest to us when times are the hardest and most difficult for us. For him who has faith, how consoling it is to be able to say: "God made me! God governs me! God wants me with Him!" Oh! Let us trust in God, our Creator and Redeemer: He does not wish us evil, but only good, so much so, that in His omnipotent love for us, He knows how to turn to our advantage even those things which we consider evil, in fact even sins, if man repents.

God is the Creator of all things, visible and invisible — of the angels, of the universe and of men. But God does not create and then leave things to take care of themselves. Quite the contrary! Although we cannot see Him nor discern His action, still, as the First Vatican Council defined it: He has the care of all things, even the smallest, and directs them to a determined end. Thus, not only does He take His place at

Dear God,
be good
to me.
The sea is so wide and my boat is so small.
Breton Fisherman's Prayer

the helm of the universe as its Steersman, but He is the Lord of history as well.

During the closing speeches of the Second Vatican Council, the Fathers affirmed their belief in Providence in these words: "God is—and more, He is real; *He lives, a personal provident God, infinitely good in Himself, but also immeasurably good to us.* He will be recognized as our Creator, our truth, our happiness; so much so, that the effort to look on Him and to center our heart in Him which we call contemplation, is the highest, the most perfect act of the spirit, the act which even today can and must be at the apex of all human activity."

The Providence of God is proved by an appeal to the following texts of Scripture.

God cares for all things in a general way. "Indeed, she [divine wisdom] reaches from end to end mightily and governs all things well " (Wis. 8:1). "For neither is there any god besides you who have care of all" (Wis. 12:13).

Providence extends to even the smallest things: "Are not two sparrows sold for a farthing? And yet not one of them will fall to the ground without your Father's leave" (Mt. 10:29).

Even things which seem to happen by chance are attributed to God: "When the lot is cast into the lap, its decision depends entirely on the Lord" (Prov. 16:33).

Providence extends particularly to mankind: "Therefore I say to you, do not be anxious for your life, what you shall eat; nor yet for your body, what you shall put on.... For your Father knows that you need all these things.... The very hairs of your head are all numbered. Therefore, do not be afraid, you are of more value than many sparrows" (Mt. 6:25; Lk. 12:7).

God so directs events that they conspire to the salvation of the elect: "You thought evil against me, but God turned it into good" (Gn. 1:20). "By me kings reign, and lawgivers establish justice" (Prov. 8:15). "For all things are for your sakes, so that the grace which abounds through the many may cause thanksgiving to abound, to the glory of God" (2 Cor. 4:15).

If God were to forget everything He created even for a second, all would be annihilated. His conservation of all that He created is an act of continuous creation! My dependence on God is so absolute that I cannot do anything without Him.

I can breathe, think, live and speak because God has created me, sustains me, conserves me in being, and gives me everything necessary so that I can do all this. The thought of God's continuous act of creating is one which should culminate in heartfelt gratitude. How great His power, His wisdom, His love! He has loved me — each one can say — with an eternal love.

The presence of evil in the world seems to deny the loving Providence of God. Under the term "evil" we include everything that injures man — sin, hunger, poverty, sickness, death and physical disasters of all kinds, as for example: floods; earthquakes; tidal waves; eruption of volcanoes; accidents, e.g., air crashes, train derailments, wars, etc. As a matter of fact, contemplation of horrors like these has contributed very much to the "Death of God" theology we hear so much about today.

There is a deep mystery in the presence of evil in the world but from its presence it does not follow that God does not exist, nor that He does not care. During one of the apparitions the Blessed Virgin said to Bernadette: "I cannot promise you happiness in this world, only in the next." We must always bear in mind that God is not and cannot be the author of evil. Whatever is bad in the world comes from the exercise of man's free will. Moreover, by His infinite wisdom and power, God draws good from evil. The supreme example of this is the death of Christ, the Son of God, upon the cross, which accomplished our Redemption.

Though evils come upon us, we must never lose sight of the fact that God still holds us in His loving care. The saints never wavered in their submission to divine Providence. Louis Veuillot, the great French author, wrote of St. Elizabeth Bichier des Ages, co-foundress of the Daughters of the Cross: "Whatever happens, she remains undisturbed. Hardships, setbacks, success, insults — they are all the same to the supreme tranquillity that is rooted in a mind that sees God in everything and so must obey." St. Madeleine Sophie Barat, who founded the Society of the Sacred Heart, used to say: "I knew nothing. I foresaw nothing. I accepted all that was given to me." St. Augustine often said: "Let us leave the past to the mercy of God, the present to His love and the future to divine Providence." When Blessed Margaret Clitherow of Yorkshire heard that she had been condemned to death for being a Catholic she said: "God be thanked. All that He shall send me shall be welcome. I am not worthy of so good a death as this."

Francis Borgia, Duke of Gandia in Spain, had twenty-two years of wonderful married life with his wife Leonora. Then she fell deathly sick. Francis was plunged in grief at the thought of being deprived of half of himself, as he put it. He prayed fervently and constantly for Leonora's recovery, giving himself to fasting for the same intention and bestowing alms. Once he went into his private room and there in secret, tears welling from the depths of his being, pleaded with God to spare his wife. At that instant he distinctly heard a voice within himself saying: "If you desire that your wife should live longer, let it be as you will — but it is not good for you." Francis believed that he had heard the voice of God rebuking him. His tears continued to flow and he said:

"When is it, O Lord, my God, that You commit to my will that which is in Your power alone? It is of the highest consequence to me to follow Your will in all things. For who knows better than You, O my God, what would come from my request? And, therefore, Your will be done, and not merely concerning my wife, but concerning my children also and myself. Do You ordain, I pray, whatever is pleasing to You. Your will be done."

It was noted that at this particular moment the disease of Francis' wife remained in such a state of equilibrium that the doctors could not tell whether she would grow better or worse. However, after Francis had said this prayer and abandoned himself to divine Providence, it was observed that Leonora's condition was past all hope. After her death, Francis entered the Society of Jesus, became its third superior general, and a canonized saint.

When he was lying in the Tower of London awaiting execution on a charge of high treason, but in reality because he had opposed the marriage of Henry VIII, king of England, and Anne Boleyn, St. Thomas More was visited often by his daughter Margaret whom he loved dearly. She employed every argument she knew to get him to make an effort to be released, but to all her pleadings he replied:

"Nothing can happen which God does not will. Moreover, what He wills, however much it may appear to us to be *evil*, is in reality the *best thing* that can happen. I will not distrust the goodness of God, my Margaret, however weak and frail I may feel myself to be. Yes, if I perceived myself to be in such a state of terror and dread that I should seem likely to fall immediately, still I would remember that St. Peter through little faith began to sink with a single blast of wind, and I would do what he did — I would call upon Christ and say 'Lord, save me!' And I trust that He would stretch forth His hand and take hold of me, and would not suffer me to sink.

"But if He should permit me even further to enact the part of Peter, and to fall entirely, and to deny Him with oaths and curses,

yet I still hope He would look upon me with the eye of His bounte-
ous mercy, and would raise me up again, so that I might confess the
truth afresh, unburden my conscience, and manfully endure the pain
and shame of my former denial. In one word, I hold it as most certain that without my own fault God will not forsake me."

St. Joseph Pignatelli, S.J., helped to restore the Society
of Jesus. He was always conscious of the workings of divine
Providence—even in the suppression of the Society to which
he belonged—and composed this beautiful prayer. We might
say it often, making it our very own:

O my God! I know not what must come to me today,
but I am certain that nothing can happen to me
which You have not foreseen, decreed and ordained from all
    eternity.
That is sufficient for me.
I adore Your impenetrable and eternal designs,
to which I submit with all my heart.
I desire, I accept them all and
I unite my sacrifice to that of Jesus Christ, my divine Savior.
I ask in His name and through His infinite merits
patience in my trials and perfect and entire submission
to all that comes to me by Your good pleasure. Amen.

CHALLENGE

A veteran of the Air Force tells of a solo flight he once
had to make during World War II—a flight over seven hundred miles of sea. He says that the fog banks were so dense
that he could see no sky above nor any ocean beneath, and
there was a moment when he felt that he would go mad. He
pushed back his helmet and rubbed his temples and eyes in
order to think of something besides the fog and the roaring
propellors and the perilous sea, which might be near at any
moment. But he tipped the tail of his plane for higher altitude
until the skies cleared—then all was serene.

You know, we are all imperfect fliers, and our varying
degrees of imperfections are due largely to our confidence as
well as our ability. Without ability, the airman would likely
have been upset. With ability and lacking confidence and
courage, he would have lost his nerve and dashed down to
the waves.

There are times when in the voyage of life, matters seem almost hopeless. But there is always our heavenly Father to cling to. The thought of God overhead reminds us that He is permanent. Man has within him a link with God who is eternal and dependable. If we tip the tail for higher altitudes, we will make port somehow, some time, and when we land, say with a smile on our face: "Well, here we are!"

REV. PATRICK FONTAINE, *Little Talks About Life*

THE
FATHER'S
PROMISE

"They broke my covenant..."

Jeremia 31

We believe that IN ADAM ALL HAVE SINNED, which means that the original offense by him caused human nature, common to all men, to fall to a state in which it bears the consequènces of that offense, and which is not the state in which it was at first in our first parents — established as they were in holiness and justice, and in which man knew neither evil nor death.

It is human nature so fallen, stripped of the grace that clothed it, injured in its own natural powers and subjected to the dominion of death, that is transmitted to all men, and it is in this sense that every man is born in sin.

We therefore hold, with the Council of Trent, that original sin, is transmitted with human nature, "not by imitation, but by propagation" and that it is thus "proper to everyone." THE CREDO

God had intended that man should be rewarded with an eternal vision of Himself. This was to be each man's supernatural reward after completing his earthly life. Right from the beginning, God aided Adam and Eve to attain this destiny by giving them special gifts over and above those which were essential to human nature.

These preternatural gifts gave man additional, more excellent perfections. They did not, however, raise him above the natural level. They were not sufficient to entitle man to the beatific vision. Clarity of intelligence, strength of will, freedom from concupiscence, immunity from suffering and death: these were the extraordinary favors given conditionally to mankind in the persons of our first parents.

In addition to the preternatural gifts God also bestowed upon Adam and Eve the state of grace. It was by far the most wonderful blessing given to them. It permitted them to share in God's life, made them heirs to the enjoyments of heaven to which they had no right *by nature. Grace was for our first parents, and is for us now, a mystery of faith.* Revelation teaches that it is a positive reality in the soul making it pleasing to God and adding to it a newer and higher life. So, Adam and Eve were lifted by grace above nature and placed in a supernatural state.

St. Augustine has graphically described all this for us as follows:

"Man lived in paradise as he pleased, as long as his pleasure lay in living as God willed him to live. Man in Eden lived in the enjoyment of God and he was good by a communication of the goodness of God. His life was free from want. There were food and drink to keep away hunger and thirst and the tree of life to hold off death. There was not a sign or a seed of decay in man's body that could be a source of any physical pain. Not a sickness assailed him from within, and he feared no harm from without. His body was perfectly healthy and his soul completely at peace.

"And as in Eden itself there was never a day too hot or too cold, so in Adam, who lived there, no fear or desire was ever so passionate as to worry his will.
Of sorrows there was none at all and of joys none that was vain, although a perpetual joy that was genuine flowed from the presence of God, because God was loved with a 'charity from a pure heart and a good conscience and faith unfeigned' (1 Tm. 1:5). Family affection was ensured by a purity of love; body and mind worked in perfect accord; and there was an effortless observance of the law of God. Finally, neither leisure nor labor had ever to suffer from boredom or sloth."

But our first parents disobeyed a command of God and the results of this act of disobedience were catastrophic in the extreme (cf. Gen. 3:1-6; 3:17-18). Immediately they lost the state of sanctifying grace and became estranged from God. The special gifts that had been granted over and above those essential to human nature were likewise lost. Their wills were weakened and their intellects clouded. They became subject to disease and death.

God formed man to be imperishable; the image of his own nature he made him. But by the envy of the devil, death entered the world. (Wis. 2:23)

In the *Constitution on the Church in the Modern World,* issued by the Second Vatican Council, this clear statement is found:

"Although he was made by God in a state of holiness, from the very onset of history, man abused his liberty, at the urging of the Evil One. What divine revelation makes known to us agrees with experience. Examining his heart, man finds that he has inclinations toward evil too, and is engulfed by manifold ills which cannot come from His good Creator" (n. 13).

There was another dreadful consequence of the fall of our first parents. Their sin was passed on to posterity. This we know from the writings of St. Paul. Thus, we read in his epistle to the Romans (5:12-21): "Therefore as through one man sin entered into the world and through sin death... thus death passed unto all men because all have sinned.... Therefore, as from the offense of one man the result was unto condemnation to all men, so from the justice of the one the result is justification of life to all men. For just as by the disobedience of one man the many were constituted sinners, so also by the obedience of the one the many will be constituted just...."

It is the teaching of the Church that original sin is passed on to posterity through generation. There have been only three exceptions to the rule that every human being is born with original sin. Jesus Christ, who, of course, is God, was preserved from its effects. So also, of course, was the Blessed Virgin Mary, who is His mother. She was conceived and born immaculately, in view of the infinite merits of her divine Son. How could He who is the Second Person of the Blessed Trinity come from a tainted source? It is also the teaching of some theologians that St. John the Baptist, though conceived in original sin, was born without it. They attribute this fact to the circumstance that when the Blessed Virgin visited her cousin St. Elizabeth, the latter, who was about to give birth to John the Baptist, felt the infant move in her womb. At that moment, due to the presence of God Himself in His Blessed Mother, the Baptist was cleansed from original sin. We read in the Gospel of St. Luke (1:39-41): "Now in those days Mary arose and went with haste into the hill country, to a town of Juda. And she entered the house of Zachary and saluted Elizabeth. And it came to pass, when Elizabeth heard the greeting of Mary, that the babe in her womb leapt. And Elizabeth was filled with the Holy Spirit."

Original sin did not destroy man's intellect, free will nor immortality of soul. Though the preternatural and supernatural gifts were lost, there was not a positive corruption of human nature as such. This means that by inheriting original sin we are born *without* sanctifying grace and *with* the consequences resulting from this loss. Thus, our minds are darkened, our wills are weakened, our passions and flesh rebel against reason; we are subject to the fatigue of labor, both mental and physical, to pain, sorrow, sickness and finally to death.

As St. Augustine so concisely puts it: "The body of man is, in accordance with God's supreme justice, his heaviest yoke because of original sin. The soul is tormented by the fear of hardships and pain which follows when this yoke is injured or disturbed and by fear of death when it is taken away or destroyed."

Stripped of grace, man is prey to a host of weaknesses and evil inclinations. He definitely needs God's help. But with grace, which restores holiness, there is no limit to the beauty and glory of human sanctity. We do not bear personal guilt for original sin, but it does leave us with a nature which is no longer strengthened by the special gifts of God. Estranged from Him, we are vulnerable to temptations and prone to actual sin for which we are fully responsible, due to our free will.

Our inheritance of Adam's sin is not contrary to God's justice or goodness.

We were deprived of gifts which were not due us at all. The human race fell to a natural level, that is, to the level of nature it would have possessed if God had never freely elevated man by grace. Moreover, even after man's offense to God, our loving Creator immediately promised a Savior who would again draw grace on mankind. Man was in no way entitled to such generosity.

Original sin consists in the privation of original grace, that is, of supernatural life, which according to divine disposition we should have but do not because the head of humanity, Adam, by his disobedience, deprived himself and all his descendants of it.

> *The offense of Adam is called "original" because it was committed by the head of the human family — by the one through whom the human race originated according to the flesh. This name distinguishes his sin from our own voluntary, personal sins which cannot be transmitted to others but for which we alone are responsible.*

God spoke to us

He [the Holy Spirit] spoke to us BY THE PROPHETS...

...these two names, "being" and "love," express ineffably the same divine reality of Him who wished to make Himself known to us... THE CREDO

The Old Testament

"The Eternal Father's plan was to raise men to a participation of the divine life. After they had fallen in Adam, God the Father did not leave men to themselves but *ceaselessly* offered helps to salvation, in view of Christ, the Redeemer" (Constitution on the Church, n. 2).

The consequences of the sin of our first parents were tragic indeed, yet the situation was not entirely without hope. For God promised a Redeemer. We know of this from Genesis (3:15): "I will put enmity between you and the woman, and your seed and her seed; he shall crush your head and you shall lie in wait for his heel." This divine promise aroused in Adam and Eve the hope of a future salvation. From then onward, although alienated from Him by original sin, the human race was still ceaselessly kept in God's care. In particular, the Jews became His Chosen People and through their patriarchs and prophets He constantly revealed Himself to them, and through them, though in an indirect manner, to the rest of mankind. This truth is clearly brought out in the following extract from Deuteronomy (18:15-22):

"A prophet like me [Moses] will the Lord, your God, raise up for you from among your kinsmen; to him you shall listen. This is exactly what you requested of the Lord, your God, at Horeb on the day of the assembly, when you said, 'Let us not again hear the voice of the Lord, our God, nor see this great fire any more, lest we die.' And the Lord said to me, 'This was well said. I will raise up for them a prophet like you from among their kinsmen, and will put my words into his mouth; he shall tell them all that I command him. If any man will not listen to my words which he speaks in my name, I myself will make him answer for it. But if a prophet presumes to speak in my name an oracle that I have not commanded him to speak, or speaks in the name of other gods, he shall die.' If you say to yourselves, 'How can we recognize an oracle which the Lord has spoken?', know that, even though a prophet speaks in the name of the Lord, if his oracle is not fulfilled or verified, it is an oracle which the Lord did not speak. The prophet has spoken it presumptuously, and you shall have no fear of him."

This coming of God into human affairs has more particularly within recent years come to be known as "salvation history." God breaks into time through the religious leaders of Israel and then, when the proper moment arrives, actually walks the earth in the person of Jesus of Nazareth. Everything we read in the Old Testament was but a preparation for this coming. The promise of a Redeemer is the central message of the Scriptures as the following quotations from the prophets will show.

According to Jeremia, the qualities of the new covenant that make it different from the old are: (a) It will not be broken, but will last forever; (b) Its law will be written in the heart, not merely on tablets of stone; (c) The knowledge of God will be so generally shown forth in the life of the people that it will no longer be necessary to put it into words of instruction. In the fullest sense, this prophecy was fulfilled only through the work of Jesus Christ.

Listen to these words of God spoken directly through the prophet Jeremia (31:31-34):

"The days are coming, says the Lord, when I will make a new covenant with the house of Israel and the house of Juda. It will not be like the covenant I made with their fathers the day I took them by the hand to lead them forth from the land of Egypt; for they broke my covenant, and I had to show myself their master, says the Lord. But this is the covenant which I will make with the house of Israel after those days, says the Lord. I will place my law within them, and write it upon their hearts: I will be their God, and they shall be my people. No longer will they have need to teach their friends and kinsmen how to know the Lord. All, from the least to the greatest, shall know me, says the Lord, for I will forgive their evildoing and remember their sin no more."

Perhaps no prophet has announced so clearly and in such great detail the coming of the Savior, what kind of a person he was to be and the sufferings he would endure, than Isaia. Thus we read in the book of that name (53:2-6):

"There was in him no stately bearing to make us look at him, nor appearance that would attract us to him. He was spurned and avoided by men, a man of suffering, accustomed to infirmity, one of those from whom men hide their faces, spurned, and we held him in no esteem.

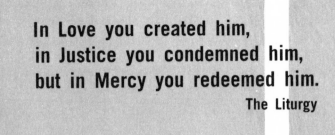

In Love you created him,
in Justice you condemned him,
but in Mercy you redeemed him.

The Liturgy

"Yet it was our infirmities that he bore, our sufferings that he endured, while we thought of him as stricken, as one smitten by God and afflicted. But he was pierced for our offenses, crushed for our sins; upon him was the chastisement that makes us whole, by his stripes we were healed. We had all gone astray like sheep, each following his own way; but the Lord laid upon him the guilt of us all."

Zacharia declares that "a spirit of grace and petition," that is, the divine blessing will be poured out on God's people through the intervention of an unnamed sufferer.

Zacharia writes (12:10):

"I will pour out on the house of David and on the inhabitants of Jerusalem a spirit of grace and petition; and they shall look on him whom they have thrust through, and they shall mourn for him as one mourns for an only son, and they shall grieve over him as one grieves over a first-born."

John the Evangelist (Jn. 19:37) sees in this passage a prophecy fulfilled in the piercing of Christ's side.

The prophet Ezechiel in speaking of a "shepherd..." is referring to a Messianic Davidic king who will rule over the restored Israel in the name of the Lord.

His words are as follows (Ez. 34:22-24):

"I will save my sheep so that they may no longer be despoiled, and I will judge between one sheep and another. I will appoint one shepherd over them to pasture them, my servant David; he shall pasture them and be their shepherd. And, the Lord, will be their God, and my servant David shall be prince among them."

There is also reference to a Redeemer in the Book of Daniel, the second part of which follows a series of visions, promising deliverance and glory to the Jews in days to come.

In chapter 7, verses 13f. the author contrasts the worldly kingdoms opposed to God, which appear as beasts, and the glorified people of God that will form His kingdom on earth, represented in human form. Just as our Lord applied the figure of the stone hewn from the mountain to Himself, He also made the title "Son of Man" His most characteristic way of referring to Himself, as the One in whom and through whom the salvation of God's people came to be realized.

Thus we discover in Daniel (9:13-14):

"I saw one like a son of man coming, on the clouds of heaven; when he reached the Ancient One and was presented before him, he received dominion, glory and kingship; nations and peoples of every language serve him. His dominion is an everlasting dominion that shall not be taken away, his kingship shall not be destroyed."

After the resurrection, during the apparition to the two disciples on the way to Emmaus (Lk. 24:13-35), Christ drew their attention to these prophecies concerning Himself in the Scriptures. And in His last instructions to His apostles before his ascension, He said: (Lk. 24:44-49):

"'These are the words which I spoke to you while I was yet with you, that all things must be fulfilled that are written in the Law of Moses and the Prophets and the Psalms concerning me.' Then he opened their minds, that they might understand the Scriptures. And he said to them, 'Thus it is written; and thus the Christ should suffer, and should rise again from the dead on the third day; and that repentance and remission of sins should be preached in his name to all the nations, beginning from Jerusalem. And you yourselves are witnesses of these things. And I send forth upon you the promise of my Father. But wait here in the city, until you are clothed with power from on high.'"

The *Dogmatic Constitution on Divine Revelation*, one of the principal documents of the Second Vatican Council, refers to what has already been said:

The principal purpose to which the plan of the old covenant was directed was to prepare for the coming of Christ, the Redeemer of all and of the messianic kingdom, to announce this coming by prophecy, and to indicate its meaning through various types. Now *the books of the Old Testament,* in accordance with the state of mankind before the time of salvation established by Christ, *reveal to all men the knowledge of God and of man and the ways in which God, just and merciful, deals with men.* These books, though they also contain some things which are incomplete and temporary, nevertheless show us true divine pedagogy. These same books, then, give expression to a lively sense of God, contain a store of sublime teachings about God, sound wisdom about human life, and a wonderful treasury of prayers, and in them the mystery of our salvation is present in a hidden way. Christians should receive them with reverence (n. 15).

The New Testament

The prophecies of the Old Testament in regard to a Redeemer were realized in Christ, whose life, words and actions have been recorded for us in the four Gospels. The paramount importance of these books was strongly emphasized by the Fathers of Vatican II. Again we read in the document on Divine Revelation:

Christ the Lord in whom the full revelation of the supreme God is brought to completion, commissioned the Apostles to preach to all men that Gospel which is the source of all saving truth and moral teaching, and to impart to them heavenly gifts. This Gospel had been promised in former times through the prophets, and Christ Himself had fulfilled it and promulgated it with His lips. This commission was faithfully fulfilled by the Apostles who, by their oral preaching, by example, and by observances handed on what they had received from the lips of Christ, from living with Him, and from what He did, or what they had learned through the prompting of the Holy Spirit. The commission was fulfilled, too, by those Apostles and apostolic men who under the inspiration of the same Holy Spirit committed the message of salvation to writing.

But in order to keep the Gospel forever whole and alive within the Church, the Apostles left bishops as their successors, "handing over" to them "the authority to teach in their own place."

Now what was handed on by the Apostles includes everything which contributes toward the holiness of life and increase in faith of the people of God; and so the Church, in her teaching, life and worship, perpetuates and hands on to all generations all that she herself is, all that she believes (nn. 7, 8).

The word of God, which is the power of God for the salvation of all who believe, is set forth and shows its power in a most excellent way in the writings of the New Testament. For when the fullness of time arrived, the Word was made flesh and dwelt among us in His fullness of grace and truth. Christ established the kingdom of God on earth, manifested His Father and Himself by deeds and words, and completed His work by His death, resurrection and glorious Ascension and by the sending of the Holy Spirit. Having been lifted up from the earth, He draws all men to Himself, He who alone has the words of eternal life. This mystery had not been manifested to other generations as it was now revealed to His holy Apostles and prophets in the Holy Spirit, so that they might preach the Gospel, stir up faith in Jesus, Christ and Lord, and gather together the Church. Now the writings of the New Testament stand as a perpetual and divine witness to these realities.

It is common knowledge that among all the Scriptures, even those of the New Testament, *the Gospels have a special pre-eminence, and rightly so, for they are the principal witness for the life and teaching of the incarnate Word, our Savior* (nn. 17, 18).

Holy Mother Church has firmly and with absolute constancy held, and continues to hold, that the four Gospels whose historical character the Church unhesitatingly asserts, faithfully hand on what Jesus Christ, while living among men, really did and taught for their eternal salvation until the day He was taken up into heaven. Indeed, after the Ascension of the Lord, the Apostles handed on to their hearers what He had said and done. This they did with that clearer understanding which they enjoyed after they had been instructed by the glorious events of Christ's life and taught by the light of the Spirit of truth. The sacred authors wrote the four Gospels, selecting some things from the many which had been handed on by word of mouth or in writing, reducing some of them to a synthesis, explaining some things in view of the situation of their churches, and preserving the form of proclamation but always in such fashion that they told us the honest truth about Jesus. For their intention in writing was that either from their own memory and recollections, or from the witness of those who "themselves from the beginning were eyewitnesses and ministers of the Word" we might know "the truth" concerning those matters about which we have been instructed (n. 19).

Inspiration

We believe all that is contained in the word of God written or handed down...   THE CREDO

We should read the Bible often, but before doing so, and especially before starting any prolonged, deep scientific study of it, we should know something about inspiration.

The word "inspiration" is explained by scriptural scholars and theologians as an impulse from God which moves certain men to communicate to others what God wishes.

In his second epistle to Timothy, (3:16-17), St. Paul says: "All Scripture is inspired by God and useful for teaching, for reproving, for correcting, for instructing in justice; that the man of God may be perfect, equipped for every good work."

The subject of inspiration is of such essential importance that the Fathers of Vatican II took especial note of it in the document on Divine Revelation. Again therein we read:

Those divinely revealed realities which are contained and presented in Sacred Scripture have been committed to writing under the inspiration of the Holy Spirit, for holy mother Church, relying on the belief of the Apostles, holds that the books of both the Old and New Testaments in their entirety, with all their parts, are sacred and canonical because, written under the inspiration of the Holy Spirit, they have God as their author and have been handed on as such to the Church herself. In composing the sacred books, God chose men and while employed by Him they made use of their powers and abilities, so that with Him acting in them and through them, they, as true authors, consigned to writing everything and only those things which He wanted.

Therefore, since everything asserted by the inspired authors or sacred writers must be held to be asserted by the Holy Spirit, it follows that the books of Scripture must be acknowledged as teaching solidly, faithfully and without error that truth which God wanted put into sacred writings for the sake of salvation. Therefore "all Scripture is divinely inspired and has its use for teaching the truth and refuting error, for reformation of manners and discipline in right living, so that the man who belongs to God may be efficient and equipped for good work of every kind" (n. 11).

Sacred Tradition, too, is inspired. Vatican II states in its document on Divine Revelation:

Sacred Scripture is the word of God inasmuch as it is consigned to writing under the inspiration of the divine Spirit, while sacred tradition takes the word of God entrusted by Christ the Lord and the Holy Spirit to the apostles, and hands it on to their successors in its full purity, so that led by the light of the Spirit of truth, they may in proclaiming it preserve this word of God faithfully, explain it, and make it more widely known. Consequently, it is not from Sacred Scripture alone that the Church draws her certainty about everything which has been revealed. Therefore, both sacred tradition and Sacred Scripture are to be accepted and venerated with the same sense of loyalty and reverence.

Sacred tradition and Sacred Scripture form one sacred deposit of the word of God, committed to the Church. Holding fast to this deposit the entire holy people united with their shepherds remain always steadfast in the teaching of the apostles, in the common life, in the breaking of the bread and in prayers so that holding to, practicing and professing the heritage of the faith, it becomes on the part of the bishops and faithful a single common effort.

Sacred tradition, Sacred Scripture and the teaching authority of the Church, in accord with God's most wise design, are so linked and joined together that one cannot stand without the others, and that all together and each in its own way under the action of the one Holy Spirit contribute effectively to the salvation of souls (nn. 9, 10).

Literary forms

Since God speaks in Sacred Scripture through men in human fashion, the interpreter of Sacred Scripture, in order to see clearly what God wanted to communicate to us, should carefully investigate what meaning the sacred writers really intended, and what God wanted to manifest by means of their words.

To search out the intention of the sacred writers, attention should be given, among other things, *to literary forms*. For truth is set forth and expressed differently in texts which are variously historical, prophetic, poetic, or of other forms of discourse. The interpreter must investigate what meaning the sacred writer intended to express and actually expressed in particular circumstances by using contemporary literary forms in accordance with the situation of his own time and culture. For the correct understanding of what the sacred author wanted to assert, due attention must be paid to the customary and characteristic styles of feeling, speaking and narrating which prevailed at the time of the sacred writer, and to the patterns men normally employed at that period in their everyday dealings with one another (Decree on Divine Revelation, n. 12).

In regard to the vital subject of biblical studies, the Fathers had these words of cautious wisdom:

But, since Holy Scripture must be read and interpreted in the same spirit in which it was written, no less serious attention must be given to the content and unity of the whole of Scripture if the meaning of the sacred texts is to be correctly worked out. The living tradition of the whole Church must be taken into account along with the harmony which exists between elements of the faith. It is the task of exegetes to work according to these rules toward a better understanding and explanation of the meaning of Sacred Scripture, so that through preparatory study the judgment of the Church may mature. For all of what has been said about the way of interpreting Scripture is subject finally to the judgment of the Church, which carries out the divine commission and ministry of guarding and interpreting the word of God.

In Sacred Scripture, therefore, while the truth and holiness of God always remains intact, the marvelous "condescension" of eternal wisdom is clearly shown, "that we may learn the gentle kindness of God, which words cannot express, and how far He has gone in adapting His language with thoughtful concern for our weak human nature." For the words of God, expressed in human language, have been made like human discourse, just as the Word of the eternal Father, when He took to Himself the flesh of human weakness, was in every way made like men (nn. 12-13).

THE BOOKS OF THE BIBLE AND THEIR ABBREVIATIONS

The Old Testament

Genesis	Gn.	Numbers	Nm.
Exodus	Ex.	Deuteronomy	Dt.
Leviticus	Lv.	Josue	Jos.

Judges	Jgs.	Sirach (Ecclesiasticus)	Sir.
Ruth	Ru.	Isaia	Is.
1 Samuel (1 Kings)	1 Sm. (1 Kgs.)	Jeremia	Jer.
2 Samuel (2 Kings)	2 Sm. (2 Kgs.)	Lamentations	Lam.
3 Kings	3 Kgs.	Baruch	Bar.
4 Kings	4 Kgs.	Ezechiel	Ez.
1 Paralipomenon	1 Par.	Daniel	Dn.
(1 Chronicles)		Osee	Os.
2 Paralipomenon	2 Par.	Joel	Jl.
(2 Chronicles)		Amos	Am.
Ezra	Ezr.	Abdia	Abd.
Nehemia (2 Ezra)	Neh.	Jona	Jon.
Tobia	Tb.	Michea	Mi.
Judith	Jdt.	Nahum	Na.
Esther	Est.	Habacuc	Hb.
Job	Jb.	Sophonia	So.
Psalms	Ps(s).	Aggai	Ag.
Proverbs	Prv.	Zacharia	Za.
Ecclesiastes	Eccl.	Malachia	Mal.
Canticle of Canticles	Ct.	1 Machabees	1 Mc.
Wisdom	Wis.	2 Machabees	2 Mc.

The New Testament

St. Matthew	Mt.	1 Timothy	1 Tm.
St. Mark	Mk.	2 Timothy	2 Tm.
St. Luke	Lk.	Titus	Ti.
St. John	Jn.	Philemon	Phlm.
Acts of the Apostles	Acts	Hebrews	Heb.
Romans	Rom.		
1 Corinthians	1 Cor.	St. James	Jas.
2 Corinthians	2 Cor.	1 St. Peter	1 Pt.
Galatians	Gal.	2 St. Peter	2 Pt.
Ephesians	Eph.	1 St. John	1 Jn.
Philippians	Phil.	2 St. John	2 Jn.
Colossians	Col.	3 St. John	3 Jn.
1 Thessalonians	1 Thes.	St. Jude	Jude
2 Thessalonians	2 Thes.	Apocalypse	Ap.

Eternal Father, You spoke to us
through Your prophets and Sacred Scripture,
and then through Your Son, the Incarnate Word,
and now through the Church
and the Holy Spirit who guides it.
I believe that the Scriptures have that meaning
which the Church teaches
and I profess my faith in the words of the Sacred Book.
O Lord, You enlighten men.
Receive my mind: I offer it to You
so that it may know You, O Father,
and He whom You sent, Jesus Christ.

CHALLENGE

God Almighty patiently instructed over several thousands of years; He deliberately and carefully and *gradually* prepared hearts and minds before disclosing His precious Word in the Flesh.

Neither faith nor discretion, nor any manifestation of spirituality can be donned in a panic, like a lifebelt. You don't get a miracle by dropping a St. Jude medal into a pinball machine; neither do you become the saint you want to be —overnight. The saints were able to meet crises with maturity, to speak perfect words of love and to enjoy the fullness of the love of God because of the patient steps of growth and development and ascension that went before.

VICTOR L. DUX, O.S.B., *What the World Needs*

6

"WHO SHALL DECLARE HIS GENERATION?"

ISAIA 53:8

**We believe in OUR LORD JESUS CHRIST, WHO IS THE
SON OF GOD. He is the Eternal Word, born of the Father
before time began, and one in substance with the Father,
and through Him all things were made.**

**...equal therefore to the Father according to His divinity,
and inferior to the Father according to His humanity...**

THE CREDO

"I and the Father"
John 10:30

We saw in the last chapter that after the fall of our first
parents, God promised a redeemer and that the prophets kept
this thought continually before the people of Israel. They
were continually looking forward to the advent of the Messia
but, scourged by tribulations and oppressed by invaders, had
come to think of him as an earthly conqueror, one who would
free them from bondage forever. However, when the Messia
did break into Israelite history He was no mere human
being — He was the Second Person of the Blessed Trinity in
the person of Jesus of Nazareth, true God and true man.

*The divinity of Christ forms the core of the historical
books called the Gospels.* Examine them closely, and you will
find that Jesus Christ did, in fact, claim to be God. He did not
do this directly — in other words, nowhere can we find Him
stating bluntly: "I am God!" But He made the claim equivalently — that is to say, He implied it by His manner of speaking and acting.

On at least four occasions did Christ claim *equality with
God the Father.* The first of these was when He cured the
beggar at the probatic pool of Bethsaida. The healing occurred
on the Sabbath, and it was objected that He had broken the

law. But Christ answered His critics: "My Father works even until now, and I work." To Hebrew ears this was blasphemy, for it implied equality with God. The crowd understood Him in this sense—and there is no mention of Christ correcting them of any misunderstanding in the matter—for we read in the Gospel of St. John: "This, then, is why the Jews were the more anxious to put him to death; because he not only broke the Sabbath, but also called God his own Father, *making himself equal to God*" (cf. Jn. 5:17-18).

The second episode took place during the third year of His public ministry during the feast of Tabernacles and again was staged in Jerusalem. It began with the seizure of a woman taken in adultery, whom Christ saved from the juridical fury of the Pharisees, who were demanding that she be stoned to death for her sin. Having dismissed the woman with a gentle and compassionate, "Sin no more," Christ began a sublime discourse, in which He promised eternal life to His followers. Once more His merciless critics objected and said: "Now we know that you have a devil. Abraham is dead, and the prophets, and you say, 'If any man keep my word he will never taste death.' Are you greater than our father Abraham, who is dead?... Whom do you make yourself?"

To this direct challenge Christ replied: "Amen, amen, I say to you, before Abraham came to be, I am" (cf. Jn. 8:52-53, 58). This is an extraordinary reply. Not only did He affirm His first statement by it, but He made it even stronger. Already we have seen in our chapter dealing with the existence of God how the Creator, in addressing Moses, referred to Himself as: "I am who am." Only too well did the Jews realize that these words could be applied to God alone. Yet here, in their opinion, was a mere creature standing before them, having the audacity to apply them to Himself! Again they called it blasphemy! In a frenzy, they bent down and seized stones to hurl at Him, for death was the penalty for blasphemy.

The third claim to equality with God was made by Christ during the feast of Dedication and once more in Jerusalem. Again the Jews had gathered around Him with their ceaseless questions. This time they asked Him squarely whether or not He was the Messia. But Jesus went much farther in His reply than they had anticipated, for He claimed to be God! "I and the Father are one" (Jn. 10:30) was the answer they received. Once more they sought to stone Him to death on a charge of blasphemy.

The fourth occasion when Christ claimed to be equal to God took place in the supper room where He and His friends had assembled to celebrate the Pasch just before His terrible sufferings and agonizing death. Addressing the apostle Philip, Christ said: "Philip, he who sees me sees also the Father. How can you say, 'Show us the Father?' Do you not believe that I am in the Father and the Father in me?" (cf. Jn. 14:9-10).

Paul VI says: "We know that Jesus is not only the revealer of Himself (the great capital question of the Gospel: 'Who do men say the Son of man is?' Mt. 16:13; 'Who are you?' Jn. 8:25), but also the revealer of God (cf. Mt. 11:27). But that which today is of interest to scholars is to observe that Jesus reveals God in Jesus Himself; he who sees Him (Jesus Himself says this) sees also the Father (cf. Jn. 14:9).

St. Paul asserts twice, He (Jesus Christ) "is the image of God" (2 Cor. 4:4; Col. 1:15).

But we are not finished. On the four above occasions Christ stated the claim equivalently Himself. On three others He accepted it without hesitation or correction, when it was applied to Him by others.

The first of these events took place early in the third year of the public ministry. Having cured a blind man, Jesus left Bethsaida and wended His way toward the River Jordan, to a bleak spot where the ground was littered with huge slabs of stone. The place was near the town of Caesarea Philippi. Jesus went to pray alone. When He had finished, He rose up and approached the twelve. They could tell that He had something on His mind, and it was not long before they found out what it was. He said to them: "Who do men say the Son of Man is?"

Instinctively they looked to Peter to answer for them. He was their leader and always voiced the thoughts of the rest. With their eyes riveted upon him, knowing full well what they expected from him, Peter, with that generous spontaneous nature of his, leaped the chasm. "You are the Christ, the Son of the living God," he exclaimed. To make such a statement, a revelation was needed, and that a revelation had been given we know from the words of Christ spoken in acceptance of the admission: "Blessed are you, Simon Bar-Jona, because flesh and blood has not revealed this to you, but my Father in heaven" (Mt. 16:13-17).

The second occasion on which Christ formally accepted the title "Son of God" is described for us by Sts. Matthew,

Mark and Luke. Jesus had been arrested and put on trial for His very life. Caiphas, the high priest for that year, looked upon the Savior and asked Him point-blank: "Are you the Christ, the Son of the blessed One? I adjure you by the living God that you tell us whether you are the Christ, the Son of God?" (Mk. 14:61; Mt. 26:63) Consider the position for a second. Christ was being asked if He were true God of true God. Not only that. He was being put upon His oath — and in public. Death was the penalty for an admission. Jesus Christ knew all this.

Calmly, weighing every word slowly and carefully, mindful of what hung upon His answer, Christ did not hesitate. "Jesus said to him: 'You have said it. I am. And you shall see the Son of Man sitting at the right hand of the Power and coming with the clouds of heaven'" (Mt. 26:64; Mk. 14:62). The Gospel story tells us what followed. "Then the high priest rent his garments, saying: 'He has blasphemed; what further need have we of witnesses? Behold, now you have heard the blasphemy. What do you think?' And they answered and said, 'He is liable to death'" (Mt. 26:65-66). The blasphemy! Guilty of death! Why? Because He had claimed to be God.

The cold fact stands out. Jesus Christ was put on His solemn oath, in public, and with His life at stake, *to say whether or not He was the* Son of God. *Under such conditions He accepted the challenge and the title. Not only that. He chose suffering and death as well for this same admission.*

For saying that He was the Son of God He underwent the most agonizing torments, the horrors of the prison, merciless beatings and mockery from the soldiery. He was scourged at the pillar, crowned with thorns, made to carry His cross along the agonizing way to Calvary and was crucified between two thieves, thus yielding up His spirit to God. Surely the most skeptical must be convinced that He meant what He said!

The third occasion on which our Lord accepted the title of God took place during the apparition to Thomas. The event as described in the Gospel of St. John (20:24-29) requires no explanation. The evangelist writes:

"Now Thomas, one of the Twelve, called the Twin, was not with them when [the risen] Jesus came. The other disciples therefore said to him: 'We have seen the Lord.' But he said to them: 'Unless I see in his hands the print of the nails, and put my finger into the place of the nails, and put my hand into his side, I will not believe.'

"And after eight days, his disciples were again inside (in the Cenacle), and Thomas with them. Jesus came, the door being closed, and stood in their midst, and said: 'Peace be to you.' Then he said to Thomas: 'Bring here your finger, and see my hands; and bring here your hand, and put it into my side; and be not unbelieving, but believing.' Thomas answered and said to him: 'My Lord and my God!' Jesus said to him: 'Because you have seen me, you have believed.'"

So much for the claim itself, but we cannot be satisfied with just this. We must investigate as to *how* the right to this claim was substantiated. Did Jesus of Nazareth have a just claim? Yes, He had. One of the strongest proofs for it consists in the testimony of Christ to Himself. Nor is this a vicious circle as might be supposed—proving something by an argument, which itself has to be proved. For having analyzed the mind of Christ and found that He was in no way mentally unbalanced and probed into His moral character and seen that with such virtues He could not have been prompted to the claim either by pride or lies, we are driven to the conclusion that the witness of Christ to Himself is one of the strongest arguments we can marshal in favor of His divinity.

But the testimony of Christ to Himself is not the only proof we possess. We can also establish it by *His prophecies and miracles.* In regard to the former, three times did our Lord predict His passion and death. He foretold the resurrection six times. The following text from St. Matthew (20:18-19) illustrates the form this kind of prediction took. "Behold, we are going up to Jerusalem, and the Son of Man will be betrayed to the chief priests and the Scribes; and they will condemn him to death, and will deliver him to the Gentiles to be mocked and scourged and crucified; and on the third day he will rise again." He also foretold the desertion of the apostles, the triple denial of Peter, the manner of the latter's death, the defection of Judas, the persecutions awaiting the Twelve. He forecast the destruction of the Temple at Jerusalem, which actually happened in 70 A.D. under the Roman generals Titus and Vespasian. He foretold the descent of the Holy Spirit on the apostles, the marvelous propagation of Christianity and the endurance of the Church until the end of time.

Then there were His miracles. Three times did our Lord prove His mastery over death—when He raised the daughter of Jairus, the son of the widow of Naim and Lazarus, His bosom friend. His greatest wonder was the resurrection

"That you may know
and believe
that the Father
is in me and
I in the Father."

John 10:38

or the raising of Himself from the dead, but this event is of such singular import, that we have left it aside for fuller treatment in the ninth chapter.

The public ministry abounds with cures of the infirm: the son of the ruler of Capharnaum, the paralytic at the pool, Simon's mother-in-law, the servant of the centurion, the man sick of the palsy, the man with the withered hand, the woman with a hemorrhage, the deaf mute, the woman troubled with an infirmity for eighteen years, and the dropsical man. Christ also restored sight to the blind. Leprosy vanished at the touch of His hand or the word from His mouth. "Go, show yourselves to the priests," He called out to ten poor men suffering from this hideous malady, and, as they went, they were made clean. On five occasions He worked mass cures among the people, healing the sick as He passed among them. Who will count the numbers that profited on these occasions by the divine charity overflowing from the heart of the God-Man? Not only that, but the evil spirits were subject to Him: the demoniac in the Temple, for instance, the man possessed by the deaf and dumb spirit, and the lunatic child, cured by Him after the transfiguration.

But the litany does not end here. There were wonders of a different kind. He changed water into wine at a marriage reception to save a newlywed couple from embarrassment. Twice He miraculously filled the nets of the apostles with fishes. He calmed the storm at sea, walked upon the waters, saved Peter from being submerged by the tumbling billows, and, on two occasions, fed vast crowds in the desert, using only a few loaves and a few fishes.

It must be understood that from the very start of the public ministry, Jesus never ceased to point to His miracles in proof of the justice of His claim. After He had cured the paralytic at the pool, He said: "The witness, however, that I have is greater than that of John. For the works which the Father has given me to accomplish, these very works that I do, bear witness to me, that the Father has sent me" (Jn. 5:36). And after He had cast out a devil He said: "If I cast out devils by the finger of God, then the kingdom of God has come upon you" (Lk. 11:20).

Later, from his dismal dungeon in the fortress of Macheronte, where he had been imprisoned by the order of Herod, John the Baptist sent messengers to inquire from Christ the nature of His mission. "Are you he who is to come, or shall we look for another?" they asked Him. And what was the reply

of Jesus? "Go and report to John what you have heard and
seen: the blind see, the lame walk, the lepers are cleansed,
the deaf hear, the dead rise, the poor have the Gospel preached
to them. And blessed is he who is not scandalized in me" (cf.
Mt. 11:3-6).

At the feast of Dedication, St. John records the following
words of Christ: "I tell you and you do not believe. The works
that I do in the name of my Father, these bear witness concerning me.... If I do not perform the works of my Father, do
not believe. But if I do perform them, and if you are not willing
to believe me, believe the works, that you may know and believe that the Father is in me and I in the Father" (10:25, 37-
38).

Again, He tells us explicitly that He raised Lazarus from
the dead, so that the Jews might believe His doctrine. "They
therefore removed the stone.... And Jesus, raising his eyes,
said: 'Father, I give you thanks that you have heard me. Yet
I knew that you always hear me; but because of the people
who stand round, I spoke, that they may believe that you
have sent me'" (Jn. 11:41-42).

We have already recounted the episode in which, speaking to Philip, Christ claimed equality with God the Father.
We will now quote once more from that same incident, as
it has a direct bearing upon this question of miracles as
proofs. Here are the words of Christ spoken on that occasion:
"Do you not believe that I am in the Father and the Father in
me? The words that I speak to you I speak not on my own authority. But the Father dwelling in me, it is he who does the
works. Do you not believe that I am in the Father and the
Father in me? Otherwise, believe because of the works themselves" (Jn. 14:10-12).

Apart from His equivalent declaration of equality with
the Father and acceptance of this title when given Him by
others, *our Lord also claimed another distinct divine attribute* — namely, *the power to forgive sin.* To the Jews, only
God could do this. Hence, we can realize their astonishment,
not to say horror, when Christ appropriated this especial
power. But not only did He claim the latter — He proved that
He had it by confirming His absolutions with miracles. This
puts the issue beyond doubt and proves that He is really and
truly God.

The first forgiving of sins occurred when He cured the
palsied man. First He forgave him his offenses. "Take courage, son; your sins are forgiven you," He told him. The Phari-

sees were dumbfounded at such presumption. Here was one daring to forgive sins, a function reserved to God alone. "And the Scribes and Pharisees began to argue, saying, 'Why does this man speak thus? Who is this man who speaks blasphemies? Who can forgive sins, but God only?'" Jesus read the shocked expressions on their faces; still He continued. The Scriptures tell us: "But Jesus, knowing their thoughts, answered and said to them, 'Why are you arguing in your hearts? Which is easier, to say to the paralytic, "Your sins are forgiven you," or to say, "Arise, take up your pallet, and walk"? But that you may know that the Son of Man has power on earth to forgive sins'"—he said to the paralytic—"'I say to you, arise, take up your pallet, and go to your house.' And immediately he arose before them, took up what he had been lying on, and went away to his house, glorifying God. And astonishment seized upon them all, and they glorified God and were filled with fear, saying: 'We have seen wonderful things today. Never did we see the like'" (cf. Mt. 9:1-8; Mk. 2:1-12; Lk. 5:18-26).

The next forgiving of sins took place during the second year of the public ministry, when, at Magdala, He absolved the woman in the city who was a sinner—Mary Magdalene. We read in the Gospels: "And behold, a woman in the town who was a sinner, upon learning that he was at table in the Pharisee's house, brought an alabaster jar of ointment; and standing behind him at his feet, she began to bathe his feet with her tears and wiped them with the hair of her head, and kissed his feet, and anointed them with ointment." Although they did not remonstrate openly, still in their minds the Pharisees condemned the entire event. "This man, were he a prophet, would surely know who and what manner of woman this is who is touching him, for she is a sinner."

But Christ had read their thoughts and seized this opportunity to prove His divinity by forgiving Magdalene her sins. "And he said to her, 'Your sins are forgiven.'" Such an assumption of spiritual power, before these rulers of the Jews, men skilled in the interpretation of the sacred books, produced its effect. The Pharisees looked at one another in stupefaction. Then they thought within themselves: "Who is this man, who even forgives sins?" When He had cured the man sick of the palsy it had been the same thing. Then also they had murmured: "Who is this man who speaks blasphemies? Who can forgive sins, but God only?" While the Pharisees still continued to discuss His words in amazed undertones of suppressed antagonism, Jesus turned to the woman and said: 'Your faith has saved you; go in peace.'" (cf. Lk. 7:36-50).

We conclude our demonstration of the divinity of Christ with the following.

Speaking one day in the Treasury, Christ said: "I am the light of the world. He who follows me does not walk in darkness, but will have the light of life." The Pharisees replied: "You bear witness to yourself. Your witness is not true."

"Even if I bear witness to myself," rejoined Christ, "my witness is true, for I know where I came from and where I go. But you do not know where I came from or where I go. You judge according to the flesh; I judge no one. And even if I do judge, my judgment is true, because I am not alone, but with me is he who sent me, the Father. And in your Law it is written that the witness of two persons is true. It is I who bear witness to myself, and he who sent me, the Father, bears witness to me" (cf. Jn. 8:12-18).

Also the Father testified to the divine mission of His Son and therefore to His Son's divinity on three occasions. The first time was at the baptism of our Lord by John in the Jordan at the start of the public ministry. "And when Jesus had been baptized, he immediately came up from the water. And behold, the heavens were opened to him, and he saw the Spirit of God descending as a dove and coming upon him. And behold, a voice from the heavens said, 'This is my beloved Son, in whom I am well pleased'" (Mt. 3:16-17).

God the Father testified to His Son a second time, at the Transfiguration on Mount Tabor. This took place before the apostles Peter, James and John. Moses and Elias came and spoke with Christ. As they conversed, a bright cloud overshadowed them, a sign that God was present with His majesty. "And as he was still speaking,...behold, a voice out of the cloud said, 'This is my beloved Son, in whom I am well pleased; hear him'" (Mt. 17:5).

The Father testified for the third time to His Son in the temple at Jerusalem on a festival day. Certain Greeks had come to see Christ, who spoke to them. Suddenly He broke off conversation and cried out to His heavenly Father: "'Father, glorify your name!' There came therefore a voice from heaven, 'I have glorified it and I will glorify it again'" (Jn. 12:28).

CHALLENGE

We must know Christ; we must know Him better; a conventional remembrance is not enough; a nominal worship is not enough. We must realize His true, profound, mysterious entity, the significance of His appearance in the world and in history, His mission in the picture of humanity, the relationship that exists between Him and us, and so forth....

Jesus is mediator between God and men (1 Tim. 2:5); Jesus is the revealer of God and man. If we truly wish to know God we must turn to Jesus; if we truly wish to know man, we still must ask Him.

There starts from Jesus Christ the way that reaches the true knowledge of the heavenly Father and of the intimate infinite life of God, the most Holy Trinity.

There starts from Jesus Christ the way which descends to the true knowledge of humanity, to man's mystery, that of his nature and of his destiny.

PAUL VI

Christ Jesus, You are the Word
begotten by the Father,
Light equal to Light.
With the Father You are the source,
the self-same ray of the Light.
Shine, too, in my mind.
Drive away the terrors of night
and show me the way of salvation.

The hypostatic union

HE WAS INCARNATE OF THE VIRGIN MARY by the power of the Holy Spirit, and was made man...

...AND HIMSELF ONE, not by some impossible confusion of His natures, but BY THE UNITY OF HIS PERSON.

THE CREDO

St. Paul states (Col. 1:15; cf. 2 Cor. 4:4): He [Christ] who is "the image of the invisible God, is himself the perfect man."

Jesus Christ's human body was conceived miraculously in the womb of the Blessed Virgin Mary. She did not conceive in the normal human way but directly by the power of God. We know this from the first chapter of St. Luke's Gospel (26-38). Therein we read that the angel said: "The Holy Spirit shall come upon you and the power of the Most High shall overshadow you, and therefore the Holy One to be born shall be called the Son of God."

The composite produced in Mary's womb by the union of a human soul and body resulted in Christ's human nature. But from the very moment of conception, the Second Person of the Blessed Trinity, the Word, united Himself to it in Mary's womb. Thus there were two natures in Christ—the one human, the other divine. But the entire being was only one Person. The Son of Mary was the Son of God.

A series of ecumenical councils convened through the ages at which the true doctrine concerning Christ was hammered out against heresies. It was in 325 that the First Ecumenical Council, held at Nicea, defined the divinity of Christ in the following terms: "And we believe in this one Lord, Jesus Christ, the Son of God, begotten as the only-begotten of the Father, i.e., of the essence of the Father, God from God, Light from Light, true God from true God, begotten not made, consubstantial with the Father, through whom all things were made."

In 431, at the Ecumenical Council of Ephesus, in Asia Minor, the Fathers spoke thus about the Incarnation: "Christ consists of one divine Person but of two distinct natures, one divine, the other human, not mixed and confounded, although intimately (hypostatically) united, so that He, true God and the Son of God by nature, was born according to the flesh of the Blessed Virgin who consequently is truly the Mother of God."

The word "hypostatic" occurs in the above formula. There is no particular difficulty about it. It comes from the Greek word "ipostasis" which means in English *substance*. The definition, therefore, means that both natures are substantially united, but that they both remain distinct.

We are now able to understand what took place in the womb of the Blessed Virgin when she replied to the announcement of the angel Gabriel: "Behold the handmaid of the Lord; be it done to me according to your word" (Lk. 1:38). In that moment, without the intervention of man, she was overshadowed by the power of the Holy Spirit, and God the Son was made flesh. True Son of the eternal Father He shared His Father's nature. Hence Jesus is divine, He is God. True son of Mary, He shared just as truly her human nature. Jesus is human, He is a man.

The following remarks may serve to clarify further some ideas we have just spoken of:

A person is an individual who thinks and acts freely and independently, one to whom is attributed his own actions (*he* walks, *he* talks, *he* thinks, etc.)

The Son of God, in taking on a human nature, remained *one individual, one Person* — a *divine Person* possessing both the nature of God and the nature of man. Each nature was complete in itself and distinct from the other. They existed together without confusion, without blending.

This union is not just an instrumental one such as a hand joined to a working implement; nor is it moral such as that produced by the love between mother and child; but it is a personal or hypostatic union, as that which unites the soul and the body. It makes only one person.

God's Son did not bring a body with Him from heaven but took it from the most pure womb of the Blessed Virgin. To this body was united a soul created directly by God. This personal or hypostatic union of the Word with a human nature was not the work of man but of the Holy Spirit.

The two natures in Jesus Christ — the divine and the human — had their corresponding operations.

Having a divine nature, Jesus acted as God: performing miracles, reading the hearts of men, predicting the future, etc.

Having a human nature He possessed an intellect that grew in the acquisition of experimental knowledge. His heart was free to love and His will was free to accept the commands of His Father.

In Christ, the union of the two natures in one Person, however, is so perfect and intimate that we attribute to Him both human and divine actions or characteristics without distinction.

If there were two persons, the human actions would come from the human person while the divine actions would be attributed to the Word. We would have to say that the man Jesus was born, suffered and died and the God Jesus is all-powerful and all-knowing and He it was who cured the sick and raised others from the dead. This, of course, is false.

From the Gospels, however, we see that this is not the case. Whether His actions were human or divine, He is spoken of as one person — Jesus Christ.

When Christ worked a miracle His divine nature was the principle cause of the miracle, while His humanity cooperated as an instrument.

One of us

The Son of God, in becoming man assumed our *passible* human nature. Here are a few texts, chosen at random, which show us how He could feel ordinary human desires and emotions.

Now, Jesus, full of the Holy Spirit, returned from the Jordan, and was led by the Spirit about the desert for forty days, being tempted the while by the devil. And he ate nothing those days; and when they were completed *he was hungry.* (Lk. 4:1-2)

Now it came to pass on one of those days, that he and his disciples got into a boat, and he said to them, "Let us cross over to the other side of the lake." And they put out into the sea. But as they were sailing, *he fell asleep.* (Lk. 8:22-23)

When, therefore, Mary came where Jesus was, and saw him, she fell at his feet, and said to him, "Lord, if you had been here, my brother would not have died." When, therefore, Jesus saw her weeping, he groaned in spirit and was troubled, and said, "Where have you laid him?" They said to him, "Lord, come and see." *And Jesus wept.* (Jn. 11:32-37)

Pointedly St. Paul tells us:

He himself has *suffered* and *has been tempted;* he is therefore able to help those who are tempted. (cf. Heb. 2:18)

Thus, by becoming man, the Son of God acquired what is proper to human nature. He felt hunger and thirst, the cold and the heat, fatigue and annoyance, but He did not suffer any human deficiency such as deafness or blindness or other abnormal conditions; nor did He have to bear the consequences of original sin, unbridled passions, a darkened intellect or a weakened will.

The body and soul assumed by the Word were perfect, with many of the gifts given to human nature before man's fall: physical and moral beauty, keenness of mind, intense vigor and sensitivity.... Jesus Christ was, without a doubt, the most perfect man, both physically and morally, that ever existed. In Him were joined all the gifts of nature and grace.

Perhaps no one has better described the human character of Christ more beautifully and simply than the famous Archbishop Goodier. He writes:

"Jesus Christ alone among men can be found wanting in nothing. His enemies looked for a flaw and acknowledged they found none; students since have been baffled in the effort to reduce Him to the ordinary category of human limitations; more than one, struck with wonder, have declared that a character such as this could never have been invented by human ingenuity, that it walks through the four Gospels with the manifest consistency of truth, that the character of Jesus Christ alone commands the homage of mankind. Let us watch Him and draw our own conclusions. First, with whom does He associate? For a man's favorite companions are often a sufficient indication of the man himself. With whom does He not? He is at home alike in the city and with the simple country people; He is welcomed alike at the tables of the rich and great and in the cottages of the poor; scholars come to argue with Him; the ignorant and unskilled find in Him an understanding mind; He is the companion of those who aspire to high thoughts and noble deeds, and yet is taunted for being an associate of publicans and sinners; men and women are equally among His friends; He is at home in the public square or discussing with a timid disciple in the silence of the night; He will magnetize an audience by the roadside with His words, friends and enemies, learned and unlearned, and even as He speaks the tiny children gather at His feet, and clamber on His knee, and cling about His neck, knowing very well that for all His greatness He is still theirs and of themselves.

"Nor is this an affectation or a studied pose; it is not the fruit of careful training; there is throughout that ring of genuineness which makes all feel that indeed His soul understands, and His heart feels and sympathizes, and the love that He shows rings deep and true. Contradictory as it may seem to some, He is at once the friend of all and the friend of each; the more He is known, the more individuals cling about Him; Peter and John, Mary and Martha, the rich young man and the woman at the well, all find in Him complete and perfect union. And as He gave to others, so are others compelled to give in return; for great as He is, there remains that sense of equality about Him; though He teaches with authority, though He works wonders, though He denounces the corrupt in high places, though He claims for Himself that which none ever dared to claim, withal He remains 'only Jesus' and in His company men find the security of mutual surrender.

"Or listen to His words and from them learn the nature of the Man. He speaks by the roadside to the ignorant passers-by, things that they understand, in language that comes from their own lips, colored with details of their own lives; yet, while He speaks, the learned in the law and the Scripture gather round the group and are baffled by the wisdom of His teaching, and the grandeur of His words, and the truth of His illustration that to this day ranks with the highest eloquence, the sublimest poetry. At once He is simple and great; familiar and of the strictest dignity; strong with the strength of a reformer, yet with the tears of weakness trickling through His words; speaking as one having authority, and yet with a note of appeal and pity and almost of despair ringing through every address; succouring the downtrodden, for they know that He knows; giving nerve to the courageous for they feel that He is with them; drawing the hesitating, for they see that He has discovered them; captivating and giving new life to the broken and disillusioned, for He seems to have gone through the same; even His enemies at times feel compelled to shake off the fascination, lest they too should be tied by the bond of His all-embracing sympathy, the rapture of His transparent truth....

"Oh! this baffling Jesus Christ! We look for His striking characteristic and we find He has none; His preferences and there is none which stands out more than another. It is not that, stoic-like He has subdued all His human longings; He possesses them all, keen and sensitive and vigorous, so that nothing that is capable of love escapes the width of His all-embracing heart. The weeping widow cannot be passed by, the wailing cripple by the roadside must be heard; the penitent sinner must be made a bosom-friend, if so she can be raised to a new life and a brighter outlook; even the traitor shall not be betrayed, but shall be called: 'Friend' to the last. Independent of them all He may be, strong to rebuke, bold to encourage, brave to face every criticism; yet the cry is in the heart, and sometimes breaks out in words, when the least of His friends is ungrateful, while for a word of recognition, a single confession of belief in Him, His thankful acknowledgment pours itself out in words and deeds that prove the depth of His human nature....

"We draw it all into one; the portrait is complete; too tremendous not to be true; too easily understood not to be stamped deep in the least sympathetic. St. Paul looks at it and is overwhelmed. Here, he says, is perfect humanity; its solution is in this only, that it is also divine; and at the end of his days he can only sum up his final message to his own in this: 'Put on the Lord Jesus Christ.' That is to be the perfect man."

The *Constitution on the Church in the Modern World* summarizes all that we have tried to say:

By His Incarnation the Son of God has united Himself in some fashion with every man. He worked with human hands, He thought with a human mind, acted by human choice and loved with a human heart. He has truly been made one of us, like us in all things except sin (n. 22).

CHALLENGE

Christ was different from the generation in which He lived. He was the very end of the old and the beginning of the new. He was so different that He could take the most shameful symbol in the world, a cross, and make it the sign of redemption.

We are in an age of the standard system. A great many people are getting standardized. They are getting to think alike, act alike, talk the same slang, getting souls and minds as standardized as hotel dinners. I am not asking you to be eccentric or funny just to be different. But I am asking you to have the courage to be different in things that matter, and it takes indeed great courage to be different.

Standardize as much as you like on externals; wear a coat exactly like a thousand others; drive a car exactly like thousands of others; but dare to be different if difference is required to be loyal to Christ, true to decencies, pure and upright. Just remember—it takes courage, great courage to be different.

REV. PATRICK FONTAINE, *Little Talks About Life*

7

THE
ENCOUNTER
WITH
CHRIST

the great commandment

He dwelt among us, full of grace and truth. He proclaimed and established the kingdom of God and made us know in Himself the Father. THE CREDO

We saw earlier that God was moved to create out of love. He wanted us to share His happiness in the next life. We also pointed out how God gave us certain commandments, through the observance of which we should come to Him. Not content with this, He finally sent us His Son, Second Person of the Blessed Trinity, born of the Virgin Mary, the God-man Jesus Christ, who in His teaching and life, in His words and actions would translate into concrete reality the will of God, showing us in intimate detail the manner in which the Creator wished us to live on earth.

This getting to know our Lord in the Scriptures has, within recent years, come to be graphically described by Catholic writers as "the encounter with Christ." By this they simply mean that, having at last come face to face with Him in the Gospels, realizing now that He is God who teaches the truth, we must follow His instructions and imitate His example. In order that we may do this perfectly, let us examine His teaching and deeds.

Christ was pre-eminently a *Teacher*. As He Himself said: "This is why I was born, and why I have come into the world, to bear witness to the truth" (Jn. 18:37). "I have not spoken on my own authority, but he who sent me, the Father, has commanded me what I should say, and what I should declare" (Jn. 12:49). He came that men "may have life and have it more abundantly" (Jn. 10:10). With this end in view He gave to mankind an unsurpassable set of truths, moral laws and counsels of perfection.

The first remarkable thing that strikes us about the teaching of Christ is the remarkable insight it gives us into the very life of the Godhead Itself. Here Christ speaks with the intimate knowledge of One who has experienced for Himself. From Him we learn about the oneness of God, His other attributes, the Trinity and Fatherhood of the Almighty. Through an acceptance of divine Providence He would have us adjust to the sorrowful and often inexplicable events of life.

Concerning Himself, as we have seen, He is no less explicit, equating Himself with and proving His consubstantial Sonship with the Father by prophecy and miracles.

Christ also explains man's place in creation, his origin, progress and destiny. He stresses the essential importance of the soul: "For what does it profit a man, if he gain the whole world, but suffer the loss of his own soul?" (Mt. 16:26). And again: "Or what will a man give in exchange for his soul?" (Mk. 8:37). Man's last end is clearly indicated. Either he is to be happy with God for eternity as the reward for having led a good life, or else, if he has behaved wickedly in the world, he will be shut out from the sight of God forever.

Confronted with the profound revelation of supernatural truths like these, most of them baffling, the human mind just seems to cease functioning, so completely paralyzed is it by the massive revelations that have been made. We can only humbly bow our heads and say with Peter in a burst of generous love:"Lord, to whom shall we go? You have words of everlasting life, and we have come to believe and to know that you are the Christ, the Son of God!"

So much for the doctrinal side of Christ's teaching in general. But what of His code of morals? To begin with, it must be noted that Christ went much farther than the ten commandments given to Moses on Mount Sinai. Jesus forbade divorce. But He did not stop there. Adultery, impure thoughts and evil desires were also outlawed by Him. Likewise anger and hatred, perjury and swearing, revenge and rash judgments. All this is contained in the Gospels, but if we were asked to sum up the teaching of Christ, we would have to say that it is contained in one word — *Charity* or *Love*. Let us examine the Sacred Books and find this out for ourselves.

He gave us His new commandment to love one another as He loved us.
THE CREDO

At the start of his Gospel, St. John tells us that the entire Incarnation and Redemption were prompted by love, the love of the Creator for man. "For God so loved the world that he gave his only-begotten Son, that those who believe in him may not perish, but may have life everlasting. For God did not send his Son into the world in order to judge the world, but that the world might be saved through him " (3:15ff.).

During the Sermon on the Mount, our Lord explicitly told His hearers that they should love their enemies. "You have heard that it was said, 'You shall love your neighbor and hate your enemy' (Lev. 19:18). But I say to you, love your enemies, do good to those that hate you, and pray for those who persecute and calumniate you, so that you may be children of your Father in heaven, who makes his sun to rise on the good and the evil, and sends rain on the just and the unjust'" (cf. Mt. 5:43-48; Lk. 6:27-28; 31-36). During the same discourse He emphasized this in the words: "Therefore all that you wish men to do to you, even so do you also to them; for this is the Law and the Prophets" (Mt. 7:12).

Christ insisted upon this fundamental truth time and time again. Not content with merely stating it, He showed us how we should put it into practice by the parable of the Good Samaritan (Lk. 10:25-37). Here is the blueprint for love of neighbor and for all social action aimed at uplifting our less fortunate brethren.

Towards the end of the public ministry, our Lord reaffirmed His teaching of charity. Both St. Matthew and St. Mark have recorded the incident as follows (Mt. 22:34-40; Mk. 12:28-34):

But the Pharisees, hearing that he had silenced the Sadducees, gathered together. And one of them, a doctor of the Law, putting him to the test, asked him, "Master, which is the great commandment in the Law?" Jesus said to him, " 'You shall love the Lord your God with your whole heart, and with your whole soul, and with your whole mind.' This is the greatest and the first commandment. And the second is like it, 'You shall love your neighbor as yourself.' On these two commandments depend the whole Law and the Prophets...." And the Scribe said to him, "Well answered, Master, you have said he should be loved with the whole heart, and with the whole understanding, and with the whole soul, and with one's whole strength; and that to love one's neighbor as oneself is a greater thing than all holocausts and sacrifices." And Jesus, seeing that he had answered wisely, said to him, "You are not far from the kingdom of God." And no one after that ventured to ask him questions.

A little later—just before His passion and death—the Master returned to the same theme, in the famous description of the Last Judgment. St. Matthew has recorded His words (25:31-46):

"But when the Son of Man shall come in his majesty, and all the angels with him, then he will sit on the throne of his glory; and before him will be gathered all the nations, and he will separate them one from another, as the shepherd separates the sheep from the goats; and he will set the sheep on his right hand, but the goats on the left.

"Then the king will say to those on his right hand, 'Come, blessed of my Father, take possession of the kingdom prepared for you from the foundation of the world; for I was hungry and you gave me to eat; I was thirsty and you gave me to drink; I was a stranger and you took me in; naked and you covered me; sick and you visited me; I was in prison and you came to me.' Then the just will answer him, saying, 'Lord, where did we see you hungry, and feed you; or thirsty, and give you drink? And when did we see you a stranger, and take you in; or naked, and clothe you? Or when did we see you sick, or in prison, and come to you?' And answering the king will say to them, 'Amen I say to you, as long as you did it for one of these, the least of my brethren, you did it for me.'

"Then he will say to those on his left hand, 'Depart from me, accursed ones, into the everlasting fire which was prepared for the devil and his angels. For I was hungry, and you did not give me to eat; I was thirsty and you gave me no drink; I was a stranger and you did not take me in; naked, and you did not clothe me; sick, and in prison, and you did not visit me.' Then they also will answer and say, 'Lord, when did we see you hungry, or thirsty, or a stranger, or naked, or sick, or in prison, and did not minister to you?' Then he will answer them, saying, 'Amen I say to you, as long as you did not do it for one of these least ones, you did not do it for me.' And these will go into everlasting punishment, but the just into everlasting life."

Not only did Christ stress the necessity of loving one's neighbor — He practiced what He preached. The whole Gospel story is proof of this, particularly His attitude toward sinners of all kinds and His working of miracles to alleviate human suffering. It is instructive to note in the Gospels how the word "love" is applied to Christ. Here are some examples. When the rich young man came to Him and wanted to follow Him, the Scriptures tell us: "And Jesus, looking upon Him, loved him" (Mk. 10:21). We also read of His relations with the family at Bethany: "Now Jesus loved Martha and her sister Mary, and Lazarus" (Jn. 11:5). When the latter was gravely ill the two sisters could think of no better way of informing our Lord than by sending someone with the message: "Lord, behold, he whom you love is sick" (Jn. 11:3).

St. John is referred to as "the disciple whom Jesus loved." And after the second miraculous catch of fishes, when He appeared by the Lake of Galilee, He asked Peter three times if he loved Him. *Jesus loved people and wanted people to love Him.* Perhaps nowhere is this more clearly indicated than by what happened during the Last Supper (Jn. 13:1-17):

Pope Paul VI comments:

"Before the feast of the Passover, Jesus, knowing that his hour had come to pass from this world to his Father, having loved his own who were in the world, he loved them until the end." "Until the end," what does this mean? Until the end of earthly life? This indicates that we are in a conscious vigil, preceding the tragedy of the Passion, that is, that final hour in which everything ends with accents and gestures of supreme sincerity, and the heart reveals its depths in the simple solemnity of complete confidence. Or does it mean: until the end of every conceivable measure, to excess, to an unheard of limit which only the heart of Christ could reach? To the total giving of self, exacted by true love, in an out-pouring that only a divine love could conceive or put into action? Whatever the interpretation we give to this expression, we must remember that it makes love the high point of Christ's last vigil, and that His own words raise it to the peak of its expression: "Greater love than this no man has than that a man lay down his life for his friend."

Loving means giving; giving means loving. Giving everything, giving up life — this is the true path of love, this is its end.

After He had instituted the Eucharist He said: "A new commandment I give you, that you love one another: that as I have loved you, you also love one another. By this will all men know that you are my disciples, if you have love one for another" (Jn. 13:31-35).

So deep an impression did this teaching about charity make on the apostles that we find many references to it scattered throughout their works. St. Paul refers to it frequently, particularly in this famous passage (1 Cor. 13:4-8):

Charity is patient, is kind;
charity does not envy, is not pretentious, is not puffed up;
is not ambitious, is not self-seeking, is not provoked;
thinks no evil, does not rejoice over wickedness,
but rejoices with the truth; bears with all things,
believes all things, hopes all things, endures all things.
Charity never fails....

It is only to be expected that St. John, the chosen disciple, he who had received such marks of love from our Lord, should himself speak of the same virtue often. The three following texts will show us how highly St. John prized charity:

He who says that he is in the light, and hates his brother, is in the darkness still. (1 Jn. 2:9)

He who loves his brother abides in the light, and for him there is no stumbling. (1 Jn. 2:10)

In this has the love of God been shown in our case, that God has sent his only-begotten Son into the world that we may live through him. In this is the love, not that we have loved God, but that he has first loved us, and sent his Son a propitiation for our sins. Beloved, *if God so loved us, we also ought to love one another.* (1 Jn. 4:9-11)

The true follower of Christ is one who loves God supremely and his neighbor as himself, that is, without limits.

Love is an inexhaustible gift of one's strength and life to others. He who loves gives, he who does not love takes to himself. Love is therefore a social impulse that unites men among themselves and with God.

Our heroism in love begins only when we lift ourselves above rancor and criticism: "Be merciful," Christ tells us, "as your heavenly Father is merciful." "Do not judge or condemn anyone," says St. John Chrysostom, "nor trust a suspicion, without first ascertaining for yourself how things really are." In fact, let us not forget St. Bernard's wise teaching: "If you cannot excuse the action, at least excuse the intention: suppose that he did not know or was deceived or perhaps made a mistake. If, however, the fault is so certain as to exclude any doubts, and cannot be hidden, even then try to excuse the offender, saying to yourself: The temptation was too strong. Who knows what a massacre it would have made of me, if it had assailed me with the same violence!"

When he was dying on the island of Patmos, being over a hundred years old, the apostle St. John called his disciples around him and left them as his most precious legacy these beautiful words: "Little children, love one another." This teaching of Christ, written down by the apostles and evident in their words and lives, had such a marvelous influence on the early believers that even the very pagans cried out: "Oh, how these Christians love one another!"

The Council Fathers, in the *Decree on the Apostolate of the Laity*, reaffirm Christ's law of love:

The greatest commandment in the law is to love God with one's whole heart and one's neighbor as oneself (cf. Mt. 22:37-40). Christ made this commandment of love of neighbor His own and enriched it with a new meaning. For He wanted to equate Himself with His brethren as the object of this love when He said, "As long as you did it for one of these, the least of my brethren, you did it for me." (Mt. 25:40) Assuming human nature, He bound the whole human race to Himself as a family through a certain supernatural solidarity and established charity as the mark of His disciples, saying, "By this will all men know that you are my disciples, if you have love for one another" (Jn. 13:35) (n. 8).

On January 18, 1961, at 9:45 in the evening, a young doctor died, just a few short moments after the priest had whispered, "Son, go now and meet your God." When the news broke, men, women and children from all over the world mourned, but particularly a certain Asiatic people who had been so dear to the youthful physician's heart. His name? Dr. Tom Dooley. At thirty-four, he was dead of cancer. A tragedy? Dr. Tom Dooley did not think so. Only two months before his death, while lying on a mattress in a hotel room, he had told a close friend, Father John Boucher, that he wanted whatever God wanted.

And after his short but selfless medical career, no one had more right to be peaceful at death than Dr. Tom Dooley.

An obscure Navy doctor, he was sent to Haiphong in 1954 with a few medical corpsmen to give medical help to thousands of refugees fleeing from North Viet Nam. That unforgettable experience changed his whole life. He realized how much understanding and brotherhood he could promote by giving the needy free medical aid.

It was then that Dr. Tom Dooley's great project of "Operation Laos" was born. "I'm resigning from the Navy, and I'm going to Laos," he told his mother. So he and three other ex-Navy corpsmen set up a medical unit in Southeast Asia in order to dedicate themselves to relieve the sufferings of the diseased, wounded and undernourished people of Laos. Their aim was not only to give these people medical aid, but to give them concrete proof of America's desire to help them on a person-to-person basis. Day after day, the young medical team strove to ease the pains of the suffering Asiatics — children miserable with smallpox, men with yaws, infants with whooping cough, women bowed under the weight of goiters, and — huddled together under the trees — the unhappy lepers.

It was not only a desire to help humanity, and advertise American brotherly love which drove Tom Dooley on; it was charity — love, and supernatural love at that.

When told he had cancer, which might possibly be fatal, he said calmly, "Walt Whitman, I think, said that it's not important what you do with the *years* of your life, but it's very important how you use each *hour.* That's how I'll live."

And so a dedicated lay apostle worked to the very last moments of his brief life to bring the compassion of Christ, the divine physician, to a suffering humanity.

the beatitudes

He taught us the way of the beatitudes of the Gospel...

THE CREDO

"In order that the faithful may reach perfection, they must use their strength accordingly as they have received it, as a gift from Christ," says the *Dogmatic Constitution on the Church.* "They must follow in His footsteps and conform themselves to His image seeking the will of the Father in all things. They must devote themselves with all their being to the glory of God and the service of their neighbor. In this way, the holiness of the People of God will grow into an abundant harvest of good. *Every person must walk unhesitatingly according to his own personal gifts and duties in the path of living faith, which arouses hope and works through charity"* (n. 40, 41).

The laws of God are heavy only for those who do not have good will; they are light for those who love. At first St. Augustine found it hard to subject himself to the law of God. He found it arduous and difficult to observe. However, when he docilely submitted to grace, he was able to experience that, "God does not order things which are impossible, but while He commands, He advises us to do what we can and to ask for that which we cannot do; then He helps us, so that we can practice it."

According to our Lord, perfect love of God and neighbor consists in putting into practice, both in the letter and spirit, the beatitudes. In the Sermon on the Mount, the Savior enumerated them as follows:

Blessed are the poor in spirit, for theirs is the kingdom of heaven.

Blessed are the meek, for they shall possess the earth.
Blessed are they who mourn, for they shall be comforted.
Blessed are they who hunger and thirst for justice, for they shall be satisfied.
Blessed are the merciful, for they shall obtain mercy.
Blessed are the clean of heart, for they shall see God.
Blessed are the peacemakers, for they shall be called children of God.
Blessed are they who suffer persecution for justice' sake, for theirs is the kingdom of heaven. (Mt. 5:3-10)

In these beatitudes Christ revealed the spirit of the Christian life. They are the clearest and most forceful examples of Christ's moral teaching. They are a positive way of perfection for they are not so much commands as counsels and the emphasis is not on the fault of transgressing them, but on the reward for keeping them. Let us examine each of these counsels in detail.

"Blessed are the poor in spirit..."

...poverty in spirit

We can look at poverty in two ways—first the practice of it in our own lives, and secondly, poverty as a world problem. We shall defer the latter for subsequent treatment. As regards personal poverty, this too has a double aspect.

First of all, it signifies being truly humble. Humility does not mean running around with a long face and telling everybody that we are no good. However, it does imply that we recognize that we come from God and depend upon Him for our very existence. Once we grasp this, all else follows in orderly fashion. Thus, if we observe good qualities in ourselves, either of body (excellence in sports, for example) or of mind (endowed with intelligence) or of personality (if people like us on account of our helpful or cheerful disposition) we must not deny these things. Humility is truth, and we must admit the good we possess, giving the credit, of course, to God.

Hand in hand with poverty in spirit goes poverty in the goods of the world. This does not mean that we should reduce ourselves to beggary. It means that we should have the proper attitude towards the goods of this world, using them as a means to an end — God's glory and the assistance of our less fortunate brethren — rather than as an end in themselves. Thus, for most of us poverty means not being extravagant about clothing, or housing, or the kind of food we eat. This is true especially of our own age, when so many people are in dire need, and who, when they see the more affluent classes wasting money and material, while their own children suffer want, starvation and even death, are tempted to resort to violence to change the state of society and ensure a more equitable distribution of the necessities of life.

In religious orders, of course, priests and nuns take vows of poverty and use things in common. But such a mode of existence is impractical for the lay person, who is counseled to embrace poverty in the way we have outlined above.

The practice of poverty was outstanding in the life of Christ. He was born of a Jewish maiden from the poor village of Nazareth, and His foster father, St. Joseph, was a trades-man, a carpenter. Christ was actually born in a stable and lived in an obscure hamlet of Galilee. During His public ministry, as He wandered from place to place, an itinerant Rabbi or teacher, He could say of Himself: "The foxes have dens, and the birds of the air have nests; but the Son of Man has nowhere to lay his head" (Mt. 8:20). He was so poor that as man He couldn't pay the tax, but, as God, worked a miracle so that the law might be observed, bidding Peter go to the water's edge and take the required coin from the mouth of the first fish caught. When the rich young man came to Him and wanted to follow Him He told him: "Go, sell what you have and give to the poor,...and come, follow me" (Mt. 19:21). The Gospels tell us that the young man turned sorrowfully away for "he had great possessions." Speaking of the danger of riches, our Lord warned: "It is easier for a camel to pass through the eye of a needle than for a rich man to enter the kingdom of heaven" (cf. Mt. 19:21-24). To the very end He practiced this virtue of poverty, for He died naked on a cross and had to be buried in another man's sepulcher!

The poor in spirit who are called blessed are those who: 1) in the intimacy of their soul are detached from exterior goods, above all, from riches and honor; 2) if they possess them, they use them with moderation and honesty; 3) if they lack them, they do not seek them with anxiety; 4) if they lose them, they suffer the loss with submission to the divine will.

Poverty of spirit makes the Christian detach his heart from created things and with firm hope direct it toward the Creator and heaven.

St. Francis of Assisi, who practiced poverty most perfectly, used to say: "So great is the good which I expect, that every pain is a pleasure to me!" True riches do not consist in the treasures of this earth...but in grace, in virtue, in merits and in the friendship of God. The liturgy says of St. Francis: "Poor and humble, Francis enters heaven rich."

"Blessed are the meek for they shall possess the land."

...meekness, suffering borne with patience...

THE CREDO

"The meek are the gentle, those who are kind to their neighbors, patiently tolerating annoyances without complaining and without avenging themselves. The meek St. Francis de Sales often repeated: "More flies are attracted with a spoon of honey than with a barrel of vinegar!" Thus he explained that men can be conquered more through gentle goodness than with severity or bitter zeal. Hence "nothing is painful," says St. Leo, "for him who loves and practices meekness."

Though Christ was fearless — witness the two occasions when He drove the money-changers from the temple and the numerous times that He denounced the corrupt in high places — yet, paradoxically, meekness was one of His most outstanding virtues. The prophets had foretold this of Him: "He shall bring forth justice to the nations, not crying out, not shouting, not making his voice heard in the street. A bruised reed he shall not break, and a smoldering wick he shall not quench, until he establishes justice on the earth" (Isa. 42:1-4). So tender is he that in the fullness of His heart He cries out: "Come to me, all you who labor and are burdened, and I will give you rest. Take my yoke upon you, and learn from me, for I am meek and humble of heart; and you will find rest for your souls. For my yoke is easy, and my burden light" (Mt. 11:28). On another occasion He said: "If someone strike you on the right cheek, turn to him the other also" (Mt. 5:39).

"Suffering can make men better or bitter."

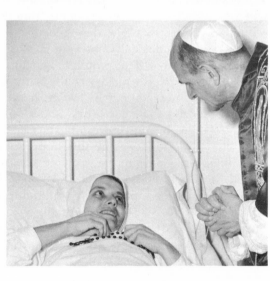

In imitation of Christ the saints also practiced the virtue of meekness. Here are some examples.

St. Francis de Sales was highstrung by nature. One day (when he was already a bishop) he was insulted and threatened. Despite his choleric temperament he remained self-composed. When his friends chided him for his silence, Francis replied: "You think I'm insensible, don't you? Put your hand on my heart, and you will see how fast it is beating. If I didn't restrain myself, I would burst out in anger. In allowing one impatient word to escape, I would lose what has taken me twenty-four years to acquire."

St. John Mary Vianney, whom we saw earlier was hounded by the devil for over thirty years, was also quick-tempered. However, he trained himself to control it. On one occasion, a person who should have known him better insulted him to his face. The saint flushed a deep red, and it was noticed how his hands kept convulsively twisting his hat in a great effort to control himself. Bystanders thought that he would explode, but the saint, by the grace of God, managed to get his feelings in order and so practiced the virtue of meekness.

Sometimes it is very difficult to curb anger and to turn the other cheek. But no matter how many times we fail, we must never give up in our efforts to be like our Lord. We should be sorry and start all over again.

Closely allied to the practice of meekness is the acceptance of suffering—not in a fatalistic way, for aided by God's grace, man must fashion his destiny in this world—but in a spirit of humble submission to the will of God, who permits everything to happen for our good.

St. Francis of Assisi used to pray that God would help him to change the things he could and to be patient when unable to change the things over which he had no control!

The following reflections of Father Victor L. Dux, O.S.B., on the practice of this type of meekness should give us much food for profound thought and, at the same time, much consolation:

It is hard for the mind of modern man to see the use in suffering. But in God's plan there is no such thing as *useless* suffering. Many passages in the Book of Job sound pessimistic and modern enough to make a syndicated column in tomorrow's newspaper, but God rebuked Job and his friends for many of the things they uttered in their philosophizing on life's ills. Take for instance a passage like Job 3:20-21: "Why is light given to the wretched, and life to the bitter in spirit? They wait for death and it comes not...they are glad when they reach the grave." This might have been written yesterday or last week to give voice to the opinion millions have on the subject of suffering. It is the attitude that causes patients suffering from an incurable disease to give up hope and faith in God; it is the frame of mind that shrivels up ambition and effort, that embitters, and that causes men to blaspheme God, who is the Absolute Good.

Yes; suffering can make men better or bitter!

The man who finds nothing but bitterness in his lot cannot say with the Psalmist: "I will sing to the Lord all my life; I will sing praises to my God while I live." (Ps. 103) Nor can he see any sense in St. Paul's declaration (2 Cor. 12): "Gladly will I glory in my infirmities that the strength of Christ may dwell in me. Wherefore I am satisfied—for Christ's sake—with infirmities, with insults, with hardships, with persecutions, with distresses. For when I am weak, then I am strong."

The modern pagan sees suffering as something degrading and mean. Like its twin-sister poverty, it is to be despised, hated, feared, shunned. Yet the Lord Christ, the God-Man, did not despise either suffering or poverty, but on the contrary embraced them both as something most dear. Those who follow Him must walk in His path.

Followers of Christ know there is a dignity in suffering that is not equalled by any other human act or endeavor. For suffering is peculiarly our own; it belongs to humanity as nothing else can. Suffering is not a part of God; it is completely foreign to His nature. But it is so much an unavoidable part of our nature that God had to take on our nature, He had to become a member of our race, before He could share suffering with us.

Precisely why a good God permits pain to torment human bodies, and particularly the bodies of innocent little children, is one of the secrets of God's many mysterious dealings with men. We cannot unravel it with satisfaction in this dim present light, but we must wait for the bright light of glory to give us a clear solution.

However, if you focus your thinking on the position we have in the Mystical Body of Christ, you will be given at least a partial answer to the problem. St. Paul says it clearly enough when he writes to the Philippians (1:29): "You have been given the favor on Christ's behalf—not only to believe in him, but also to suffer for him." And again, to the Colossians (1:24): "What is lacking of the sufferings of Christ, I fill up in my flesh for his Body which is the Church."

*"Blessed are they who hunger and thirst after
justice for they shall have their fill."*

...thirst after justice...

THE CREDO

Love for the virtue of justice was another of Christ's
characteristics. He warned the people: "Unless your justice
exceeds that of the Scribes and Pharisees, you shall not enter
the kingdom of heaven" (Mt. 5:20).

The word *justice* here signifies sanctity, that is, that
interior justice which renders man dear to God when he forces
himself always to fulfill the law and the will of God. Hence,
those who daily try to progress with good works in perfection
and in charity toward God and their neighbor, have hunger
and thirst for justice. "The just man," says St. Bernard,
"never thinks he has reached his goal nor does he say: 'It
is enough now!' But he continually feels a greater hunger and
thirst for justice. If he should live forever, he would always
strive to grow in justice and sanctity."

*"Blessed are the merciful
for they shall obtain mercy."*

...mercy...

THE CREDO

The virtues of meekness and mercy are so akin, that
what we have said of the former could equally apply here.
Read through the Gospels and you will find that Christ never
condemned harshly. He thundered against the religious
leaders of His time for their hypocrisy, but then the latter is
a hateful vice, especially in those in whom we expect to find
only virtue. Jesus never treated repentant sinners in this way.
Think of the woman at the well who had been divorced and
remarried so often, of the woman taken in adultery, of Mary
Magdalene, and, above all, of Peter, who had denied Him
three times. Think of how He treated Judas, the traitor. He
could have exposed him to the other apostles, yet all He said
to him was: "That which you have to do, do quickly" (Jn.
13:27) Think of His treatment of the good thief: "This day you
shall be with me in paradise!" (Lk. 23:43) To Zacchaeus, the

chief tax collector of Jericho, detested by the Jews for his profession, He said: "Zacchaeus, make haste and come down; for
I must stay in your house today." We read in St. Luke: "And
upon seeing it, all began to murmur, saying, 'He has gone to
be the guest of a man who is a sinner" (cf. Lk. 19:5-7). It was
not the first time that such a remark had been made, for we
read earlier in the Gospels, "Why does your Master eat with
publicans and sinners?" (Mt. 9:11). When He allowed Magdalene to anoint His feet, the Pharisees said inwardly, "This
man, were he a prophet, would surely know who and what
manner of woman this is" (Lk. 7:39).

In the parable of the unjust steward, our Lord by impli-
cation shows how God the just Judge will treat all those
who refuse to show mercy towards their neighbor:

> The kingdom of heaven is likened to a king who desired to set-
> tle accounts with his servants. And when he had begun the settle-
> ment, one was brought to him who owed him ten thousand talents.
> And as he had no means of paying, his master ordered him to be
> sold, with his wife and children and all that he had, and payment to
> be made. But the servant fell down and besought him, saying, "Have
> patience with me and I will pay you all!" And moved with compas-
> sion, the master of that servant released him, and forgave him the
> debt.
>
> But as that servant went out, he met one of his fellow-servants
> who owed him a hundred denarii, and he laid hold of him and throt-
> tled him, saying, "Pay what you owe!" His fellow-servant therefore
> fell down and began to entreat him, saying, "Have patience with me
> and I will pay you all." But he would not; but went away and cast
> him into prison until he should pay what was due.
>
> His fellow-servants therefore, seeing what had happened, were
> very much saddened, and they went and informed their master of
> what had taken place. Then his master called him, and said to him,
> "Wicked servant! I forgave you all the debt, because you entreated
> me. Should not you also have had pity on your fellow-servant, even
> as I had pity on you?" And his master, being angry, handed him over
> to the torturers until he should pay all that was due to him. So also
> my heavenly Father will do to you, if you do not each forgive your
> brothers from your hearts (Mt. 18:23-35).

On the contrary, those who are merciful towards their
fellowmen will be rewarded by Christ. This we know from
the intimate details of the Last Judgment recorded earlier
in this chapter.

"Blessed are the clean of heart
for they shall see God."

...purity of heart...

THE CREDO

Those who have a pure heart will see Him here below through His grace. They will see Him in heaven through the beatific vision and through the enjoyment of the celestial glory.

Let us therefore say with St. Augustine: "You, O Lord, command that I be pure; hence give me the strength to be so, and then command whatever You wish."

Our Lord loved and preached the virtue of holy purity. During the Sermon on the Mount He told the assembled multitudes: "You have heard that it was said to the ancients, 'You shall not commit adultery' (Ex. 20:14). But I say to you that anyone who so much as looks with lust at a woman has already committed adultery with her in his heart.

"So if your right eye is an occasion of sin to you, pluck it out and cast it from you; for it is better for you that one of your members should perish than that your whole body should be thrown into hell. And if your right hand is an occasion of sin to you, cut it off and cast it from you; for it is better for you that one of your members should be lost than that your whole body should go into hell.

"It was said, moreover, 'Whoever puts away his wife, let him give her a written notice of dismissal' (Deut. 24:1). But I say to you that everyone who puts away his wife, save on account of immorality, causes her to commit adultery; and he who marries a woman who has been put away commits adultery" (Mt. 5:27-32).

In our modern world, purity seems to be a forgotten virtue. It is imperiled from every direction, particularly by the mass communications media. About three years after the Fatima apparitions, Jacinta was ill in an orphanage. Here the Blessed Virgin appeared to her many times. "Did our Lady say anything about sin?" asked a nun. "Yes!" said Jacinta. "She said that more souls were going to hell because of sins of impurity, than any other." It is apt that we once more contemplate the teaching of our Lord on purity and give a few words of advice about temptations of this kind.

It is only common sense to keep away from all occasions of sin, whether these be persons, places or things. "He who loves the danger shall perish in it" warns the Bible, and never were truer words uttered. There is no use in telling yourself that you will be strong in such and such a circumstance if the occasion is deliberately chosen. Human nature is not built that way and its innate weakness soon becomes manifest.

There is much practical wisdom in the fables of Aesop, a Greek slave who lived in the sixth century B.C. We can learn a lesson from the following. On one occasion the lion proclaimed that he was going to hold a convention and invited the animals of the forest to attend. All went except the fox. A few days after, the latter appeared before the lion's den but did not enter. From within, the lion spied him and called out, "All the other animals came to the meeting except you? What kept you away?" Still keeping a safe distance the fox replied: "I see many footprints entering your den but none coming out!" The moral? Keep away from the occasion of sin – otherwise you will perish therein!

However there are types of temptation from which we cannot escape. We carry them around with us in our own bodies. We are necessary occasions of sin to ourselves simply because we just cannot get up and walk away from ourselves. In cases of this nature, we must use common sense. Sexual temptations should not be fought directly – this only imbeds them more in the mind. As soon as possible, when one finds that a temptation is forming, one should divert the attention. Throw a barrier across it. If this is not done, if the thought is allowed to dally, the imagination gets stronger and this then affects the body. If we can form the habit of diverting the mind as quickly as possible – by taking exercise, for example, or reading a good book, or trying to solve a difficult problem in mathematics, the battle is half won. And this is so, because psychology tells us that two ideas cannot exist in the mind simultaneously. One has to drive the other out.

The other half of the battle consists in learning how to use the will properly.

We must train our wills to be strong. A good start can be made here by going against ourselves in little things, things which do not injure health, but count, nevertheless. For instance, you can form the habit of doing without certain things you like at meals—passing up a certain dessert, refusing an extra coke, ordering a hot dog when you would have preferred a hamburger and so on. All this strengthens character.

A prayer, said quietly, in the secrecy of the heart, asking God for His grace not to sin, should always be made. The prayer need not be long—a few short aspirations will suffice. God sees your circumstances, knows that you are calling upon Him, and will come to your aid.

Always remember that God has not placed an impossible burden on your shoulders. "I can do *all* things in him who strengthens me," says St. Paul (Phil. 4:13), and in another place he writes, "God is faithful and will not permit you to be tempted beyond your strength, but with the temptation will also give you a way out that you may be able to bear it" (1 Cor. 10:13).

St. Teresa of Avila used to repeat:

"Teresa by herself can do nothing, but Teresa with God can do everything."

One should also have a tender love for the Blessed Mother, go to confession often and receive Holy Communion as frequently as possible.

The great St. Augustine, who before his conversion failed to keep the sixth commandment, has given us excellent advice as to what we must do in order to preserve purity intact. He writes:

"If evil concupiscence occasions a pleasant sensation, let no consent be given; if it flames into passion, let God be implored against it that the heart may be inwardly aroused and cleansed, for it is within the heart that petition is made to God Himself."

Again he says:

"Let there be nothing in the heart to offend the eyes of God, nothing to displease Him. If you are earnestly striving to make your heart pure, call upon Him who will not disdain to make it a clean abode for Himself."

We must learn to control panic in these matters. Fear of the temptation can bring it on; fear of consenting can contribute to a fall during its progress. We must have a holy fear of sin. God wants us to have this. But this type of fear is completely different from the irrational, panicky fear that results sometimes when temptation becomes strong. The mind must always be kept calm and in control of the body. It is the jockey who rides the horse, the driver who steers the car. Let them lose control for one moment, and disaster will ensue. Should a fall take place, again there must be no panic, no giving way to despair, but one must remain calm, always confident in God. An act of perfect contrition should be made on the spot—quietly, sincerely and without agitation—and the person should have the intention of going to confession as soon as possible. After confession the entire matter should be dismissed from the mind. Grace overcomes everything. Who is more powerful than God?

The following story is told about St. Philip Neri.

A certain young man, who had an impure habit, used to go to confession to him. Once this youth fell into despair. He became convinced that he would never be cured and told St. Philip that he would not cause him any more trouble by confessing. To this the saint wisely replied: "You must come to confession as often as you need it. Then we will see who will tire first—you of the habit, or me of absolving you!"

Let us do the best we can then and leave the final judgment in these matters to the infinitely merciful God Himself. He knows the clay of which we are formed and judges accurately all the circumstances involved.

We should recite often the following beautiful prayer of Blessed Claude de la Colombiere:

"Though temptations should assail me, I will hope in You.
Though I should sink beneath my weakness,
I will hope in You still.
Though I should break my resolutions, I will look
to You confidently for the grace to keep them at last.
Though You should kill me, even then will I trust in You.
For You are my Father, my God,
the support of my salvation. You are my kind,
my tender, my indulgent parent,
and I am Your loving child
who casts myself into Your arms and begs Your blessing,
who puts my trust in You
and, so trusting, shall not be confounded."

ACT OF CONFIDENCE IN GOD
BY BLESSED CLAUDE DE LA COLOMBIERE

Earlier we suggested the cultivation of habits of mortification to aid us in resisting temptations against chastity. At this point we include the following for two reasons. Since TV can be a source of good or evil as the case may be, proper ob-servance of these regulations will *help us to practice self-denial* and also will *lessen occasions of sin.* These regulations are really worth thinking about and adopting:

TV code of ethics

I am a Christian. How should I act before the TV screen?

1. Fully aware of my Christian responsibilities, I will select the programs I want to view with care. I will not watch programs harmful to faith or morality, even if they are the most popular or receive the highest general ratings.

2. I will make every effort to form an exact judgment of programs. To do so I will read the articles, judgments and criticisms found in reliable Catholic papers and magazines.

3. I will impose on myself wise moderation in using the television set. The time for family meals, conversation with relatives and friends, reading, rest and good manners among the members of the family in deciding programs to watch, must be respected. These are priceless things for which I will have due regard and will pay close attention to my own way of acting.

4. I will avoid frequently watching "late, late shows." They only result in loss of sleep, and cause me to neglect those brief moments of quiet reflection that should close my day. The next morning I get up later than usual in a bad mood, and am late for work, class, church, etc.

5. I will not assist at a TV Mass when I have every pos-sibility of participating at Mass in my own parish. A Mass on TV does not fulfill one's Sunday obligations.

6. I will not eat and drink continually while watching TV.

7. I will faithfully and attentively watch religious tele-casts. They are produced for the glory of God and to enkindle in me the desire for Christian perfection. I will encourage my friends to do likewise. I will discuss them with those who are lax in religion, particularly when I know they appreciate the spiritual values found in these programs.

8. I will encourage those responsible for the production of religious programs. A good telecast that made me more fer-vent, left me serene or made me better deserves at least a warm "thank you." Thus, too, I will also take on the part of the

televiewer who speaks out against the displeasing, ridiculous or immoral aspects of a particular program. I should formulate my criticisms in such a way that they will always be constructive. The letters I write to TV studios or producers must bear my signature.

9. I will discuss the merit of TV programs with my parents, teachers and others who will help me formulate solid judgments. This will help me develop my own critical spirit, better perceive the moral, intellectual and artistic worth of every production.

10. Courtesy demands that young people do not impose "their" programs on the older members of the family. I must lead by my good example and show my younger brothers and sisters how to make reasonable use of the TV. Religious duties, study, outdoor life, family recreations, sports and contacts with friends must always hold a prominent place in my day. The TV is only one means of recreation and ideas, and must not be abused.

(International Catholic Association for Radio and TV)

"Blessed are they who suffer persecution for justice's sake, for theirs is the kingdom of heaven."

...persecution suffered for justice sake.

THE CREDO

In this world the good will always be persecuted, just as their Mother the Church is persecuted, as were the Apostles and as was Jesus the Redeemer. "If they have persecuted me, they will persecute you also" (Jn 15:20). Nevertheless, not all the persecuted are blessed, only those who suffer persecution for justice's sake; that is, they who patiently suffer derisions, calumnies and persecutions *for the love of Jesus Christ.*

What we have said already in regard to suffering borne with patience is equally applicable here. However, we add the following paternal words of wisdom uttered by Pope Paul VI:

We Christians should not feel less happy than other people because we have accepted Christ's yoke — a yoke that He bears with us and which He describes as 'light' and 'easy.' On the contrary, we should feel happier than others because we have positive reasons for being so. The salvation that Christ won for us, and through it, light on the most difficult problems of our existence, justify us in looking at everything with optimism.

St. Paul encourages us (2 Cor. 3:17-18): "Our present light affliction, which is for the moment, prepares for us an eternal weight of glory that is beyond all measure, while we look not at the things that are seen, but at the things that are not seen. For the things that are seen are temporal, but the things that are not seen are eternal."

As a help towards the preservation of virtue and perfect observance of the beatitudes, we should frequently examine our consciences. By forming the habit of self-examination — done without worry or meticulous scrupulosity — we will all the more easily see wherein we have failed and can resolve not to succumb in the future.

Who is it that is contented at his last moment? The soul who has led a good life. But if we take the wrong road, especially in our youth, what will happen to us? "Wide is the gate and broad is the way that leads to destruction" (Mt. 7:13); "Strive to enter by the narrow gate" (Lk. 13:24).

We read: "Fear God and keep his commandments" (Eccl. 12:13). All our works, good and bad, will be brought to judgment.

Let us analyze our thoughts, desires, words and actions and never be content with a superficial look at appearances. Our hearts must be probed well and everything pulled out for inspection. The more bad points we discover and detest now, the less we shall carry to the judgment.

Where conscience finds evil, no excuses are to be attempted, no self-deception permitted. What a properly-instructed upright conscience pronounces good must be continued, without compromise.

The famous pagan philosopher Cicero advised going into one's room at night, in the quiet dark, and putting every act of the day through an inspection, a merciless inspection — every act, every word, every sentiment, every place visited.... How few judge themselves dispassionately!

Let us remember that at the judgment we shall be defenseless, but here on this earth we have a great means at our disposal: the possibility of examining ourselves, repenting, and being forgiven. Let us fear God. Realizing how little merit we have, let us work intensely and diligently to acquire it, begging Jesus Christ, meanwhile, to give us His own. Then we shall meet our judge with peaceful hearts, for He will be our rewarder, our father, coming to lead us into our blessed home in heaven.

CHALLENGE

Give me courage to do what is hard; courage to say no to sin; courage to hold off the quitter in me.

Give me a clean mind and clean speech; clean eyes and clean hands. Let me cherish cleanness, and recognize that it brings happiness. Let me appreciate that in purity all good things grow.

Give me a gift for kindness, so I may never hurt another. Teach me to control my temper and my tongue, so they do not become the instruments of cruelty. I know my own importance, Lord; but let me never fail to see that others have importance, too.

Give me strength of spirit to defeat self-pity. If I am lonesome, lead me to the knowledge that to be loved I must be lovable; that I will have no real friends until I earn them.

Give me that bigness I will need to be cheerfully obedient. Remove from my personality a sullen spirit. Teach me to take orders, so that some day I will know how to give them reasonably.

Give me zest and drive to conquer laziness. Never let me feel that I can be served without serving, or get without giving. Instruct my heart in the love of work, so I may know the joy of rest.

Give me that peace of mind which comes from knowing that I will never lead another to sin. By Your grace, may no one be cheapened because he kept my company. Let all who love me, learn to love You more.

Give me, finally, such brightness, laughter, and grace, that You will find in me a temple which will please You as Mary pleased You. Amen.

JOHN MICHAEL MURPHY, *Ready or Not!*

8

HIS
LIFE
FOR
THE
WORLD

Even unto death

Under Pontius Pilate He suffered—the Lamb of God bearing on Himself the sins of the world, and HE DIED FOR US ON THE CROSS ...
THE CREDO

How can we be sure that Christ really died on Calvary? That question can only be answered by recounting in full the horrors of the passion. First came the agony of Jesus in the Garden. The apostles tell us that "he began to be saddened and exceedingly troubled. Then he said to them, 'My soul is sad, even unto death. Wait here and watch with me.'" Continuing the account we read: "And falling into an agony he prayed the more earnestly. And his sweat became as drops of blood running down upon the ground" (cf. Mt. 26:37; Lk. 22:43-44).

Medicine explains to us how a person can sweat blood. Under intense emotion, due to terror, small blood vessels in the sweat glands burst. The blood then exudes along with the sweat through the pores. Because this happened to Christ, we can form some idea as to the tremendous pressure to which He was subjected as He foresaw what was going to happen to Him.

After His arrest and trial, we know that He spent the night in jail. It was a time of horrors, as we gather from the sacred text. "And the men who had him in custody began to mock him and beat him. And they blindfolded him, and kept striking his face and asking him, saying, 'Prophesy, who is it that struck you?' And many other things they said against him, reviling him" (Lk. 22:63-65).

The next morning worse took place. The evangelists refer to it in the minimum of words. "Pilate then took Jesus and had him scourged" (Jn. 19:1). It is generally believed that this event was the most cruel episode of the whole passion. The Roman writer Horace calls the whip — which was composed of four leather thongs, to which were attached leaden balls — "horribile flagellum," or "the terrible scourge." Not infrequently people died as a result of this merciless form of castigation. It is commonly accepted that those who scourged Christ took it in relays. Not only did the Redeemer receive lashes on His chest, back and shoulders, but likewise on His face, where the skin is the most sensitive.

The scourging was followed by other atrocities. Again the sacred text enumerates these: "Now the soldiers led him away into the courtyard of the praetorium, and they called together the whole cohort. And they clothed him in purple, and plaiting a crown of thorns, they put it upon him, and began to greet him, 'Hail, King of the Jews.' And they kept striking him on the head with a reed, and spitting upon him; and bending their knees, they did homage to him" (Mk. 15:16-19).

The trial before Pontius Pilate began at seven in the morning of the day that we now refer to as Good Friday. Christ is believed to have received His sentence, either standing upright tied to a pillar, or forced to lean across a very low abutment. Then began the journey to Calvary, a distance of about six hundred yards, or slightly under half a mile. Authorities are of the opinion that He did not carry the entire gibbet but only the crossbar, or "patibulum" which weighed from eighty to ninety pounds.

From what has been said, it must be obvious that by the time Jesus arrived at the place of His immolation, He must have been considerably weakened both by suffering and more especially by loss of blood. In fact, many experts say that the torments He had endured would have been enough to cause death in an ordinary man, not to speak of One so sensitive to pain as our Lord.

The crucifixion, however, was the fatal event which brought His life to an end. It was a most barbarous punishment, so excruciating and degrading that Roman law forbade application of it to citizens of the empire. It would seem more probable that Christ was fastened with but three nails — one each for the hands, the other to affix the feet. The latter were pinned with the soles flat to the wood, so that He hung upon the tree in a crouching position, the knees bent outward.

Opinions differ as to what kind of cross was used, the high or the low. Most researchers think it was the latter form, so that after He had been nailed and hoisted into position, His head would not have been more than about eight feet above the ground.

Despite all that we have said, still some have maintained that Christ did not really die upon the cross. But it is impossible to conceive how He could have survived such an ordeal. Indeed, so sure was the centurion that He had died, that he cried out: "Truly this man was the Son of God" (Mk. 15:39). Moreover, the soldiers were bound to see that the victim was dead by a certain hour, and Roman law prescribed that if such were not the case, then the executioners themselves incurred the death penalty. With such a threat hanging over them, it is hardly likely that they would bungle their task. It is significant also that when the soldiers came to break the legs of the condemned, they did so in the case of the two thieves, but left untouched those of Christ, for the simple reason that He had already expired.

The period of time it took Christ to die must have been comparatively short. Even Pilate was surprised that He had breathed His last so soon, since it was not uncommon for criminals to hang writhing on the tree from one to three days, their agony increased by loss of blood, hunger, thirst, cramps, and gnawing of the nails. Again, before anyone could be handed over to the relatives for burial, the law stipulated that death was to be made certain by a spear-thrust. This was done in the case of Christ, leaving behind a large gash, so gaping in fact, that later, Christ in the apparition to Thomas, invited him to put his hand into it.

This latter circumstance certainly puts the issue beyond all doubt, but from medical sources we obtain another strong argument which proves that Christ really died on the cross. Doctors testify that water gathers in the pericardium (a sac composed of two layers surrounding the heart) of those who die after a long and painful agony. In the case of Christ, the spear thrust must have been delivered soon after death, for blood and water gushed forth.

Moreover, on being taken down from the cross, the body passed through the hands of His holy mother, the devout women, Nicodemus and Joseph of Arimathea. Had there been a spark of life left, beyond question the Blessed Virgin and friends of the Savior would have expended all their energy to make it spurt into flame. As a matter of fact, the very burial ceremonies to which the body was subjected—the wrapping in winding sheets, the weight of the spices used in the embalming process (a hundred pounds of myrrh and aloes) would have been enough to suffocate Him were He not already dead.

In addition, we must mention that Pilate only permitted Jesus to be interred when he was officially certain that death had taken place. Moreover, the hatred of His enemies was so venomous, that they would have left no stone unturned to ensure the certain destruction of Him whom they contemptuously referred to as "the Nazarene" and of whom the chief priest had said: "It is expedient for us that one man die for the people." As a matter of fact, so convinced were they that they had wrought His ruin that they persuaded Pilate to appoint a night guard, lest the apostles should come, steal away the body and say that their Master had arisen.

There is but one conclusion to these insurmountable facts—Jesus Christ really and truly died upon the cross.

The following observations will give us some insights as to what is implied by Christ's death:

Death means separation of the parts of a living composite. The death of man is the separation of the spiritual soul and the material body. God, who is Pure Spirit, has no parts and cannot die. Jesus Christ *as God*, therefore, *did not die.*

Suffering and death cause a feeling of repugnance and sorrow. Since God *is* Happiness, Jesus Christ, *as God,* was unable to experience these things. *Only as man did Jesus Christ die.* He suffered all the oppression of Gethsemane, the wounds of the scourging, the crowning with thorns and the piercing of the nails through His flesh.

At the death of Christ, the soul separated itself from the body, but the *Word* remained really and hypostatically united to His body in the tomb and to His soul in limbo.

In the *Apostles' Creed* we say that Christ descended into "hell" but this does not mean hell in the strict sense as we understand it. Christ did not go to the hell of the damned but to the hell of the just. Scripture calls it "Abraham's bosom" and we sometimes call it "limbo." There the souls of the just awaited news of redemption. Since the fall of our first parents, the gates of heaven had been closed but with Christ's death the just of the Old Testament were finally liberated. At the ascension of Jesus they all entered into the glory of heaven.

the reason for Christ's passion and death

...SAVING US BY HIS REDEEMING BLOOD.
We believe that OUR LORD JESUS CHRIST, BY THE SACRI-
FICE OF THE CROSS, REDEEMED US FROM ORIGINAL SIN
AND ALL THE PERSONAL SINS committed by each one of
us, so that, in accordance with the word of the apostle,
"where sin abounded, grace did more abound." THE CREDO

Sin, both original and actual, explains the necessity for the Redemption. Christ came to release man from the eternal punishment of original sin and to regain for him divine grace. Adam had lost grace, light and strength for posterity; but Christ, the new Adam restored these gifts. His sacrifice and sacraments are the means of grace; His doctrine banishes the darkness of the mind. The power of His grace overcomes our weakness of will.

Death still remains, but it becomes the gateway to eternal happiness through Christ's resurrection and ascension. Suffering and labor remain part of the human condition but through Christ they act as a means of earning merit—hence, greater glory in heaven. Satan is still permitted to tempt man, but his dominion over the human race has been broken by Christ the King.

An offense is measured by the dignity of the one who is offended, and reparation is measured by the dignity of the one who makes the reparation.

Sin is an offense against divine justice that no mere creature could repay with equal satisfaction.

Only a man who is also God is able to offer fitting reparation and satisfy the debt. Only a God-man is able to acquire a sufficient amount of merit to gain pardon for us, grace and heavenly glory. Only a human being can suffer, but suffering without participation of a Divine Person could not have given to God a satisfaction proportionate to the sin.

As a man Jesus Christ endured poverty, fatigue, hunger, thirst, plus the torments of the passion and crucifixion. As God He gave an infinite value to all of His prayers and actions and, therefore, He merited for us the forgiveness of sins, original and personal, the acquisition of grace and our salvation.

The Church has enshrined all this in her official teaching. Thus she has made it a dogma that Christ truly and properly redeemed us by His passion and expiatory death, all undertaken through obedience and love. In proof of this she points to the words of Isaia:

"Yet it was our infirmities that he bore, our sufferings that he endured, while we thought of him as stricken, as one smitten by God and afflicted. But *he was pierced for our offenses, crushed for our sins;* upon him was the chastisement that makes us whole, by his stripes we were healed. We had all gone astray like sheep, each following his own way; but the Lord laid upon him the guilt of us all...he surrendered himself to death and was counted among the wicked and he shall take away the sins of many, and win pardon for their offenses" (53:4, 12).

She strengthens it by an appeal to St. Luke (19:10) where Christ Himself says: "For the Son of Man is come to seek and to save what was lost."

"You have been bought at a great price," writes St. Paul (1 Cor. 6:20). St. Peter reechoes this (1 Peter 1:18): "You were redeemed not with perishable things, with silver or gold, but with the precious blood of Christ," and St. John perhaps makes the strongest and most arresting remark of all: "Because he loved us, he washed us from our sins in his own blood" (Apoc. 1:5).

The Fathers of the Council of Trent were most anxious that these facts should be clearly understood by all, and defined the doctrine of the Redemption, making it an article of faith as follows: "the sin of Adam, which in its origin is one, and by propagation, not by imitation, transfused into all, which is in each one as something that is his own, is not taken away either by the forces of nature, or by a remedy other than the merit of the one mediator, our Lord Jesus Christ, who has reconciled us to God in His own blood, made unto justice, sanctification and redemption...."

It is also a revealed truth that *Christ died for all men without exception.* By the infinite value of Christ's sacrifice on mankind's behalf, the sin of Adam which we inherit is erased. And not only is original sin forgiven, but also our own personal mortal and venial sins. How? *Certainly Christ did not take away unconditionally the sins of future men, but He provided the means by which our sins could be forgiven as*

"He was pierced for our offenses,

long as each man corresponded with grace. This particular grace we receive through the sacraments of Baptism and Penance.

The redemption accomplished by Christ was something objective. It did not consist in the moral example of His virtues such as patience in suffering. No, Christ actually died on a cross for the specific purpose of saving mankind from eternal punishment. *Real changes in man's relationship with God resulted.* The *benefits of the Redemption* can be summarized in this way: Christ fully satisfied the justice of God for the infinite offense of sin; He freed man from its slavery; He made it possible for man to be united with God on earth by regaining for him the gift of divine life, grace. Thus man became an adopted son of God and an heir to heaven.

Basic truths like these need to be reiterated in every age. Especially does this hold even more of our own with its emphasis on the materialistic. It was for this reason that the Fathers of the Second Vatican Council decided to stress the significance of the Redemption. They did so in the following words from the *Constitution on the Church in the Modern World:*

crushed for our sins."　Isaia 53:4

As an innocent lamb, Christ merited for us life by the free
shedding of His own blood. In Him God reconciled us to Himself and among ourselves; from bondage to the devil and sin
He delivered us, so that each one of us can say with the Apostle: "The Son of God loved me and gave Himself up for me "
(Gal. 2:20) (n. 22).

St. Augustine exhorts us to contemplate the scene of
Jesus who has just expired: "See the wounds of the divine
Crucified, the blood of the dead Christ, the price of your
ransom, the scars of the future resuscitated. He has His head
bowed to kiss you. His heart is pierced to love you. His arms
are widespread in order to embrace you. His whole body is a
mass of wounds in order to redeem you. Think of it, O men,
what divine attestations of love!"

Pope Paul VI also stressed the same theme, when he said:

"We must understand the 'why' of Christ's passion, its real
meaning and its universal import.
The passion of Christ is not merely a tragic shedding of blood.
It is a *sacrifice*, an *expiation* and a *holocaust*. If we accept this
aspect of our Lord's passion, we shall see in it a boundless
religious and moral value. And we will arrive at this unique

and extraordinary conclusion: Jesus suffered and died for us. We are part of this drama of the cross. We also are responsible. What it comes to is this. *Our sins are reflected in the sufferings and death of Christ.* If we should have lost the sense of sin, like so many today, we would intuitively recover it by discovering in Christ's sufferings and in the folly of His death our real moral condition, the consequences to which it leads, and the price that had to be paid for our redemption.

Christ took upon Himself what was due to us; He bore our chastisement. Jesus is the victim of man's sin. He is the Lamb which expiates our sin with its blood. We are the ones who are guilty of His immolation.

But here is a strange thing. This tremendous discovery of ours which should make us remorseful and drive us to despair, fills us instead with joy and love. It was for us that He suffered and died. By His cross we are saved.

A torrent of mercy gushes forth from the foot of the cross and offers to all – to all of us – the priceless good fortune of being pardoned and of being redeemed. So true is this, indeed, that we call that cruel passion a 'blessed' one."

"I will take his place"

We have outlined the purpose of the Redemption. We should think about these things often and try to make them part of our very lives. In order to help us do this, we narrate the two following episodes, which will serve to impress upon us in startling fashion just what our Redemption by Jesus Christ means.

After the Civil War ended, a farmer from Illinois used to go to Nashville, Tennesse, every year to pray at the tomb of a certain soldier.

One day someone asked him, "Is that your son?" "No," replied the farmer, "he was – just a friend. When the war broke out I was supposed to go and fight but I had seven small children and my wife was very sick.

"I knew my family couldn't survive during the war years without me so I went to my friend who lived alone and had no family and asked him if he would go in my place. He agreed without any hesitation.

"A short time afterwards he was wounded and brought to a hospital not far from here, where later he died.

"This is his grave and this is the inscription I wanted carved on the tombstone... 'He died for me.' "

Each one of us can say the same... "He (Jesus Christ) died for me."

The next incident, in many ways like the one just described, also took place in the last century, but this time in Russia.

On one occasion a young soldier – a mere boy of seventeen – was caught stealing. The penalty was flogging. On the appointed day – a bitterly cold one in winter – the regiment was assembled. The culprit was marched to the front, stripped to the waist and tethered to the whipping post. The lash was known to the Russians as the "knout" – a dreadful flail of thick, leather thongs. A shudder ran through the infantrymen and they groaned. All knew that the boy would never survive this ordeal. The terrible scene was about to be enacted when suddenly a shout came from somewhere in the rear ranks: "I will take his place!" and a tall, strong, well-built soldier strode forward. He was stripped to the waist and the punishment began. The cruel thongs bit into the back of the courageous soldier, pieces of his flesh flew off, and the snow was soaked in blood. Twenty-one strokes were given, the number required by law. When it was over, the youth who had been saved crawled over the scarlet snow in the sub-freezing temperature, clasped the feet of his deliverer and with sobs shaking his whole body cried out: "You took my place! You saved my life! I will be your slave forever!"

Here indeed was an example of heroic mercy. But there was an even greater one – *Christ took my place on the cross.*

Let us try to make sure that the fruits of the Redemption will always remain with us. This we do by refusing to commit mortal sin. Listen to these strong words of St. Paul which he wrote in his epistle to the Romans:

Therefore do not let sin reign in your mortal body so that you obey its lusts. And do not yield your members to sin as weapons of iniquity, but present yourselves to God as those who have come to life from the dead and your members as weapons of justice for God; for sin shall not have dominion over you, since you are not under the Law but under grace.

For when you were the slaves of sin, you were free as regards justice. But what fruit had you then from those things of which you are now ashamed? For the end of these things is death. But now set free from sin and become slaves to God, you have your fruit unto sanctification, and as your end, life everlasting. For the wages of sin is death, but the gift of God is life everlasting in Christ Jesus our Lord....

You, however, are not carnal but spiritual, if indeed the Spirit of God dwells in you. But if anyone does not have the Spirit of Christ, he does not belong to Christ. But if Christ is in you, the body, it is true, is dead by reason of sin, but the spirit is life by reason of justification. But if the Spirit of him who raised Jesus from the dead dwells in you, then he who raised Jesus Christ from the dead will also bring to life your mortal bodies because of his Spirit who dwells in you (6:12-14; 20-23; 8:9-11).

Linked with the fact of sin and the Redemption by Christ is the important doctrine of indulgences. To help us understand this teaching, the following must be stated. Sin is an offense against God and His laws. The guilt of sin refers to the personal responsibility which a person bears for breaking God's laws. Punishment is the penalty exacted of the offender by God.

An *indulgence is concerned only with the temporal punishment due to sin.* It has nothing to do with the nature of sin, the guilt of or the eternal punishment due to it.

We may summarize by saying that mortal sin results in personal guilt for the sinner and liability to both temporal and eternal punishment. An indulgence affects only the former, which still remains, even after both the guilt of sin and the eternal punishment due to it have been removed in the sacrament of Penance or by a perfect act of sorrow, with the intention of going to confession. An indulgence is therefore a means we have of reducing temporal punishment—the debt we owe to God.

The *Apostolic Constitution on Indulgences,* issued by Pope Paul VI, January 1, 1967, referred to indulgences as follows:

An indulgence is the remission before God of the temporal punishment due to sins already forgiven as far as their guilt is concerned, which the follower of Christ with the proper dispositions and under certain determined conditions acquired through the intervention of the Church which, as minister of the Redemption, authoritatively dispenses and applies the treasury of the satisfaction won by Christ and the saints. An indulgence is partial or plenary according as it removes either part or all of the temporal punishment due to sin (1, 2).

Likewise bound up with the subject of the Redemption is the doctrine of voluntary suffering for our personal sins. The

mystery of iniquity is always with us. Although the satisfaction for our offenses which Christ made by His bitter
passion and death was most perfect, the Church teaches that
adult Christians should imitate the suffering Christ and with
Him satisfy for their sins by their good works, if they wish to
be saved. Our Lord Himself said: "If anyone wishes to come
after me, let him deny himself, and take up his cross, and
follow me" (Mt. 16:24). St. Peter, who was very close to Christ,
re-echoed this when he wrote: "For Christ also suffered for
you, leaving you an example that you may follow in his steps"
(1 Pet. 2:21).

In addition, there is the question of suffering in expiation
for the sins of others. The genesis of this doctrine we find in
the text of St. Paul: "But now he has reconciled you in his
body of flesh through his death, to present you holy and un-
defiled and irreproachable before him. Only you must remain
firmly founded in the faith and steadfast and not withdrawing
from the hope of the Gospel which you have heard. It has been
preached to every creature under heaven, and of it I, Paul,
have become a minister. I rejoice now in the sufferings I bear
for your sake; and what is lacking of the sufferings of Christ I
fill up in my flesh for his body, which is the Church" (Col.
1:22-24). These words clearly show that the satisfaction of
Christ, though perfect in itself, must be completed by us.
We must be configured to Christ, who is the head of the
Mystical Body, which is the Church. In this way will His
satisfaction and merits be applied to us.

In the light of this doctrine we can understand suffering
in the lives of the saints. For them it was a means of saving
their own souls and those of others.

Here are the words of St. Margaret Mary: "The world of
love is measured by its willingness to suffer. Without suffering we cannot live the life of God."

The value of suffering to expiate the sins of others is
clearly brought out in the events that happened at Fatima
in 1917.

On the occasion of the first apparition, the Blessed Virgin
asked the children, "Do you wish to offer yourselves to God in order
to accept all the sufferings He wishes to send you, in reparation for
sin and for the conversion of sinners?" To this the three little ones—
Lucia, Jacinta and Francisco—replied, "Yes, we want to!"

At once the Blessed Virgin replied, "Then you will suffer much,
but God's grace will strengthen you." She continued, "My children,

go on always saying the rosary, as you have just done." During the fourth visitation she said, "Pray, pray very much and make sacrifices for sinners. For many souls go to hell because there is no one to make sacrifices for them."

The children did not have long to wait before sufferings came to them. They had to bear the unbelief and hostility, not only of the villagers, but also of their own relatives and parents. Indeed, the only one who stood by them in this excruciating ordeal was Ti Marto, the father of Francisco and Jacinta. Apart from this type of pain, which came to them in the natural order of God's Providence, the children also embraced voluntary suffering for the salvation of souls. In this they were but fulfilling the wishes of the Blessed Mother, whose attitude they understood quite plainly from the apparitions. In reparation for sin they decided not to dance – an innocent recreation in which they used to indulge while tending the sheep.

We know that when Jacinta was in the hospital, although she disliked milk, she drank it, and although she relished grapes, she refused to eat them, in order that she might embrace voluntary suffering in reparation for sin and for the salvation of souls. Later, she was operated on and had two ribs removed. The daily dressing of these wounds caused her indescribable anguish, but she would cry out: "Oh! Our Lady! Patience! We must suffer to go to heaven!" Then, speaking to our Lord as if He were present she would say: "Now You can convert many sinners, for I suffer greatly, my Jesus!" All this from a child scarcely eleven years old!

In his ardor for suffering, little Francisco went so far as to wind a rope around his body, so he could not sleep at night. But the Blessed Mother appeared to Jacinta and told her that he should use the rope only during the day, as our Lord was already pleased with what he was doing. Francisco was hardly ten years old!

All this, of course, is anathema to a modern world bent on pleasure, anxious to "live it up." In many ways our present era is reminiscent of the state of the Roman Empire just before it collapsed in ruins. The slogan then was: "Eat, drink and be merry for tomorrow we die!" Even many Catholics do not grasp the meaning of suffering and its place in the plan of our salvation. They are inclined to look upon people who practice mortification as perhaps not being just right in the head! After all they will tell you, it's not the American way of life! Haven't we been blessed with all the good things of the earth! Let's enjoy them! Don't be a square! Join the crowd and have fun!

No one is condemning lawful recreation. It is essential in God's scheme of things. It is good for soul and body. But the mad craze for pleasure and activity at any cost fills many clear-sighted, right-thinking people with alarm. "Bread and the circus" was another cry of ancient Rome. Today there is nothing left of that once-proud civilization that dominated a great part of the then-known world.

But herein lies a challenge for those who feel they want to do much more for the cause of our Lord and Savior Jesus Christ. All through the Christian ages there have been found rare souls willing to pay the highest ransom for the vices of men. The calendar of the saints is replete with names of this kind: St. Frances of Rome, St. Catherine of Genoa, St. Mary Magdalene dei Pazzi, Blessed Anna Maria Taigi, St. Catherine of Siena, St. Teresa of Avila, St. John of the Cross, and, in our days, St. Therese or the Little Flower and St. Gemma Galgani are examples which spring to mind.

We may not be able to follow absolutely in the footsteps of these great servants of God. But at least we can keep their sterling example before our eyes and try to do our best in this struggle against evil. Infallibly we must suffer. In the designs of God, as long as we remain in this vale of tears, we shall experience spiritual, mental or physical suffering of some kind or other. The emphasis may be on one or the others of these — it may be even all three combined. That depends upon the Providence of God. Knowingly and willingly then, let us take all our trials and tribulations, unite them to the infinite merits of Christ upon the cross and also to His merits in all the Masses that are celebrated daily and offer them up to God, in reparation for sin, for the salvation of our own souls, as well as those of others.

Doing this, we will approach the realization of that ideal of Pope Pius XII for which he appealed in these words:

"Today more than ever, as in the first centuries of her existence, the Church has need of witnesses, more even than apologists, of witnesses, who by their entire life, will make the true image of Christ and the Church shine before the eyes of the pagan world surrounding them" (July 4, 1947).

The wonders of His love

We cannot leave this section on the Redemption without some reference, however slight, to devotion to the Sacred Heart, which is so intimately bound up with the passion and death of Christ.

The story opens in France, where in the town of Janots, Burgundy, Margaret Alacoque was born in the year 1647. At the age of twenty-four she joined the Visitation Order. During her religious life she was privileged to have a series of visions of our Lord, and as a result of these the feast of the Sacred Heart was established, on which day every year, reparation is offered to God for the sins of men. The life and visions of St. Margaret Mary have been approved by the Church. The subject matter of the revelations is of extraordinary interest and if acted upon today would help to solve many of the world's ills.

One day during the octave of the feast of Corpus Christi, in the year 1674, St. Margaret Mary was kneeling in adoration before the Blessed Sacrament exposed on the altar.

Before her our Lord appeared, brilliant in glory. The light surrounding Him was so dazzling that the sun would have been dim in comparison with it. The sight of Him filled her heart with an indescribable joy. He did not resemble any pictures that she had ever seen before. Radiant with light were the sacred wounds in His hands and feet; burning with fire was His heart.

St. Margaret Mary writes: "He showed me the inexplicable wonders of His pure love and to what extremes He had gone in loving man, from whom He received nothing but ingratitude."

Our Lord spoke to her as follows: "This wounds me more than all I suffered in my passion. All I did for them I count as little and would wish, if possible, to do more. But in return for my eagerness, they give me nothing but coldness and rebuffs. You at least rejoice me by making up for their ingratitude so far as you can."

In his encyclical on the Sacred Heart, Pope Pius XI referred to these complaints of Christ as follows: "Behold this heart, which has loved men so much and has loaded them with every favor, and for this boundless love receives not merely no return of gratitude, but on the contrary, forgetfulness, neglect, contumely and that at times at the hands of those who were bound by the debt and duty of a special love."

There is a great lesson for all of us in these revelations to St. Margaret Mary. Every individual has been redeemed by Jesus Christ? How do we repay Him?

We conclude with the prayer taught by the Blessed Virgin to the children of Fatima:

"O my Jesus, forgive us our sins. Save us from the fires of hell. Lead all souls to heaven, especially those who have most need of Your mercy."

CHALLENGE

One morning a strange masterpiece, painted by an unknown artist was discovered in the men's holdover of the central police district in St. Louis, Missouri. That day in 1932, on the rear wall of cell number 8, there was found an amazingly life-like drawing of Christ dying upon the cross. The artist had executed his drawing with great care, skill and perhaps pain. Art experts who saw it felt that it had taken a long time and great determination to complete. The police blotter did not record the presence of any artist in that cell at any time, and those who were detained in number 8 never remained for more than a few hours.

The most curious feature of the prisoner's picture is that ordinary artist's materials, such as pencil, pastel or paint, were not used to render this picture, but the entire sketch was done with nothing but burned out matches.

Cell number 8 has almost become a shrine, and it is no longer used to detain offenders. The picture has been covered with glass and illumined with a spotlight, since it has attracted many visitors. The curious, who come to gaze upon this unique labor of love, leave feeling like pilgrims. Many have tried to penetrate the riddle of this puzzling picture. What must have been the great conflict and the deep repentance which moved a man in his darkest hour to draw this study of Christ, the same Christ who, in the last minutes of His life on earth, promised an eternal reward to another repentant criminal?

The identity of the unknown but repentant artist may always remain a mystery. Perhaps the reason for its creation may never be satisfactorily explained. Both are known only to God. But the picture, far from being mute, gives eloquent testimony of its creator's sorrow for his sins.

There are no crimes, however foul, nor sins, however serious, for which a sorrowful man cannot find forgiveness from God. Although God did not spare the angels that sinned, yet, as a merciful Father, He has compassion on His children who love and fear Him.

St. Vincent de Paul was no betting man but on one occasion he made a wager with a habitual sinner, who claimed that he was too weak to stop sinning. The saint told the sinner that when he was tempted to sin he should look at the cross and say: "I do not care that You died for me." "In a week's time," he told that man, "you will give up your sinful life and repent."

St. Francis de Sales had a great devotion to the cross and he would frequently point to the cross bearing his crucified Savior and ask: "How can I look at the cross and deny Him anything?"

J.J. AMATO, Ready or Not!

9

"I
LIVE
AND
YOU
SHALL
LIVE"

JOHN 14:18

the Gospels and the resurrection

HE was buried, and, of His own power, ROSE ON THE THIRD DAY, raising us by His resurrection to that sharing in the divine life which is the life of grace.

THE CREDO

"It is not a difficult thing," St. Augustine has said, "to believe that Christ died. In fact, pagans, Jews, and even the wicked, all believe that He died. But the faith of the Catholics rests in the resurrection of Christ: for us, this is great, to believe that He is risen."

For this reason, Jesus frequently spoke of the resurrection, and He almost never spoke of His passion to His disciples without alluding to the resurrection. "Believe, then, in His resurrection," exhorts this saint, and with St. Paul he confesses with joy: "For we know that Christ having risen from the dead, dies now no more, death shall no longer have dominion over him" (Rom. 6:9).

"Mankind was used to seeing everyone die, but had never seen anyone come back to life. It therefore had something to fear and did not know what to hope for. But in order that I might have the hope of resurrecting, which I lacked, You, O my God, came back to life before me, so that, where You preceded me, I may hope to follow You." (St. Augustine)

We saw how Jesus Christ claimed to be God and proved it by His miracles. We pointed out that the greatest of these miracles was the resurrection and we left it aside for fuller treatment. The time has now come to examine it in detail.

The fact that our Lord by His own power raised Himself from the dead, taken along with the Incarnation and institution of the Blessed Eucharist, ranks as the most important episode in the history of the world. It is the seal which stamps the mark of truth upon the whole life of the Carpenter of Nazareth. It is the cornerstone upon which the Church is built.

St. Paul, in that forceful, direct way of his, has well summed up the significance of the resurrection. Here are his words taken from the first epistle to the Corinthians (15:12-17): "Now if Christ is preached as risen from the dead, how do some among you say that there is no resurrection of the dead? But if there is no resurrection of the dead, neither has Christ risen; and if Christ has not risen, vain then is our preaching, and vain, too, is your faith. Yes, and we are found false witnesses as to God, in that we have borne witness against God that he raised Christ—whom he did not raise up, if the dead do not rise. For if the dead do not rise, neither has Christ risen; and if Christ has not risen again, vain is your faith, for you are still in your sins."

As we have already pointed out, on six occasions our Lord prophesied the resurrection. Let us examine each of them in detail.

Christ first foretold the resurrection after Peter's confession of faith in Him at Dalmanutha. Sts. Matthew (16:21-23), Mark (8:31-33) and Luke (9:22) tell us: [1] "And from that time Jesus began to teach His disciples, saying: 'The Son of Man must go to Jerusalem, suffer many things and be rejected by the ancients and the high priests and the Scribes and be killed, and after three days rise again.' And he spoke the word openly."

The second prediction came after the Transfiguration on Mount Tabor. Again these three evangelists (Mt. 17:1-9; Mk. 9:1-8 and Lk. 9:28-36) have described the actual Transfiguration and the words of Christ which followed it. We read: "And as they were coming down from the mountain, Jesus charged them saying: 'Tell the vision to no man, till the Son of Man be risen from the dead.' And they held their peace and told no man in those days any of the things which they had seen."

The third prophecy was made after He had cured the man born blind. Once more it is the three same evangelists who record the incident (Mt. 17:21-22; Mk. 9:30-31; Lk. 9:44-45). They tell us: "And when they abode in Galilee, and all were

1. Where the writers are mentioned in triple, the quotes are taken from: "Jesus the Messiah": The Four Gospels in One Narrative, by J.M. Bover, S.J., English Adaptation by J. Burgers, S.T.L.

astonished at the mighty power of God, Jesus taught his disciples and said to them: 'Lay up on your hearts these words: The Son of Man shall be betrayed into the hands of men, and they shall kill him, and the third day he shall rise again.' But they understood not this word and it was hid from them so that they perceived it not. And they were afraid to ask him concerning this word. And they were troubled exceedingly."

The fourth prediction concerning the resurrection took place early in the third year of the public ministry after He had cast the devil out of the mute man. St. Matthew (12:38-42) and St. Luke (11:29-32) tell us: "Then some of the Scribes and Pharisees answered him saying: 'Master, we would see a sign from you.' Who answering said to them: 'An evil and adulterous generation seeks a sign: and a sign shall not be given it, but the sign of Jona the prophet. For even as Jona became a sign to the Ninivites, so shall the Son of Man be to this generation. For as Jona was in the whale's belly three days and three nights, so shall the Son of Man be in the heart of the earth three days and three nights.... Behold a greater than Jona here.' "

The fifth prediction took place near Jerusalem after the scene with the rich young man who would not leave all to follow Him. Again the incident is outlined for us by the same three writers (Mt. 20:17-19; Mk. 10:32-34 and Lk. 18:31-34). "And they were in the way going up to Jerusalem: and Jesus went before them and they were astonished and following, were afraid. And taking again the twelve disciples apart, he began to tell them the things that should befall him, saying: 'Behold we go up to Jerusalem and all things shall be accomplished which were written by the prophets concerning the Son of Man, for the Son of Man shall be betrayed to the chief priests and the Scribes and the ancients and they shall condemn him to death, and shall deliver him to the Gentiles. And they shall mock him and spit on him and scourge him. And after they have scourged him, they will put him to death; and the third day he shall rise again.' "

Just before the Last Supper He made a prophecy about the crucifixion: "You know that after two days shall be the pasch, and the Son of Man shall be delivered up to be crucified" (Mt. 26:1-5; Mk. 14:1-2; Lk. 22:1-6). This He followed up with a sixth prediction, this time a general reference to the resurrection. It was spoken on the way from the supper room to the Garden of Gethsemane. He said to the disciples:

"A little while and you shall see me no longer; and again a little while and you shall see me, because I go to the Father" (Jn. 16:16).

So well known was this prophecy of Christ that after the crucifixion, His enemies said to Pilate: "Sir, we have remembered how that deceiver said while he was yet alive, 'After three days I will rise again' "(Mt. 27:63). The resurrection is a double argument for the genuineness of Christ's claim. It is a proof in so far as it is the greatest miracle recorded, and it also compels our assent as being the fulfillment of prophecy.

Since the resurrection is of such crucial importance, we quote from the three evangelists who have described it.

The Testimony of St. Matthew (28:1-6):

Now late in the night of the Sabbath, as the first day of the week began to dawn, Mary Magdalene and the other Mary came to see the sepulcher. And behold, there was a great earthquake; for an angel of the Lord came down from heaven, and drawing near rolled back the stone, and sat upon it. His countenance was like lightning, and his raiment like snow. And for fear of him the guards were terrified, and became like dead men. But the angel spoke and said to the women, "Do not be afraid; for I know that you seek Jesus, who was crucified. He is not here, for he has risen even as he said. Come, see the place where the Lord was laid.

The Testimony of St. Mark (16:1-6):

And when the Sabbath was past, Mary Magdalene, Mary the mother of James, and Salome, bought spices, that they might go and anoint him. And very early on the first day of the week, they came to the tomb, when the sun had just risen. And they were saying to one another, "Who will roll the stone back from the entrance of the tomb for us?" And looking up they saw that the stone had been rolled back, for it was very large. But on entering the tomb, they saw a young man sitting at the right side, clothed in a white robe, and they were amazed. He said to them, "Do not be terrified. You are looking for Jesus of Nazareth, who was crucified. He has risen, he is not here. Behold the place where they laid him."

The Testimony of St. Luke (24:1-8):

But on the first day of the week at early dawn, they came to the tomb, taking the spices that they had prepared, and they found the stone rolled back from the tomb. But on entering, they did not find the body of the Lord Jesus. And it came to pass, while they were wondering what to make of this, that, behold, two men stood by them in dazzling raiment. And when the women were struck with fear and bowed their faces to the ground, they said to them, "Why do you seek the living one among the dead? He is not here, but has risen. Remember how he spoke to you while he was yet in Galilee, saying that the Son of Man must be betrayed into the hands of sinful men, and be crucified, and on the third day rise."

And they remembered his words.

Referring to the extended accounts of the resurrection, i.e., what we have quoted above plus the narration of the apparitions, we must add the following. First, there is substantial agreement as to a number of items. Thus, it is said that the women first discovered the empty tomb, that the resurrection was announced to them by a messenger, that shortly after Christ appeared to the women, and they brought the astounding news to the apostles.

Apart from these facts, each Gospel contains material that the others do not. For example, Matthew mentions the guard at the tomb, the bribery of the soldiers by the Jewish leaders and Christ's apparition on the mountain in Galilee. St. Luke recounts the apparition to the two disciples on the way to Emmaus. He also tells of the appearance to Simon, to the apostles in Jerusalem and narrates the ascension. St. John informs us that both Peter and John inspected the tomb, describes two apparitions which took place in Jerusalem on Easter Sunday, and includes two others — that to Thomas in the supper room, the other by the Sea of Galilee, where Christ also worked a miracle involving the catch of fishes. Early as these texts are in the history of the Church, there are others earlier still. The earliest reference occurs in St. Paul's first epistle to the Corinthians (15:3-8). It runs: "For I delivered to you first of all, what I also received, that Christ died for our sins according to the Scriptures, and that he was buried, and that he rose again the third day, according to the Scriptures, and that he appeared to Cephas, and after that to the Eleven. Then was he seen by more than five hundred brethren at one time, many of whom are with us still, but some have

"I arose and am still with you."

The Liturgy

fallen asleep. After that he was seen by James, then by all the apostles. And last of all, as by one born out of due time, he was seen also by me." Verses 3-5 in the above were in very, very early Church use. They were originally composed in Aramaic and, in accordance with Jewish belief, could only refer to a bodily resurrection.

At the very beginning of Christianity, the believers fashioned simple creeds, and there are traces of these in the New Testament. The text: "For if you confess with your mouth that Jesus is Lord, and believe in your heart that God has raised him from the dead, you shall be saved" (Rom. 10:9) is of this nature. So also, in the Acts of the Apostles, which book was composed before the four Gospels, there are frequent references to the resurrection: 1:22; 2:24-28; 3:15, 26; 4:10, 33; 5:30 ff.; 10:41 ff.; 13:31-37; 17:3, 31; 26:22 ff. All this extra data proves that the resurrection was believed in and preached from the very beginning of Christianity.

The careful reader will note that in none of the accounts of the resurrection that we have given is the actual resurrection itself described. This is so, because, as a matter of fact, no one saw it with his own eyes. The whole truth of the resurrection rests upon two things, which cannot be explained away either by biblical exegesis or critical historical analysis. These two points are — the fact of the empty tomb, and the witness of the apostles due to the apparitions of Christ.

The earliest evidence for the empty tomb is contained in Mark 16:1-8. In passing, it should be made clear that the early Christians never used the fact of the empty tomb as an apologetical argument, in other words, to prove that Christ had actually risen, for the discovery was made by women, and at that period of Jewish history, women could not be witnesses. That is why we read in Luke 24:10-11: "Now, it was Mary Magdalene and Joanna and Mary, the mother of James, and the other women who were with them, who were telling these things to the apostles. But this tale seemed to them nonsense, and they did not believe the women."

At the same time, the report of an empty tomb could have been checked in Jerusalem by the authorities, and we know that the foes of Christ never combatted the story of an empty tomb. It must also be stressed that the apostles and holy women declared their faith in the risen Christ, not because they found an empty tomb, but by reason of their personal experiences when they were favored with the apparitions of the risen Lord.

These various appearances as described in the Gospels confirm the fact of the resurrection. At least twelve of them are recorded. Our Lord was first seen by Mary Magdalene who mistook Him for the gardener and later by the holy women as they returned from the tomb. He next came to Peter and then walked with two disciples as far as the little village of Emmaus, breaking bread with them at the inn. After that He visited the apostles in the supper room, St. Thomas being absent, and came to them again, Thomas being present. Later He was seen by five disciples and two apostles at the Sea of Tiberias and then by the Eleven as they went into Galilee to the spot whereunto He had appointed them. We also hear of Him appearing to more than five hundred brethren at once, then to "James the brother of the Lord" and again to the apostles in the Holy City, from whence He told them not to depart until they should have received the Holy Spirit. Finally, He led them into Bethania and before their eyes ascended into heaven. There was another apparition. It happened to St. Paul on the road to Damascus. See Acts 9:1-7; 22:6-16; 26:12-18.

Such are the facts in bare outline, but it will be essential to go more into particulars about these apparitions. For if they had always taken place under a definite set of circumstances, in a restricted area say, or if He had only been seen by a certain group of persons — say women — then we might have some grounds for doubt. But the very differences only serve to convince us the more that they are genuine. Some of these apparitions occurred in Galilee, others at more than a distance of seventy miles away in Jerusalem. Some were in the open, others behind closed doors, some by the Lake of Genesareth and one on a mountain in Galilee. At varying hours of the day we read of Christ coming to His friends — in the morning, at noon and in the evening. Many of the appearances were granted to individuals, but not all. He was seen by groups of the brethren and once by a multitude of five hundred. Both men and women beheld Him, touched His body, spoke with Him for a considerable time and even dined with Him.

These apparitions of our Lord are the most heartwarming and most colorful episodes in all Scripture. We will speak of three of them.

The following is an amalgamation of accounts by St. Mark (16:9-11) and St. John (20:11-18).

Early the first day of the week, he appeared first to Mary Magdalene, out of whom he had cast seven devils. But Mary stood at the sepulcher outside, weeping. Now, as she was weeping, she stooped down and looked into the sepulcher. And she saw two angels in white, sitting one at the head and one at the feet, where the body of Jesus had been laid. They said to her: 'Woman, why do you weep?'

She said to them: 'Because they have taken away my Lord, and I know not where they have laid him.'

When she said this, she turned back, and saw Jesus standing, and she knew not that it was Jesus. Jesus said to her: 'Woman, why do you weep? Whom do you seek?'

She, thinking it was the gardener, said to him: 'Sir, if you have taken him hence, tell me where you have laid him, and I will take him away.

Jesus said to her: 'Mary.'

She turning said to him: 'Rabboni' (which is to say, Master).

Jesus said to her: 'Do not touch me, for I am not yet ascended to my Father, but go to my brethren and say to them, 'I ascend to my father and to your Father, to my God and your God.'

Mary Magdalene came and told the disciples that had been with him, who were mourning and weeping: 'I have seen the Lord and these things he said to me.

And they, hearing that he was alive and had been seen by her, did not believe.

The next account is constructed from the Gospels of St. Mark (16:14), Luke (24:36-45) and John (20:19-21):

Now while they were speaking these things, when it was late that same day, the first of the week, and the doors were shut, where the disciples were gathered together for fear of the Jews, at length while they were at table, Jesus stood in the midst of them and said to them: "Peace be to you. It is I, fear not."

But they, being troubled and frightened, supposed that they saw a spirit. And he said to them: "Why are you troubled and why do thoughts arise in your hearts? See my hands and feet, that it is I myself; handle and see, for a spirit has not flesh and bones, as you see me to have." And when he had said this, he showed them his hands and feet and his side. But while they yet believed not, and wondered with joy, he said: "Have you here anything to eat?"

And they offered him a piece of a broiled fish and a honeycomb. And when he had eaten before them, taking what remained he gave it to them. The disciples therefore were glad, when they saw the Lord. And he said to them: "These are the words which I spoke to you while I was yet with you, that all things must be fulfilled, which are written in the law of Moses, and in the prophets and in the psalms concerning me."

Then he opened their understanding, that they might understand the Scriptures. He said therefore to them again: "Peace be to you. As the Father has sent me, I also send you." When he had said this, he breathed on them and said to them: "Receive the Holy Spirit; whose sins you shall forgive, they are forgiven them; and whose sins you shall retain, they are retained."

The third appearance which we include is that of Christ to Thomas. In his work, *The Risen Lord,* the author, James Sullivan has described how an artist vividly portrayed the above incident. The entire quotation reads as follows:

In 1881 Carl Bloch painted his unforgettable conception of this apparition to Thomas. The plan of the canvas is simple. It is rectangular in shape, the vertical axis being the longer. Christ stands just a little off center, filling most of the right-hand space. Behind his left shoulder are two apostles, one with his hands joined in an attitude of humble, respectful love, gazing upon him with profound reverence, afraid to get too near lest he touch Him; the other—the higher part of whose face beginning from the nose upward can just be seen almost in shadow—has an excited look mingled with fear, his lively, inquisitive eyes, almost starting from their sockets, carefully following every movement of the Master.

Just left of the vertical axis stands Peter, partly hidden behind Christ and just visible from the right waist upward. His right arm is bent and the hand—upon which the knuckles and veins stand out boldly—rather tensely clutches his cloak just below the left shoulder. Peter's features are taut. His vivid eyes, in which one can read bafflement, expectancy and a certain helplessness, are fixed intently upon the face of Jesus.

Thomas occupies the lower left portion of the picture, the rectangle made by the intersection of the vertical and horizontal axes. He is clad in a full, dark red garment, held around the waist by a cord into which are tucked the flowing folds of his faded blue cloak, the latter slung loosely over the left shoulder. He is on his knees in a posture of utter abasement, reverence and adoration. His head, matted with thick black hair, is averted from Christ—he is too ashamed to look upon Him, too ashamed that he has doubted such a gentle, sympathetic, forgiving Master, whom he now knows to be his God. His eyes are closed, as from the waist downward he inclines abjectly toward the ground. Both arms are raised—one gets the impression that they are trembling with fear and emotion—somewhat halfway between cinture and head, the outstretched though not rigid right hand, on a level with the right eye, hiding the lower part of his features—the right jaw and portion of the mouth to be precise. Between the hands is depicted His long, ample, flowing beard.

The background of the work is executed in dark brown colors and these serve to accentuate the resplendent figure of Christ, this same effect being heightened by the suppliant attitude of Thomas.

With overpowering presence, our Lord dominates the entire scene. He stands erect and tall—tallest in the picture—full of grace and poise, a perfect specimen of manhood, despite the scars which He has won in the battle with sin. He looks almost like a soldier at attention, but lacking the tension and rigidity usually associated with such a stance. Radiating imperial dignity, He is complete master of the situation. He is garbed in a long, flowing cream-colored garment, an edge of which He holds in His pierced left hand, the entire left arm extended full length downward. Obviously He has just swung it in a sweeping, majestic arc, baring the whole of His left side from the waist up. Just below the left breast is a livid mark—the wound caused by the spear-thrust. The garment also drapes over His right shoulder and is caught in His right hand—also gashed—His long slender index finger pointing to the rupture in His side. Emerging from underneath the garment is the left foot, sealed with the print of the nail.

His long, copious auburn hair, parted in the middle, streams down His neck and over His shoulders. The artist has depicted him with moustache and beard, the former somewhat light, the latter quite abundant. The chin, protruding a little is strong, as is also the mouth, which is set in a firm, though not severe or repelling line. The nose is long and aquiline, the forehead high and noble. His eyes, shaded by heavy though not bushy brows gaze down solemnly, compellingly and in a somewhat mildly reproving manner on Thomas. The face is, in a masculine way, beautiful, stamped with unearthly splendor and massive strength of character—the face of a God Incarnate, of a God in human flesh. In it one discerns infinite power and authority but tempered by compassion, understanding and, above all, love. This is how the artist imagined the apparition of Christ to Thomas; the apostle who played such a vital part in the whole drama, had the unique privilege of experiencing much, much more.

Modern objections to the resurrection can be reduced to four main classes. First, there are those who say that it just could not possibly have happened. Others point to the discrepancies within the apparition stories and on this account try to discredit them. A third band has misgivings about the empty tomb and say that the story was inserted comparatively late into the Gospels. The fourth group says that the story of a bodily resurrection came about as the result of the way in which the disciples described their personal experiences. We will deal with each of these criticisms in particular.

The first objection comes from those who rule out any possibility of the supernatural. For them there are only natural laws. They only accept what they can verify by their senses. For them, the resurrection never occurred. When a person dies, certain laws take over and the body begins to disintegrate. These laws do not reverse themselves. The laws of astronomy, chemistry, mathematics and physics are immutable. So are those of biology. Dead men just do not return to life again.

This is the type of mind which does not stop to think that the God who made the physical laws can make exceptions to them. Such people refuse to look at a thing impartially, to meet a situation with open eyes. They refuse to consult even the records. Today, along the course of the Amazon, deep in the Brazilian jungles, there are Indian tribes who have never come in contact with white men. Suppose that having met them and learned their language, you were to tell them that men have landed on the moon and returned to earth? Would they believe you? They wouldn't! And why? Because to them it is impossible; it just cannot be done. The man who denies the possibility of raising the dead is in exactly the same position. Probably he is in a worse one, for the chances are that he does not believe in the existence of God who could work such a wonder, while most likely the Brazilian primitive has some idea, even though a faint one, of an omnipotent Creator.

There is only one cure for such an attitude. A person like this must first learn to shed his prejudices and approach the question with an open mind. Given this, the way is clear for dialogue and progress can be made.

What of those who discount the resurrection on account of the discrepancies in the apparition stories? Briefly, the objection runs like this. The six accounts in the Gospels covering the apparitions fall into two groups—the appearances that took place in Jerusalem, and those that happened in Galilee. Neither of these two versions shows any awareness of appearances in the other region. How can there be such a discrepancy if we are dealing with historical records?

The best answer to this objection is simply to admit that no sequence in the apparitions can be established with any accuracy. Each of the six Gospel accounts emphasizes an all-important appearance to the disciples, during which they were instructed what to do for the future. This method of answering is in keeping with the best modern analytical approaches to the historical value of the Gospels.

The third objection centers around the tomb. Here, undoubtedly, there are certain discrepancies in the various reports. Seizing on this, modern objectors hold that in actual fact the body of Christ remained in the tomb, that it never left it! But there is absolutely no warrant for any such statement. There is nothing whatever in the New Testament which could even remotely lead to such a conclusion. As Wolfhart Pannenberg, a popular German theologian, so neatly puts it: "We have only to try to imagine how the disciples of Jesus could proclaim His resurrection if they could be constantly refuted by the evidence of the very tomb itself wherein lay the corpse of Jesus." Despite the diversity of their sources, the writers of the Gospels unanimously accepted the story of the empty tomb.

The belief that Christ's body was still in the sepulcher seems to have gained some ground even among Catholics. They say: "My faith in the resurrection could never be disturbed, even if Christ's body were found in Palestine today!" But in view of what we have just said, such a statement is completely without foundation. Indeed, if this had been the case, if the body had been still in the tomb, the faith of the apostles in the resurrection would have been shattered. But it wasn't. They constantly preached their invincible belief in the risen Lord. There can be only one possible conclusion. The tomb was empty, because Jesus had risen from the dead.

The fourth objection takes the following form. In reality, Jesus did conquer death but not through a physical resurrection. Those who had known Him were full of faith and fervor and experienced His resurrection in the following peculiar way. Actually they did not see Him with their own eyes, but they tried to explain their belief in Him in terms of a bodily resurrection. When they experienced the majesty of the glorified Jesus in their inmost souls, the best and only way for them to describe this sensation was to say that they had seen His resurrected body. Thus, a mere subjective experience was given the status of an historical fact.

The tenor of the entire Gospel story is against such an interpretation. Instead of confusing feeling with fact, the apostles proved themselves to be practical, hard-headed, common-sense men throughout the entire event. They began with utter incredulity in the women's stories that Christ had risen. Is there any reason here for assuming intense interior exaltation? Then, when Christ Himself did appear to them, there is no mention of great spiritual uplift. In fact, just the opposite is recorded, for they were troubled, frightened and thought they saw a spirit! Christ had to eat before them to convince them that it was really He who was in their presence. Moreover, they failed to recognize Him on four occasions during the apparitions (cf. Mk. 16:12; Lk. 24:16; Jn. 20:14 and Jn. 21:4). Thus, instead of transforming their feelings into a belief in bodily appearances, they did not even know that it was Christ when He appeared before them!

The material contained in the Gospel accounts, which, as we saw, were written very, very early in the life of the Church, show us how the apparitions were being interpreted at that particular period. It is clear that the evangelists went out of their way to forestall a non-corporeal interpretation of the appearances. Thus, this fourth. objection has no real substance. It is completely opposed to the New Testament. It too decides beforehand that the resurrection could not have happened and so denies the omnipotence of God.

> On the side of Golgotha's hill there is a sepulcher hewn in the stone; on it one reads, "He was born in Bethlehem of Juda. He died on Calvary," and then that which makes it different from all other tombs,

"HE IS RISEN, HE IS NOT HERE."

The true interpretation of the resurrection is as follows. Christ rose from the dead with the same body which He had previous to the crucifixion. But this was not a simple resuscitation, like what happened in the case of the daughter of Jairus, the son of the widow of Naim, and Lazarus, all of whom Christ restored to life. They all returned to a normal mode of existence — they merely continued on where they had left off. With Christ it was completely different, for He did not return to the former existence that had been His. He was now outside of time, with His Father who was in heaven and with His body glorified. The latter was also changed and this explains why Mary Magdalene did not recognize Him in the garden, why the apostles failed to recognize Him when He stood before them (cf. Lk. 24:16; Jn. 20:14; Jn. 21:4); why the disciples on the way to Emmaus did not know that it was He (cf. Lk. 24:13-25); why some among the disciples doubted (cf. Mt. 27:17; Lk. 24:41; Jn. 21:12); and why Mark speaks of Him appearing in "another form" (cf. 16:12).

Dwelling upon the effects of the resurrection, Pope Paul VI said:

There is one aspect of this fact of the resurrection of Christ and our own which we wish to recall; namely, that it is a deed of power, nay more, of the divine omnipotence. The agency of natural causes does not suffice to engender it, or to give it at least an appearance of probability. Death is of such a nature and exercises so catastrophic a dominion, that it seems absurd to presume its defeat. And yet it was truly so in Jesus: who was dead, buried, and then, at dawn on the third day, risen and glorious. Thus, too, will it be for us, if in Him, by faith, by grace, by honest conduct, we graft our mortal life into His immortal life. The enemy, the great foe, will be defeated in the end (cf. 1 Cor. 15:26)

The resurrection of Christ is the clinching proof that Jesus of Nazareth was divine, that He was God. However, we must not permit this aspect of the miracle to hide from us the other values that it possesses. As we have already pointed out, the resurrection, in the primitive Church, was not stressed for its force as a proof. It was understood more in the light of its impact upon the personal life of the believer.

St. Augustine put it very concisely when he wrote: "Christ made His resurrection the symbol of our new life." The meaning is this. By dying on the cross, Christ conquered sin. By raising Himself from the dead, He showed His dominion over death. All this has profound spiritual significance for us. Applied to ourselves, it means that we must die to sin and rise to a new life. This we do when we receive the sacrament of baptism which blots out original sin.

We also die to sin and rise to the life of grace each time we go to confession and through absolution are restored to the friendship of God. This is why St. Paul wrote in his epistle to the Romans (6:34): "All of us who have been baptized into Christ Jesus have been baptized into his death. For we were buried with him by means of Baptism into death, in order that, just as Christ has risen from the dead through the glory of the Father, so we also may walk in newness of life."

St. Thomas Aquinas has this: "Jesus Christ did not come on earth simply to die; He came to unite us to Himself and to associate us with His triumph.... Death is but one-half of the work of redemption that claims the resurrection as its necessary complement.... Without the resurrection, faith lacks its true object; without the resurrection Baptism lacks its complete symbolism!"

In the Easter preface, the Church sings: "He is the true Lamb who has taken away the sins of the world, who overcame death for us by dying himself and who restored us to life by his own resurrection."

With this quotation we bring to an end this section on the resurrection. Its meaning for us is that we have been released from the dominion of sin, which is death to the soul. We must now continue to live in the resurrected life of grace, persevering to the end, when in the kingdom of heaven, we shall live eternally with Christ. For here, indeed, is another fruit of the resurrection: it is the guarantee of being forever united to God. Our Lord Himself has said it: "I am the resurrection and the life; he who believes in me, even if he die, shall live; and whoever lives and believes in me shall never die" (Jn. 11:25-26).

St. Paul sums it all up in his second epistle to the Corinthians. Referring to God the Father he says: "For we know that he who raised up Jesus will raise up us also with Jesus, and place us with you" (4:14).

The ascension

He ascended into heaven.

THE CREDO

Christ's ascension into heaven, another dogma of the Catholic Faith is clearly mentioned in Scripture. The following composite account is taken from St. Mark (16:19-20); St. Luke (24:50-53); and Acts (1:9-12).

"And when he had said these things, he led them out as far as Bethania, and lifting up his hands he blessed them. And it came to pass, while he blessed them and while they looked on, he departed from them, and he was raised up, and was carried up to heaven. And a cloud received him out of their sight. And the Lord Jesus was taken up to heaven, and sits on the right hand of God."

When dealing with the resurrection we saw how it becomes a part of our very lives, for it symbolizes our resurrection from the death of sin to the life of grace. The ascension, likewise has a personal message, for it reinforces the lesson of the resurrection. If we are faithful to our baptismal promises and avoid sin or, having the misfortune to fall, if we at once seek resuscitation in the sacrament of penance, then we, too, will ascend into glory.

Father James Alberione has expressed all this clearly:

"When His mission on earth was complete, He ascended into heaven by His own divine power where He sits at the right hand of the Father." Because He is God, Jesus is equal to the Father and even as man He holds the place of honor in heaven and shares in the power and glory of the heavenly Father.

Inasmuch as He is God, Jesus Christ is present everywhere. In heaven and in the Eucharist He is present as God and man since the human and divine natures are inseparable.

The ascension puts the finishing touches on the way which God has shown to man. Jesus Christ, who is the Way to go to the Father—way in example, doctrine, grace, and in His living humanity itself—now shines forth as Way in His marvelous ascension: "ascending on high."

After the resurrection of the dead, body and soul reunited, we, too, will ascend into heaven, if we live now our own paschal mystery, "dying to sin and becoming conformed to Christ."

CHALLENGE

If Christ truly dominates your life, as your name of *Christian* pretends that He does, that fact must make a difference in your personal life and work, whatever that life may be, and it must make a difference in your relation to the community with which you are identified.

Once your purposes, your interests are identified with those of Christ, your trade, your profession, your calling in life will acquire the sanctity of a *vocation*. The contacts with other men which arise from your temporal callings will give you opportunities to answer your eternal vocation to be *apostles* of Christ in this age when *all men are seeking Him* and when He needs us to fulfill His purpose: to preach in towns and villages and private places and public, and to restore all things to His spiritual kingdom.

If you become a *doctor* to men, you will be a *man of God* to other doctors. If you are a *teacher* of children, you will be an *apostle* to other teachers. If you are an *engineer*, a *tradesman*, a *technician*, a *laborer* in the City of Man, you will influence the men of your *unions*, your *syndicates*, your *professional groups* to aid you and to aid *Christ* in the building of the City of God. If you are a *business man* in the marts and the market places of the world, you will become the *associate of Christ* in promoting His Father's business wherever men of good will are to be found.

You will merge all the *purposes* that give your life meaning with the *purpose* of the Church that gives meaning to the life of the world, with the constant effort of the Church to grow to the full stature of Jesus Christ, to make Christ *all* and *in all*.

RICHARD CARDINAL CUSHING, *The Purpose of Living*

10

MARY — MOTHER, TEACHER AND QUEEN

We believe that MARY is the Mother, who REMAINED EVER A VIRGIN, of the Incarnate Word, our God and Savior Jesus Christ... THE CREDO

Ever Virgin

While still very young, Mary was enlightened by God to understand the *value of virginity.* Regardless of the opinion of men and without previous example, she offered her body and soul to God in an unprecedented consecration.

This Jewish maiden so loved this virtue that she would rather renounce the dignity of becoming the Mother of God if this meant losing her virginity and breaking her perpetual vow. It is no wonder that she readily asked an explanation of the angel's announcement before giving that *yes* upon which so much depended.

The conception of Christ is vividly described for us by St. Luke:

Now in the sixth month the angel Gabriel was sent from God to a town of Galilee called Nazareth, to a virgin betrothed to a man named Joseph, of the house of David, and the virgin's name was Mary. And when the angel had come to her, he said, "Hail, full of grace, the Lord is with you. Blessed are you among women." When she had heard him she was troubled at his word, and kept pondering what manner of greeting this might be.

And the angel said to her, "Do not be afraid, Mary, for you have found grace with God. Behold, you shall conceive in your womb and shall bring forth a son; and you shall call his name Jesus. He shall be great, and shall be king over the house of Jacob forever; and of his kingdom there shall be no end."

But Mary said to the angel, "How shall this happen, since I do not know man?"

And the angel answered and said to her, "The Holy Spirit shall come upon you and the power of the Most High shall overshadow you; and therefore the Holy One to be born shall be called the Son of God. And behold, Elizabeth your kinswoman also has conceived a son in her old age, and she who was called barren is now in her sixth month; for nothing shall be impossible with God."

But Mary said, "Behold the handmaid of the Lord: be it done to me according to your word." And the angel departed from her (1:26-38).

In the account by Saint Matthew we get some further details.

Now the origin of Christ was in this wise. When Mary his mother had been betrothed to Joseph, before they came together, she was found to be with child by the Holy Spirit. But Joseph her husband, being a just man, and not wishing to expose her to reproach, was minded to put her away privately. But while he thought on these things, behold, an angel of the Lord appeared to him in a dream, saying, "Do not be afraid, Joseph, son of David, to take to yourself Mary your wife, for that which is begotten in her is of the Holy Spirit. And she shall bring forth a son, and you shall call his name Jesus; for he shall save his people from their sins." Now all this came to pass that what was spoken by the Lord through the prophet might be fulfilled, "Behold, *the virgin shall be with child, and shall bring forth a son;* and they shall call his name Emmanuel"; which is interpreted, "God with us." (1:18-23).

From these words we see how Joseph was enlightened by God as to the exact nature of what had happened to his intended spouse. Mary and Joseph were now lawfully married, but in accord with Jewish custom, they did not live together during the first year of their marriage, which was called betrothal. Throughout the ancient world for a woman to live alone was unknown. Women in all classes and states of life were attached to some man: a husband, a father, a son, a brother—only a woman of bad repute lived alone.

Among the Hebrews in particular, marriage was honorable since for many generations every Jewish woman had hoped to be the mother of the Messia. So it was that Mary at about the age of fifteen was betrothed to Joseph in order that no accusation might be made against her by the world and that he might be her protector. Tradition informs us that Mary's parents, Joachim and Anna, were by that time deceased.

Clearly then, we know from divine revelation that the Son of God had a human mother but not a human father. Joseph was the *foster-father* of Jesus and guardian of Mary's purity. As the Apostles' Creed repeats: Our Lord was conceived by the Holy Spirit, born of the Virgin Mary.

We are told by St. Luke how Christ was born.

Now it came to pass in those days, that a decree went forth from Caesar Augustus that a census of the whole world should be taken. This first census took place while Cyrinus was governor of Syria. And all were going, each to his own town, to register.

And Joseph also went from Galilee out of the town of Nazareth into Judea to the town of David, which is called Bethlehem — because he was of the house and family of David — to register, together with Mary his espoused wife, who was with child. And it came to pass while they were there, that the days for her to be delivered were fulfilled. And she brought forth her firstborn son, and wrapped him in swaddling clothes, and laid him in a manger, because there was no room for them in the inn" (2:1-7).

By God's intervention, Mary's virginity was in no way marred *before, during* or *after* the birth of Jesus. He came forth from her womb miraculously just as He had entered it by the power of the Holy Spirit.

Human nature had never known such a wonder nor will it ever experience it again. The birth of God's Son may be likened to a ray of light passing through crystal without breaking or dimming it. Jesus' birth not only did not harm Mary's immaculate body but actually made it more resplendent.

Because of her sinlessness and because her Son had no human father, Mary by the power of the Holy Spirit was exempt from the law of nature concerning which we read in Genesis 3:16: "In pain shall you bring forth children."

St. Peter Chrysologus summed it up beautifully when he wrote:

The virgin conceives, the virgin brings forth her child, and she remains a virgin. Consequently, her body is conscious of strength, not pain. By her child-bearing she receives an increase of integrity, and suffers no harm to her modesty. She is, rather, the witness of her motherhood who suffered none of its customary pains. The new mother marvels at her having a part in heavenly mysteries.

St. Bernard gave his opinion by the following simile:

She is most beautifully likened to a star, for a star pours forth its light without losing anything of its nature. She gave us her Son without losing anything of her virginity. The glowing rays of a star take nothing away from its beauty. Neither has the Son taken anything away from His mother's integrity.

St. Ambrose asks:

Who is more noble than the Mother of God? Who is more splendid than she, whom Splendor Itself selected? Who is more chaste than she, who generated the body of Christ without human intervention? What shall I say of her other virtues? She was a virgin, not only in body but also in mind. All her affections were untarnished. She was humble of heart, grave and sparing in speech, prudent of mind, placing all her hope in the prayer of the poor, rather than in the uncertainty of riches. Industrious at work and modest in behavior, she sought God in all things. She wished well to everyone, gave honor to age, envied not her equals, never boasted, and loved virtue. There was no deceit in her eyes, nothing impetuous in her character. All her actions were graceful and dignified.

Immaculate

...preserved from all stain of original sin and filled with the gifts of grace more than all other creatures.

THE CREDO

From the very beginning, it has been the teaching of the Church that the Blessed Virgin was conceived free from all stain of original sin. This privilege was granted to her because she was to become the Mother of God and in virtue of her Son's infinite merits. It was inconceivable that God should take His human nature from anyone who had been tainted with sin. As St. John Damascene says: "The desires of the world and the concupiscence of the flesh never touched her pure soul, as was fitting for one who would someday receive her God into her bosom."

In the same connection St. Cyril of Alexandria poses the question:

Whoever heard of an architect who built himself a palace and then allowed his greatest enemy to occupy it?

St. Bernard gives us this precise explanation: "If for a very moment the Blessed Virgin was touched by sin, in that very moment she would not have been 'full of grace' as the angel affirmed, but rather 'empty.' Our Lord at least for that moment, would not have been with her and she would not have been 'blessed among women.'"

Duns Scotus, the great medieval Franciscan philosopher, put the argument for the Immaculate Conception very concisely in four Latin words: "Potuit. Decuit. Ergo fecit." A free translation runs as follows: *God could [have preserved Mary immaculate]. It was becoming that He do so. Therefore, He did it.*

It was Pope Pius IX who defined the dogma of the Immaculate Conception thus: "We declare, pronounce and define that the doctrine which holds that the most Blessed Virgin Mary, in the first instant of her Conception, by a singular grace and privilege granted by almighty God, in view of the merits of Jesus Christ, the Savior of the human race, was preserved free from all stain of original sin, is a doctrine revealed by God and therefore to be believed firmly and constantly by all the faithful."

The revealed truth of the Immaculate Conception of the Blessed Virgin does not mean that Mary was begotten or born in a different manner from the rest of men or that original sin was taken away from her after her conception.

No, Mary was born normally, of human parents and hence liable to original sin according to nature. But she was supernaturally preserved from sin, both original and actual. She was not *freed* from sin in the strict sense of the word — rather her soul possessed grace from the first moment of its existence and for the duration of her life. In short, Mary was irreconcilably opposed to sin.

We must also remember, as Pope Paul puts it in the Credo:

...that, by reason of this singular election, SHE WAS, IN CONSIDERATION OF THE MERITS OF HER SON, REDEEMED IN A MORE EMINENT MANNER.   THE CREDO

Like all other persons, Mary was in need of redemption; unlike them, however, she was not *cleansed* by Christ's merits from original sin but *preserved* from it even before His coming. Since God had chosen her to be the mother of the Redeemer, He fitted her with graces necessary for that office in a unique manner—by the way of prevention. In other words, sin was blocked from reaching Mary's soul. God the Son, who would assume a human nature through Mary, extended His future redeeming graces to her at her conception. This is what we mean by saying that Mary was redeemed in view of the merits of her divine Son.

St. Francis de Sales clearly summarized this truth when he wrote:

"God bestowed upon His glorious Mother the Blessedness of the two states of human nature; for she possessed the innocence which the first Adam lost, but also enjoyed in a most excellent manner the Redemption which the second Adam obtained for men."

Assumed body and soul into heaven

...the Blessed Virgin, the Immaculate, WAS AT THE END OF HER EARTHLY LIFE RAISED BODY AND SOUL TO HEAVENLY GLORY and likened to her Son in anticipation of the future lot of all the just...   THE CREDO

Just as from the beginning of Christianity, there had always been belief in the Immaculate Conception, so also had there been acceptance of her glorious assumption. The reason given for this was that just as it was fitting that Christ as man should take His human origin from an untainted source, so also was it most becoming that this untainted source should never experience the corruption that follows death.

Never could it happen that the body which enveloped the Word-made-flesh, which was perfectly sanctified on earth, could ever return to dust, to be the food of worms.

The Fathers of the Church always maintained this doctrine. Listen to these words of St. John Damascene: "It was fitting that the body of her whose virginity was kept intact in childbirth should be kept free from all corruption even after death."

Conscious of this weighty and noble tradition, weighing all the issues involved and after consulting the Catholic world, Pope Pius XII proceeded to define the dogma of the Assumption, on November 1, 1950. The papal statement went as follows:

"Wherefore, having offered to God continual prayers of supplication, and having invoked the light of the Spirit of truth, to the glory of almighty God who has enriched the Virgin Mary with His special favor; in honor of His Son, the immortal King of ages and Victor over sin and death; for the increase of the glory of the same august Mother, and for the joy and exultation of the whole Church; by the authority of our Lord Jesus Christ, of the holy apostles, Peter and Paul, and by our own authority, we pronounce, declare and define it to be a divinely revealed dogma that the Immaculate Mother of God, Mary ever a virgin, was, at the end of her earthly life, assumed body and soul into heavenly glory."

The dogma of the Assumption states that Mary was taken bodily into heaven at the *end of her earthly life.* It does not define whether or not our Blessed Mother first underwent death.

It was original sin which brought to man the punishment of death with its corruption of the body and Mary never incurred original sin. Therefore, it was not necessary that she face death as other men must but theologians generally agree that Mary underwent death in order to be more conformed to her Son.

Of course, in no sense must it be understood that Mary ascended to heaven by her own power. She was taken up by Christ in virtue of a special privilege.

Her maternal role

...and we believe that THE BLESSED MOTHER OF GOD, the New Eve...joined by a close and indissoluble bond to the Mysteries of the Incarnation and Redemption... CONTINUES IN HEAVEN HER MATERNAL ROLE WITH RE-GARD TO CHRIST'S MEMBERS, cooperating with the birth and growth of divine life in the souls of the redeemed.

THE CREDO

Christ is the sole and principal mediator between God and man, but many theologians see Mary, the Mother of God,

She sought God in all things.

in the role of a secondary mediator. She is dependent on Christ, but her influence is universal, so much so, say these writers that, without her intervention, no graces are given to men. The argument offered for this belief is quite simple. It is pointed out that Mary gave us Christ, the source and meritorious cause of all grace. It is fitting that she who gave us the river, that is, the font of grace, Jesus Christ, should also give us the little streams, that is, the particular graces we need.

This doctrine, too, is traditional in the Church. St. Anselm says:

> *Many graces, if we ask them of God, we will not obtain; if we ask them of Mary, we will obtain them, not because she is more powerful but because God intends to honor her in this manner.*

St. Bonaventure teaches: "The grace of God, so necessary to heal mankind, is dispensed to us through her. As from an aqueduct, grace flows through Mary. What her Son won by strict right, Mary dispenses as a most merciful queen, compassionating her needy people."

"Nobody knows and comprehends so well as she everything that concerns us," wrote Pope Leo XIII, "what help we need in life; what dangers, public and private, threaten our welfare; what difficulties and evils surround us; above all, how fierce is the fight we wage with the ruthless enemies of our salvation. In these and in all other troubles of life her power is most far-reaching. She has the most ardent desire to bring consolation, strength and help to every race of children so dear to her.

"Accordingly, let us approach Mary confidently, wholeheartedly beseeching her by her motherhood which unites her so closely to Jesus and at the same time to us. Let us with deepest devotion invoke her constant aid in the prayer which she herself has indicated and which is most acceptable to her. Then with good reason shall we rest with an easy and joyful mind under the protection of the best of mothers."

In the *Dogmatic Constitution on the Church*, a Vatican II document, the Fathers referred to Mary's mediation in these words:

There is but one Mediator as we know from the words of the apostles, 'for there is one God and one mediator of God and men, the man Christ Jesus, who gave himself a redemption for all" (1 Tim. 2:5-6). The maternal duty of Mary toward men in no wise obscures or diminishes this unique mediation of Christ, but rather shows His power. For all the salvific influence of the Blessed Virgin on men originates not from some inner necessity, but from the divine pleasure. It flows forth from the superabundance of the merits of Christ, rests on His mediation, depends entirely on it and draws all its power from it. In no way does it impede, but rather does it foster the immediate union of the faithful with Christ (n. 60).

Pope Paul has spoken of Mary's mediation thus:

"Just as no human mother can limit her task to the generation of a new man but must extend it to the function of nourishing and educating her offspring, thus the blessed Virgin Mary, after participating in the redeeming sacrifice of the Son, and in such an intimate way as to deserve to be proclaimed by Him the Mother not only of His disciple John, but of mankind which he in some way represents, now continues to fulfill from heaven her maternal function as the *cooperator in the birth and development of divine life in the individual souls of redeemed men*. This is a most consoling truth which, by the free consent of God the all-wise, is an integrating part of the mystery of human salvation; therefore it must be held by all Christians" (The Great Sign).

Mother of the Church

...Mother of the Church... THE CREDO

In his speech closing the third session of the Second Vatican Council, Pope Paul proclaimed Mary "Mother of the Church." He did it in the following terms:

"For the glory of the Virgin Mary, and for Our own consolation, We proclaim Mary *Mother of the Church*, that is, of the whole People of God, of the faithful as well as of the pastors....

"Mary, then, as Mother of Christ, is mother also of all the faithful and of all shepherds, that is to say, of the Church. Just as she has given us Christ Jesus, the fountainhead of grace, so will she not fail to assist the Church, now that it is flourishing through the abundance of the gifts of the Holy Spirit and is setting itself with new zeal to the accomplishment of its mission of salvation."

St. Augustine compares the benefits brought us by Mary with the harm done by Eve:

Eve mourned, but Mary exulted. Eve carried tears in her womb; Mary carried joy. Eve gave birth to a sinner; Mary gave us the Innocent One. The mother of our race brought punishment to mankind; the Mother of our Lord brought salvation to mankind. From Eve came sin; from Mary, grace. Eve was the source of death; Mary was the source of Life. One hurt us, the other helped us. The faith and obedience of Mary compensates for the pride and disobedience of Eve.

The episode of the wedding feast of Cana shows us Mary exercising her maternal role:

Left a widow by the death of St. Joseph, Mary changed her way of life very little. She tended to her home and went out only for errands of charity or religious duties.

It must not be believed, however, that Mary was negligent regarding her social duties such as visiting relatives and friends. Thus, as the Gospel narrates, she attended the marriage feast at Cana. "And on the third day a marriage took place at Cana of Galilee, and the Mother of Jesus was there." (Jn. 2:1)

It is a great joy for oriental women to participate in wedding preparations. Sisters, cousins and friends of the bride and groom assume the responsibility for the preparation of choice foods. They arrive at the home where the wedding is to take place on the eve of the feast, or even a few days before, and stay until the end, which is usually for about a week. The evangelist has us suppose that Mary was already there with that family when her Son Jesus was invited. And Jesus went there with His disciples.

On that feast Mary proved the goodness of her heart toward the newlyweds, by inducing her Son to work a delicate miracle so as not to spoil the sweet joy of the day.

At a certain point, Mary noticed that there was no more wine. With a few words she pointed out to Jesus the young couple's preoccupation, and tactfully, as only she knew how to do it, begged Him to help them: "And the wine having run short, the mother of Jesus said to him, 'They have no wine.'" (Jn. 2:3) Such a statement was obviously made to demand a miracle, and it reveals Mary's great confidence in her Jesus. She had always believed in her Son's divine power, and for thirty years she had experienced the goodness of His heart and His readiness to grant her least desire. She was, thus, certain of obtaining the miracle. Jesus, however, answered Mary in a way that emphasized the independence of His own action: "What would you have me do, woman? My hour has not yet come" (Jn. 2:4).

Mary understood that He was postponing the miracle for a later time, but certain of being heeded, she told the servants: "Do whatever he tells you." And Jesus, indeed, gave them orders to fill the jars with water. There were six large stone jars prepared in accordance with the Jewish manner of purification, each holding two or three measures.

The servants filled the jars to the brim. Then Jesus said to them, "Draw out now, and take to the chief steward." (Jn. 2:8)

As soon as the latter had tasted the wine, not knowing where it had come from, he chided the groom for having saved the best wine for the last, contrary to custom: "Every man at first sets forth the good wine, and when they have drunk freely, then that which is poorer. But you have kept the good wine until now." (Jn. 2:10)

Thus in Cana of Galilee, Jesus worked the first of His miracles, and manifested His glory, and His disciples believed in Him.

This episode teaches us a valuable lesson. Jesus willed to perform His first miracle at Mary's urging in order to teach us with what trust we should have recourse to this mother of goodness to obtain the graces we need.

Mary is good; she thinks of us, sees and provides for our needs. Mary knows our wants. Assumed into heaven in soul and body, and admitted to the beatific vision, Mary sees in God all our thoughts, feelings, aspirations, difficulties, dangers, temptations and resolutions.

We are not excused by this fact from praying to her or enumerating the graces we need. Mary knows what is best for us, so let us tell her of our needs and trust in her. Let us abandon ourselves completely to her maternal heart.

The fact that the Second Vatican Council gave Mary a special place in its magnificent document on the Church should stimulate us to increase our trust in her help. Pope Paul VI says:

All of us know that the Second Vatican Council devoted to the Blessed Mother the entire eighth and last chapter of the *Dogmatic Constitution on the Church*, thus almost placing at the zenith of this marvelous doctrinal structure the sweet and shining figure of Mary. And this is sufficient for us to feel bound — also because of the council's authority for renewal — to *renew our concept and our devotion to the Virgin.*

The council did not wish to expound new doctrines with reference to the Blessed Mother, just as it did not intend to say all that could be said of Mary.

The council, however, presented Mary most holy in such form and with such title that every one who is faithful to the council's teachings should not only feel strengthened in his profession of the Marian devotion that always was held in such great honor and fervor in the Catholic Church, but should furthermore feel himself drawn

"Mary, joined by a close and indissoluble bond to the Mysteries of the Incarnation and Redemption, continues her maternal role in the Church..." (The Credo)

to mold his devotion according to the broad, genuine and enrapturing visions which the magnificent and meaningful council pages offer to a thoughtful Christian for meditation and devotion.

The power of the rosary

Among the practices of piety of the Christian, the rosary holds the third place, as John XXIII expressed himself: "As a practice of Christian devotion among the faithful of the Latin rite (who constitute a notable portion of the Catholic family), the rosary holds the place, among ecclesiastics, after the Holy Mass and the breviary, and among the laity after the participation in the sacraments (Mass, Communion and Penance). It is a devout form of union with God, and always of high spiritual elevation."

The rosary instructs and vivifies faith.
The rosary is a guide to Christian life.
The rosary obtains spiritual and material graces for the individual, for society and for all humanity.

For six centuries, the Popes have written and spoken on the rosary, urged and exhorted the faithful to recite it, granted indulgences and approved confraternities of the rosary.

In a special manner we recall Pope Leo XIII at the end of the last century, who wrote thirteen documents, some encyclicals and some letters, on the rosary. The Popes of our century, too, have always recommended it, particularly John XXIII, who wrote a series of meditations on the mysteries.

Pope Paul VI in an encyclical, *Rosaries to the Mother of Christ,* said "The Second Vatican Council clearly referred to the rosary, though not in express terms, when it reminded the faithful that 'practices and exercises of devotion towards her (Mary), recommended by the teaching authority of the Church in the course of the centuries, are to be held in high esteem' (Dogmatic Constitution on the Church, n. 67)."

If you want a sign of salvation for the life to come, faithfully practice the recitation of the rosary. When a family recites the rosary, be sure that that family will not be lost. All will obtain a holy death. And the reason is this: in the rosary we repeat one hundred fifty times: "Pray for us sinners now and at the hour of our death."

The purpose of the rosary is to make us consider life for what it is. Our life is always to be considered in its complete

meaning. It is a test. This trial can be undergone in difficulties, fatigue and labors; it can be undergone in a vocation,
a mission which God has entrusted to each soul. It ends with
pains and then with death. And finally one arrives at the eternal glory, paradise. That paradise is happiness, complete
blessedness. It will entirely satisfy our desires and our
faculties — intellectual faculties as well as sensitive, human,
physical and corporal.

They say that Americans are practical people; it is true.
However, one must be completely practical — practical not
only in what is useful for the present life, but also in what
is useful for the complete life, and the complete life extends
into eternity. It will never end.

The rosary should obtain this grace for us: to super-
naturalize our life, considering life for what it is, a preparation for heaven.

This is the general thought of the rosary, which makes
us consider *fifteen mysteries, divided into three series: the
joyful, the sorrowful and the glorious mysteries.*

The rosary places before our eyes some happy events
(joyful mysteries), and it also makes us consider some sad
events, sorrowful and painful. It makes us consider the
weariness which we must put up with here below, the sacrifices which we must make, and then it presents us with the
eternal happiness of heaven.

Life on earth is spent amid things which please us and
things which displease us, but people who have the spirit
of God sanctify both pleasant and unpleasant events and derive merit from everything. Others are happy and fervent
only when everything goes according to their feelings, desires and views, only when the sky is serene. When there is a
storm, when there are delusions, when things go contrary to
our views, we who see only a short way into the things of God
perhaps attempt to guide ourselves. And who knows where
we will end up! We must let ourselves be guided by God,
even through things not pleasing to our tastes, not according to our views.

What practical things do the mysteries of the rosary teach
us? The mysteries tell us: your model is Jesus, who became
man, who was born of a Virgin, who was the Master, the Priest,
the Divine Host, who accomplished the mission entrusted
to Him by the Father until He could say: "It is consummated" — now, Father, I give back my spirit into Your hands.
And behold His glorious entrance into heaven on the day of

the Ascension, accompanied by the patriarchs and the just of the Old Testament. There He received His glory: "Sit at my right hand."

The other lesson these mysteries teach us comes from Mary. What did Mary do? She had a vocation, manifested by an angel on the day of the Annunciation, and she accepted it: I am the servant of God, the handmaid of God. And probably she did not repeat this declaration in words many times; rather, she always showed herself in her actions to be the servant of God. By her deeds she would repeat at every instant: "Behold the handmaid of the Lord, be it done to me according to your word," which means, as the Lord wills. She accepted her mission and carried it to the end through many sufferings.

Her Baby was born in extreme poverty, and then His life was sought. Yet there were consolations, too, as when she saw the Child adored by the shepherds and the Magi. Next came exile in a strange land among pagans. Then, when the persecutor died, the angel invited Joseph to return to Palestine. Jesus was taken to Nazareth, a hidden village, so as not to be too conspicuous, lest the successor of Herod, Archelaus, also grow suspicious and seek to kill Him. Just as He had been hidden in the stable, Jesus lived hidden at Nazareth for thirty years in His private life of prayer, work, recollection, obedience and practice of every domestic virtue. He grew in wisdom, age and grace.

Thus Jesus prepared Himself for the public ministry and Mary was His companion.

Mary listened to the Master in His sermons, and Mary was with Him in the accomplishment of His sacrifice on Calvary as victim and eternal High Priest.

Mary also assisted at the glorious mysteries of Jesus. Authors say that she received the first visit of the risen Christ. The Gospel does not record this, but it is probable. Mary was also present at the Ascension of Jesus into heaven, and from that day she took the Church into her arms because her mission had not been completed. Besides being the Mother of Jesus, Mary was to be the Mother of the infant Church, and just as she had led Jesus in His youth, so she guided the Church in its youth—that is, in its first years— assisting it with prayers and good example, encouraging the apostles, sustaining them in persecution, etc.

What practical teachings do the mysteries impart in general? That it is necessary to live by the example of Jesus and

Mary and fulfill our vocation on earth as they fulfilled theirs. Our exemplars are Jesus and Mary.

Let us be like prudent and wise business people who let slip no opportunity to make a gain. During all the moments of life, we can always obtain something, that is, we can always gain merit. Did not Jesus do this during His lifetime, from those first moments in the manger until He returned His spirit into the hands of His Father and died? This was always His fervent prayer: "I thank You, O Father!" Always. In regard to everything.

And did not our mother Mary do likewise? Was everything in her life joyful? No. There were many happy events: the Annunciation of the angel, the miraculous birth of the Divine Child, the grace of being in the company of Jesus in the house of Nazareth for so many years, the joy of hearing Him preach with such wisdom and seeing Him work so many miracles. And then came the sorrowful mysteries: Mary witnessed Jesus' condemnation to death, His journey to Calvary, His crucifixion, agony and burial, the seeming triumph of His enemies. Was everything happy? No.

Joy and sorrow are always mixed, because the Lord is good; He is very good. He does not let us experience only sufferings, but He also gives us consolations, and if these do not come exteriorly, they may come interiorly.

Jesus wants us to try to really love Him, accepting crosses also, working, denying ourselves — eyes, ears, tongue, sentiments of the heart, etc. God works in us.

Through the various occurrences of our day our hearts are fixed on high, where joys are true and everlasting. This is the general effect of the rosary.

CHALLENGE

Whoever you are, who are in the sea of this world, feel yourself rather tossed about between storms and tempests than walking on the earth, do not look away from the brightness of this Star if you do not want to be submerged by the waves.

If the winds of temptation blow, if you stumble against the reefs of tribulation, look at the Star, call Mary. If you are agitated by waves of pride, of ambition, of murmuring, of envy, look at the Star, call Mary. If anger or avarice or seduction of the flesh agitate the fragile ship of the soul, look at the Star, call Mary. If disturbed by the enormity of crimes, confused by the guilt of the soul, terrified by the severity of the judgment, you feel yourself pulled into the vortex of melancholy, into the abyss of despair, think of Mary.

In dangers, in troubles, in doubts, think of Mary, call Mary. Let her not depart from your lips, let her not depart from your heart; and to obtain the help of her prayers, do not lose sight of the examples of her life. Following her you do not go astray; by praying to her you do not despair; thinking of her you do not err. If she upholds you, you do not fall; if she protects you, you have nothing to fear; if she accompanies you, you do not tire; if she is propitious to you, you will arrive at the goal and thus experience in yourself how rightly it was said: "and the Virgin was called Mary."

ST. BERNARD

11

**THIS
BELOVED
CHURCH
OF GOD!**

"If there exists a route of ours toward God," exclaims Pope Paul VI, "there is *also* the more valid, the more mysterious and beautiful *route of God toward us!*"

Our heavenly Father, loving and vigilant, is in search of humanity. Today He seeks each one of us through the Church which is alive in Christ, His beloved Son.

Has the Church come to take on an ever deeper meaning for you as Christ increasingly means more and more to you? In this case, you no longer think of the Church in terms of buildings or places. You think of the Church in terms of Christ. You accept the Church as Christ still *teaching* in the world. You love the Church as Christ still *healing* in the world. You cooperate with the Church as Christ still *at work* in the world.

The Church, as you know, is God's people.

The *Constitution on the Church* affirms that it has pleased God to bring men together as one people (n. 9). This union of God with a people all His own began many, many years before He sent His Son to consolidate the pact between mankind and its God. Let us, with humble and grateful hearts, look into the history of Israel, whose relationship to God under the Old Covenant prefigures our ecclesial union with Him in the New Economy...

The foreshadowing

HEIRESS OF THE DIVINE PROMISES and daughter of Abraham according to the Spirit, through that Israel whose Scriptures she lovingly guards, and whose patriarchs and prophets she venerates...

THE CREDO

The founding of the Church by Christ was foreshadowed in the Old Testament. St. Augustine speaks of this as follows: "*Abraham,* a devout and faithful servant of God, *was chosen that to him might be made the revelation concerning the Son of God,* so that by imitating his faith all the faithful of all nations in time to come might be called his children. From him was born a people who should worship the one true God, who made heaven and earth, while all the other nations served idols and evil spirits. In that people, without doubt, the future Church was clearly figured."

All future history flowed from Abraham. He was "the father of us all...our father in the sight of God" (Rom. 4:16-17). God first spoke to this tribal chief at Haran in Northern Mesopotamia, and the same mercy shown to Abraham is extended from generation to generation.

"*The Church of Christ acknowledges that,* according to God's saving design, *the beginnings of her faith and her election are found already among the patriarchs, Moses and the prophets.* She professes that all who believe in Christ — Abraham's sons according to faith — are included in the same patriarch's call" (Declaration on Relation of Church to Non-Christian Religions, n. 4).

When the Virgin Mary concluded her canticle of thanksgiving after her cousin Elizabeth had called her blessed — for she was the Woman of the Promise (cf. Gen. 3:15) — she jubilantly recalled God's faithfulness to His promises: "He has given help to Israel, his servant, *mindful of his mercy* — Even as he spoke to *our fathers — to Abraham and to his posterity forever* (Lk. 1:54-55).

The help which God gave to the Israelites, His Chosen People, during their journey from slavery in Egypt to life in the Promised Land has also a significance for us. The Council Fathers added that "the salvation of the Church is mysteriously foreshadowed by the Chosen People's exodus from the land of bondage" (n. 4).

As the *Dogmatic Constitution on the Church* says, "Israel according to the flesh, which wandered as an exile in the desert, was already called the Church of God. So likewise the *new Israel* which while living *in this present age* goes in search of a future and abiding city *is called the Church of Christ*" (n. 9).

Moses, who led God's people out of Egypt, is extolled by St. Paul as one who "persevered as if seeing him who cannot be seen." The Apostle emphasizes the fact that "God had something better in view for us," so that all his faithful people of the Old Covenant might not be perfected without us (cf. Heb. 11:27, 40).

When God chose his servant David, He took him from the sheepfolds. From following the ewes he brought him to shepherd Jacob, his people, and Israel, his inheritance. And he tended them with a sincere heart, and with skillful hands he guided them (Ps. 77).

In a vibrant passage of the *Constitution on the Church*, we discover that "the Church is a *sheepfold* whose one and indispensable door is Christ. It is a flock of which God Himself foretold He would be the shepherd, and whose sheep, although ruled by human shepherds, are nevertheless continuously led and nourished by Christ Himself, the Good Shepherd and the Prince of the shepherds, who gave His life for the sheep" (n. 6).

God's family

She is the Mystical Body of Christ...

THE CREDO

By His preaching of the kingdom of God, Christ prepared the way for the foundation of the Church. As the collective pastoral letter of the U.S. bishops, *The Church in Our Day,* issued January 11, 1968, so clearly puts it:

> *"The Church does not think it too bold to declare that she was brought into being, structured, commissioned, and given her life by the Lord Himself. Her faithfulness to herself, therefore, becomes faithfulness to Him. Her total mission in history begins and ends with Jesus.*

"The Apostle Paul did not hesitate to call the Church *the Body of Christ.* Of all the many images of the Church, surely this is the most difficult to comprehend and yet the most eloquent. It reminds us that the Church has a sanctity, a holiness which no one of us would have imagined had not the Apostle assured us of this under God's own inspiration. *We have been* chosen as a body, indeed *as the Body of Christ, to be the People of God....* United to Christ by Baptism, really and truly partaking of the Body of the Lord in the sacred Eucharist, we are raised into fellowship with Him and with one another. In this way, all of us are made members of Christ and through

I am the vine, you are the branches...without me you can do nothing.

(John 15:5)

Him, members of one another. This union we call the Mystical
Body of Christ."

The doctrine is based on the words of Christ as recorded
for us by St. John (15:1-5). "I am the true vine, and my Father
is the vinedresser. Every branch in me that bears no fruit he
will take away; and every branch that bears fruit he will
cleanse, that it may bear more fruit.... Abide in me, and I in
you. As the branch cannot bear fruit of itself unless it remain
on the vine, so neither can you unless you abide in me. I am
the vine, you are the branches. He who abides in me, and I
in him, he bears much fruit, for without me you can do
nothing."

What a marvelous union Christ desires to have with us!
We his friends form with Him a closely-knit spiritual community.

It was precisely around a group of His close friends that
Jesus began building the family of the sons of God. To His
apostles, on the evening before His consummating sacrifice
on the cross, He confided: "I have called you friends, because all things I have heard from my father I have made
known to you. You have not chosen me, but I have chosen
you, and have appointed you that you should go and bear
fruit, and that your fruit should remain" (Jn. 15:15-16).

Pope Pius XII, in his encyclical, *Mystici Corporis Christi*
(On the Mystical Body of Christ), explains that this union
between Christ and the members of His Church "is the closest
possible: for in Sacred Scripture it is not only compared to the
bond of chaste wedlock, to the vital union of the vine and the
branches, and to the organic unity of the body (cf. Eph.
5:22-23; Jn. 15:1-5; Eph. 4:16), but it is also shown to be so
intimate that—according to the words of the Apostle—"He
(Christ) is the Head of the Body which is the Church" (Col.
1:18). The very ancient and constant teaching of the documents received from the Fathers shows us that the Divine
Redeemer together with his social Body constitutes one
mystical person, or, as Augustine has it, the *whole Christ*."

The Church in Our Day says that "if we see ourselves as
the Body of Jesus, then we shall strive to be one with Christ
in His consecration to the Father, one with Him in His open-
ness to the Spirit, one with Him in His love for His brethren
even unto death."

To be conscious of the reality of our membership in the
Mystical Body of Christ means to see things from Christ's
viewpoint as much as we are able to do so. How, then, our

attitudes toward all others improve once we have this truth and love in our hearts as a living principle for daily life! How we love every human being, because he or she is an actual or potential member of the Mystical Body of Christ; has a part to play in the great drama of our Savior; has a work to do that no one but he or she can do; is dear to our Father, beloved of our Savior Jesus and dear to our mother, Mary.

How can jealousy, envy, bitterness, enmity enter one's soul? Your soul, my soul? Christ is watching. You will rather rejoice in the good you see others doing. All smallness leaves your life when you make the effort to live as Christ would say, "in union with Me." We must never forget, we are His members.

Whatever the past may have been, or whatever the future could bring, there is *today's* happiness in living the doctrine of the Mystical Body. As members of this Body, even the smallest action has its eternal value. They are all acts of the Mystical Christ. Can any assignment, then, be a just cause for unhappiness? Our Lord wants us to realize that this doctrine covers everything: ourselves, others, our work, their work, our sufferings, their sufferings, our joy and their joy.

How does Christ look upon human beings? Does He not see them as either actual or potential members of His Body? Can we see them in the same light? How does He see the "feeble" and "less honorable members"? Christ wants to help them all. St. Paul tells us, "Those that seem the more feeble members of the body are more necessary" (1 Cor. 12:22). St. Paul eliminates the possibility of looking down on anyone, of having a low or mean opinion of anyone. At all times, he was Christ-conscious. This is only possible by living the truth of the Mystical Body.

That's the point, to live it! We know that the life of Christ pulsates within the soul of the person in the state of grace. We know that in the depth of those souls the Holy Trinity dwells, that the light of their eyes tells the same tremendous truth as the sanctuary lamp: God is here. We know this but do we live day by day conscious of the fact? Do we at least try to make the effort of looking out on the world around us with the eyes of Christ?

He continues to identify Himself with all the different members of His Church. I was hungry and you gave *Me* to eat; thirsty and you gave *Me* to drink; sick and you visited *Me*.

Is it any wonder that St. Paul spoke so earnestly regarding the fact that the same life of Christ is shared by all in the state of grace? (cf. 1 Cor. 10:15-16). What a different world it would be among Catholics if they realized the presence of Christ in one another. Christ in the heart and Christ in the home, this is to be individually and socially Christ-conscious.

Dear Lord, You are still being born in other Bethlehems through baptism. You are still coming into Your own, and Your own are sometimes receiving You not. You are still instructing the teachers of the people and answering their questions. You are still laboring at a carpenter's bench. You are still going about doing good. You are still bringing souls their courage and strength. You are still the loyal martyr of the faith. You are still climbing other Calvarys. You are still rising triumphantly in the souls of the just. There is for us, thank God, no mistaken identity.

With Pope Paul's words of his encyclical letter, *Paths of His Church,* we can exclaim: "Oh, it is neither pride nor presumption nor obstinacy nor folly but a luminous certitude and our joyous conviction that we are indeed living members of the Body of Christ, that we are the authentic heirs of the Gospel of Christ, those who truly continue the work of the apostles, that there dwells in us the great inheritance of truth and morality characterizing the Catholic Church, which today possesses intact the living heritage of the original apostolic tradition. If all this redounds to our glory or to use a better expression, the reason for which we must 'always give thanks to God' (Eph. 5:20), it also constitutes our responsibility before God Himself to whom we are accountable for so great a benefit and also before the Church, in which we must instill the firm desire and resolution to guard the 'deposit' about which St. Paul speaks (1 Tim. 6:20). We have a responsibility, also, before our brothers who are still separated from us, and before the entire world so that all share with us the gift of God."

God is the common Father of all. The following words spoken by Pope John XXIII are addressed to each member of the Mystical Body: "Hear the voice of your Father, the common Father of all, as we urge and exhort you to abound in doing good to all men, as we appeal to you in behalf of our children to whom equal blessings of earthly prosperity have been denied, as we beg in their name—promising in the words of the Master: 'Amen, I say to you, you shall not lose your reward'" (cf. Mk. 9:40).

If Pope John were so solicitous regarding even temporal goods, how great must have been his desire for the spiritual welfare of souls! Let us pray to be more and more Christ-conscious. If so, our membership in the Mystical Body of Christ will have its fullest meaning.

...at the same time a visible society instituted with hierarchical organs, and a spiritual community.

THE CREDO

"If the Church is a body," Pius XII explains, "*it must be an organism*, one and indivisible, according to the words of St. Paul, 'We, being many, are one body in Christ' (Rom. 12:5). Nor is it sufficient to say one and indivisible; *it must also be concrete and perceptible to the senses*, as Our Predecessor of holy memory, Leo XIII, in his encyclical letter *Satis cognitum* affirms: 'It is because the Church is a body that she is *visible* to our eyes.'"

As a body requires many members united under one head, *so the Body of the Church has a well-ordered structure united under its Head, Jesus Christ.* "The Divine Redeemer," says Pius XII, "began the building of the mystical temple of the Church when He gave His doctrine in His preaching; He completed it when He hung publicly suspended from the cross; and finally He procured its manifestation and promulgation when He sent the Spirit Paraclete down on His disciples.... In the same way that the head—to use the words of St. Ambrose—is the "royal summit" of the body, and all the members over which it presides to provide for their needs are naturally directed by the head, and the head is endowed with superior qualities for this end, so the Divine Redeemer holds the key of the entire Christian community and directs its course. And since to rule a community of men is nothing other than to direct them to their proper end by an effective providence, by suitable assistance, and by right methods, it is easy to see that our Savior, archetype and model of good shepherds, acquits Himself of these functions in a marvelous way.

"For when He was on earth, by His laws, His counsel, His warnings, He taught us in words which will never pass away and which will be for men of every age, spirit and life. Beyond this, He communicated to the apostles and their successors a triple power, that of teaching, ruling and guiding men to sanctity; and this power, made explicit by peculiar precepts, laws and duties, constitutes the primary law of the whole Church.

"But it is directly also and in His own person that *our Divine Savior rules and directs the society He established.* For He rules in the minds and souls of men, subjects to His good pleasure and compels even stubborn wills. By this internal direction He not only cares for each individual, but also provides for the entire Church....

"*The Divine Redeemer also governs His Mystical Body in a visible and ordinary way through His Vicar on earth....* He who was so wise could never leave without a visible head the social body which He had founded.... That Christ and His Vicar form only one single Head, Our Predecessor of immortal memory, Boniface VIII, solemnly taught in his Apostolic Letter *Unam Sanctam,* and his successors have never ceased to repeat it after him.... For those who would remove the visible Head of the Church and break off the bonds of visible unity, obscure and deform the Mystical Body of the Redeemer, so that it cannot be seen or recognized by men who seek the port of eternal salvation....

"As Christ wishes each one of His members to be like Himself, so He wills it also for the entire Body of the Church."

In the *Dogmatic Constitution on the Church,* we find that Christ enables us to be renewed in Him unceasingly because "He has shared with us His Spirit who, existing as one and the same being in the Head and in the members, gives life to, unifies and moves through the whole body" (n. 7).

Amid the whirlwind— a steadfast Rock

...built by Jesus Christ ON THAT ROCK WHICH IS PETER.

THE CREDO

The Divine Master had singled out one member of His chosen group to be the visible head of His newly-founded community—Simon Bar-Jona. "Blessed are you, Simon Bar-Jona.... I say to you, you are Peter, and upon this rock I will build my Church, and the gates of hell shall not prevail against it. And I will give you the keys of the kingdom of heaven; and whatever you shall bind on earth shall be bound in heaven; and whatever you shall loose on earth shall be loosed in heaven" (Mt. 16:13-19).

Since a rock symbolizes stability, Pope Paul VI asks us to probe the significance of Simon's new name:

Let us ask you a question. Have you understood the meaning of the symbolic name of Peter, which Jesus gave to His principal disciple, Simon, son of Jona: "And I say to you, you are Peter, and upon this *rock* I will build my Church" (Mt. 16:18), in other words, the society of those who believe in me and are gathered together in my name—in fact, founded on you?

The meaning which Jesus wanted to express is clear, though looked at closely, it is a very complex and profound meaning. It is, in other words, the concept of *soundness, stability, steadfastness,* let us even say, of *fixedness.*

In giving to Simon, son of Jona—a good man, but, from what we know of him, an enthusiastic and changeable man, generous and timid—the title, in fact the gift, the charism of strength, of solidity and of the ability to withstand and to uphold, such as precisely is the nature of rock, stone, or reef, Jesus linked the message of His word to the new and prodigious virtue of this apostle who, together with those who would be his legitimate successors, was to bear witness with incomparable certainty to that very message, which, by a comprehensive term, we call the Gospel.

Think well. We are recalling and experiencing the truth of the structural word of Jesus. Here that rock (also an image and derivation of that other rock—the cornerstone, center, basis, the force of all Christianity, that is, Christ Himself), that rock, we were saying, is still firm, solid, secure. It is a historical, psychological, theological, marvelous prodigy.

That rock is what we might call an experimental proof of another prophetic and solemn word of Jesus: "Heaven and earth will pass away, but my words will not pass away" (Mt. 24:35).

St. Ephrem paraphrases the prophetic words of the Divine Master thus:

"Simon, my disciple, I have made you the foundation of the holy Church. I have called you rock, because you will sustain all the edifices. You will be the superintendent of those who will build my Church on earth. If they should desire to build something blameworthy, you, the foundation, reprove them. You are the source of the fountain from which my doctrine is drawn; you are the head of my disciples. By means of you I will quench the thirst of all peoples...I have given you the keys of my kingdom. Behold, I have elected you prince over all my treasures."

How was Peter's position understood in the early Church? This is a most important question, which we will now try to answer. We do not hesitate to affirm that after the ascension, Peter immediately appears as the leader. This is clear from the Scriptures. For example, it was Peter who pro-posed nomination of a successor to Judas (cf. Acts 1:15-26). It was Peter who first addressed the crowds after the coming of the Holy Spirit at Pentecost.

The episode involving Ananias and Sapphira also points to the preeminence of Peter. The story is told in Acts 5:1-10.

When the apostles were brought before the council and questioned by the high priest, the Acts (5:29) tell us: "But Peter and the apostles answered and said, 'We must obey God rather than men.'"

When Simon Magus wanted to buy the power to confer the Holy Spirit, Peter said to him: "Your money go to destruc-tion with you, because you have thought that the gift of God could be purchased with money.... Repent therefore of this wickedness of yours and pray to God, that perhaps this thought of your heart may be forgiven you" (Acts 8:20-22).

As the result of a heavenly revelation, described in Acts 11:1-18, Peter was the first to preach to the gentiles.

A remarkable example, showing us in what respect Peter was held in the primitive Church has been preserved for us in Acts 15:1-12. A dispute arose as to whether new converts should be circumcised. After a long debate, Peter spoke and the Scriptures conclude: *Then the whole meeting quieted down...."*

With such a scriptural background, it was inevitable that the doctrine of the primacy should develop as it did. In Christ's words to Peter, theologians and canonists saw ir-refutable proof of the primacy of the Roman See, and of him who occupied it, the successor of St. Peter. This primacy in-volves the triple power of teaching, ruling and sanctifying the faithful. From the very first the Popes claimed and exercised supremacy in spiritual matters.

"The Church has but one ruler and governor, the in-visible one, Christ, whom the eternal Father has made head over all the Church, which is his body; the visible one, the Pope, who, as legitimate successor of Peter, the Prince of the apostles, fills the apostolic chair" (Council of Trent).

Since there are attempts to minimize the Holy Father's authority today, the certain teaching of the Church, as de-fined by the First Vatican, should be fresh in our minds:

"We renew the definition of the ecumenical Council of Florence, in virtue of which all the faithful of Christ must believe that the Holy, Apostolic See and the Roman Pontiff possess the primacy over the whole world, and that the Roman Pontiff is the successor of Blessed Peter, Prince of the apostles, and is the true vicar of Christ and Head of the whole Church, the Father and Teacher of all Christians; and that full power was given to him in Blessed Peter to feed, rule and govern the universal Church, by Jesus Christ our Lord, as is also written in the acts of the general councils and in the sacred canons."

The Savior confided to Peter the whole Church, and with St. Jerome we can exclaim to Peter's successor today, "I speak to the successor of the fisherman and to the disciple of the cross. I am joined in communion with the See of Peter. Upon *that rock* I know the Church is built."

One in Christ

We believe that the Church founded by Jesus Christ and for which He prayed is indefectibly ONE IN FAITH, WORSHIP AND THE BOND OF HIERARCHICAL COMMUNION.

THE CREDO

In Vatican II's *Decree on Ecumenism,* we read: "Christ perfects His people's fellowship in unity: *in their confessing the one faith, celebrating divine worship in common, and keeping the fraternal harmony of the family of God"* (n. 2).

At the very start of Christianity, in his epistle to the Ephesians, St. Paul referred to the unity of the Church in these words:

I, the prisoner in the Lord, exhort you to walk in a manner worthy of the calling with which you were called...careful to preserve the unity of the Spirit in the bond of peace: one body and one Spirit, even as you were called in one hope of your calling: one Lord, one faith, one Baptism; one God and Father of all (4:1-6).

"The Church, which is spread abroad far and wide into a multitude through the increase of her fruitfulness," explains St. Cyprian, "is one. Just as the sun has many rays, but one light; and as a tree has many boughs, but one strength derived from its tenacious root—unity is preserved in the source."

In his encyclical letter, *Near the Chair of Peter,* Pope John XXIII pointed with satisfaction to the Church's unity.

Speaking of the Church's *unity of doctrine*, he said: "The Church clearly knows and maintains that there is but one truth, and consequently that contrary 'truth' cannot exist.

"With regard to *unity of religious practices*," he continues, "everyone knows that the Catholic Church, from its earliest period down through the centuries, has always had seven, neither more nor fewer, sacraments, received as a sacred legacy from Jesus Christ. She has never ceased to dispense these throughout the Catholic world for the nourishing and fostering of the supernatural life of the faithful.

"It is likewise known that in the Church is celebrated *only one sacrifice*. This is the eucharistic sacrifice by which Christ Himself, our Savior and our Redeemer, daily sacrifices Himself for us all in an unbloody manner but truly, as He did when hanging from the cross on Calvary; and thus in His mercy He pours out on us the immeasurable treasures of His grace.

"Hence St. Cyprian with complete truth declares: 'It is impossible for another altar to be set up or a new priesthood to be established apart from the one altar and the one priesthood.'"

"Further, the *unity of government* in the Catholic Church is obvious to all. For just as the faithful are subject to their priests, and the priests to their bishops, whom 'the Holy Spirit has placed...to rule the Church of God' (Acts 20:28), so each and all the bishops are subject to the Roman Pontiff, who is regarded as the successor of St. Peter, whom Christ our Lord set as the rock and foundation of His Church (cf. Mt. 16:18)."

A message to be spread

We believe that the Church is necessary for salvation, because Christ, who is the sole mediator and way of salvation, renders Himself present for us in His body which is the Church. But THE DIVINE DESIGN OF SALVATION EMBRACES ALL MEN; and those who without fault on their part do not know the Gospel of Christ and His Church, but seek God sincerely, and under the influence of grace endeavor to do His will as recognized through the promptings of their conscience, they, in a number known only to God, can obtain salvation.

THE CREDO

Recognizing also the existence, outside the organism of the Church of Christ, of numerous elements of truth and sanctification which belong to her as her own and tend to Catholic unity, and believing in the action of the Holy Spirit who stirs up in the heart of the disciples of Christ love of this unity, we entertain the hope that the Christians who are not yet in the full communion of the one only Church will one day be reunited in one flock with one only shepherd.

THE CREDO

"No one who believes in God is totally estranged from the Church," is a statement in the U.S. Bishops' Pastoral, *The Church in Our Day.*

However, since the Church is charged with the mission of witnessing to God by her sacramental, social and sacrificial deeds and the suasion of her words, "she bears a certain responsibility for belief and unbelief in the world. She yearns," continues the Pastoral of the U.S. Bishops, "to bring *all believers* into ever more complete communion with herself, and *all men* into an ever more conscious communion with God."

In his encyclical letter, *Paths of the Church,* Pope Paul VI writes: "If the Church has a true realization of what the Lord wishes it to be, then within the Church there arises a unique sense of fullness and a need for outpouring, together with the clear awareness of a mission which transcends the Church, of a message to be spread. It is the duty of evangelization.

"The duty consonant with the patrimony received from Christ is that of spreading, offering, announcing it to others. Well do we know that 'Going, therefore, make disciples of all nations' (Mt. 28:19) is the last command of Christ to His apostles. By the very term 'apostles' these men define their inescapable mission. To this internal drive of charity which tends to become the external gift of charity We will give the name of dialogue, which has in these days come into common usage.

"The Church should enter into dialogue with the world in which it exists and labors. The Church has something to say; the Church has a message to deliver; the Church has a communication to offer.

"And how is the dialogue to be carried on?

"Many, indeed, are the forms that the dialogue of salvation can take. It adapts itself to the needs of a concrete situation, it chooses the appropriate means, it does not bind itself to ineffectual theories and does not cling to hard and fast forms when these have lost their power to speak to men and move them. The question is of great importance, for it concerns the relation of the Church's mission to the lives of men in a given time and place, in a given culture and social setting.

"To what extent should the Church adapt itself to the historic and local circumstances in which its mission is exercised? How should it guard against the danger of a relativism which would falsify its moral and dogmatic truth? And yet, at the same time, how can it fit itself to approach all men so as to save all, according to the example of the Apostle: 'I became all things to all men that I might save all' (1 Cor. 9:22)?

"The world cannot be saved from the outside. As the Word of God became man, so must a man to a certain degree identify himself with the forms of life of those to whom he wishes to bring the message of Christ. Without invoking privileges which would but widen the separation, without employing unintelligible terminology, he must share the common way of life — provided that it is human and honorable — especially of the most humble, if he wishes to be listened to and understood. And before speaking, it is necessary to listen, not only to a man's voice, but to his heart. A man must first be understood; and, where he merits it, agreed with. In the very act of trying to make ourselves pastors, fathers and teachers of men, we must make ourselves their brothers. The spirit of dialogue is friendship and, even more, it is service. All this we must remember and strive to put into practice according to the example and commandment that Christ left to us (cf. Jn. 13:14-17).

"But the danger remains. The apostle's art is a risky one. The desire to come together as brothers must not lead to a watering-down or subtracting from the truth. Our dialogue must not weaken our attachment to our faith. In our apostolate we cannot make vague compromises about the principles of faith and action on which our profession of Christianity is based. An immoderate desire to make peace and sink differences at all costs is fundamentally a kind of skepticism about the power and content of the Word of God which we desire to preach. Only the man who is completely faithful to the teaching of Christ can be an apostle. And only he who lives his Christian life to the full can remain uncontaminated by the errors with which he comes into contact.

"The Church is not unaware of the formidable dimensions of such a mission; it knows the disproportion in numbers between those who are its members and those who are not; it knows the limitations of its power; it knows, likewise, its own human weaknesses and failings. It recognizes, too, that the acceptance of the Gospel depends, ultimately, not upon any apostolic efforts of its own nor upon any favorable temporal conditions, for faith is a gift of God and God alone defines in the world the times and limits of salvation. But the Church knows that it is the seed, the leaven, the salt and light of the world. It sees clearly enough the astounding newness of modern times, but with frank confidence it stands upon the paths of history and says to men: 'I have that for which you search, that which you lack.' It does not thereby promise earthly felicity, but it does offer something—its lights and its grace—which makes the attainment as easy as possible; and then it speaks to men of their transcendent destiny. In doing this it speaks to them of truth, justice, freedom, progress, concord, peace and civilization. These are words whose secret is known to the Church, for Christ has entrusted the secret to its keeping. And so the Church has a message for every category of humanity: for children, for youth, for men of science and learning, for the world of labor and for every social class, for artists, for statesmen and for rulers. Most of all, the Church has words for the poor, the outcast, the suffering and the dying: for all men."

"In order to dialogue we must acquire a sense of humility," says the Vatican Document *Towards the Meeting of Religions,* "which counteracts in us the natural tendency to consider ourselves superior because we alone possess revelation and certitude, while others are groping their way in the dark. Humility, which is truth, shows us all men as brothers, all of them created by God, all of them equally loved by Him, destined by Him for eternal life. We know that on the day of judgment publicans and sinners will pass before the children of the kingdom and the Ninivites will have the right to condemn our generation. The benefit of truth and of the faith is a gratuitous gift and we have received it in order that we may share it with others.

"In its *Declaration on the Attitude of the Church to Non-Christian Religions,* the Second Vatican Council has pointed out some of the merits of each of the principal religions, the zeal of the Hindus in scrutinizing the mystery of God by meditation, in Buddhism the recognition of the vanity of this world, in Islamism adoration of the one God and total submission to His will, and in all religions in general, the effort to furnish an answer to the anxieties of the human heart. His Holiness Pope Paul VI, on his part, points out the glimmerings of truth in these religions which the Church recognizes and appreciates.

"If there is a point on which the other religions can serve as an example and stimulus to us, it is perhaps their zeal for the preservation of their spiritual heritage, a point on which we are often too negligent. They are similar to those who take extreme pains to produce fire and watch attentively and lovingly over the live coals on their hearth, whereas when flames can be produced instantly by striking a match we are inclined to lose sight of the importance of fire.

To be able to extend our hand with success, "we must never forget that no matter what external form our activity may assume, we are God's laborers, working for His glory and for the good of men. Our mission is one of grace and if the Lord does not operate and build we are wasting our time.

"We must also distinguish all the time between the divine and the human without ever unduly mixing these two elements. This will prevent us from intervening in what is outside our province.

"It is not sufficient that we ourselves be convinced of the divine character of our work. We must convince others of this, leading them to true prayer, to real contact with God in order to obtain from Him what is beyond our own powers as, for example, the gift of faith, or the remission of their sins. Examples are not lacking of people who are still fully attached to their own creed, but are pleased to recite the Our Father and Act of Contrition" (Toward the Meeting of Religions, Chapter 6, issued by the Vatican Secretariat for Non-Christians, September 21, 1967).

In the bosom of this Church, the rich variety of liturgical rites and the legitimate diversity of theological and spiritual heritages and special disciplines, far from injuring her unity, make it more manifest.

THE CREDO

While it is true to say that the Church enjoys unity, this does not mean that it is uniform. The Church is not a monolithic structure. It is not like a factory which makes only the same type of objects and assembles them into a standardized finished product. Quite the contrary. The *Constitution on the Sacred Liturgy* of Vatican II speaks of legitimate diversity in forms of worship in these terms:

Even in the liturgy, the Church has no wish to impose a rigid uniformity in matters which do not implicate the faith or the good of the whole community; rather does she respect and foster the genius and talents of the various races and peoples. Anything in these peoples' way of life which is not indissolubly bound up with superstition and error she studies with sympathy and, if possible, preserves intact. Sometimes in fact she admits such things into the liturgy itself, so long as they harmonize with its true and authentic spirit (n. 37).

The Roman Rite prevails in the Western or Latin Church, but there is also a Milanese rite (named after the city of Milan in Italy) and a Mozarabic rite in Spain. The various Eastern churches in communion with Rome also have their own distinctive rites. Some of these rites are the Byzantine, the Armenian, the Caldean, the Maronite, and the Syrian, to name a few.

Speaking of these rites, the *Decree on Eastern Catholic Churches* of Vatican II says:

The Holy Catholic Church, which is the Mystical Body of Christ, is made up of the faithful who are organically united in the Holy Spirit by the same faith, the same sacraments and the same government and who, combining together into various groups which are held together by a hierarchy, form separate churches or rites. Between these there exists an admirable bond of union, such that the variety within the Church in no way harms its unity; rather it manifests it, for it is the mind of the Catholic Church that *each individual church or rite should retain its traditions whole and entire* and likewise that it should adapt its way of life to the different needs of time and place.

These individual churches, whether of the *East* or the *West*, although they differ somewhat among themselves in *rite* (to use the current phrase), *that is, in liturgy, ecclesiastical discipline, and spiritual heritage*, are, nevertheless, each as much as the others, entrusted to the pastoral government of the Roman Pontiff, the divinely appointed successor of St. Peter in primacy over the universal Church. They are consequently of equal dignity, so that none of them is superior to the others as regards rite and they enjoy the same rights and are under the same obligations, also in respect of preaching the Gospel to the whole world under the guidance of the Roman Pontiff.

History, tradition and abundant ecclesiastical institutions bear outstanding witness to the great merit owing to the Eastern Churches by the universal Church. The Sacred

Council, therefore, not only accords to this ecclesiastical and spiritual heritage the high regard which is its due and rightful praise, but also unhesitatingly looks on it as the heritage of the universal Church. For this reason it solemnly declares that the Churches of the East, as much as those of the West, have a full right and are in duty bound to rule themselves, each in accordance with its own established disciplines, since all these are praiseworthy by reason of their venerable antiquity, more harmonious with the character of their faithful and more suited to the promotion of the good of souls (nn. 2, 3, 5).

"They shall hear my voice"
John 10

...founded upon the apostles and handing on from century to century their ever-living word and their powers as pastors in the successor of Peter and the bishops in communion with him...

We believe in one, holy, catholic, and APOSTOLIC Church...

THE CREDO

The Good Shepherd, Jesus Christ, who calls Himself the door of the sheepfold, was quite emphatic when He said, "And they [the sheep] shall hear my voice" (Jn. 10:16).

How? From the reliable teachers—the apostles and their successors—to whom He entrusted His doctrines.

In the following passage from the *Constitution on the Church*, we read:

"Jesus Christ, the eternal Shepherd, established His holy Church, having sent forth the apostles as He Himself had been sent by the Father; and He willed that their successors, namely the bishops, should be shepherds in His Church even to the consummation of the world" (n. 18).

The bishops are successors of the apostles as pastors of souls. Together with the supreme Pontiff and under his authority they are sent to continue throughout the ages the work of Christ, the eternal pastor. Christ gave the apostles and their successors the command and the power to teach all nations, to sanctify men in the truth, and to feed them.

"Bishops, therefore, have been made true and authentic teachers of the faith, pontiffs, and pastors through the Holy

Spirit, who has been given to them" (Decree on Pastoral Office of Bishops in the Church, n. 2).

To announce Christ and arouse faith in Him—this was the mission of the apostles. Pope Paul VI says that faith was the heritage of the apostles; it was the gift of their apostolate, of their charity. Addressing us, he urges that by accepting the faith, "we put ourselves in communion with the apostles. We enter their school. We take part in the plan of salvation which Jesus Christ entrusted to them to be developed and to be established in humanity."

We are under a mandate from the Lord which requires that "in all we are and all we do for and among men, we become the light of the world, the lamp illumined to show where Christ is to be found" (The Church in Our Day).

...perpetually assisted by the Holy Spirit, she has the charge of guarding, teaching, explaining and spreading the Truth which God revealed in a then veiled manner by the prophets, and fully in the Lord Jesus.

We believe...all that the Church proposes for belief as divinely revealed whether by a solemn judgment or by the ordinary and universal magisterium.

We believe in the infallibility enjoyed by the successor of Peter when he teaches ex cathedra as pastor and teacher of all the faithful, and which is assured also to the episcopal body when it exercises with him the supreme magisterium. THE CREDO

Protection from error is assured by Christ to all of His sheep who adhere unwaveringly to the voice He designates as authentic and infallible, which is the voice of His Vicar and bishops in communion with him.

Our security guard

The nature and scope of papal infallibility is clearly outlined in this extract from the *Dogmatic Constitution on the Church*, issued during the Second Vatican Council. The statement runs:

The infallibility with which the Divine Redeemer willed His Church to be endowed in defining doctrine of faith and morals, extends as far as the deposit of revelation extends, which must be religiously guarded and faithfully expounded. And this is *the infallibility* which the Roman Pontiff, the head of the college of bishops, enjoys in virtue of his office, when, as the supreme shepherd and teacher of all the faithful, who confirms his brethren in their faith, by a definitive act he proclaims a doctrine of faith or morals (n. 25).

The same document states that the bishops, united under their head, the Pope, and gathered in ecumenical council, are also infallible, when they too solemnly decree that a certain doctrine concerning faith or morals must be accepted by the whole Church:

When *either the Roman Pontiff or the body of bishops together with him* defines a judgment, they pronounce it in accordance with revelation itself, which all are obliged to abide by and be in conformity with, that is, the revelation which as written or orally handed down is transmitted in its entirety through the legitimate succession of bishops and especially in care of the Roman Pontiff himself, and which under the guiding light of the Spirit of truth is religiously preserved and faithfully expounded in the Church. The Roman Pontiff and the bishops, in view of their office and the importance of the matter, by fitting means diligently strive to inquire properly into that revelation and to give apt expression to its contents; but a new public revelation they do not accept as pertaining to the divine deposit of faith (n. 25).

The above mentioned document also made all this clear when it stated:

Our Lord placed Simon alone as the rock and the bearer of the keys of the Church, and made him shepherd of the whole flock; it is evident, however, that the power of binding and loosing, which was given to Peter, was granted also to the college of apostles, joined with their head. This college, insofar as it is composed of many, expresses the variety and universality of the People of God, but insofar as it is assembled under one head, it expresses the unity of the flock of Christ. In it, the bishops, faithfully recognizing the primacy and preeminence of their head, exercise their own authority for the good of their own faithful, and indeed of the whole Church, the Holy Spirit supporting its organic structure and harmony with moderation. The supreme power in the universal Church, which this college enjoys, is exercised in a solemn way in an ecumenical council. A council is never ecumenical unless it is confirmed or at least accepted as such by the successor of

Peter; and it is the prerogative of the Roman Pontiff to con-
voke these councils, to preside over them and to confirm them
(n. 22).

The unqualified "yes"

The Pope also exercises an ordinary magisterium. This
takes place when he issues grave statements contained in
papal documents, such as encyclicals. Technically, these
assertions are not infallible, but they must be given respectful
consideration and compliance since they are issued only in
grave circumstances and given weighty thought before publication.

Pope Pius XII drew attention to the importance of pronouncements of the ordinary magisterium in the following
words:

"It must not be thought that what is expounded in encyclical
letters does not of itself demand consent, since in writing
such letters the Popes do not exercise the supreme power of
their teaching authority. For these matters are taught with
the ordinary teaching authority, of which it is true to say:
'He who hears you, hears me'; and generally what is expounded and inculcated in encyclical letters already for other
reasons appertains to Catholic doctrine.

*"But if the Supreme Pontiffs in their official docu-
ments purposely pass judgment on a matter up to
that time under dispute, it is obvious that that matter, according to the mind and will of the same Pontiff, cannot be any longer considered a question open
to discussion among theologians."*

The Fathers of Vatican II also wished to emphasize the
importance of the ordinary teaching of the Church. Hence we
read in the *Dogmatic Constitution on the Church* as follows:

The *religious submission of mind and will* must be shown in a
special way *to the authentic magisterium of the Roman Pontiff, even when he is not speaking ex cathedra;* that is, it must
be shown in such a way that his supreme magisterium is
acknowledged with reverence, the judgments made by him
are sincerely adhered to, according to his manifest mind and
will. His mind and will in the matter may be known either
from the character of the documents, from his frequent repe-
tition of the same doctrine, or from his manner of speaking
(n. 25).

Bishops exercise their ordinary magisterium when in their own dioceses they preach the usual truths of the Church or urge the faithful to belief in and compliance with what the Pope has spoken of in an encyclical. No bishop is infallible by himself, except, of course, when he is teaching an already infallibly defined doctrine of faith or morals.

The *Dogmatic Constitution on Divine Revelation* has this:

The task of authentically interpreting the word of God, whether written or handed on, has been entrusted exclusively to the living teaching office of the Church, whose authority is exercised in the name of Jesus Christ. This teaching office is not above the word of God, but serves it, teaching only what has been handed on, listening to it devoutly, guarding it scrupulously and explaining it faithfully in accord with a divine commission and with the help of the Holy Spirit, it draws from this one deposit of faith everything which it presents for belief as divinely revealed.

> *It is clear, therefore, that sacred tradition, Sacred Scripture and the teaching authority of the Church, in accord with God's most wise design, are so linked and joined together that one cannot stand without the others, and that all together and each in its own way under the action of the one Holy Spirit contribute effectively to the salvation of souls (n. 10).*

In their collective pastoral, *The Church in Our Day,* the American bishops drew the attention of the faithful to the existence of the teaching function of the Church and pointed out the duty of obedience to it in the following words:

The Church is the object of our loyalty. Loyalty includes obedience, not the merely exterior obedience which could be passive and simply carry out instructions, but an inner, spontaneous spirit of obedience which continues among His members the fundamental act of Christ, His unqualified "Yes" to the will of His Father. It is this "Yes" which dominates the whole scheme of salvation, the Incarnation and the Redemption through which, by His obedience, Christ won for us our place in the Church and our restoration to the friendship of God. The loyalty to the Church of which we speak is therefore loyalty to Christ.

The folly of courage and love

We believe in one, holy CATHOLIC...Church.

THE CREDO

The Church of Christ is called catholic, that is, universal.

"The characteristic of universality which adorns the people of God is a gift from the Lord Himself. By reason of it, the Catholic Church strives constantly and with due effect to bring all humanity and all its possessions back to its source in Christ, with Him as its head and united in His Spirit" (Constitution on the Church, n. 13).

The Church is catholic by her very nature, by her actual global extension and by the numbers she possesses. She contains all kinds—the learned and the unlearned, the rich and the poor, all races. The words that St. Paul uttered almost two thousand years ago are just as true today—perhaps even more so—than they were in his time:

> For all you who have been baptized into Christ, have put on Christ. There is neither Jew nor Greek; there is neither slave nor freeman; there is neither male nor female. For you are all one in Christ Jesus (Gal. 3:27-28).

It is true that the Church is more solidly founded and perhaps better organized in those areas where Western culture predominates—Europe, the United States, Latin America and Australia. But to think of the Church as being *Caucasian* only is a grave error. From the very start, the Gospel was meant for every creature. Due to certain historical and geographical causes it took root earliest in the Mediterranean countries of Europe and from there spread northward to the Germanic, Scandinavian, Slavic and Celtic tribes. But the Church no more *belongs* to these regions or peoples than it does to any other region or people in the world.

Although the present Catholic population of the world is large—over 566,775,000—still there are billions outside it. Contemplate for a moment those densely peopled sectors of the Far East—China with over 700,000,000; India with over 400,000,000; Japan with close to 100,000,000; Oceania with South East Asia running close to 150,000,000—and you will get some idea of the vast amount of missionary work that has to be done to get the Gospel to these people! Add to these the more than 471,340,000 Moslems over the earth plus the

244,308,000 non-Christians of the African continent and the enormity of the problem simply staggers the human mind!

The complex state of the missionary world is ever before the eyes of the Holy Father, as the vicar of Christ he is entrusted with the task of seeing that the Gospel be preached to all peoples and at all times insofar as this is possible. In an address delivered June 2, 1968, he referred to the missions.

The Church of Christ is called catholic, i.e., universal. It is called to be in fact, in history, in the successive generations of mankind, what it is by right and by duty: the witness of Christ for all men, the means of salvation for all, the mystic and human society open to all. It is called, not to dominate, not to substitute itself for or place itself over the earthly city, but to penetrate men's minds with its light of truth, its ferment of liberty, its encouragement to work in justice and brotherhood; to give to the world a religious unity in the harmony of ethnic, cultural and political differences, which should always be respected. It is Catholic by institution, and it should be Catholic in fact. This divine purpose that the Church bears in herself has been awakened in recent times, and she has become more conscious of it.

As the paths of the world have opened up new possibilities of communication among peoples, the Church has felt in herself the "urgency of charity" to travel those paths – often, in fact, to be the first to walk them. She has felt this through her very nature, which is missionary. St. Paul's cry, *"Woe to me if I preach not the Gospel,"* (1 Cor. 9:16) has echoed in the Church's heart, and has reminded her of her original vocation. The history of the missions during the past few centuries shows this – an epic, as it is, full of risks, adventures, heroism and martyrdom. Missionary endeavor has, one might say, exploded, braving superhuman difficulties, putting to the task the most rudimentary means, and *men with the folly of courage and love.* Faith has become what it ought to be – *dynamic, irresistible, even rash.* The joy of spreading the Gospel has repaid every effort, every sacrifice.

Then came the Council, to clarify the theological basis of this phenomenon, to remind the People of God of their native duty to expand, and to give criteria, norms and exhortations to pursue with greater vigor and system the great work of the evangelization of peoples to whom the name of Christ has not yet been announced, and in whom the Church has not yet struck roots of autonomous life.

Brothers and children! This picture, which represents a marvelous and, in certain ways, miraculous aspect of the contemporary life of our Church, deserves to be observed and meditated upon with great interest. *He who would be indifferent or detached before this epiphany of the Church ought to doubt his faithfulness to Christ and to his own baptism. The missions belong to us, to each of us, to each community of believers.*

In the following ringing words of praise, on World Mission Day, October 20, 1968, the Pope paid sterling tribute to missionaries. He said:

They are champions, even to the point of heroism, of the saving truth and charity. They are the pioneers of universality, that is, of the effective catholicity of the Church. They are the most assiduous, humble, disinterested, efficacious promoters of brotherhood and peace among men.... They are the masters of life who teach the value of time, work, pain, forgiveness, prayer and love without asking for payment. They are the bearers of the cross which is heavy and a sacrifice for themselves, but bright and beneficial for those who receive and welcome it. They are the prophets of the Word, of eternity, goodness and hope. No other mission is equal to theirs.

We must, all of us, think of these missionaries. A duty, and, in the economy of salvation, a self-interest binds us to them. A thought, a prayer, an offering, a little admiration and support — who will deny them these things?

Let us then proceed to the task, to the struggle and to the danger. There is not a day, nor an hour, nor a moment to be lost. Father Damian, the leper priest, despite constant ill-health, refused to cease his missionary tasks. Touched by sympathy, a friend once asked him to rest for a little while. The reply, which should give us endless food for thought, considering the immense issues involved, was characteristic: "There is so much to do, and so little time left in which to do it." The theater of war is immense, the contest for souls intense, and if the missionaries are to be victorious in their grim, bloodless battles for those who sit in darkness, their lines of communication must be kept open and along them must flow, in ever increasing volume, resources of all kinds to aid them to triumph! Think often, then, of those lonely front-line forts which Christ's spiritual commandos have thrown up against the ramparts of error. Let the reflection be a spur to redoubled efforts for the missionary apostolate. For, to borrow a slogan which Father Keller, founder of the Christopher Movement, made famous: "You can change the world!"

A stronger faith, a mightier love, a richer life

We believe in one, HOLY...Church.

She is therefore holy...because she herself has no other

life but that of grace: it is by living by her life that her members are sanctified...
THE CREDO

Our human nature thirsts for perfection. In Christ our brother we have our model, our help and our reward. As members of His Church, we find in it "a stronger faith, a mightier love, a richer life" (The Church in Our Day). If we collaborate with the grace of Christ as we find it in the Church, our dream of becoming Christlike — or in other words, "holy" — will turn into a reality.

Holiness or sanctity has always been present in the Church. This holiness flows from the sanctity of Jesus Christ, her founder. The Church is holy in its sacraments which are the channels of grace, in its doctrines, in its morality, in its liturgy and institutions. St. Paul refers to the holiness of the Church thus:

Christ loved the Church, and delivered himself up for her, cleansing her in the bath of water by means of the word; in order that he might present to himself the Church in all her glory, not having spot or wrinkle or any such thing, but that she might be holy and without blemish. (Eph. 5:25-27)

St. John writes of the Church in the Apocalypse (21:2):
I saw the holy city, New Jerusalem, coming down out of heaven from God, made ready as a bride adorned for her husband.

The *Dogmatic Constitution on the Church* says:
The Church is believed to be indefectibly holy. Christ, the Son of God, who with the Father and the Spirit is praised as uniquely holy, loved the Church as His bride, delivering Himself up for her. He did this that He might sanctify her. (n. 39).

The holiness of the Church is clearly seen in the lives of the saints. They are of both sexes, old and young, and come from all parts of the world, from all walks of life. As St. John describes them in the Apocalypse (7:9-12):
"After this I saw a great multitude which no man could number, out of all nations and tribes and peoples and tongues, standing before the throne and before the Lamb, clothed in white robes, and with palms in their hands. And they cried with a loud voice, saying, "Salvation belongs to our God who sits upon the throne, and to the Lamb." And all the angels were standing round about the throne, and the elders and

The Holy Catholic Church, which is the Mystical Body of Christ is made up of the faithful who are organically united in the Holy Spirit by the same faith, the same sacraments, the same government ... and held together by a hierarchy.

(Vatican II)

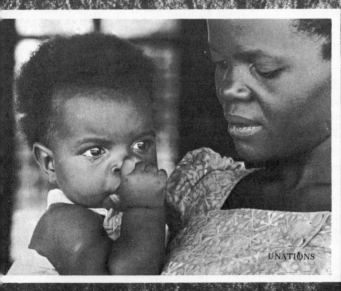

UNATIONS

the four living creatures; and they fell on their faces before the throne and worshiped God, saying, "Amen. Blessing and glory and wisdom and thanksgiving and honor and power and strength to our God forever and ever. Amen."

Many of us are familiar in some way or other with the biographies of certain saints — those whom we like particularly or those whose names we bear or those associated with certain nationalities — St. Boniface with Germany, for example; Saints Cyril and Methodius, apostles of the Slavic peoples; St. Patrick and St. Bridget, so well-known to the Irish; St. Joan of Arc to the French; St. Francis of Assisi to the Italians; St. Ignatius of Loyola to the Spaniards; St. Martin de Porres, St. Benedict of Philadelphia and the Uganda Martyrs to the Negro peoples. These were all great saints and we would like to give capsule biographies of them, as of certain others. But this would be impossible in a volume of this kind. There is one saint however who cannot be passed over in silence — St. Joseph, the foster father of our Lord and Savior, Jesus Christ.

In a recent address, Pope Paul VI eulogized this great saint and held him up for our imitation.

This most elect figure appears to us at the end of the period preparatory to Redemption. It is a focal point in history, a most solemn, decisive period rich in great things and lofty mysteries.

St. Joseph presents himself to us under the most unexpected aspects. We might have imagined him a powerful man in the act of opening the way to the new-born Christ, or perhaps a prophet, a wise man, a man of priestly activities ready to receive the Son of God into the human race. Instead, he is the most ordinary, humble, modest person one could imagine.

It is well for us to consider the singular coming of Christ on earth. He arranged that his private and personal environment for such an event should be one of extreme simplicity.

Joseph was to give our Lord, shall we say, his civil status in human society. Since Joseph belonged to the house of David, one might have thought he would have been accustomed to royalty, war, political struggles. Instead we find ourselves on the threshold of a poor craftsman's shop in Nazareth. Here is Joseph, who indeed belongs to the lineage of David, but he derives no title or motive of glory from it. One would almost say it is a source of antithesis which puts him on a level with everyone else without fame or glory.

Furthermore, even in his capacity as head of the earthly family in which Jesus deigned to live, no detail is given us about him in the Gospel.

He was a quiet and poor man, faithful to his duty despite his royal lineage. He was a *righteous* man. This is the only attribute the

Gospel gives him, but it is sufficient to give us the social environment chosen by our Lord for Himself.

Can we then ignore this figure and not pause a moment before it? Indeed not. For in doing so we would not understand the doctrine of the Divine Master, that of announcing the Gospel to the poor, the humble, those in need of consolation and redemption. Therefore, the Gospel of the Beatitudes begins with this forerunner called Joseph. We find ourselves before a charming tableau which each one of us could represent only inadequately if we were artists. But lo and behold, our Lord Himself presents His forerunner to us, His foster- father and guardian in the most human and simple way which all of us can understand.

Nonetheless there is a special aspect which deserves to be observed and understood. This quiet life which is interwoven with that of the new-born Jesus and the most blessed life of the Virgin, has something unique, most beautiful and mysterious.

Three times the Gospel speaks of an angel appearing to Joseph in his sleep.

What does this mean? It means that Joseph was guided and intimately counselled by the heavenly messenger. He received a dictation of the will of God which placed itself before his actions. Therefore his ordinary actions were moved by a mysterious dialogue which told him what to do: "Fear not, Joseph; do this; go; return!"

What do we perceive then in this humble personage so dear to us? We see a great meekness, an exceptional readiness to obey and perform God's will.

He does not argue or hesitate, he does not allege rights or aspirations. He is ever ready and willing to perform what is required of him. He knows his life will unfold in a series of dramatic events transfigured at an extraordinary level of purity and loftiness well above any human expectation or calculation. Joseph accepts his destiny, for it was said unto him: "Do not be afraid to take Mary as your wife, for what is born of her is the work of the Holy Spirit."

And Joseph obeys. Later on he will be told: "You must leave, for the new-born Savior is in danger." And he faces a long journey, crossing burning deserts, without any means or acquaintances, an exile in a foreign and heathen land. He is always faithful and ready at the voice of the Lord who later will order him to return.

As soon as he goes back to Nazareth, he resumes his usual life as a reserved craftsman. His is the task to "educate" the Messia to work and to life's experiences. He will watch over him and will have the sublime prerogative to be the one who will guide, direct and assist the Redeemer in the world. And Jesus was subject to them.

The typical conformity of Joseph to the will of God is the example on which we should ponder.

God's lofty designs can coexist with the most common conditions of life. *No one is excluded from carrying out the divine call to perfection.* Indeed, everyone should be so attentive to the voices from heaven to ask himself the question: "Have I been called?" In clearer language: "What is God's will for my life?" How must I direct my days and talents in order to be in complete accordance with the will of our Lord?

The saints deliberately set out to be saints — with the help of God, of course. Take, for instance, St. Ignatius Loyola, founder of the Society of Jesus. As a soldier, however, he was not remarkable for Christian virtue. When he was wounded at the siege of Pamplona, and was disfigured, he was so vain about his appearance that he underwent two very severe operations to have the leg straightened, but he had a limp for the rest of his life. As he lay recuperating he chanced to come across a volume of the lives of the saints. He read it avidly and decided that he, too, with the help of God would become a saint. "What these have done, why can't I?" he kept saying to himself. Today he is canonized.

St. Therese of Lisieux, too, set herself to become a saint. She wrote: "The good God would not fill me with desires that cannot be accomplished. In spite of my smallness I may aspire to sanctity." It was thus that she found her way to heaven by doing ordinary things extraordinarily well — like St. John Berchmans and St. Stanislaus Kostka — for the pure love of God. Thus she was able to write of herself: "I am a very little soul, who can only offer very little things to our Lord."

What is a saint?

A saint is simply a person who clearly grasps the significance of the Gospel messages and realizes them thoroughly through constant reflection upon them. *Then he acts on them — he puts them into practice — no matter what the cost!* It is as simple and as difficult as that! Father Alberione, S.S.P., S.T.D., declares:

Sanctity is not a privilege reserved to a few. All of us are called to it.

A saint is not one who is worn-out, an irresponsible person who cannot make up his mind to do his share in life. For St. Paul, sanctity is the full maturity of the man, the perfect man: "perfect manhood" (Eph. 4:13). The saint does not wrap himself up in himself; he opens himself up to development. He does not stay still; rather his motto is growth and progress. Sanctity is life, movement, nobility, dynamic enthusiasm — not the kind that falls off but the good kind that keeps rising upward! But sanctity will be only and always in proportion *to the spirit of faith* and *to will power.* God is with us! We cooperate with Him.

Never without sinners

...though she has sinners in her bosom...

...it is by removing themselves from her life that they fall into sins and disorders that prevent the radiation of her sanctity.

THE CREDO

Though the Church is holy, simultaneously and paradoxically, sin exists within it. When confronted with the fact of evil in the Church — and history shows there has been enough of it! — we must not act like the ostrich which buries its head in the sand until the storm passes. No! We must face up to the truth squarely and never try to sweep it under the rug! As long as human nature is the way it is, there will always be sin in the world. There *need* not be sin, but it will forever rear its ugly head, in one way or another. Our Lord Himself has told us this (Mt. 18:6-9; Mk. 9:41-47). "And whosoever shall scandalize one of these little ones, that believes in me, it were better for him that a millstone were hanged about his neck and he were cast into the sea. Woe to the world because of scandals. For it must needs be that scandals come; but nevertheless woe to that man by whom the scandal comes."

The U.S. bishops did not hesitate to draw attention to the existence of evil. We read in the already mentioned *The Church in Our Day:*

"We are painfully aware of the shortcomings of some among us, the excesses of a few. There is neither possiblity of concealing these nor point to apology for them. But we can and do ask that people, beginning with people within the Church, be more mindful of our saints, notably the saints in the making among our priests. *The Church never promised to be without sinners and she is the last to repudiate them; it was promised that she would give the world many and great saints.* In this time of adjustment and self-scrutiny, God is faithful to His promise to raise up in our midst the saints He has never denied us. Future generations may yet envy us the opportunities for sanctity we had and the number of saints God gave us."

The existence of sin in the Church is one of the greatest crosses that the people of God have to bear. It bows them down in anguish until they are almost at the breaking point. Pope John XXIII once referred to this in an address thus:

Listen to this lament of St. Jean Marie Vianney, the Curé of Ars: "The dear God is so much offended that one might be tempted to invoke the end of the world.... You have to come to Ars to know what sin is.... One does not know what to do. All you can do is cry and pray." The saint forgot to say that he also took upon himself a part of the expiation: "As for me," he confided to a person who came to him for advice, "I assign a small penance to them and the rest I do myself for them."

And truly the Curé of Ars lived only for his "poor sinners," as he called them, in the hope of seeing them converted and repentant. Their conversion was the objective on which all his hopes converged and the work on which he spent all his time and all his efforts. And this because he knew from his experience of the confessional all the harm of sin and the dreadful ruin wrought by it in the world of souls. He spoke of it in frightening terms: "If we had faith and could see a soul in the state of mortal sin, we would die of fright."

But the bitterness of his sorrow and the vehemence of his words were due less to the fear of the eternal sorrows that threaten hardened sinners than to the emotion he felt at the thought of divine love ignored and offended. In the face of the sinner's obstinacy and his ungratefulness toward such a kind God, the tears would flow from his eyes. "Oh, my friend," he would say, "I cry precisely because you do not cry."

On the other hand, with how much delicacy and how much fervor did he bring back the rebirth of hope in penitent hearts. That is why he made himself the untiring minister of divine mercy, which is, he said, powerful, "like a swirling torrent that carries away hearts in its passage," and more tender than the solicitude of a mother, because God is "more ready to forgive than a mother would be to retrieve one of her children from the fire."

What is sin? We know that it is an offense against God, but it is so much of a mystery that actually we can only get an idea of it from examples. For one mortal sin of pride, committed in an instant, the Almighty created hell and condemned the rebellious angels there for eternity! The person who touched the ark of the covenant in defiance of the will of God was slain on the spot by Him. Already we have seen how Ananias and Sapphira were struck dead for theft and deception. "I would rather die than sin," said the great Saint Augustine of Hippo, who himself had been estranged from God for sixteen years and had then become converted. St. John Chrysostom wrote that sin, insofar as in it lies, aims at the destruction of God. St. Bernard of Clairvaux reiterated the same thought when he said: "Were He capable of destruction, a single mortal sin would annihilate God." The great St. Dominic prayed that God would place him as a stone in the mouth of hell, if that would prevent sinners from falling into it, and St. Ignatius Loyola was once heard to say that if the entire Society of Jesus should succeed in preventing only *one* mortal sin, then it had not been founded in vain!

The greatest tragedy of the twentieth century lies in the fact that not only have many people lost their horror of sin — but the very concept of it. No calamity, no matter how great — not even the loss of life itself — is equal in horror to the turpitude of one mortal sin. Yet it is a fact that often only lip-service, if indeed that, is paid to this definition. Grave sins are committed against the various commandments in different ways as if there were no such thing as a standard of morality given us by God Himself!

In a homily delivered on Ash Wednesday, 1968, Pope Paul VI drew attention to this disastrous state of affairs in the following weighty words:

Sin is clearly a Christian concept. *Anyone who has accepted Christianity, God's revelation, possesses a precise awareness of sin.* Elsewhere there may be approximate ideas of sin, but they are always vague and uncertain. With us it is quite definite. Sin implies two elements that are truly religious. The first is that of our relationship with God, not only the God of the Law, the powerful and severe God, the God of justice, who judges our human actions inflexibly and infallibly, but the God of love, of goodness, the God who, in order to blot out our sins, came among us and took upon Himself the weight of our faults and atoned for them by His death. God cannot ignore our sins — He would not be God if He were indifferent to them. But, We repeat, He is the God of goodness, of infinite love, to the point of immolating Himself on the gibbet of the cross to blot out our sins. Therefore, we must renew in our souls the sense of sin, that is, a conscience sensitive of our relationship with God.

The other concept which sin implies is one of extraordinary enormity. It tells us that human guilt is a drama — for freedom is involved. Sin is an abuse of our responsible liberty. It is a challenge to God, transgression of His law, indifference to His love. It is, therefore, a case of evil turning back upon ourselves. Our real evil is the sin committed by us.

We must renew in ourselves this sense of a true Christian conscience which accuses us of guilt and gives us no peace until we have found a remedy to our erring nature. It is then that penance becomes not only a remedy, but a necessity. We must do penance in order to declare to ourselves, to

heaven and earth, that we are miserable sinners. We are
obliged to implore mercy and to show by some act of ours
that we repudiate the evil we have committed....

Perhaps the saying, "A saint is a sinner who kept on trying," is the realistic position for us. If we admit our faults,
our failures, our transgressions, and yet fly repentant to the
merciful embrace of the Lord, who is swift to pardon and slow
to punish, we gain courage in our efforts towards sanctity.
And there is never any reason to quit trying!

As often as we sin, we blur the image of Christ in us. As
often as we repent, we bring Him into focus again in our lives.

As soon as we start to deny ourselves we begin to find
God, Thomas Merton wrote, and his own life story reveals
the truth of his words.

This is why she suffers and does penance for these offenses... THE CREDO

The Church is composed of weak human beings who are
subject to error and fault. Therefore, she always stands in
need of reform, sometimes more, sometimes less. Concerning
this we read in the *Pastoral Constitution on the Church in the
Modern World:*

Although by the power of the Holy Spirit the Church will
remain the faithful spouse of her Lord and will never cease
to be the sign of salvation on earth, still she is very well aware
that among her members, both clerical and lay, some have
been unfaithful to the Spirit of God during the course of many
centuries. In the present age, too, it does not escape the
Church how great a distance lies between the message she
offers and the human failings of those to whom the Gospel
is entrusted. Whatever be the judgment of history on these
defects, we ought to be conscious of them, and struggle
against them energetically, lest they inflict harm on the spread
of the Gospel. The Church also realizes that in working out
her relationship with the world she always has great need
of the ripening which comes with the experience of the centuries. Led by the Holy Spirit, Mother Church unceasingly
exhorts her sons to purify and renew themselves so that the
sign of Christ can shine more brightly on the face of the
Church (n. 43).

...and the Church filled with heavenly blessings.

...the germ and the first fruits of the kingdom of God, through which the work and the sufferings of Redemption are continued throughout human history, and which looks for its perfect accomplishment beyond time in glory.   THE CREDO

One day the Church's pilgrimage will be over, as will also the pilgrimage of every individual soul. Then shall we all enter into heavenly glory. For as we read in Isaia:

No longer shall the sun be your light by day, nor the brightness of the moon shine upon you at night; the Lord shall be your light forever, your God shall be your glory. No longer shall your sun go down, or your moon withdraw, for the Lord will be your light forever, and the days of your mourning shall be at an end. Your people shall all be just, they shall always possess the land, they, the bud of my planting, my handiwork to show my glory. The smallest shall become a thousand, the youngest, a mighty nation; I, the Lord, will swiftly accomplish these things when their time comes. (Is. 60:19-22)

Lo, I am about to create new heavens and a new earth; the things of the past shall not be remembered or come to mind. Instead, there shall always be rejoicing and happiness in what I create; for I create Jerusalem to be a joy and its people to be a delight; I will rejoice in Jerusalem and exult in my people. No longer shall the sound of weeping be heard there, or the sound of crying. (Is. 65:17-19)

CHALLENGE

The human heart beats with superhuman desires. No creature can satisfy it; God alone can completely fulfill its yearning for love.

Saints are people who make God's love the reason for their life and labors. Sanctity is for all men. There have been and there are in our own day many souls who love Christ very much. They are generous, pure and diligent in the duties of their state in life. Souls such as these merit the reward of heaven. Let us have courage and follow their example. Despite our personal weaknesses, faults and lack of special training, we, too, can become holy, and by renewing our own faith and commitment to Christ, we can also witness to Him.

Indeed, many forms of apostolate are open to us. We can "announce Christ" in our conversations, in our social life.... We can do all that we do with higher motives: for love of God, for love of our brothers in Christ. And we can suggest these richer, deeper values to others so that their lives will be more God-filled—and consequently, more grace and joy-filled.

Every member of the Church, far from judging his neighbor, should strive, instead, to purify himself and be a real apostle to as many people as he can.

12

THE
ISSUES
TODAY

Poverty

Without ceasing to recall to her children that they have not here a lasting dwelling, she [the Church] also urges them to contribute, each according to his vocation and his means, to the welfare of their earthly city,...

...to give their aid freely to their brothers, especially to the poorest and most unfortunate.
THE CREDO

It is one of the greatest paradoxes of the twentieth century, that in a world filled with plenty and with the technological capacity to produce unlimited supplies of goods and services, hunger and poverty should afflict such a great segment of mankind. Let us quote a few statistics in regard to the United States alone. By government standards a family is poor when its yearly income is below $3000.00 Taking that figure as a yardstick, then some 36 million Americans are poor. Half the number of Negro families in the United States earn less than $3000.00 per annum. Over 25% of them are crammed into large city slum areas both in the North and South. Things are bad enough in America; they are much worse in other parts of the world, where all forms of disease complicate the already existing hunger situation.

In addition to what we said about poverty when treating of the beatitudes, we mention the following. The question of poverty was very much in the mind of our Lord. He saw plenty of poverty around Him and was moved to say: "The poor you have always with you" (Mt. 26:11). In His discourses He drew attention to the poor and strove to improve their lot. Thus we read His words in St. Luke (14:12-14): "When you give a dinner or a supper, do not invite your friends, nor your brethren, nor your relatives, or your rich neighbors, lest perhaps they also invite you in return, and a recompense be made to you. But when you give a feast, invite the poor, the crippled, the lame, the blind; and blessed shall you be, because they have nothing to repay you with; for you shall be repaid at the resurrection of the just." How pleased He must have been, when after telling Zacchaeus that He was going to dine with him, the latter said: "Behold, Lord, I give one-half of my goods to the poor, and if I have defrauded anyone of anything, I restore it fourfold" (Lk. 19:8).

How strongly our Lord felt about the subject of poverty is revealed to us in the parable which He preached concerning Dives and Lazarus. We read in the Gospel of St. Luke:

> There was a certain rich man who used to clothe himself in purple and fine linen, and who feasted every day in splendid fashion. And there was a certain poor man, named Lazarus, who lay at his gate, covered with sores, and longing to be filled with the crumbs that fell from the rich man's table; even the dogs would come and lick his sores. And it came to pass that the poor man died and was borne away by the angels into Abraham's bosom; but the rich man also died and was buried in hell. And lifting up his eyes, being in torments, he saw Abraham afar off and Lazarus in his bosom. And he cried out and said, "Father Abraham, have pity on me, and send Lazarus to dip the tip of his finger in water and cool my tongue, for I am tormented in this flame."
>
> But Abraham said to him, "Son, remember that you in your lifetime have received good things, and Lazarus in like manner evil things; but now here he is comforted whereas you are tormented. And besides all that, between us and you a great gulf is fixed, so that they who wish to pass over from this side to you cannot, and they cannot cross from your side to us." (16:19-26)

Speaking of Lazarus, St. John Chrysostom exclaimed: "Whoever you are, rich or poor, you saw him despised in the rich man's vestibule; now look at him radiant in Abraham's bosom. You saw him when he was lying at the gate, surrounded by dogs which licked his sores; now contemplate him surrounded by the angels. Then you saw him in the most squalid poverty; now look at him among the sweetest delights. You saw him in hunger; now look at him with an abundance of every good. You saw him in the struggle; now observe him as the crowned victor. You saw his afflictions; now see his reward."

For those who bear poverty patiently, a great reward is undoubtedly prepared. But this fact does not excuse us from doing all we can to help the poor.

Mindful of the exhortations and actions of her Founder in this regard, the Church has always tried to better the lot of the poor. Particularly is this true of the saints. We could give many examples but will content ourselves with one—that of St. Richard.

The youth Richard almost singlehandedly supported the family after his parents' early death. His love for study took second place as he tackled hard labor. Years went by, and Richard turned everything over to his brother, leaving for Oxford University. There he began to satisfy his thirst for learning, proceeding also to Paris and Bologna. Upon his return to Oxford he was asked by the Archbishop of Canterbury, St. Edmund Rich, to become his chancellor. The ailing archbishop had to face Henry III's tactics concerning bishoprics and Church revenues. Richard assisted his archbishop in many ways until the latter's death, retiring then to a Dominican house of studies, where he was ordained in 1243.

Elected to the See of Chichester against Henry III's wishes, Richard was consecrated by Pope Innocent IV on March 5, 1245. The king refused him his revenues and his house. But the homeless bishop was given refuge by the good priest, Simon of Tarring. Richard spent two years as a missionary bishop, travelling his entire diocese on foot, visiting fisherfolk and workmen. He corrected abuses and became loved as a father by all. When Henry finally restored his bishopric to him, Richard made use of it only to help the poor. When chided for the fact that his alms exceeded his income, he gave the order to sell all his gold and silver dishes, adding, "Take my horse, too; he's in good condition, and we should get a good price for him. The money will go for the poor." In addition to his many duties, he was asked by the Pope to preach a crusade. Fever seized him on this journey and the fifty-five-year-old bishop died at a house for poor priests and pilgrims. His canonization took place only nine years later.

The subject of global poverty was discussed in depth by the Fathers of the Second Vatican Council. During one of the sessions, Valerian Cardinal Gracias of Bombay, India, made the following strong statement:

"Let me remind you of some facts, facts which are indeed grim. I quote from a recent publication (*Christian Responsibility and World Poverty*). 'In the underdeveloped countries, 150,000,000 families are living in sub-human conditions; two-thirds of the population of the world are not receiving the 2500 calories daily, considered to be a vital minimum; infant mortality still stands at 185 per 1000 in India and the expectation of life of the new-born is only thirty-two years in India. The nineteen richest countries representing together only 16% of the world's population control 75% of the world's income. In the underdeveloped countries, 150,000,000 families are living under sub-human conditions and 30,000,000 in countries called prosperous. India has an illiteracy percentage of 83.4%.'"

Moved by considerations of this nature, the Council Fathers vehemently urged improvement of these appalling conditions. Thus we read in the *Constitution on the Church in the Modern World*:

Never has the human race enjoyed such an abundance of wealth, resources and economic power, and yet a huge proportion of the world's citizens are still tormented by hunger and poverty, while countless numbers suffer from total illiteracy (n. 4).

God intended the earth with everything contained in it for the use of all human beings and peoples. Thus, under the leadership of justice and in the company of charity, created goods should be in abundance for all in like manner. Whatever the forms of property may be, as adapted to the legitimate institutions of peoples, according to diverse and changeable circumstances, attention must always be paid to this universal destination of earthly goods. In using them, therefore, man should regard the external things that he legitimately possesses not only as his own but also as common in the sense that they should be able to benefit not only him but also others. On the other hand, the right of having a share of earthly goods sufficient for oneself and one's family belongs to everyone.

The Fathers and Doctors of the Church held this opinion, teaching that *men are obliged to come to the relief of the poor and to do so not merely out of their superfluous goods.* If one is in extreme necessity, he has the right to procure for himself what he needs out of the riches of others. Since there are so many people prostrate with hunger in the world, this sacred council urges all, both individuals and governments, to remember the aphorism of the Fathers, "Feed the man dying of hunger, because if you have not fed him, you have killed him," and really to share and employ their earthly goods, according to the ability of each, especially by supporting individuals or peoples with the aid by which they may be able to help and develop themselves (n. 69).

The question of poverty weighs constantly and heavily on the mind of the Popes. Since the end of the Council Paul VI has made many references to it.

In October 1968, he spoke thus to a general audience:

The possession and the pursuit of wealth, as an end in itself, as the only guarantee of present welfare and of human fulfillment, is the paralysis of love. The dramas of contemporary sociology prove this, with dark, tragic proofs. They prove that Christian education to poverty can distinguish free and praiseworthy renunciation of temporal goods, inasmuch as they are a hindrance to man in the pursuit and attainment of his ultimate end, which is God, and his immediate end, which is loving and serving his brother, from the lack of those temporal goods which are indispensable to human life, that is from want and hunger, for which it is a duty, it is charity, to provide.

As you see, the topic is becoming wide and complex. We will stop here; at the praise of *poverty,* which *purifies the Church from superfluous and unedifying temporal interests;* which teaches her not to put her heart and her trust in the goods of this world (cf. Lk. 12:20); which turns the Christian away from all theft and dishonest administration, from all illegal and often obsessing speculation; which makes hearts sensitive to the needs and injustice from which so many humble people are suffering, which accustoms everyone to treat persons of a lower social standing as brothers (cf. Jas. 2:1, 16); which rids the heart of so many unimportant worries and restores to it peace and the joy of prayer.

In an address during 1968, Patrick Cardinal O'Boyle drew attention to the existence of widespread poverty in the United States, pointed the finger of blame and urged efforts at assistance. He said:

For some people, the night really is cold and dark, and the talk about "love, sweet love," does sound quite hollow. I mean for the poor.

In a sense, many of us were poor once. When I was a boy in Scranton, a man had to work hard twelve hours a day to make a living. A boy was proud of the new patches on the seat of his pants and he was glad if his dad gave him a dime a week out of the money he earned selling papers.

But we didn't know we were poor. We were happy and in a sense we weren't poor. We didn't have steak or chops often but we didn't starve. We did have a chance to work and a chance to move up the ladder.

Today there are people — too many people — who are really poor, miserably poor. Their poverty is all the worse because they know they're poor, they know how much better off the rest of us are, and they don't know how they can better themselves.

The contrast between poverty and luxury is no mere fact of nature like the difference between winter and summer. To a great extent poverty resulted from injustices in the past and it continues to exist because of injustices we have not yet taken the trouble to end.

> *We forget about the "guilt of the good," the failure of decent people to do the things we ought to do, our apathy in the face of those social evils and injustices we don't find it difficult to live with, evils and injustices we have come to take for granted.*

When our Lord describes the last judgment, He does not condemn people for what they did, but asks them about what they failed to do. And in the parable of the Good Samaritan, Christ is more concerned about the two pious men who passed the victim by as they headed toward church along the road to Jericho than He is about the robbers who had waylaid the traveler.

I think that when we look at the contrast between poverty and affluence, we ought to bear in mind the "guilt of the good." Miserable, hopeless poverty is demoralizing. There is no doubt about it, and that is one of the worst things about such poverty.

Behind a good part of the "guilt of the bad" is poverty, misery, and hopelessness. The report of the National Advisory Commission on Civil Disorders showed that clearly enough. Behind poverty and misery and hopelessness, and worse than the "guilt of the bad," is the "guilt of the good," of the good and decent people who want law and order—quite rightly so—but who don't care enough about the frustration of others who suffer under injustices they see no way of surmounting.

We too often imagine that anything we do about poverty is a matter of charity, of pure benevolence, of sheer generosity. For this reason our consciences don't bother us if we do little or nothing. We think that since we came by what we have honestly, we can justly do as we please with our wealth, even if that is installing a second heated swimming pool while a family living in a basement on the other side of town doesn't even have a cold water faucet to call its own.

I wish to assert very clearly that doing something about stark poverty that still exists in the midst of affluence is not a matter of kindness on our part. It is a matter of *justice.*

In America, one often hears the remark that the poor are such because they have no initiative, that they are too lazy to work. This is as unjust as it is untrue. Not all people have had the same opportunities in life and not all possess the same ability to profit by them when they do present themselves. Most people — even the poorest — have independent principles and would rather work, when work is available, than subsist on doles and hand-outs. Moreover, many less fortunate people have been thrown to the ground and trampled underfoot by the rest of us, ambitious for the better things in life, marching ever upward and onward to higher levels of comfort and luxury within the affluent and status-seeking society. Viewed from this angle the contemptuous objection, "Why don't they stand on their own feet?" aimed at the poor, is baseless.

Race relations

...to promote justice...

...He [God] is "love" as the Apostle John teaches us...

THE CREDO

The difficulty of racial tensions is one that has been very much before the public in recent times. It is a complicated problem with many facets — economic, historical, psychological and political. Irrespective of all this, we must be guided by the words of Christ. Everything that we said when dealing with the great commandment applies, of course, here.

We must always have sympathy for the downtrodden and the forgotten, especially in the matter of basic human rights. A balanced, Christian outlook on questions like these will go a long way towards eliminating the crippling disadvantages under which less fortunate people than ourselves labor. The Second Vatican Council did not explicitly treat the race issue in a separate session; nevertheless, important references were made to it. Here are some excerpts from various documents:

We cannot truly call on God, the Father of all, if we refuse to treat in a brotherly way any man, created as he is in the image of God. Man's relation to God and his relation to men his brothers are so linked together that Scripture says "he who does not love does not know God" (1 Jn. 4:8) (Declaration on Relation of Church to Non-Christian Religions, nn. 4-5).

Christ Himself revealed to us that "God is love" and at the same time taught us that the new command of love was the basic law of human perfection and hence of the world's transformation (Constitution on Church in Modern World, n. 38).

In America the race question has grown to vast, complex and almost insoluble proportions. Yet we must never be deterred by the magnitude of the task but press onward with hope for an ultimate solution. Patrick Cardinal O'Boyle has outlined the following immediate program for us:

We ought to ask ourselves whether a proposal will overcome injustice, and we should not turn it down unless there is a better way to overcome injustice. We should ask whether a proposal really respects the *dignity of people,* whether it will help people who have been pushed down to get on their own feet.

We should look very closely at any program to see whether it is a mere sop to our consciences and a matter of good publicity or whether it is really serious and big enough to do the job. I am beginning more and more to appreciate the importance of public relations, but we need more than a good image, and we have to be careful that we are not just putting a good face on injustice instead of really fighting it.

Therefore, here is part of your job as Christians in today's world. The Church, I mean *you,* must fight injustice not only in the South but also in the North, and we must fight to win. The "guilt of the good" is apathy—that is, not acting as a light of justice in the world.

What I am asserting is that we have some strict obligations in social justice and I do not think we take these obligations nearly seriously enough. The Church has always taught that we have such obligations. In the past hundred years, there has been a series of encyclicals reaffirming, explaining, and applying to new conditions the constant teaching of the Church about justice.

You know these encyclicals. There was Leo XIII's *Rerum Novarum,* on the condition of the laboring classes. Recently, we received Paul VI's *Populorum Progressio,* on development in less developed countries and the obligations of social justice among nations. Pope John XXIII's *Mater et Magistra* was such an excellent treatment of some of these questions that at the time of the council it wasn't considered necessary to go into them as fully as other questions that had not been given such thorough recent treatment. And yet when Pope John's *Mater et Magistra* (Mother and Teacher) appeared, someone said: "Mater, sì; magistra, no!"

I wish to say clearly that such a rejection of the supreme teacher of the Church, the vicar of Christ on earth, is never acceptable. For faithful Catholics it is always: "Mater, sì; magistra, sì."

We love the Church as a mother and listen to her as a teacher, just as we listened to our own mothers when we were children. For when the teacher whom God Himself appointed for mankind speaks to us, we are all children, however clever or expert we may be, however we may pride ourselves on our maturity, and however much we may talk about mankind-become-adult.

"I was eyes to the blind and feet to the lame was

I was a father to the needy." (Job 29:15-16)

The Church has always taught and still teaches that one may never deprive workers of their *fair wage*, enough to live on — that is one of the sins that "cries to heaven for vengeance."

Racial discrimination, which is so deeply tied up with the injustices of poverty in our own land, also is always wrong. Nobody can claim to be a faithful Catholic if he says that citizens may responsibly decide in accord with their consciences that racial discrimination in some circumstances is permissible and indeed necessary to preserve and foster something or other. Racial discrimination is always wrong.

On the other hand, however, the social encyclicals suggest many things that should be done, or might be done, to help bring about justice.

While we labor for the betterment of race relations, we must be careful to avoid violence. As Pope Pius XII so aptly put it:

"Salvation and justice are not to be found in revolution.... Violence has always achieved only destruction, not construction; the kindling of passions, not their pacification; the accumulation of hate and ruin, not the reconciliation of the contending parties. And it has reduced men and parties to the difficult task of rebuilding, after sad experience, on the ruins of discord."

Inspired by God, the Apostle St. John wrote:

Beloved, no new commandment am I writing to you, but an old commandment which you had from the beginning. The old commandment is the word which you have heard. Again, a new commandment I am writing to you, and this is true both in him and in you. Because the darkness has passed away and the true light is now shining.

He who says that he is in the light, and hates his brothers,
is in the darkness still. He who loves his brother abides in
the light, and for him there is no stumbling. But he who
hates his brother is in the darkness, and walks in the dark-
ness, and he does not know whither he goes; because the
darkness has blinded his eyes (1 Jn. 2:7-11).

On one occasion, early in the present century, an elderly Negro lady was struggling to make her way to Union Station in Washington, D.C. She was carrying very heavy bags and evidently was in great difficulty. A white man approached her, took her luggage and escorted her to the depot. Upon arrival, wishing to thank her benefactor, she asked his name. "Theodore Roosevelt, Madam," he replied. It was the President of the United States.

Technology

We confess that the kingdom of God begun here below in the Church of Christ is not of this world whose form is passing, and that its proper growth cannot be confounded with the progress of civilization, of science or of human technology, but that it consists in an ever more profound knowledge of the unfathomable riches of Christ...

THE CREDO

Twentieth century man is prone to believe only in what he can see, touch and measure — in other words, he is motivated to credit only that knowledge which comes to him through the senses, or which he can verify by the laws of chemistry, mathematics and physics.

In his encyclical letter, *Mater et Magistra*, issued May 15, 1961, Pope John drew attention to this state of affairs in the following clear manner:

There is no doubt that when a nation makes *progress in science, technology, economic life, and the prosperity of its citizens*, a great contribution is made to civilization. But all should realize that these things *are not the highest goods, but only instruments for pursuing such goods.*

Accordingly we note with sorrow that in some nations economic life indeed progresses, but that not a few men are there to be found, who have no concern at all for the just ordering of goods. No doubt, these men either completely ignore spiritual values, or put these out of their minds, or else deny they exist. Nevertheless, while they pursue progress in science, technology, and economic life, they make so much of external benefits that for the most part they regard these as the highest goods of life. Accordingly, there are not lacking grave dangers in the help provided by more affluent nations for development of the poorer ones. For among the citizens of these latter nations, there is operative a general awareness of the higher values on which moral teaching rests — an awareness derived from ancient traditional custom which provides them with motivation.

Thus, those who seek to undermine in some measure the right instincts of these peoples, assuredly do something immoral. Rather, those attitudes, besides being held in honor, should be perfected and refined, since upon them true civilization depends (nn. 175-177).

Pope Paul also, in June, 1968, referred to the technological problem when he enumerated the causes of modern
incredulity:

We refer to the technological mentality, which has its roots in
the scientific mentality and which rejoices in its flowering in the
wonderful, innumerable and powerful instruments placed in the
hands of man, proud of his inventions, set free from physical toil and
launched into the realm of science-fiction, where everything seems
understandable and everything seems possible without turning
either in thought or in prayer to a transcendent and mysterious God.

*Mastery over things and natural forces, the primacy at-
tached to practical and useful action, the completely new
mode of life resulting from the manifold applications of
technology deprive man of the memory of God, and extin-
guish in him the need for faith and religion.*

Our predecessor Pius XII, of revered memory, in an admirable
analysis of this subject treated in the Christmas radio message of
1953, spoke of the "technological spirit" with which the modern
mentality is filled. He defined it as "considering life exclusively
for its technological values, as an element and factor in technology."

And again: The "technological concept of life is therefore nothing else than a particular form of materialism insofar as it offers a
mathematical formula and utilitarian calculations as the ultimate
answer to the question of existence."

But if this, as the council acknowledged, "often complicates the
the approach to God" (Pastoral Constitution on the Church in the
Modern World, n. 19), it does not in itself obstruct it, rather it should
make it easier through the stimulation of the discovery of the existen-
tial depths of nature and through the experience of human intelligence that does not invent such depths but discovers them and
makes use of them.

In order to be able to appreciate the true values of religion, the Holy Father counseled men to cultivate the art of
correct thinking. And correct thinking demands that they approach the entire subject with an open mind. By doing this,
and with God's help, they would arrive at a proper evaluation
of the things of the spirit.

**It is this same love which induces the Church to concern
herself constantly about the true temporal welfare of men.**

THE CREDO

From what has been said, the student must not conclude
that the Church is the enemy of progress and science. Far
from it. It is the duty of the Church to point out where tech-

nology ends and God begins. If she did not do so, she would be denying her divine mission. This attitude is clearly expressed in Pope Paul's encyclical letter, *On the Development of Peoples*, issued March 26, 1967:

Founded to establish on earth the kingdom of heaven and not to conquer any earthly power, the Church clearly states that the two realms are distinct, just as the two powers, ecclesiastical and civil, are supreme, each in its own domain. But, since the Church lives in history, she ought to scrutinize the signs of the times and interpret them in the light of the Gospel. Sharing the noblest aspirations of men and suffering when she sees them not satisfied, she wishes to help them attain their full flowering, and that is why she offers men what she possesses as her characteristic attribute: a global vision of man and of the human race (nn. 12, 13).

Not only this — the Church positively lauds the advances of science. We read in *Mater et Magistra* of Pope John XXIII:

The Church has always taught and continues to teach that advances in science and technology and the prosperity resulting therefrom, are truly to be counted as good things and regarded as signs of the progress of civilization. But the Church likewise teaches that goods of this kind are to be judged properly in accordance with their natures: they are always to be considered as *instruments for man's use,* the better to achieve his highest end: that he can the more easily improve himself, in both the natural and supernatural orders (n. 246).

Pope John actually encouraged Christians to become a part of the technological age and to influence it from within. We read in *Pacem in Terris,* another encyclical letter of Pope John XXIII:

"In order to imbue civilization with sound principles and enliven it *with the spirit of the Gospel,* it is not enough to be illumined with the gift of faith and enkindled with the desire of forwarding a good cause. For this end it is necessary to take an active part in the various organizations and influence them from within. And since our present age is one of outstanding scientific and technical progress and excellence, one will not be able to enter these organizations and work effectively from within unless he is scientifically competent, technically capable and skilled in the practice of his own profession."

Pope Paul has sincerely re-echoed all this. Addressing a scientific group on April 27, 1968, he said:

Behold in what light the council views your vocation as researchers: "Indeed, whoever labors to penetrate the secrets of reality with a humble and steady mind, is, even unawares, being led by the hand of God, who holds all things in existence, and gives them their identity." These words are read in the *Constitution on the Church in the Modern World*, which devotes an entire chapter to the problem of culture. Analyzing the developments of that culture, the conciliar document does not hesitate to make note, with great satisfaction, of the positive acquisitions due to the present progress of science and technology, and it mentions explicitly "scientific study and strict fidelity toward truth in scientific research, the necessity of working together with others in technical groups, a sense of international solidarity, an ever clearer awareness of the responsibility of experts to aid men and even to protect them, the desire to make the conditions of life more favorable for all, especially for those who are deprived of the opportunity to exercise responsibility or who are culturally poor" (Constitution on Church in Modern World, nn. 36, 57). The conciliar document indeed puts Christians on guard against the peril of a purely earthly humanism; but it shows them at the same time how the faith that they profess, "in no way decreases, but rather increases, the weight of their obligation to work with all men in constructing a more human world (ibid. n. 57).

Contemplation of the unique though different roles of religion and science should be a source of extreme consolation and encouragement to us. Not only does God tell us to love and worship Him, He also commands us to "subdue the earth" (cf. Gen. 1:28). For this reason there is a trend in modern Catholic theology to note God's influence and man's response to it, not merely in the religious field, but in the secular city as well, in the effort man makes here to improve life and unravel the secrets of the cosmos. Who knows, but it may be God's design that man should people the other planets of the solar system — those celestial bodies at least which give a chance for survival. In truth then, the Kingdom of God begins here below and begets in us, in the words of the Credo of Pope Paul:

The Church's proper growth...consists of...an ever stronger hope in eternal blessings, an ever more ardent response to the love of God, and an ever more generous bestowal of grace and holiness among men.   THE CREDO

Though the picture may be blurred in many places, still the Holy Father is very optimistic. He expressed himself thus on this point on April 17, 1968:

Yes, we Christians should not feel more unhappy than others, because we have agreed to bear the yoke of Christ — that yoke which He bears with us and which, therefore, He defines as being: "easy, and my burden light" (Mt. 11:30). We should be happier, precisely because we have splendid and safe reasons to be so. The salvation which Christ merited for us, and with it the light on the most arduous problems of our life, gives us the right to look on everything with optimism.

We are better equipped than others who are deprived of the Gospel light, to look at the panorama of the world and of life with joyous wonder and to enjoy all that life holds in store for us, including the trials in which it abounds, with a grateful and informed serenity.

The Christian is a fortunate person. The Christian knows how to find the reasons for God's goodness in every event, in every phase of history and of experience. And he knows that "all things work together unto good for those who, according to His purpose, are saints through his call" (cf. Rom. 8:28).

The Christian should always give witness of superior assurance, which will let others see where he gets such a serene spiritual superiority: from Christ's joy.

Fortunately, this attitude of a happy vigor of soul today is spreading among modern Christians; they are freer (more unconstrained) and more cheerful than in the past. And this is good.

However, let this be so on the condition that they will not fall into a jolly naturalism, which can easily become pagan and illusory. It is a condition that one must derive his inner joy and his external serenity from the faith and not so much as from fortunate contingencies of temporal well-being.

Christ is our happiness. We repeat to His honor and to our comfort: Alleluia!

War

The Church urges her children...to promote...peace and brotherhood among men. THE CREDO

When dealing with the beatitudes we did not discuss the saying of Christ: "Blessed are the peacemakers, for they shall be called the children of God" (Mt. 5:9). The topic of peace can best be dealt with in conjunction with that of war, so here we will go into detail about them both.

Since the day that Cain slew his brother Abel (cf. Gen. 4:1-16), there has been strife among men. Hatred spread, so that it became a question of family against family, of tribe against tribe, of nation against nation. No century has been free from wars, and the more civilization progresses, the more deadly become the weapons. In earlier times, combats were decided by the bow and arrow. Today, millions of people as far apart as New York and Moscow are threatened with instant incineration by thermonuclear bombardment. "War," said Napoleon grimly, and no one knew better than he, "is the science of destruction."

The ideal would be to abolish all wars. Given the condition of human nature, this is hardly likely to occur. Failing this, the next best thing would be to localize them as much and as quickly as possible, lest they consume the world in an inextinguishable conflagration. No effort should be spared, of course, to prevent their outbreak by peaceful means: the calling together of possible warring parties to discuss their differences in an atmosphere of friendly trust and with good will on each side.

Pope Paul has proved himself a sincere advocate of true and lasting peace. He traveled to the United Nations in New York and issued an impassioned plea for it. *"Never again war!"* he cried out. *"Never again!"* Pope Paul's predecessor, Pope John, was also an ardent apostle of peace.

The Fathers of the Second Vatican Council were very much preoccupied with the danger of war and the threat it presents to human survival. It is true that no separate paper was devoted to the subject, but there are weighty references to it scattered throughout the Council documents. For instance, we read in the *Pastoral Constitution on the Church in the Modern World:*

Insofar as men are sinful, the threat of war hangs over them, and hang over them it will until the return of Christ. But insofar as men vanquish sin by a union of love, they will vanquish violence as well and make these words come true: "They shall turn their swords into plough-shares, and their spears into sickles. Nation shall not lift up sword against nation, neither shall they learn war any more" (Is. 2:4). Certainly, war has not been rooted out of human affairs. As long as the danger of war remains and there is no competent and sufficiently powerful authority at the international level, governments cannot be denied the right to legitimate defense once every means of peaceful settlement has been exhausted. State authorities and others who share public responsibility have the duty to conduct such grave matters soberly and to protect the welfare of the people entrusted to their care. But it is one thing to undertake military action for the just defense of the people, and something else again to seek the subjugation of other nations. Nor, by the same token, does the mere fact that war has unhappily begun mean that all is fair between the warring parties.

Those too who devote themselves to the military service of their country should regard themselves as the agents of security and freedom of peoples. As long as they fulfill this role properly, they are making a genuine contribution to the establishment of peace.

Peace is not merely the absence of war; nor can it be reduced solely to the maintenance of a balance of power between enemies; nor is it brought about by dictatorship. Instead, it *is rightly and appropriately called an enterprise of justice.* Peace results from that order structured into human society by its divine Founder, and actualized by men as they thirst after ever greater justice. The common good of humanity finds its ultimate meaning in the eternal law. But since the concrete demands of this common good are constantly changing as time goes on, peace is never attained once and for all, but must be built up ceaselessly...(Constitution on the Church in the Modern World, nn. 78,79).

As individuals we can influence the decisions of men in government, and in our own private lives as Catholics we can do a lot. The Blessed Virgin revealed to the children of Fatima that sin is the cause of all the evils in the world, including wars. She said: "Say the rosary every day to obtain peace for the world and the end of the war." We can always pray for peace, saying the rosary for that intention. We can also say from time to time the beautiful prayer of St. Francis of Assisi for peace as well as that composed by Pope John, both of which follow.

Prayer of St. Francis for peace

Lord, make me an instrument of Your peace.
Where there is hatred, let me sow love;
where there is injury, pardon;
where there is doubt, faith;
where there is despair, hope;

where there is darkness, light;
and where there is sadness, joy.
O Divine Master, grant that
I may not so much seek
to be consoled as to console;
to be understood as to understand;
to be loved as to love;
for it is in giving that we receive;
it is in pardoning that we are pardoned;
and it is in dying that we are born to eternal life.

Prayer of Pope John for peace

May Christ our Peace banish from the hearts of men
whatever might endanger peace.
May He transform them into witnesses
of truth, justice and brotherly love.
May He enlighten the rulers of peoples
so that in addition to their solicitude
for the proper welfare of their citizens,
they may guarantee and defend the great gift of peace.
May He enkindle the wills of all
so that they may overcome the barriers that divide,
cherish the bonds of mutual charity,
understand others,
and pardon those who have done them wrong.
By virtue of His action,
may all peoples of the earth become as brothers,
and may the most longed-for peace blossom forth
and reign always between them.   Pope John XXIII

Salvation and service

The deep solicitude of the Church, the Spouse of Christ, for the needs of men, for their joys and hopes, their griefs and efforts, is therefore nothing other than her great desire to be present to them, in order to illuminate them with the light of Christ...   THE CREDO

We have discussed some of the problems which confront today's Church. We have tried to indicate the attitude of Vatican II towards them, as well as that of Paul VI and Pope John.

The Church wants to be and is by her very nature, *a mother and a teacher.* As Pope John put it in his encyclical *Mater et Magistra:*

It is a question here of the teaching of the Catholic and Apostolic Church, mother and teacher of all nations, whose light illumines, sets on fire, inflames. Her warning voice, filled with heavenly wisdom, reaches out to every age. Her power always provides efficacious and appropriate remedies for the growing needs of men, for the cares and solicitudes of this mortal life. With this voice, the age-old song of the Psalmist is in marvelous accord, to strengthen at all times and to uplift our souls: "I will hear what God proclaims; the Lord—for He proclaims peace to His people, and to His faithful ones, and to those who put in Him their hope. Near indeed is His salvation to those who fear Him, glory dwelling in our land. Kindness and truth shall meet, justice and peace shall kiss. Truth shall spring out of the earth, and justice shall look down from heaven. The Lord Himself will give His benefits; our land shall yield its increase. Justice shall walk before Him, and salvation, along the way of His steps" (Ps. 84:9ff) (n. 262).

Not all the efforts of the Church are appreciated, however, and there is a certain estrangement between her and the world. Pope Paul, most anxious to iron out all the differences, has said that if the Church is to be of service to modern man, she must state her doctrine and position in a way that he can comprehend, simultaneously helping him to solve the problems which trouble him. The Pope stated these views in a general audience held July 12, 1967. He said:

One of the results of the Second Vatican Council, and under certain aspects perhaps the most widespread and the most important, is the conviction that the Church must approach the world in which it lives and in which all of us live.

The Council, with its by now famous *Pastoral Constitution on the Church in the Modern World,* regarding relations which occur and which need to be established between the Church and the contemporary world, has given to the Church a great and difficult commitment, that of re-establishing the bridge between the Church and mankind today.... How to regain the trust of man, the Church asks itself; how to persuade man that the Church is mother to him, his friend, that the Church is necessary to him?

Two words sum up the psychology of the Church in the face of this problem: salvation and service. The Church will try to draw close to mankind once more, offering mankind the salvation of which it is the depository, and the service which mankind needs, and which in a way, only the Church can give to it.

To go to the world! This, therefore, is the mission which the Church, following the Council, proposes to undertake with a new, clear outlook, and with a new spirit of charity and of sacrifice.

Yes, indeed! The Church wishes to be vitally present to twentieth-century men and in the Pope's words:

...to gather them all in Him, their only Savior.   THE CREDO

In all this, however, the Church must keep in mind her specific religious nature. For as the Holy Father again says:

This solicitude can never mean that the Church conform herself to the things of this world, or that she lessen her ardor of her expectation of her Lord and of the eternal kingdom.

The Fathers of Vatican II, in the *Pastoral Constitution on the Church in the Modern World,* put it all very neatly thus:

> *The Church truly knows that only God, whom she serves, meets the deepest longings of the human heart, which is never fully satisfied by what this world has to offer* (n. 41).

CHALLENGE

Those who escaped from God are approaching. I can hear their mournful voices. Out of the darkness there comes a chorus of blasphemous sneers jeering at the followers of Christ: "*Show us by your lives that Christ is really alive.*" I see them, their eyes clouded in darkness, splashed with hatred and with blood; corpses craving for salvation, looking for God but finding only despair.

That unknown God they seek is our Christ! How often have we tried to tell them, but the truth always meets with the same old sarcastic echo: "Only by your lives can you convince us that Christ is alive." We must speak the whole truth to those who have strayed before their smouldering confidence in us is completely extinguished. Speak the truth to them.

Oh no! Tell them nothing! It is useless talking to them. The time has come to act—to act in silence, quietly, with discretion. But it is essential, it is vital, that we act effectively. By our fruits we shall be known. Let no one shirk the serious responsibility which rests upon the shoulders of every man, woman and child baptized into the faith of Christ. Are you ready for action?

Don't let your life be barren. Be useful. Make yourself felt. Shine forth with the torch of your faith and your love. With your apostle's life, wipe out the trail of filth and slime left by the corrupt sowers of hatred. And set aflame all the ways of the earth with the fire of Christ that you bear in your heart.

RICHARD CARDINAL CUSHING, *Show Us by Your Lives That Christ Lives*

13

PRELUDE TO ETERNAL FRIENDSHIP

In the course of time, the Lord Jesus forms His Church by means of the sacraments emanating from His plenitude.

THE CREDO

"Nothing ever happens in my life!" This is a common complaint and sometimes you hear it from men and women or boys and girls whose days seem to be as full as possible. "Nothing exciting ever happens to me!" They are looking for something different, something out of the ordinary — a meeting that will change their lives.

Meetings *are* exciting. The French word for an encounter, *rendezvous,* has a whiff of the mysterious and exciting about it. To think that *someone* is waiting for you, looking for you, counting the minutes until you arrive — this is a great feeling.

Here we come to the reason why life should never be dull, routine, empty. Someone *has* arranged for meetings with us, for a rendezvous that will put life into our existence. These *encounters* are the sacraments. Christ — the Son of God and God Himself! Christ, true God and true man! — is waiting for *me,* each of us can say. He first came to me in Baptism and He followed up that initial encounter with more: in Confirmation, Penance and Holy Communion.

You need at least *two* people for an encounter. And if it is to *mean* something, if it is to make a difference, both parties have to look forward to it and get ready for it. The sacraments, the most marvelous, life-transforming encounters imaginable, will be in many respects, as tremendously meaningful as we let them be. It is up to us to *get ready* for these encounters with Christ. Then life will never be dull!

It is easy to see now the importance of refreshing our minds about the nature of the sacraments, which is what this chapter aims to do.

The word "sacrament" in English derives from the Latin word *sacramentum,* which with the ancient Romans signified a sacred obligation, for example, an oath of allegiance taken by soldiers to serve the state. The meaning of the word gradually underwent a change in the early Church and came to imply any sacred thing that manifested God's power, as well as the workings of grace in the soul. As time passed, this latter came to be the sole and definitive meaning for a while, but gradually it underwent another change, so that it came to be understood in one sense only—an external sign of inward grace, instituted by God for the sanctification of mankind. It is in this final way that it is understood today.

The Council of Trent has defined as an article of faith that there are *seven sacraments*—neither more nor less. Although it is true that nowhere in Scripture are all the seven sacraments specifically designated, yet their institution by Christ can be deduced by inference. Baptism and the Eucharist are clearly mentioned in the New Testament. Confirmation is referred to in Acts 8:15-17. We know of penance from the power to forgive sin conferred by Christ (cf. Jn. 20:22-23). Anointing of the Sick is mentioned by St. James (cf. 5:14-15), Holy Orders by St. Paul (cf. 2 Tim. 1:6) and marriage, again by St. Paul (cf. Eph. 5:25-32). These various texts, taken alone, do not conclusively manifest the exact nature of the sacrament in question, but taken along with Tradition in the Church, which is also the word of God, they form a moral argument for the existence of each sacrament. Another strong proof for the existence of seven sacraments come from the Eastern Orthodox Churches, which have always held to the number seven. Since the roots of these churches go straight back to apostolic antiquity, it is a very sound demonstration indeed.

In each sacrament there are two elements—*matter and form,* or to put it another way, things and words. By things are usually meant common elements, such as water and oil, or even human acts—the imposition of hands at ordination, for example. In the sacrament of matrimony, the matter is the respective persons of both contracting parties. The words (or if you like, the specific formulae) are those uttered by the person administering the sacrament. Thus Baptism consists in the pouring of water on the head of the recipient, saying at the same time the words: "I baptize you, etc." It should be borne in mind that in each case, God has chosen the matter in such a way that it symbolizes outwardly what is really taking place inwardly in the soul. In the physical order, water cleanses; in the supernatural order, used in Baptism, it washes away original sin. Bread nourishes the body in the natural order; the Eucharist nourishes the soul in the spiritual. It is the same for the other sacraments.

The sacraments produce supernatural effects in the soul. *Sanctifying grace* reigns, provided that the subject does not place an obstacle to worthy reception of the sacrament in question. Thus, for anyone to receive the Eucharist in the state of mortal sin would be worthless. It would produce no effect on the soul and really the person so acting would be guilty of sacrilege. There is also a special grace for each sacrament. It is known as *sacramental* grace. Thus, the sacramental grace of Matrimony entitles the parties to receive all those graces from God which are necessary in order that they may live properly in the married state. The same holds for the other sacraments.

The *minister* of the sacraments is usually a priest duly authorized by the Church. But there are exceptions. Thus, any layman or lay woman can administer the sacrament of Baptism in danger of death. Confirmation, which by express order of the Holy See is reserved to the bishop, can be administered by a priest duly delegated. In the case of Matrimony, the ministers of the sacrament are the contracting parties themselves.

By the *subject* of the sacraments is meant the person who is capable of receiving them. Infants—and under this heading come all who have not reached the use of reason—can receive Baptism and Confirmation.

Some sacraments can be received only once. These are Baptism, Confirmation and Orders. They can only be received once because they imprint a character, an indelible mark on the soul. Marriage may be received more than once and, of course, Penance as well as the Eucharist. Anointing of the Sick may also be received more than once, though not within the same illness.

To receive a sacrament validly, one must have the right intention, though obviously this would not hold for the reception of Baptism and Confirmation by infants. To receive a sacrament fruitfully, one must be in the state of grace and free from mortal sin. Two exceptions—Baptism and Penance.

Freed from the slavery of sin and thrust upward by the impulse of grace the human soul lifts itself daringly toward God.

These are designed to raise the soul from the death of sin and, therefore, the state of grace is not necessary for their reception.

The purpose of the sacraments, as we said, is to sanctify men. The *Constitution on the Sacred Liturgy*, issued during Vatican II, brings this out very clearly:

The purpose of the sacraments is to sanctify men, to build up the Body of Christ, and, finally, *to give worship to God;* because they are signs they also instruct. They not only presuppose faith, but by words and objects they also nourish, strengthen, and express it; that is why they are called "sacraments of faith." They do indeed impart grace, but, in addition, the very act of celebrating them most effectively disposes the faithful to receive this grace in a fruitful manner, to worship God duly, and to practice charity.
It is therefore of the highest importance that the faithful should easily understand the sacramental signs, and should frequent with great eagerness those sacraments which were instituted to nourish the Christian life (n. 59).

The life given us by Jesus in the sacraments is the life of grace — God's life in us — which renders him who possesses it a participant of divine life on earth and prepares him for the superabundance of the life of glory in heaven (cf. Jn. 10:10).

What an irreparable disappointment we would have at the judgment, if we should labor all our life, but not in the grace of God! Yet this is given such little thought!... What blindness! The merits and eternal glory are lost....

And what must we do to preserve the grace of the sacraments? We must go to confession and receive Holy Communion often, pray and correspond with one's own actions, do good and avoid evil, because as St. Augustine says, "He who has created us without us, will not save us without our cooperation."

Through grace, man ceases to be weak and vain and becomes, we would almost say, a God" (St. Jerome). Man, then, is elevated not to the angelic, but to the divine order. Let us therefore, greatly esteem grace and the means to receive it, that is, the sacraments and prayer.

Prayer is the elevation of our mind to God. But if our mind thinks of something else while our mouth prays, can we say that it is elevated to God? Certainly not. Although God is so good and condescending, nevertheless there are certain rules to be followed which cannot be neglected when treating with

Him, if we wish to obtain what we ask. "As you prepare your-self to appear before God, in prayer, so God will show Him-self to you; as He will find you, so you will find Him. God alone is never sought in vain, and when He is sought with hope, He is always found" (St. Bernard).

In Matthew 6:9, Jesus teaches us to pray: *Therefore shall you pray: Our Father...:* Our Father and not my Father, be-cause Jesus wants that each one should pray for all, as He be-came flesh, suffered and died for all; and in Him all of us form one Mystical Body. Praying for all, we also participate in ev-eryone's prayers. How beautiful and consoling is this invisible but real communication among the members of the Church! The Our Father is the prayer taught and recommended by Jesus Christ, which is therefore called the Lord's Prayer. The Our Father is the most excellent prayer, because it issued from the mind and heart of Jesus Christ, and in seven brief requests contains that which we must ask of God as His children and as brothers among ourselves. Jesus Christ made us invoke God as our Father to remind us that God is truly everyone's Father, especially of us Christians who in Baptism, were adopted by Him as His sons; and to inspire in us great love for and trust in Him. What an honor it is for us to call God our Father! But let us not forget that to call God our Father im-plies that we are obliged to conduct ourselves as children of God, so that, if we are happy to have God as our Father, He will be happy to have us as His children. Jesus said: "'What-soever you shall ask the Father in my name, you shall receive it': how much more efficaciously then will we receive that which we ask in the name of Christ if we pray with His own words?" (St. Cyprian)

Pope Paul beautifully explained what it means to be in the state of grace:

The state of grace is that quality in which the soul is enfolded when the new, supernatural relationship into which God wishes to elevate the man who abandons himself to Him is established — in the effort of conversion, in confident readiness to serve, in the accept-ance of His word through faith, in humble, imploring love, to which infinite love, which God Himself, immediately answers with the fire of the Holy Spirit.

Grace is a divine Presence, which pours into the soul that is made into a temple for the Spirit: it is an extraordinary per-manence of the living God in the humblest life, struck by an ineffable and divine light. There is no way to define fully the state of grace. It is a gift, riches, beauty, a wonderful transfiguration of the soul associated with the life of God Himself, by which to a certain extent we share in His transcendant nature. It means being elevated to the position of adopted sons of the celestial Father, of brothers of Christ, of living members of the Mystical Body through the animation of the Holy Spirit. It is a personal relationship; but think — a personal relationship between the living God, mysterious and inaccessible in His infinite power, and our base persons. It is a relationship that should become conscious.

Only the pure in heart can tell us something about it. It does not fall within the sphere of sentient experience, although the educated conscience acquires a certain spiritual sensibility; it feels within itself the "fruits of the spirit," of which St. Paul made a long list: "love, joy, peace" (especially these: interior joy and then peace, a tranquil conscience), "patience, goodness, longsuffering, meekness, faith, modesty, temperance and chastity" (Gal. 5:22): we seem to glimpse the picture of a saint. This is grace; this is the transfiguration of a man who lives in Christ.

No wonder if this condition, in itself strong and permanent ("nothing can separate us from the love of God," says St. Paul, Rom. 8:39), is, all the same, delicate and demanding. It projects over the mortal life of man special duties, very fine sensibilities; and fortunately it instills, too, new and suitable energies, so that the balance of this supernatural position may be firm and joyful. But the fact remains that it can be disturbed and upset when, unhappily, we despise it, and prefer to sink to the level of our corrupted and animal nature; when we voluntarily detach ourselves from the order to which God has associated us, from His life that flows through ours, when we commit a real and deliberate sin, which, when serious, we therefore call mortal....

By these [sacraments] she makes her members participants in the Mystery of the death and resurrection of Christ, in the grace of the Holy Spirit who gives her life and movement. THE CREDO

To sum up then, we can classify the sacraments as loving creations of the heart of Jesus through which He encounters us and gives us a share, even on this earth, in the divine life of God Himself, which is a prelude and preparation for fulfillment of heavenly bliss.

With Baptism, Jesus unites us to Himself and causes us to be born to the life of grace by which we are "called children of God; and such we are" (1 Jn. 3:1).

In Confirmation He strengthens this supernatural life in us and brings it to full maturity.

In the Holy Eucharist, He makes Himself the food of our souls and strengthens us against the attacks of our enemies: "O saving Victim," sings the Church: "O saving Victim, opening wide the gates of heaven to man below, our foes press on from every side; Your aid supply, Your strength bestow."

In the sacrament of Penance, our Lord gives us the embrace of His forgiveness and the restoration of that divine life when we have had the misfortune to lose or diminish it by sin.

Finally, in the Anointing of the Sick He comes to visit us when we are seriously ill and comforts us, sometimes even restoring us to health or else, if our hour has come, preparing us for the all-important passage into eternity.

While these five sacraments are ordered to our personal sanctification, the other *two* have a social character as well. Jesus instituted them expressly for the good of the Christian community. In fact, with the sacrament of Matrimony Jesus gives the Church holy parents and families modeled on that of Nazareth. With the sacrament of Orders, He provides the Church with shepherds who are His ministers and who will perpetuate His eucharistic presence in the world till the end of time.

There also exist what are known as *sacramentals.* They are defined as actions or things which the Church is accustomed to use, to obtain certain effects—chiefly of a spiritual nature—by her prayers. Among the sacramentals are liturgical prayers, and rites used in administration of the sacraments themselves, exorcisms, various blessings, (of persons or objects). The *Constitution on the Sacred Liturgy* refers to their efficacy and that of the sacraments as follows:

Holy Mother Church has, moreover, instituted *sacramentals.* These are sacred signs which bear a resemblance to the sacraments: they signify effects, particularly of a spiritual kind, which are obtained through the Church's intercession. By them men are disposed to receive the chief effect of the sacraments, and various occasions in life are rendered holy.

Thus, for *well-disposed members of the faithful,* the liturgy of the sacraments and sacramentals signifies almost every event in their lives; they *are given access to the stream of divine grace which flows from the paschal mystery* of the passion, death, the resurrection of Christ, the font from which all sacraments and sacramentals draw their power. There is hardly any proper use of material things which cannot thus be directed toward the sanctification of men and the praise of God (nn. 60, 61).

CHALLENGE

How can a life remain mediocre which is called to communion with the life of Christ? How can one ever become
bored with life or remain indifferent to action when he has
received a place in Christ's own purpose, a destiny identified with the destiny of God's own Son?

Never complain that you have nothing to live for, nothing
worth dying for, nothing to love. The trouble with our lives
as Christians is that, while we profess to believe Christ worth
living and dying for, while we declare Christ and His kingdom
to be the purpose of our lives, in point of fact we rarely give
Him the dominant place in our scheme of things. We seek the
same purposes, we respond to the same motives, we give ourselves up to the same interests and live by the same limited
values as those who have never heard of Christ and have felt
no call to His kingdom.

If once we would overthrow Self or Sin or whatever false
god dominates us in order to sincerely and completely make
Christ our true center of gravity, the point of our lives, the
supreme object of our striving, the purpose inspiring us, how
changed we would be! How changed the Church would be!
How changed the world would be!—changed as only *Christ*
can change things.

RICHARD CARDINAL CUSHING, *The Purpose of Living*

14

THE
NEW
MAN

Born again

We believe in one Baptism instituted by our Lord Jesus Christ for the remission of sins.

THE CREDO

Anniversaries are special occasions only when the people involved are still glad the original event took place. A couple who became engaged last year but are on the verge of breaking up certainly won't celebrate the anniversary of their engagement!

When we celebrate someone's birthday, it's a way of saying that we're glad he or she was born. When a man takes his wife out to dinner on their wedding anniversary, it's his way of telling her how glad he is that she married him. The love that is *a real thing in the here and now* makes people celebrate events of the past. They will never forget the wonderful occasion which made possible their present happiness!

Today in catechetical classes students are being urged to celebrate each year the anniversary of their Baptism. The reason is obvious. Baptism was the beginning of our life with Christ, the day He claimed us for His own. He has never regretted it either, even though He may have seen us quite forgetful at times of our relationship to Him. We have every reason, then, to rejoice when we recall our Baptism; it was really a great day.

Something wonderful began then which is still going strong. And Confirmation strengthened that love between Christ and us, that bond of unity, that unique relationship.

We're glad these events are part of our personal history. And in order to appreciate ever better the *present* relationship we have with Christ, it helps to ponder again the significance of those great events.

"Remember, O Christian," said St. Leo the Great, "that upon receiving Baptism you become the temple of the Holy Spirit. Take care not to put Him out with sin and do not renew your slavery to the devil, because you cost the blood of Jesus Christ."

The English word "baptism" comes from the Greek word *baptizo*, meaning "I wash." It is defined in theology as "a sacrament of the New Law instituted by Christ, in which, through the external ablution of water, with the invocation of the most holy Trinity, a person is spiritually regenerated and signed as a disciple of Christ."

During the discourse with Nicodemus, Christ Himself spoke of this sacrament. We read in the third chapter of St. John's Gospel:

There was a certain man among the Pharisees, Nicodemus by name, a ruler of the Jews. This man came to Jesus at night, and said to him, "Rabbi, we know that you have come a teacher from God, for no one can work these signs that you work unless God be with him." Jesus answered and said to him, "Amen, amen, I say to you, unless a man be born again, he cannot see the kingdom of God." Nicodemus said to him, "How can a man be born when he is old? Can he enter a second time into his mother's womb and be born again?"

Jesus answered, "Amen, amen, I say to you, unless a man be born again of water and the Spirit, he cannot enter into the kingdom of God. That which is born of the flesh is flesh; and that which is born of the Spirit is spirit. Do not wonder that I said to you, 'You must be born again.' The wind blows where it will, and you hear its sound but do not know where it comes from or where it goes. So is everyone who is born of the Spirit" (3:1-8).

After the resurrection He commissioned the apostles to go forth as follows:

All power in heaven and on earth has been given to me. Go, therefore, and make disciples of all nations, *baptizing them* in the name of the Father, and of the Son, and of the Holy Spirit. (Mt. 28:18-19)

And we read in St. Mark :

He who believes and is baptized shall be saved, but he who does not believe shall be condemned. (Mk. 16:16)

Only true and natural water *is valid matter* for conferring the sacrament of Baptism. As Christ Himself said to Nicodemus, "Unless a man be born again of *water* and the Spirit, he cannot enter into the kingdom of God" (Jn. 3:5). Thus, liquids such as wine, milk, blood, coffee, tea are not valid matter.

For the *lawful* (as distinct from the *valid)* conferring of baptism, baptismal water must be used, i.e., water especially blessed for this purpose on Holy Saturday. In danger of death, of course, where this baptismal water is not available, ordinary water would suffice. The sacrament can be administered in any of three ways — by immersion, by aspersion or sprinkling, or by infusion or pouring. This latter method is the one in common use in the Latin or Western Church. In baptizing, care must be taken that *the water touches the skin, that it flows, that it be poured on the head of the person* since this is the principal part of the body, *and that the words of the form be uttered during the act of pouring the water.*

The words of the form must include four things: the distinct invocation of the Three Divine Persons of the Trinity, the act of baptizing or washing, the subject who is receiving the sacrament, and the person who is conferring it. All these are taken care of by the recital of the words: "(John), I baptize you in the name of the Father and of the Son and of the Holy Spirit." The word "Amen" is not used at the end.

The first effect of Baptism is to imprint a character on the soul, which is the indelible spiritual imprint that consecrates the believer, with a certain priestly power, to the worship of God and makes him a member of the Mystical Body of Christ. The second effect is to confer sanctifying grace on the recipient. This latter is also called "regenerative grace," because in the case of children it wipes out original sin, and in the case of adults, not only original sin, but all actual sins as well, and the penalties due to these latter.

Speaking of these effects of the sacrament, St. Augustine says: "The gift of *Baptism is an antidote against original sin,* so that what is contracted by birth should by a second birth be taken away. *Baptism, too, takes away whatever actual sins have been committed prior to it* in thought, word and deed."

The *Dogmatic Constitution on the Church* of Vatican II also refers to the effects of Baptism in these words:

The baptized, by regeneration and the anointing of the Holy Spirit, are consecrated as a spiritual house and a holy priesthood, in order that through all those works which are those of the Christian man they may offer spiritual sacrifices and proclaim the power of Him who has called them out of darkness into His marvelous light. Therefore all the disciples of Christ, persevering in prayer and praising God, should present themselves as a living sacrifice, holy and pleasing to God. Everywhere on earth they must bear witness to Christ and give an answer to those who seek an account of that hope of eternal life which is in them (n. 10).

There are two other forms of Baptism which do not imprint an indelible character on the soul as the sacrament of Baptism by water does. These are Baptism by blood and Baptism of desire. They also remove original sin from the soul and make it possible to enter heaven.

Baptism of blood is martyrdom for the sake of Christ. One who freely sacrifices his life as a witness for Jesus is assured of salvation by our Lord: "He that shall lose his life for me, shall find it." (Mt. 10:39) A person willing to give up his life rather than deny Christ would wish to receive Baptism of water if it were possible.

Baptism of desire springs from *perfect love of God.* One who loves God perfectly desires to do all that God commanded for salvation. However, a person through no fault of his own may not know that God has made it obligatory to be baptized in order to be saved. Hence, he does not explicitly desire Baptism as does a convert preparing to receive the sacrament. Nevertheless, his love for God and conformity to the divine will contains an implicit desire for Baptism. This desire supplies for Baptism of water if the person dies without the latter. Christ said: "He who loves me, shall be loved by my Father, and I will love him and will manifest myself to him" (Jn. 14:21). Apart from martyrdom, the sacrament of Baptism either in fact or in desire is absolutely necessary for salvation. *Christ gave no other positive means by which we may enter His kingdom.* And the Baptism *of water* is absolutely necessary for the *valid* reception of *all other* sacraments.

The *ordinary minister* of Baptism is a priest. Its extraordinary minister is a deacon. As has already been pointed out, in case of necessity, any lay person, man or woman can administer it. This latter is certain doctrine, proved by the common practice of the Church and also from the Councils of Lateran IV and Florence.

Baptism should be administered even to little children who have not yet been able to be guilty of any personal sin, in order that, though born deprived of supernatural grace, they may be reborn "of water and the Holy Spirit" to the divine life in Christ Jesus.

THE CREDO

The subject of Baptism, i.e., the person capable of receiving the sacrament, is any person not already baptized. Baptism is a sacrament necessary for salvation, and this has been made an article of faith by the Council of Trent. In order that adults may receive Baptism validly and fruitfully, they should have the right intention, be properly instructed in Christian doctrine and should be sorry for their sins. It is certain that an explicit intention suffices, i.e., not only an actual or virtual intention, but even an habitual one, once expressed and never retracted. Thus a person who is known to be of this frame of mind, even though unconscious and in danger of death, can be lawfully baptized.

Persons who have been baptized in non-Catholic religions are usually baptized conditionally when they are received into the Catholic Church since it is extremely difficult in most cases to be sure that the requirements of a valid administration of Baptism were fulfilled in non-Catholic Baptism. (The Greek Orthodox are an exception.)

Converts are baptized conditionally in this way: "If you are not baptized, I baptize you in the name of the Father, and of the Son, and of the Holy Spirit." In other words, the priest leaves the entire matter up to God. If the former Baptism was not valid, the sacrament is now actually received.

The absolute necessity of Baptism for salvation explains conditional Baptism. The Church will not take a chance.

God does not punish with the torments of hell infants or those without the use of reason who die with only original sin. On the other hand, this soul does not possess grace and so cannot enter heaven.

The souls of unbaptized children do not suffer the pain of sense or fire because they did not deliberately turn from God. They enjoy a merely *natural happiness* in a place called limbo.

Parents should not neglect to have a child baptized as soon as possible after birth. If the infant dies without Baptism because of this neglect, the parents are responsible before God for depriving a soul of the *supernatural end* for which it was created. St. Cyprian says:

"If even to those who are very grave sinners and those who sinned much against God, when they have subsequently believed, forgiveness of sins is granted, and nobody is prevented from Baptism and from grace, how much more should an infant not be prevented who, newly born, has not sinned except that, being born according to the flesh according to Adam, he has contracted the contagion of the ancient death at the very first moment of his birth, who approaches the more easily on this very account to the reception of the forgiveness of sins, because to him are forgiven, not his own sins, but the sins of another."

Furthermore, it must not be supposed that our Lord would withhold the sacrament and grace of Baptism from children of whom we read in the Gospel: And they were bringing little children to him that he might touch them, but the disciples rebuked those who brought them. But when Jesus saw them, he was indignant and said to them, *"Let the little children be, and do not hinder them from coming to me, for of such is the kingdom of heaven.... Amen I say to you, unless you turn and become like little children, you will not enter into the kingdom of heaven."* And he put his arms about them, and laying his hands upon them, he began to bless them. (cf. Mt. 19:14-15; 18:3)

Let us take to heart this wise admonition of St. Gregory Nazianzen:

"Have you an infant? Do not let sin get an opportunity, but let him be sanctified from his childhood; from his most tender age let him be consecrated by the Spirit."

It is a good custom to renew our Baptismal vows privately from time to time.

> *O Christ, in whom all human life is grafted,*
> *You have given me a share in divine life*
> *through the wonderful sacrament of Baptism.*
> *To do this, you came down from heaven,*
> *became man, died and rose again in triumph*
> *over the death of sin.*
> *By Baptism, I became a member*
> *of Your Mystical Body, the Church.*
> *I promised to avoid sin and follow You.*

"Grace is a divine presence; it is an extraordinary permanence of the living God in the humblest life."

(Paul VI)

Help me to live my commitment always
by the grace of Your other sacraments.
Then, one day I too will rise to eternal glory.

Forming Christian athletes

Confirmation is a true and proper sacrament of the New Law. In the Acts of the Apostles there are at least two references to the conferring of this sacrament—Acts 8:12-18 and Acts 19:1-6. The remote matter of Confirmation is *chrism* blessed by the bishop. This is certain from the Council of Florence which laid it down that chrism is *a mixture of oil and balsam.* The oil should be olive oil, for the oil used in apostolic times was of this nature. Balsam is a perfumed spice taken from certain trees.

There is a special significance attached to this mixture. Athletes were always rubbed with it before engaging in sports contests. The spiritual significance at once becomes obvious. The Christian is an athlete engaged in a much more vital struggle, a duel to the death with the powers of darkness and with himself, for the weakness of his own fallen nature tempts him to sin. The inward grace, symbolized by the outward anointing, strengthens him for the contest and is an aid to victory. Balsam, being a perfume, signifies the sweet odor of the virtues which the recipient should practice.

The proximate or immediate matter of the sacrament consists in the actual anointing on the forehead with the chrism along with the imposition of hands which accompanies this action. The form of the sacrament consists in the appropriate use of the special words which accompany application of the matter. They are: "I sign you with the sign of the cross and confirm you with the chrism of salvation, in the name of the Father, and of the Son and of the Holy Spirit."

The first effect of Confirmation is the granting of an habitual grace which strengthens the recipient. The gifts of the Holy Spirit are also infused and he obtains the right to special helps to zealously proclaim his faith. There is also another effect—a character is imprinted on the soul. With regard to Confirmation, the *Dogmatic Constitution on the Church* says:

The faithful are more perfectly bound to the Church by the sacrament of Confirmation, and the Holy Spirit endows them with special strength so that they are more strictly obliged to spread and defend the faith, both by word and by deed, as true witnesses of Christ (n.11).

Millions and millions of martyrs have sacrificed their lives for love of God.

Mary Sulan, a young Chinese school teacher, was one of these. Her first and impressive contact with Christianity was through fellow students, Catholics and members of the Legion of Mary at college. Before she graduated, however, these friends of hers had been arrested and heard of no more. She herself had received Baptism by showing one of her own pagan pupils how to baptize her! Now she was under arrest....

Sulan was not unprepared for prison. She knew the pressure that would be exerted, the periods of torture alternated with periods of "kindness" and "soft treatment." Proud of her faith, she was yet well aware of the dangers she now faced. Perhaps she made her own the prayer said by so many threatened Chinese Catholics:

"O my God, I fear my fear. It may induce me to abandon you.

"O my God, I fear my fear. It may keep me from remaining firm until the end.

"O my God, I beg You not to forget me in Your glory. Fill me with Your love. Give me strength to give up my life for You. Amen."

In May of 1953, when every attempt to persuade this "unbelievably stubborn reactionary" had failed, Sulan was brought before a people's court. Invited once more to sign a "confession" and save her life, she proudly told the story of her Baptism instead.

Before she had finished, an astonished cry interrupted her. "Sulan!" Whirling, she realized that it had come from the other prisoners on the platform. Weakened from the months of prison life, she was afraid her eyes were playing tricks on her. Could it really be the missionary priest and her Legion of Mary friends from Sinceng? Yes! It was they!

All together again, there on a prisoners' platform, the little group received their death sentences with that unflinching serenity that had marked the martyrs before them—from Ignatius of Antioch in a Roman arena to Theophane Venard in Vietnam and the Jesuit martyrs in America.

Thus a courageous young Chinese teacher chose God while surrounded by those who hated Him, and joyfully embraced the faith at a time when it meant death.

In the Latin rite, the ordinary minister of Confirmation is the bishop, but by special delegation, the *extraordinary* minister can be the parish priest. In most Eastern rites, the priest is the ordinary minister.

The subject of Confirmation is any baptized person. It was a practice in the early Church to give Confirmation to infants, since it is the completion of Baptism, but this custom fell into disuse in the West, and Confirmation was deferred to an age considered a more apt time for administering it.

Recommended to the Lord

We have looked at two great gifts of Christ's love, Baptism and Confirmation, gifts whose effects will always be with us. Now we look ahead to the high point of life, to the tremendous moment when Christ will meet us in the Anointing of the Sick to prepare us for our death, which will bring us into *real life* – with Him forever, in heaven.

There are two scriptural passages usually given as proofs that Anointing of the Sick (formerly called Extreme Unction) is truly and properly a sacrament of the New Law, instituted by Christ. One text is taken from St. Mark, the other from St. James. They are as follows:

And he summoned the Twelve and began to send them forth two by two; and he gave them power over the unclean spirits. And going forth, they preached that men should repent, and they cast out many devils, and anointed with oil many sick people, and healed them. (Mk. 6:7, 12-13)

Is any one among you sick? Let him bring in the presbyters of the Church, and let them pray over him, anointing him with oil in the name of the Lord. And the prayer of faith will save the sick man, and the Lord will raise him up, and if he be in sins, they shall be forgiven him. (Jas. 5:13-15)

Tradition is also invoked as an argument for the existence of this sacrament, for it has always been recognized in both East and West. During the first three centuries it must be admitted that testimonies in the writings of the Fathers are few and some of them not very clear. From the fourth to the ninth centuries, however, the references are more precise. Thus – St. Serapion in the fourth century, Pope Innocent I and Victor of Antioch in the fifth, Cassiodorus in the sixth, St. Eligius in the seventh, and the Venerable Bede in the eighth – all testify to the existence of Anointing of the Sick as a sacrament.

St. Caesarius of Arles, who also lived in the sixth century, wrote:

"As soon as some infirmity overtakes him, a sick man should receive the body and blood of Christ, humbly and devoutly ask the presbyter for blessed oil, and anoint his body with it.

Thus will be fulfilled in him what we read (cf. Jas. 5:13). See to it, brethren, that a man hastens to the Church in infirmity, and he will merit to receive both bodily health and the remission of his sins."

The remote matter of this sacrament is oil blessed by the bishop. It must be renewed each year. The proximate matter is the actual anointing of the person with this especial oil. The use of oil is symbolic. Oil is used in medicine for curative purposes. In like manner, external application of oil which has medicinal properties symbolizes the curing of the soul within.

The minister of the sacrament of Anointing of the Sick is a priest.

The primary effect of anointing of the sick is the granting of *a grace which strengthens the soul* against those difficulties which confront it at the hour of death. (To be fruitful, the sacrament must be received in the state of grace.) There is also a secondary effect. It does not always take place, but sometimes it does happen. It is this. The bodily sickness may depart and health be restored to the person who is gravely ill. There is still another effect. Anointing of the Sick *remits venial sins* as well as the penalties due to them. It also takes away mortal sin when the sick person is unconscious or otherwise unaware that he is not properly disposed, but has made an act of imperfect contrition.

The subject of Anointing of the Sick is *any baptized person*, having the use of reason and in danger of death by sickness, accident or old age.

The following quotation from the *Constitution on the Sacred Liturgy* is very important:

"Extreme Unction," which may also and more fittingly be called "anointing of the sick" is not a sacrament for those only who are at the point of death. Hence, as soon as any one of the faithful begins to be in danger of death from sickness or old age, the fitting time for him to receive this sacrament has certainly already arrived (n. 73).

So also is this one from the *Dogmatic Constitution on the Church:*

By the sacred *anointing of the sick* and the prayer of her priests the whole Church commends the sick to the suffering and glorified Lord, asking that He may lighten their suffering and save them; she exhorts them, moreover, to contribute to the welfare of the whole people of God by associating themselves freely with the passion and death of Christ (n. 11).

CHALLENGE

The change that Christ can bring into a life when He becomes its center and when His purpose becomes its inspiration is as radical and as revolutionary as being born all over again. In fact, that is how Christ described the effect that He would have on the lives of those who accept Him literally and completely: *They will be born again* — their dreary, defeated, mediocre lives will be off to a fresh start, *re-created, made entirely new.*

That faith fired the first Christians. St. Paul spoke for them when he said: "If, then, any man is in Christ, he is a new creature; the old things are passed away; behold they are all made new!" The early Christians believed passionately in Christ's power to make all things new, but they realized that before He could do so He would have to become the controlling purpose of their lives, the center of all their thoughts and actions, their loyalty and their love.

We call ourselves *Christians*. The word should mean that Christ is as much a part of us as we are a part of ourselves. It should mean that self and class and family and nation and every other interest which may move a man's heart hold second place to Christ in our lives — we are *renewed* in Him. If we are, though the renewal may be on the hidden level of the soul and of sanctifying grace, its effects will be visible to all; the whole world will be able to witness the change Christ makes in us.

When the purpose that is Christ's dominates the life of a Christian, everything about him is made different. All that he *is* and all that he *does* — all that he is at *home*, all that he does *outside* — all the things and all the people he knows and loves are affected and made better. They are themselves renewed by the contagious power of Jesus Christ at work through the convinced Christian man.

RICHARD CARDINAL CUSHING, *The Purpose of Living*

15

"HE LOVED ME
AND
GAVE HIMSELF
FOR ME"

GALATIANS 2:20

The unique and indivisible existence of the Lord glorious in heaven is not multiplied, but is rendered present by the sacrament in the many places on earth where Mass is celebrated.

Pursued by love

A girl with the missionary ideal deeply rooted in her heart was told that among her college courses she should include a study of the world's great religions. Already familiar with Protestant theology and Biblical studies, having been a serious student of everything her minister had suggested she read, she thought that there would be little in Catholic interpretation of Scripture that would be new.

To her surprise, however, she found herself deeply affected by certain words of Christ—as though she had never read them before: "He who eats my flesh and drinks my blood has life everlasting and I will raise him up on the last day. For my flesh is food indeed, and my blood is drink indeed." (Jn. 6:55-56)

Suddenly those words seemed so obvious, so clear. Christ must have meant exactly what He was saying! She noted that when many of His disciples left Him because they could not accept those plain words in their literal meaning, Christ let them go. He did not retract one word of what He had said. He added nothing to it and subtracted nothing from it. The statement remained as He had uttered it: "My flesh is food indeed and my blood is drink indeed."

That college student did become a missionary but not before the doctrine of Christ's presence in the Eucharist had drawn her to study the Catholic faith further and finally embrace it wholeheartedly. The love of Christ, pouring itself into the sacrament of the Holy Eucharist, became the center of her whole life.

"He loved me and gave Himself for me." It is impossible to understand this Sacrament unless we grasp the depths of the love that invented this extraordinary way of communicating itself. Pope Paul does not hesitate to say:

"We are *pursued* by this ineffable, unrestrainable love. We are well known, well remembered, assailed by this powerful, silent love, that gives us no rest, that wishes to be understood, received, returned. The whole of Christianity is here. *Christianity is the communion to the divine life in Christ with our own life. Christianity means to possess God; and God is charity, God is love.*"

Such a love on the part of Christ calls for the fullest response we know how to give. Such an act of almighty power calls for an act of deep faith from us. We must take Christ *at His word.* Theodore of Mopsuestia, an early witness to the belief of the Church on this point, declared: "The Lord did *not* say: This is a symbol of my body, and this is a symbol of my blood but: *This is my body and my blood.*" He teaches us not to look to the nature of those things which lie before us and are perceived by the senses, for by the prayer of thanksgiving and the words spoken over them at the Consecration of the Mass by the priest, they have been changed into Christ's flesh and blood.

His presence is "for real"

...and we believe that the mysterious presence of the Lord, under what continues to appear to our senses as before, is a true, real and substantial presence.

Christ cannot be thus present in this sacrament except by the change into His body of the reality itself of the bread and the change into His blood of the reality itself of the wine, leaving unchanged only the properties of the bread and wine which our senses perceive. This mysterious change is very appropriately called by the Church "transubstantiation."

THE CREDO

Christ becomes present in the Eucharist through the mystery of transubstantiation, i.e., by the conversion of the total substance of the bread and wine into the body and blood of Christ, the species of these two elements — bread and wine — still remaining.

Before the consecration of the Mass, the substance of bread is there, with the accidents — color, shape, weight, etc. The same holds for the wine. After the words of Consecration have been pronounced, both the substance of the bread and that of the wine mysteriously are changed entirely into the body and blood of Christ. But the accidents (qualities such as color, weight, etc.) remain and these we can still recognize by our senses.

How is this possible? The Church explains it through the omnipotent power of God, who miraculously preserves the accidents in being, even though they have no longer their natural substance of bread and wine in which to inhere. This is known as the doctrine of Transubstantiation which explains what takes place during the holy sacrifice of the Mass at the moment of Consecration.

Christ is whole in the entire sacred Host and whole in all its parts. That is why sometimes you see the priest breaking hosts to communicate to people when a mistake has been made in the number presenting themselves for Holy Communion. Christ is also present in the whole chalice of wine and in each drop of it.

As St. Thomas expressed it in his Eucharistic hymn, sung on the Feast of Corpus Christi:

Not a single doubt retain
When they break the Host in two
That in each part there remains
What was in the whole before.
Since the simple sign alone
Suffers change in state or form
The signified remaining one
And the same for evermore.

Every theological explanation which seeks some understanding ot this mystery must, in order to be in accord with the Catholic faith, maintain that in the reality itself, independently of our mind, the bread and wine have ceased to exist after the Consecration, so that it is the

adorable body and blood of the Lord Jesus that from then on are really before us under the sacramental species of bread and wine, as the Lord willed it...   THE CREDO

Within recent years, certain theories about Christ's Presence in the Eucharist have been advocated which are not in accord with traditional teaching of transubstantiation. In his encyclical, *Mystery of Faith*, Pope Paul referred to them as follows:

"It is not allowable...to exaggerate the element of sacramental *sign* as if the symbolism, which all certainly admit in the Eucharist, expresses fully and exhausts completely the mode of Christ's presence in this sacrament.

"Nor is it allowable to discuss the mystery of transubstantiation without mentioning what the Council of Trent stated about the marvelous conversion of the whole substance of the bread into the body and of the whole substance of the wine into the blood of Christ, speaking rather only of what is called 'transignification' and 'transfiguration,' or finally to propose and act upon the opinion according to which, in the Consecrated Hosts which remain after the celebration of the sacrifice of the Mass, Christ our Lord is no longer present.

"It would therefore be wrong to explain this presence by having recourse to the "spiritual" nature, as it is called, of the glorified Body of Christ, which is present everywhere, or by reducing it to a kind of symbolism, as if this most august Sacrament consisted of nothing else than an efficacious sign, of the spiritual presence of Christ and of His intimate union with the faithful, members of His Mystical Body.

"To avoid misunderstanding this sacramental presence which surpasses the laws of nature and constitutes the greatest miracle of its kind, we must listen with docility to the voice of the teaching and praying Church. This voice, which constantly echoes the voice of Christ, assures us that the way Christ is made present in this Sacrament is none other than by the change of the whole substance of the bread into His Body, and of the whole substance of the wine into His Blood, and that this unique and truly wonderful change the Catholic Church rightly calls *transubstantiation.* As a result of transubstantiation, the species of bread and wine undoubtedly take on a new meaning and a new finality, for they no longer remain ordinary bread and ordinary wine, but become the sign of something sacred, the sign of a spiritual food.

"However, the reason they take on this new significance and this new finality is simply because they contain a new 'reality.' Not that there lies under those species what was already there before, but something quite different; and that not only because of the faith of the Church, but in objective reality, since after the change of the substance or nature of the bread and wine into the body and blood of Christ, nothing remains of the bread and wine but the appearances, under which Christ, whole and entire, in His physical 'reality' is bodily present, although not in the same way that bodies are present in a given place."

...We believe that as the bread and wine consecrated by the Lord at the Last Supper were changed into His body and His blood which were to be offered for us on the cross, likewise the bread and wine consecrated by the priest are changed into the body and blood of Christ enthroned gloriously in heaven.

...[the Mass] is the sacrifice of Calvary rendered sacramentally present on our altars.

THE CREDO

The daily Paschal Mystery

Loving us as much as He does, Christ did not will that the sacrifice of His love should be renewed only year by year, but rather day by day.

Every day the Lord renews the Sacrifice of the Cross to pay for our daily sins. And every day He invites us: "Take and eat, this is my body; he who eats my flesh and drinks my blood has life everlasting" (Mt. 26:26; Jn. 6:55).

The *Constitution on the Sacred Liturgy* says: "At the Last Supper, on the night when He was betrayed, *our Savior instituted the eucharistic sacrifice* of His body and blood. He did this in order *to perpetuate the sacrifice of the cross* throughout the centuries until He should come again, and so to entrust to His beloved spouse, the Church, a memorial of His death and resurrection: a sacrament of love, a sign of unity, a bond of charity, a paschal banquet in which Christ is eaten, the mind is filled with grace, and a pledge of future glory is given to us" (n. 47).

Christ is present in the Sacrifice of the Mass, declares the *Constitution on the Sacred Liturgy,* "not only in the person of His minister, 'the same now offering, through the ministry of priests, who formerly offered Himself on the cross' (Council of Trent), but especially under the eucharistic species."

Jesus Christ offers Himself to the Father in each Mass with a special act of His will — through that same most ardent desire for the glory of God and salvation of men which was His on the cross.

The differences between the Sacrifice of the Cross and the Sacrifice of the Mass are accidental. On the cross the victim was mortal, passible, visible; in the Mass, instead, He is present in His sacramental state — immortal, impassible, invisible.

On the cross the Redemption was accomplished; in the Mass it is applied.

The Eucharistic Sacrifice is offered to adore, thank, propitiate and supplicate God.

God is the supreme good; there is nothing good which does not come from Him. He is the source of all, just as He is the destiny of all. Infinite is the number of His perfections, and each perfection is infinite in itself. God needs nothing, for He is utterly happy; yet His love expressed itself in the creation of every being.

We, His creatures, therefore, owe Him the gratitude, honor, and adoration He deserves. Yet we cannot render to God an honor proportional to His greatness. This honor only Jesus Christ, true man yet also true God, can give. And this He does *in the holy Mass where He is represented in a state of immolation.* This state acknowledges God's supreme dominion over all things; they are for Him alone.

"Through him (Christ), therefore, let us offer up a sacrifice of praise always to God" (Heb. 13:15).

The Mass also has the purpose of thanksgiving — its eucharistic end. The word, *Eucharist,* means thanksgiving. All that we have, has come from God: "What have you that you have not received?" (1 Cor. 4:7) Creation, redemption and sanctification are from God. From Him come life, the soul with its faculties, the body with its senses, and all the blessings showered upon the world, the Church and ourselves: "How shall I make a return to the Lord for all the good he has done for me? The cup of salvation I will take up, and I will call upon the name of the Lord" (Ps. 115:12-13).

Before consecrating the bread, Jesus Christ gave thanks to the Father; before consecrating the wine, He likewise gave thanks. Thus, this sacrifice is eucharistic. What thanksgiving is more worthy than that which is offered to the Father by His Incarnate Son? *It has an infinite value;* God is pleased with it, as is said in the prayer: "Through him we ask you to accept and bless these gifts we offer you in sacrifice."

The Eucharistic Sacrifice is propitiatory. Every time the sacrifice is repeated, the work of our redemption is renewed. Consecrating the bread and wine at the Last Supper, Jesus Christ said of His body: "which shall be given up for you" (1 Cor. 11:24). Of His blood, He said: "which shall be shed for you" (Lk. 22:20).

"By means of the mystery of the Eucharist," wrote Pope Paul in *Mystery of Faith,* "the Sacrifice of the Cross, which was once offered on Calvary, is marvelously re-enacted and its saving power is constantly recalled and applied for the forgiveness of those sins which we daily commit."

Liturgy of the Word

The Mass is the breviary of the Incarnation, life, ministry and Paschal Mystery of Jesus Christ. In this light let us consider its main parts, the Liturgy of the Word and the eucharistic liturgy, which are so closely connected that they form one single act of worship.

In the *Liturgy of the Word,* we perceive the divine truths — the food of our minds and substance of our faith. Just as Jesus Christ preached the Good News before offering the Sacrifice of the Cross, so in the Mass the sacrifice is preceded by instruction. The *Constitution on the Sacred Liturgy* declares: "The faithful should be instructed by God's word."

In readings of the Mass, the bread of God's word is distributed to His people, while the entrance hymn and prayer stress what we should learn and profess. "In the liturgy," states the same document, "God speaks to His people and Christ is still proclaiming His Gospel. And the people reply to God both by song and prayer."

Every Mass has a message, and if this is followed well, the teachings of God are grasped, at least in some degree.

Unfortunately, we often have thoughts that are not the thoughts of Christ our Divine Master! If we analyze His teachings in the Gospel and ask ourselves if our thoughts are like His, what will the answer be?...

The Christlike way of thinking depends on the Liturgy of the Word. The readings at Mass should lead us to think like Christ.

In this first part of Mass, the Liturgy of the Word, let us ask for an increase of faith and supernatural wisdom.

We will thus prepare well for the *Liturgy of the Eucharist,* as the instruction on the eucharistic worship reminds us: "When the faithful hear the word of God, they should realize that the wonders it proclaims culminate in the Paschal Mystery, of which the memorial is sacramentally celebrated in the Mass. In this way the faithful will be nourished by the word of God which they have received and in a spirit of thanksgiving will be led on to a fruitful participation in the mysteries of salvation. Thus the Church is nourished by the bread of life which she finds at the table both of the word of God and of the body of Christ."

Liturgy of the Eucharist

Jesus Christ defined Himself as "the Way, the Truth and the Life" (Jn. 14:6). In the liturgy of the word, He is especially our Truth. In the eucharistic liturgy He is especially our Way and our Life.

In the second part of the Mass, the Liturgy of the Eucharist, Christ marks out the way for us, which is to follow in His footsteps: "If anyone wishes to come after me, let him... take up his cross and follow me" (Mt. 16:24). Up to what point has Jesus Christ loved the Father? To the point of sacrificing Himself: "Your will be done" (Lk. 22:42). Up to what point has He loved man? To the point of giving Himself completely: "who loved me and gave himself up for me" (Gal. 2:20).

During the Liturgy of the Eucharist we should ask the love of God that reserves nothing — that love which brings us to accept weariness, sorrows, privations and death all in the spirit of Christ Jesus our Lord.

"By offering the Immaculate Victim," states the *Constitution on the Sacred Liturgy,* "not only through the hands of the priest, but also with him, the faithful should learn also to offer themselves."

"Let all the disciples of Christ, persevering in prayer and praising God (Acts 2:42-47), present themselves as a living sacrifice, holy and pleasing to God" (Rom. 12:1).

In the great Eucharistic prayer, together with Christ, we give thanks to the Father in the Holy Spirit for all the blessings He gives us in creation and especially in the Paschal Mystery, and we pray to Him for the coming of His kingdom.

The Eucharistic Sacrifice is offered to God, whose extrinsic glory is increased, by the priest in the name of the Church for the benefit of all. Every need was provided for by our Redeemer on the cross; the same is true on the altars; and the priest offers the divine Victim with the heart of Jesus Christ Himself.

"In offering this sacrifice," writes Pope Paul in his oft-quoted *Mystery of Faith*, "the Church learns to offer herself as a sacrifice for all and applies the single, boundless, redemptive power of the sacrifice of the cross for the salvation of the entire world. For every Mass which is celebrated is offered not for the salvation of ourselves alone, but also for that of the whole world."

At the Consecration, Christ is made sacramentally present. The *Mystery of Faith* explains: "In an unbloody representation of the Sacrifice of the cross and in application of its saving power, in the Sacrifice of the Mass the Lord is immolated when, through the words of consecration, He becomes present in a sacramental form under the appearances of bread and wine to become the spiritual food of the faithful....

"This Sacrifice, no matter who offers it, be it Peter or Paul, is always the same as that which Christ gave His disciples and which priests now offer: the offering of today is in no way inferior to that which Christ offered, because it is not men who sanctify the offering of today; it is the same Christ who sanctified His own. For just as the words which God spoke are the very same as those which the priest now speaks, so too the oblation is the very same."

It is our privilege to give ourselves to the Father with Christ our Mediator, the great Priest and glorified Victim. States the *Instruction on Eucharistic Worship:*

"It is indeed the priest alone who, acting in the person of Christ, consecrates the bread and wine, but the role of the faithful in the Eucharist is to recall the passion, resurrection, the glorification of the Lord, to give thanks to God, and to offer the immaculate Victim not only through the hands of the priest, but also together with him and finally, by receiving the body of the Lord, to perfect that communion with God and among themselves which should be the product of participation in the Sacrifice of the Mass."

The Mass should be for us always the privileged occasion to make more strong the bonds of love that unite us one with another and all of us with our Lord. When one goes to Mass, he must recall that he is praying for his brothers, present and absent, for those who are already in fact his brothers in the faith, for those who, since they are men for whom Christ died, are, likewise, those for whom he must pray.

After the Consecration, we offer up to the Father Christ sacrificed for our sins, and implore God, in His loving kindness towards men, to be propitious to them, as well as to ourselves and to the dead.

Our response, "Amen," at the minor elevation at the end of the Canon signifies the total offering of ourselves, our cares, our sorrows, our distresses and our necessities in union with our divine Savior on the cross. In Christ let us render adoration, worthy thanksgiving, satisfaction and supplication. Through Him, our Mediator, supreme honor and glory are given to the eternal Father.

The Holy Eucharist presents to us Jesus Christ, immolated for our salvation, from whom flows in abundance all things good and joyous.

Intimate union in Communion

We read in the *Instruction on the Worship of the Eucharistic Mystery:*

"The Eucharistic Sacrifice is the source and the summit of the whole of the Church's worship and of the Christian life. The faithful participate more fully in this sacrament of thanksgiving, propitiation, petition and praise, not only when they wholeheartedly offer the Sacred Victim, and in it themselves, to the Father with the priest, but also when they receive this same victim sacramentally."

The eucharistic celebration, in addition to being the sacrifice of the cross, re-enacted in an unbloody manner, is also a eucharistic meal. If we examine more closely descriptions of eucharistic celebrations in the apostolic period, as they are recorded in the New Testament, we will find that the meal aspect is a basic and common characteristic. Even at a later period this aspect was quite prominent, as we know from the visit of St. Paul to Troas (Acts 20:7-12). The same is true for the Christian community at Corinth, where Paul insisted upon proper conduct of the community meal (1 Cor. 11:17ff).

This common meal was designed to reach its climax in the Eucharist, from which it derived its name: "The Lord's Supper." Abuses crept in, however, threatening to destroy the banquet character of the whole ritual. It was for this reason that St. Paul warned offenders of the rigors of divine judgment (27:34).

Since at a meal all join and partake of the same food, so, too, at the eucharistic meal all partake of Christ and by so doing become one with Him and one with each other.

As material food nourishes life, the eucharistic food strengthens our life in Christ. Besides approaching this sacrament in the state of grace, we should receive It with sincere faith and a desire to let Christ transform us — to take over in our life. His interests must constitute our overriding purpose in life.

Frequent Communion is necessary in order to grow in love of Christ. We need It not as a reward for our goodness, but as a remedy for our weakness.

The Eucharist brings about an intimate union and close friendship between the soul and Jesus Christ: "He who eats my flesh, and drinks my blood, abides in me and I in him" (Jn. 6:57).

The love of God is not idle; when it is present, it accomplishes great things; therefore, not only grace and holiness are bestowed lavishly by this sacrament, but also one is impelled to action: "The love of Christ impels us" (2 Cor. 5:14).

Thus is realized the exhortation of the instruction on eucharistic worship: "What the faithful have received by faith and sacrament in the celebration of the Eucharist should have its effect on their way of life. They should seek to live joyfully and gratefully by the strength of this heavenly food, sharing in the death and resurrection of the Lord. And so everyone who has participated in the Mass should be 'eager to do good works, to please God, and to live honestly, devoted to the Church, putting into practice what he has learned, and growing in piety.' He will seek to fill the world with the Spirit of Christ and 'in all things, in the very midst of human affairs' to become a witness of Christ."

Holy Communion is also a sign of unity, a bond of charity among the faithful. Through Holy Communion we become, member by member, united to the Head, Jesus Christ. "In the sacrament of the Eucharistic Bread," says the *Constitution on the Church*, "the unity of all believers who form one

"Christ Himself, our Paschal living Bread, by the action of the Holy Spirit through His very flesh vital and vitalizing, gives life to men...." (Vatican II)

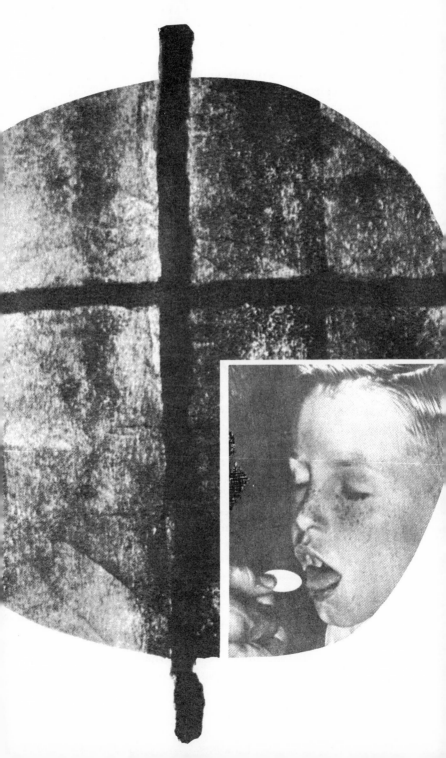

body in Christ (1 Cor. 10:17) is both expressed and brought about. All men are called to this union with Christ."

As many grains combine to form one loaf of bread and many clusters of grapes unite to produce the eucharistic wine, so we all form but one body in Christ: "that all may be one" (Jn. 17:21).

It is well in a world in which there is so much of loneliness to realize that in the Last Supper and in every Mass that renews the Last Supper, there is the symbol and the reality of fraternal love. We have only to think of the washing of the feet, of the symbol of the supper in common, by which we can understand that we do not go to Communion singly and alone, but as those who are united by the bonds of love.

The *Decree on the Ministry and Life of Priests* declares: the Holy Eucharist "contains the entire spiritual boon of the Church, that is, Christ Himself, our Pasch and Living Bread, by the action of the Holy Spirit through His very flesh vital and vitalizing, giving life to men...."

Thus Holy Communion brings about a growth in the spiritual life — strengthening man and perfecting the union of the soul with God: "He who eats me, he also shall live because of me" (Jn. 6:58).

Our paschal mystery

When we assemble for Holy Mass, holy thoughts and dispositions should be cultivated. The Lord Jesus told the apostles: "Go and prepare" (Lk. 22:8) — go and prepare for the Supper.

Therefore, we should come to the Eucharistic Sacrifice recollected in thoughts both sublime and humble — sublime because of the sublimity of this sacred action; humble, because we are aware of our needs.

The instruction on eucharistic worship tells us: "Like the passion of Christ itself, this sacrifice, though offered for all, 'has no effect except in those united to the passion of Christ by faith and charity.... To these it brings a greater or less benefit in proportion to their devotion.'"

The Paschal Mystery: passion, death, resurrection and ascension of the Lord, celebrated in the Holy Mass, is to be extended into our life — a life of faith, love and sacrifice.

The Paschal Mystery should permeate our entire life, which is also a mystery of passion, death and resurrection.

We ought to look suffering in the face, to meet it squarely, or at least accept it, giving it the greatest value. One day we will bless it. Thus did the saints, who have suffered and been glorified with Christ, and with them all the souls who journey with fatigue but decision on this earthly pilgrimage to heaven.

St. Paul coined the right phrase to express this truth which can be understood only by people of faith. He tells us that we must suffer together with Christ, and be crucified with Him: "With Christ I am nailed to the cross" (Gal. 2:19). He also tells us that we must die with Him and be buried with Him to resurrect with Him: "If we have died with him, we shall also live with him; if we endure, we shall also reign with him" (2 Tim. 2:11-12).

"We must model our whole life on the life of Christ," Pope Paul said in a sermon which he gave when still a cardinal, "in a union real and *vital*. This is Christianity; this is religion. We must *co-live* with Christ."

"It is no longer I who live, but Christ lives in me," wrote St. Paul (Gal. 2:20). Our lives should not be distinguishable from Jesus Christ, in whom we have been "grafted," so that like St. Paul we will be able to say: Christ is my life, Christ is my thought, Christ is my desire, Christ is my love, my wish, my speech. My very actions are Christ.

We must form one body with Him, become His mystical body, the whole Christ, as St. Augustine used to say. We must be members of Christ.

"From this stems our dignity, our transfiguration, our redemption, our sanctity and our hope of the future immortal life," continued Cardinal Montini.

The life of Jesus in us, fruit of divine grace and of our correspondence to it, primarily brought about through a loving obedience, is dynamic: it brings us to an ever greater and more perfect love for our heavenly Father. It induces us to do His will and to seek *His* glory only, always and in everything.

Our entire life is a Mass, to be lived daily and completed only on our deathbed.

And then there will be the vision of God, and participation in the eternal Mass celebrated by the great High Priest, Jesus Christ and assisted at by all the heavenly court.

Declares the *Constitution on the Sacred Liturgy:* "We take part in a foretaste of that heavenly liturgy which is celebrated in the holy city of Jerusalem toward which we journey as pilgrims, where Christ is sitting at the right hand of God...

we sing a hymn to the Lord's glory with all the warriors of the heavenly army...we eagerly await the Savior, our Lord Jesus Christ, until He, our life, shall appear and we too will appear with Him in glory."

Life is one great Mass that will be prolonged in eternity!

Devotion to the Blessed Sacrament

And it is our very sweet duty to honor and adore in the blessed Host which our eyes see, the Incarnate Word, whom they cannot see, and who, without leaving heaven, is made present before us.

And this existence remains present, after the sacrifice, in the Blessed Sacrament which is, in the tabernacle, the living heart of each of our churches.

THE CREDO

From time immemorial there has been a custom in the Church of reserving the Blessed Sacrament in the tabernacle on the altar. The practice can be traced as far back as the beginning of the second century. The Host was kept thus to communicate the sick and also to give Communion to those who for a good reason could not receive at Mass. Since the eleventh century there has been another reason for reserving the Host — that It might become a center of private and public devotion. The last mentioned gave rise to the custom of holding eucharistic congresses at various places throughout the world.

Christ exists in the Eucharist independently of its use, i.e., even though He is not received in Holy Communion, as long as the species (accidents) of bread and wine remain incorrupt.

Speaking of reservation of the Blessed Sacrament, Pope Paul says in his encyclical on the Eucharist:

"The Catholic Church has always offered and still offers the cult of latria to the sacrament of the Eucharist, not only during Mass, but also outside of it, reserving consecrated Hosts with the utmost care, exposing them to solemn veneration, and carrying them processionally to the joy of great crowds of the faithful.

"St. Cyril of Alexandria rejects as folly the opinion of those who maintained that if a part of the Eucharist was left over for the following day it did not confer sanctification. 'For,' he says, 'neither Christ is altered nor His body changed, but the force and power and vivifying grace always remain with it.'"

Continuing, the Holy Father answered the objections of certain theologians who held that since the Eucharist was a meal as well as a sacrifice therefore no consecrated Hosts should be preserved after the celebration:

"No one can fail to understand that the Divine Eucharist bestows upon the Christian people an incomparable dignity. Not only while the sacrifice is offered and the sacrament is received, but as long as the Eucharist is kept in our churches and oratories, Christ is truly the Emmanuel, that is, 'God with us.' Day and night He is in our midst, He dwells with us, full of grace and truth. He restores morality, nourishes virtues, consoles the afflicted, strengthens the weak. He proposes His own example to those who come to Him that all may learn to be, like Himself, meek and humble of heart and to seek not their own interests but those of God."

The Eucharistic Instruction also upholds this practice:

It would be well to recall that the primary and original purpose of the reserving of the sacred species in church outside Mass is the administration of the Viaticum. Secondary ends are the distribution of communion outside Mass and the adoration of our Lord Jesus Christ concealed beneath these same species. For the reservation of the sacred species for the sick...led to the praiseworthy custom of adoring the heavenly food which is preserved in churches. This practice of adoration has a valid and firm foundation, especially since belief in the real presence of the Lord has as its natural consequence the external and public manifestation of that belief (n. 49).

Benediction or Solemn Exposition of the Blessed Sacrament, therefore, can never be considered an out-dated custom, for, as the *Instruction on the Eucharist* declares, it "stimulates the faithful to an awareness of the marvelous presence of Christ, and is an invitation to spiritual communion with Him. It is, therefore, an excellent encouragement to offer Him that worship in spirit and truth which is His due" (n. 60).

Visits to the Blessed Sacrament, too, should always be a part of your life, for Christ always wants to see you—any time, any hour, in any "mood" you're in. The visit may be long or short, as you wish. Let it be a renewal of your intimate union with Him in Mass and Holy Communion.

Adore your Christ, offer Him reparation for sin, thank Him for everything He does for us, ask Him for what you need. Don't worry about what to say or how to say it. There are many books with suggested prayers, but actually, your own words, your own thoughts, your own expressions — the real you talking is "good enough" in Christ's opinion.

CHALLENGE

At the altar, as we deepen our union with Christ and with one another, we should be aware that this step, this action of coming forward to share in the love feast of the Lord, implies also that we are willing and ready to accept the social consequences of our communion.

The Christian who in love and faith comes to the altar of Christ must be aware, must know that he is also stepping forward at that moment, as an apostle about to receive an assignment, that he is committing himself to work for whatever is his share in the responsibility of building up the body of Christ, which is the Church.

RICHARD CARDINAL CUSHING, *Liturgy and Life*

16

CONVERSION
AND
PROGRESS

His action [the Holy Spirit], which penetrates to the inmost of the soul, enables man to respond to the call of Jesus: Be perfect as your heavenly Father is perfect (Mt. 5:48).

...she [the Church] has the power to heal her children through the blood of Christ and the gift of the Holy Spirit.
THE CREDO

The Church talks about "healing us" in the sacrament of Penance. Does a person in sin — in this money-crazy, pleasure-crazy world of ours — really feel "sick" or in need of being "healed"? Does a sinner in an expensive suit who hops into his expensive car and drives off to his expensive house really suffer from his rejection of God's friendship?

That is a good question. And it is not an easy one to answer. The person himself might not realize that "what's eating him" is his rejection of the Source of all joy. He may keep telling himself: "Relax! You've got everything you ever wanted — what more do you want?"

Coming closer to home, don't *we* find *ourselves* sometimes running after anything and everything rather than admit that it is guilt and remorse which are making us miserable?

A successful New York manufacturer had long ago decided that he could do whatever he wanted with his life despite God's commandments. He was not at all hesitant about telling people that he had left the Church years ago, especially if he knew this would bring on a reaction. Indeed, he liked what he called a "good argument about religion."

Good-natured and generous, he enjoyed donating some of his products to charitable organizations. One day, when a Sister expressed her gratitude for his contributions, he told her smilingly, "You'd be surprised to know that I've been away from the Church for most of my life." For some reason, he found himself waiting to see what she would reply, because he admired her and her community for the hard work they always did so cheerfully.

He didn't have to wait long. Without wasting words she told him, "The best thing for you to do is to go to Confession quick." He laughed it off, but that night he found himself unable to sleep. Three things were on his mind: the peace on the Sister's face despite her long, sacrifice-filled days; the way she had said, "the *best* thing for *you* to do..."; and the thought of returning to God through sorrow for sin in confession. He found himself facing the fact that someone who was practically a stranger had realized that he wasn't the happy man he had always said he was.

"The best thing for you...." And he did it. Afterwards, to describe the difference in himself, he could only say that he was a new man. The Church *is* still exercising her "power to heal her children through the blood of Christ and the gift of the Holy Spirit" (Credo).

The Council of Trent has defined it as an article of faith that Christ gave to the Church the power of remitting and retaining all sins committed after baptism and that this takes place through a judicial process. The statement is based on the words of Christ in St. Matthew:

Whatever you shall bind on earth shall be bound in heaven, and whatever you shall loose on earth shall be loosed in heaven (16:18-19).

We read also in St. John:

Jesus said to the apostles, "Peace be to you! As the Father has sent me, I also send you." When he had said this, he breathed upon them, and said to them, "Receive the Holy Spirit; whose sins you shall forgive, they are forgiven them; and whose sins you shall retain, they are retained" (20:21-23).

That this has been the constant teaching of the Church since apostolic times is easily established. From the second century onward there are abundant testimonies from the Fathers in support of it. As an example, listen to St. Cyprian, bishop of Carthage in North Africa:

"The Lord proves and declares in his Gospel that sins can be forgiven through them alone who have the Holy Spirit. For, after the resurrection, sending his disciples, he spoke to them, saying, 'As the Father has sent me, I also send you.' When he had said this, he breathed upon them, and said to them, 'Receive the Holy Spirit; whose sins you shall forgive, they are forgiven them; and whose sins you shall retain they are retained' (Jn. 20:21-23). In this place, he shows that he alone who has the Holy Spirit can baptize and give the remission."

"God knows all things," St. Augustine explains, "yet He requires a sincere confession of our sins. Whoever reveals the burden of his sins unburdens himself. He impedes all other accusations, no matter how just, because he himself forestalls all accusers. In vain you will seek to deceive Him who sees all. You run no risk in telling Him what He already knows."

After Jesus had cleaned the ten lepers, He said to them: *"Go, show yourselves to the priests"* (cf. Lk. 17:14). He sent them to show themselves because the Mosaic Law did not permit the lepers to return to society without first showing themselves to the priests who judged whether they were clean. Leprosy is to the body what sin is to the soul. Therefore, in the new Law, Jesus Christ imposed the obligation upon us to confess our sins to the priest in order to be forgiven. "Let no one say: I confess my sins secretly to God, it is enough that He who is to forgive me knows the penance I make in my heart. If this were the case, Jesus would not have sent the lepers to the priests nor would He have said to the apostles: That which you loose on earth will be loosed in heaven. If God had given us the power to open heaven by ourselves, His having given the keys to the Church would be useless. It is not enough to confess ourselves to God, therefore, but we must confess ourselves to those who received from Him the power to loose and to bind." (St. Augustine)

Eventually the Council of Trent defined the doctrine in these words:

"The *fruit of baptism is one thing; that of penance is another thing.* For by putting on Christ by Baptism, we are made an entirely new creature in Him, obtaining a full and complete remission of all sins, to which newness and integrity, however, we can in no way arrive by the sacrament of Penance without many tears and labors on our part, for divine justice demands this, so that Penance has justly been called by the holy Fathers, 'a laborious kind of Baptism.' The sacrament of Penance, moreover, is necessary for the salvation of those who have fallen after Baptism, as Baptism itself is for those as not yet regenerated." (Denz. 895)

Actual confession of sin is preceded by an examination of conscience. This should not be done in a scrupulous manner, but one should employ the same care as a business man expends attending to his affairs. In the examination of conscience, usually the commandments can be taken in order, for in that way one remembers more easily how each one may have been broken.

The Council of Trent has also laid it down—and as an article of faith—that by divine law, sacramental confession is essential for all those who after Baptism have committed grave sins and that there is a grave obligation to confess each and every mortal sin. Trent also prescribed that these sins must be confessed according to the number of times and also according to their kind, i.e., against what particular commandment the offense has been performed. Circumstances which add to the guilt must also be confessed. For example, a married person who is guilty of adultery must mention the fact that either he or the accomplice (or both) are married, for there are sins of injustice involved here, too.

An inward look

On May 25, 1967, the Sacred Congregation of Rites issued the following directive on frequent confession:

"The precept 'Let a man examine himself' (1 Cor. 11:28) should be called to mind for those who wish to receive Communion. The custom of the Church declares this to be necessary so that no one who is conscious of having committed mortal sin, even if he believes himself to be contrite, should approach the Holy Eucharist without first making a sacramental confession. If someone finds himself in a case of necessity, however, and there is no confessor to whom he can go, then he should first make an act of perfect contrition.

"The faithful are to be constantly encouraged to accustom themselves to going to confession outside the celebration of Mass, and especially at the prescribed times. In this way, the sacrament of Penance will be administered calmly and with genuine profit, and will not interfere with participation in the Mass. Those who receive Communion daily or very frequently, should be counseled to go to confession at times suitable to the individual case."

Pope John had this to say about the confession of venial sins: "One should also remember that our predecessor, Pius XII, condemned in 'Gravissimis verbis' the mistaken opinion that states there is no great value in the frequent confession of venial sins:

> "'For an ever greater progress on the road of virtue, we earnestly recommend the pious custom of frequent confession, introduced by the Church not without the inspiration of the Holy Spirit.'

The penitent must be truly sorry for his sins. Contrition is defined as "sorrow for sin and a detestation of it with the intention of sinning no more." There are two kinds of contrition—perfect and imperfect. The first is based on a truly supernatural motive—the love of God, for example. The second rests on a less sublime motive—the loss of heaven, fear of the pains of hell, a consideration of the moral turpitude of sin. The second kind of sorrow is sufficient in confession. But when we sin and cannot go to confession immediately, in order to recover the state of grace we must make an act of perfect contrition and must have the intention of going to confession as soon as possible.

We must also have the *firm* intention of not committing sin any more. If we comprehend the psychology of temptation, then this will be a great help in forming a determined resolve. In the following words St. Augustine explains how temptations arise.

"There are *three steps toward the complete commission of sin:* suggestion, pleasure, consent. Suggestion comes about either through our memory or our senses—when we see, hear, smell, taste or touch something. If to enjoy any of these sensations brings pleasure, the pleasure, if forbidden, must be checked. Were we to yield to it, we would surely commit sin, a sin in the heart known to God, though actually it may remain unknown to man.... To yield consent to a forbidden pleasure is a sin; the sin which a person commits in yielding consent is in his heart. If he goes further and puts this into action, his passion appears to be satisfied. Later on, when the suggestion is repeated, there is enkindled a more intense pleasure, though this pleasure is still much less formidable than the pleasure that comes when repeated acts have formed a habit."

Our Lord made all this quite clear, for we read in St. Mark:

The action of the Holy Spirit which penetrates to the inmost of the soul, enables
man to respond to the call of Jesus: "Be

perfect as your heavenly
Father is perfect " (Mt. 5:48)

(The Credo)

Jesus called the crowd to him and said to them, "Hear me, all of you, and understand. There is nothing outside a man that, entering into him, can defile him; but the things that come out of a man, these are what defile a man. If anyone has ears to hear, let him hear."

And when he had entered the house away from the crowd, his disciples began to ask him about the parable. And he said to them, "Are you also, then, without understanding? Do you not realize that nothing from outside, by entering a man, can defile him? For it does not enter his heart, but his belly, and passes out into the drain." Thus he declared all foods clean. "And," he said, "the things that come out of a man are what defile a man. *For from within, out of the heart of men, come evil thoughts, adulteries, immorality, murders, thefts, covetousness, wickedness, deceit, shamelessness, jealousy, blasphemy, pride, foolishness. All these evil things come from within, and defile a man* (7:14-23).

Once you have made up your mind not to sin any more, you should launch yourself on your new career with as strong and as decided an initiative as possible. Strive not to allow an exception to occur to any good habit that you are forming. Keep repeating your resolutions to yourself and act on every emotional prompting that directs you towards the formation of the habit you have in mind. For example, you may find sudden surges of desire within you to live as perfectly as possible, or a humble feeling of satisfaction over the fact that, with God's grace, you resisted a temptation. Capitalize on these feelings to urge you to greater efforts in the struggle.

Keep the effort alive within you by some little daily practice of your own choosing. We have already spoken of this in another way — going against yourself in little things, with the object of strengthening the will and building up character. For example, you can refuse a coke, or a sundae, or refrain from going to the movies. Or you can eat something at dinner that you don't particularly care for. By acting in this manner, and by using prayer of course, you are toughening yourself for the battles that lie ahead and when they come, God will be on your side, for He never allows Himself to be outdone in generosity. Father James Alberione gives some sound advice about the role the mind plays:

> The mind is wasted in useless reading.
> The mind is wasted in useless talk.
> The mind is wasted in indecision.

The mind is wasted in recreation and vacations prolonged beyond measure, in useless movies, television and radio programs.

The mind is wasted in daydreaming.

The mind is wasted in fears, in frantic worrying about the future, in scruples.

Mental laziness, inactivity and lack of intellectual interest leave the mind open to receive everything, irrational or shameful though it be. Instead, if the mind is kept busy in wholesome activity, and if its interest is constantly engaged, many temptations and regrettable happenings will be avoided.

The grace of God always backs up those who make use of common sense and prudence.

This is especially true when danger approaches or is already present. Fill the mind with wholesome thoughts, of both the natural and supernatural order.

As the thoughts go, so goes the mind. By the fruit, the tree is known. A healthy, vigorous mind produces wholesome thoughts; a sick mind, instead, produces defective thoughts.

Are thoughts weak, unchecked, ignoble? They are caused by an unhealthy physical condition or poor mental education. To yield better fruit, one must improve in health and re-educate his mind, in order to possess a "sound mind in a sound body."

Because of good principles, many souls have achieved sanctity; due to bad thoughts, many have become base. Character depends on thought.

The greatest battles are fought in the mind. It is here that we must concentrate our efforts.

Change of heart

"Many," said St. Augustine, "frequently confess to be sinners, but in the meantime they take pleasure in sinning. Their word is a confession, not a change; they uncover the wounds of their soul, but they do not cure them; they confess the offense, but they do not cancel it. Only hatred of sin and love of God constitute a real contrition."

St. Bernard adds: "Sincere sorrow for having sinned is an infinitely desirable treasure. It brings an infinite joy to the soul of man and obtains great energy for the will."

In confession, a penance is imposed by the priest. Implementation of this penance on the part of the subject is known as "satisfaction." God forgives us our sins, but the temporal punishment due to them remains. This must be expiated, either in this life by penance, or in the next, by suffering in purgatory. Performance of the penance imposed by the priest does not mean that in fact *all* the temporal punishment due to sin has been remitted. *Much* of it may remain, even after the penance has been done, and the remainder of this temporal punishment can be curtailed either by further voluntary penance or by the gaining of indulgences. The *Apostolic Constitution on Fast and Abstinence,* issued by Paul VI, February 17, 1966 says of satisfaction:

Since the Church is closely linked to Christ, the penitence of the individual Christian also has an intimate relationship of its own with the whole ecclesial community. In fact, not only does he receive in the bosom of the Church through Baptism the fundamental gift of "metanoia" ["change of heart"], but this gift is restored and reinvigorated through the sacrament of Penance in those members of the Body of Christ who have fallen into sin.

And in the Church the *little acts of penitence imposed each time in the sacrament become a form of participation of Christ,* while, by a general disposition of the Church, the penitent can intimately join to the sacramental satisfaction itself every other action he performs, his every suffering and sorrow. Thus the task of bearing in his body and soul the death of the Lord (cf. 2 Cor. 4:10) affects the whole life of the baptized person at every instant and in every aspect (n. 1).

The *Apostolic Constitution on Indulgences* continues in the same vein:

Sins bring punishments inflicted by God's sanctity and justice.... These *punishments are imposed by the just and merciful judgment of God for the purification of souls, the defense of the sanctity of the moral order and the restoration of the glory of God....* It is therefore necessary for the full remission and — as it is called — reparation of sins not only that friendship with God be reestablished by a sincere conversion of the mind and amends made for the offense against His wisdom and goodness, but also that all the personal as well as social values and those of the universal order itself, which have been diminished or destroyed by sin, be fully reintegrated whether through *voluntary reparation* which will involve punishment or through acceptance of the punishments established by the just and most holy wisdom of God, from which there will shine forth throughout the world the sanctity and the splendor of His glory (nn. 2, 3).

New dimensions

We must do penance for our own sins, but we can also do penance for the sins of others.

The *Apostolic Constitution on Fast and Abstinence* speaks of voluntary penance thus:

"We find among the just ones of the Old Testament those who offered themselves to satisfy with their own personal penitence for the sins of the community. This is what *Moses* did in the forty days when he fasted to placate the Lord for the guilt of his unfaithful people. This above all is how the character of the Servant of Yahweh is presented, 'Who took on our infirmities,' and in whom 'the Lord has laid on him the iniquity of us all.'

"All this, however, was but a foreshadowing of things to come. *Penitence* — required by the inner life, confirmed by the religious experience of mankind and the object of a particular precept of divine revelation — *assumes 'in Christ and the Church' new dimensions infinitely broader and more profound.*

"Christ, who always practiced in His life what He preached, before beginning His ministry spent forty days and forty nights in prayer and fasting, and began His public mission with the joyful message: "The kingdom of God is at hand." To this He added the command: "Repent and believe in the Gospel." These words constitute, in a way, a compendium of the whole Christian life."

The example of Judith in the Old Testament who offered herself as a voluntary victim for sin is a stirring and appealing one:

A widow for three and a half-years, Judith fasted every day except the Sabbaths and the feasts of the house of Israel. She was greatly renowned among all, because she feared the Lord very much. When her city was threatened with destruction, she addressed the elders thus:

"For as much as the Lord is patient, let us be penitent, and with many tears let us beg his pardon.... Let us humble our souls before him, and continuing in a humble spirit in his service, let us ask the Lord with tears, that according to his will so he would show his mercy to us.... Tell the people to remember how our father Abraham was tempted, and being proved by many tribulations, was made the friend of God. So Isaac, so Jacob, so Moses, and all that have pleased God, passed through many tribulations, remaining faithful. But they that did not receive the trials with the fear of the Lord, but uttered their impatience and the reproach of their murmuring against the Lord, were destroyed by the destroyer, and perished by serpents. As for us, therefore, let us not revenge ourselves for these things which we suffer. But esteeming these very punishments to be less than our sins deserve, let us believe that these scourges of the Lord, with which we are chastised, have happened for our amendment, and not for our destruction."

Judith secured the victory over Holofernes and his followers because she trusted in God, not in herself, and because she added to her confident prayer the mortifications she inflicted on her body by fasting. (cf. Judith 8-13)

The sacrament of penance, received with the necessary proper dispositions, remits all mortal and venial sins. It also lessens the temporal punishment due to them. We know, from the teaching of the Church, that any good done by a person in the state of mortal sin receives no merit. However, once a good confession has been made, all the merit earned before the mortal sin was committed revives.

Since the Second Vatican Council there has been in certain quarters a new approach to the sacrament of Penance. It does not abolish private confession to a priest, commanded by the Council of Trent and reaffirmed many times, as in the recent pastoral norms. In April, 1974, Pope Paul VI described three forms of reconciliation:

"The first form is the individual one, still in use, but with emphasis on the necessity of personal dispositions and of reference to that Word of God from which the blessed message of divine goodness comes to us and on which our soul, first converted and then justified, must be focused. It is the usual form, but enriched with awareness, earnestness, listening as well as confession, tasting, if we may say so, divine love and the ineffable joy knowing that one is reborn to divine life. We could never praise enough the sacrament of reconciliation, which is for us sinners a renewed baptism of supernatural rebirth.

"The second form is that of collective preparation, followed by individual confession and absolution. It unites the double merit of the community act and the personal act. This is the best form for our people, when it is possible; but it usually presupposes the simultaneous presence of several ministers of the sacrament; and that is not always easy. But we hope, especially in the case of homogeneous groups: children, young people, workers, sick people, pilgrims, etc., that it will be celebrated more often, because it facilitates preparation and a more orderly procedure.

"Then there is the third form, with collective reconciliation and one general absolution. But this form is of an exceptional nature, for cases of necessity, with the authorization of the bishop and with the obligation of individual confession of grave or mortal sins later."

Communitarian penance was known in the Old Testament. We read once more in the *Apostolic Constitution on Fast and Abstinence:*

"The social aspect of penitence is not lacking in the Old Testament. In fact, the penitential liturgies of the Old Covenant are not only a collective awareness of sin but constitute in reality a condition for belonging to the people of God."

Neither was the idea foreign to the early Church, for as St. Augustine tells us:

"The whole Body of Christ, diffused through the entire world, that is, the whole Church, *practices penance as that corporate unity* which says in the psalm: 'To you have I cried from the ends of the earth; when my heart was in anguish.' Hence, light begins to dawn upon us as to why the Lenten season was inaugurated as the solemnity of this humiliation."

Although in recent years the traditional Church stand on certain practices of penance has been modified, this certainly does *not* mean that the Church gives less importance to penance nowadays. Pope Paul VI in his *Constitution on Fast and Abstinence* outlined the true position as follows:

The Church invites all Christians without distinction to respond to the divine precept of penitence by some voluntary act, apart from the renunciation imposed by the burdens of everyday life.

To recall and urge all the faithful to the observance of the divine precept of penitence, the Apostolic See intends to reorganize penitential discipline with practices more suited to our times. It is up to the bishops – gathered in their episcopal conferences – to establish the norms which, in their pastoral solicitude and prudence, and with the direct knowledge they have of local conditions, they consider the most opportune and efficacious. The following, however, is established:

In the first place, holy mother Church, although it has always observed in a special way abstinence from meat and fasting, nevertheless wants to indicate in the traditional triad of "prayer – fasting – charity" the fundamental means of complying with the divine precepts of penitence. These means were the same throughout the centuries, but in our time there are special reasons whereby, according to the demands of various localities, it is necessary to inculcate some special form of penitence in preference to others. Therefore, *where economic well-being is greater, so much more will the witness of asceticism have to be given* in order that the sons of the Church may not be involved in the spirit of the world, *and at the same time the witness of charity will have to be given to the brethren who suffer poverty and hunger beyond any barrier of nation or continent.* On the other hand, in countries where the standard of living is lower, it will be more pleasing to God the Father and more useful to the members of the Body of Christ if Christians – while they seek in every way to promote better social justice — offer their suffering in prayer to the Lord in close union with the cross of Christ.

Therefore, the Church, while preserving — where it can be more readily observed — the custom (observed for many centuries with canonical norms) of practicing penitence also through abstinence from meat and fasting, intends to ratify with its prescriptions other forms of penitence as well, provided that it seems opportune to episcopal conferences to replace the observance of fast and abstinence with exercises of prayer and works of charity.

In order that all the faithful, however, may be united in common celebration of penitence, the Apostolic See intends to establish certain penitential days and seasons chosen among those which in the course of the liturgical year are closer to the paschal mystery of Christ or might be required by the special needs of the ecclesial community.

Therefore, the following is declared and established:

By divine law all the faithful are required to do penance.

The prescriptions of ecclesiastical law regarding penitence are totally reorganized according to the following norms:

The time of Lent preserves its penitential character. The days of penitence to be observed under obligation throughout the Church are all Fridays and Ash Wednesday, that is to say the first days of "Grande Quaresima" (Great Lent), according to the diversity of the rites. Their substantial observance binds gravely.

Apart from the faculties referred to in VI and VIII regarding the manner of fulfilling the precept of penitence on such days, abstinence is to be observed on every Friday which does not fall on a day of obligation, while abstinence and fast is to be observed on Ash Wednesday or, according to the various practices of the rites, on the first day of "Grande Quaresima" (Great Lent) and on Good Friday.

The law of abstinence forbids the use of meat, but not of eggs, the products of milk or condiments made of animal fat.

The law of fasting allows only one full meal a day, but does not prohibit taking some food in the morning and evening, observing — as far as quantity and quality are concerned — approved local custom.

To the law of abstinence those are bound who have completed their fourteenth year of age. To the law of fast those of the faithful are bound who have completed their twenty-first year and up until the beginning of their sixtieth year.

As regards those of a lesser age, pastors of souls and parents should see to it with particular care that they are educated to a true sense of penitence.

Elsewhere in these pages we have spoken of our encounter with Christ (chapters 7 and 18). But nowhere is our encounter with Him more profound and personal (with the exception of the Eucharist wherein we receive His very body and blood) than in the sacrament of Penance. Many people keep away from confession through a false fear of God, through a conviction of hopelessness, or through plain inertia. But what a pity, when here ready to meet us is Jesus Himself, the Jesus of the Gospels, the Jesus who would not break the bruised reed, nor quench the smoldering wick! Read and re-read the Gospels and see what our Lord has to say about the sinner and how personally He treats him.

What a wealth of material there is for us on this important subject in Matthew, Mark, Luke and John. Five of our Lord's parables deal with forgiveness for the offender. They are the parables of the lost sheep, of the unmerciful servant, of the lost drachma, of the prodigal son, and of the laborers hired for work in the vineyard. In all these our Lord shows how eager He is for our return, waiting to welcome us with open arms. In the parable of the lost sheep He Himself goes after the strayed one, and in the parable of the prodigal son, the joy of the father — symbolic of our heavenly Father — at the return of his wayward and sinning son is unbounded.

Our Lord's actions were totally in keeping with His words. He chose Matthew, a publican, to be His disciple. He chatted with the woman at the well and tried to lead her to a better life. He forgave the sins of the man sick of the palsy and also cured him of his bodily infirmity. He pardoned the woman who washed His feet, saved the woman taken in adultery from being stoned, absolving her and telling her to sin no more, dined with Zacchaeus, one who was hated for his tax-gathering profession — and made clean the penitent thief.

Let us never fear, then, our encounter with Christ in the confessional. "Though your sins are like scarlet, they may become white as snow" we read in the Old Testament (Is. 1:18).

O Jesus, my suffering Savior,
I see what sin has done to you.
Make me understand the duty I have
of making reparation
for my many sins
and for all offenses
to your divine Majesty.
Impress on my heart
and on that of every penitent soul
the virtues of your Sacred Heart.

Prayer of St. Augustine

God addresses the soul thus:

See how weak you are!
See how strong you are!
In you is all your weakness,
In me is all your strength.
And as I am infinitely greater than you are,
By so much is your strength greater than your weakness!

CHALLENGE

It is the lot of most of us to have to face temptations daily. Let's remember that there is no new miracle drug against temptation on the market, no moral penicillin that will make a person immune by taking a weekly or daily injection. We still have to oppose it with the old reliable remedies of prayer, self-discipline, and flight.

It's like Will Rogers used to say: "The best remedy against temptation is cowardice—run away from it!" Send in the fire alarm by prayer, and then get away from the fire, because you are not covered with asbestos. Christ's presence may be reinforcing you in every encounter, but your poor human weakness is sticking out just the same. It's vulnerable, and the old devil knows it.

REV. VICTOR L. DUX, O.S.B., *What the World Needs*

17

"SET
APART
FOR ME..."
ACTS 13

...celebrated by the priest representing the person of Christ by virtue of the power received through the SACRAMENT OF ORDERS...

"A priest forever..." those words thrilled young Karl Leisner to the bone. As he lay on the dirty, evil-smelling pallet that was his bed, Karl kept dreaming about the priesthood. He had been a seminarian; in fact, he was already a deacon. But to become a priest.... That seemed utterly impossible now. For here he was, racked with tuberculosis, in the prison hospital of one of the most horrible of Nazi concentration camps – Dachau. Mere mention of the place sent chills of horror up and down one's spine. Here priests were horribly mistreated. Some of them had even been whipped to death. Karl had already had tuberculosis at the time of his arrest by the Nazi secret police in 1941, and after three years in prison the disease was far advanced. Yet the young deacon could only wish, hope and pray that his great desire might someday come true.

Then it happened, almost like a miracle. The prisoners (many of whom were priests) discovered that among them was a Bishop Piquet, a Frenchman. After interviewing Karl and obtaining the required certificates (they were somehow smuggled into the prison), Bishop Piquet agreed to ordain Karl to the priesthood.

December 17, 1944, dawned bleak and cold. To any other inmate of Dachau, it was just the beginning of another dreadful day, but to Karl Leisner, this raw, chilly winter morning was the most wonderful day of his life – ordination day! A few hours later, the ceremony was over. Just steps away from the prison guards, in the presence of a select number of prisoner priests, His Excellency, Bishop Piquet, secretly ordained Karl Leisner a priest. From now on, he would be Father Karl.

Greatly weakened by the disease which he had endured for so long, Father Karl died soon afterwards. And do you know how many Masses Father Karl said before he died? *Just one.*

The priest-prisoners and bishop had risked their lives so that he could become a priest. To be caught at a secret ordination ceremony could have meant terrible punishments if not death, for all of them. And after all that, Father Karl said only one Mass. Was it worth all that the other prisoners had gone through?

Yes! For just one Mass gives God our Father more glory than the combined praises of the angels, the saints, the Blessed Virgin, and all of us, the People of God. For at Mass our Lord Jesus Christ, the Son of God, offers Himself, the perfect Gift, to our heavenly Father.

The priesthood may be defined as a sacred order conferring the power to consecrate the body and blood of Christ and to forgive sin. There are numerous references to the existence of the priesthood in the New Testament. We read of it in Acts 6:6; 13:3 and 14:22. There are many allusions in St. Paul: 1 Cor. 4:1, 17; 1 Thes. 3:2; Heb. 5:1; 1 Tim. 3:1-12; 4:14; 5:19-22; 2 Tim. 5:6; Tit. 1:5-9. When the sacrament of ordination came under fire during the Reformation, the Council of Trent made it an article of faith that Orders is a sacrament of the New Law instituted by Christ.

Priestly dignity

The collective pastoral letter of the U.S. bishops, *The Church in Our Day,"* issued January 11, 1968, had this to say of the dignity and function of the priesthood:

"There is an essential difference between priest and people no matter how much the heart of the priest identifies with his people. In a dramatic and altogether decisive manner, the ordained priest is a man of the Church; he becomes the sign of the Church as no other Christian does, he gives expression in his priesthood to special ministries of Jesus Christ, the sole High Priest. His ultimate responsibility is not alone to his people, great though his duties to them, nor is it to himself nor to any priestly caste; his responsibility is to God, by whom he has been called, as Aaron was, to a mission apart from that of the unordained and yet within the community of God's people — a mission to which he is called and ordered by those appointed by God to rule His Church."

What is the function of the priest in today's modern world? The answer to that question is abundantly contained in the documents of the Second Vatican Council. From them we quote a representative sample. The *Dogmatic Constitution on the Church* says:

Priests exercise their sacred function especially in the eucharistic worship or the celebration of the Mass by which *acting in the person of Christ and proclaiming His Mystery* they unite the prayers of the faithful with the sacrifice of their

Head and renew and apply in the sacrifice of the Mass until the coming of the Lord the only sacrifice of the New Testament namely that of Christ offering Himself once for all a spotless Victim to the Father (n. 28).

The *Decree on the Ministry and Life of Priests* has this: *In the liturgy priests continue to carry on Christ's priestly office by the action of His Spirit.* By Baptism men are truly brought into the People of God; by the sacrament of Penance sinners are reconciled to God and His Church; by the Anointing of the Sick, the ill are given solace; and especially by the celebration of Mass they offer sacramentally the Sacrifice of Christ. In administering all sacraments, as St. Ignatius Martyr has borne witness from the early days of the Church, priests by various titles are bound together hierarchically with the bishop. And so in a certain way they make him present in every congregation (n. 5).

In another place the same document reads: ·*The purpose which priests pursue* in their ministry and by their life *is to procure the glory of God the Father in Christ.* That glory consists in this — that men working freely and with a grateful spirit receive the work of God made perfect in Christ and then manifest it in their whole lives. Hence, priests, while engaging in prayer and adoration, or preaching the word, or offering the Eucharistic sacrifice and administering the other sacraments, or performing other works of the ministry for men, devote all this energy to the increase of the glory of God and to man's progress in the divine life. All of this, since it comes from the Pasch of Christ, will be crowned by the glorious coming of the same Lord, when He hands over the Kingdom to God the Father (n. 2).

Imitation of the Master

Priests of the Latin or Western Rite do not marry. The reasons for this are given in the Council's document on the priesthood:

Through virginity, then, or *celibacy observed for the kingdom of heaven,* priests are consecrated to Christ by a new and exceptional reason. They adhere to Him more easily with an undivided heart, they dedicate themselves more freely in Him and through Him to the service of God and men, and they more expeditiously minister to His kingdom and the work of heavenly regeneration, and thus they are apt to accept, in a broad sense, paternity in Christ. They give, moreover, a living sign of the world to come, by a faith and charity already made present, in which the children of the resurrection neither marry nor take wives (n. 16).

It would be wrong to so dramatize and exaggerate the life of a priest as to give a wrong idea as to what such a life really means. Here, as in all else, we must be realistically truthful. In their collective pastoral letter, the United States bishops were forthrightly frank in their statements about the life of a priest. They wrote as follows:

No one knows better than the priest the loneliness of the aged, the imprisoned, those unmarried despite their preference, the exiled, the abandoned, the dedicated who have renounced consolation to pursue art, science or the service of neighbor.

However, mindful precisely of priests, the council speaks of the "bitter loneliness," and even of the "seeming sterility of the past labors" which priests may sometimes experience. Pope Paul also cautions that "loneliness will weigh heavily on the priest" (Priestly Celibacy, n. 59). But it is well to keep certain realities in mind when there is consideration of the loneliness involved in the human condition; even more, it is bound up with the vocation of the Christian, always a pilgrim and stranger on the face of the earth. We are not yet, in the fullest sense of the word, "home"; we have not here a lasting dwelling place and ours is the unrest of those who seek a city. Nor do we yet so completely experience the effects of redemption that estrangement from God, from one another, and even from our true selves is no longer to be feared.

Married or single, religious or lay, priest or people, all must come to terms with loneliness. Often the sustaining of loneliness results in human and Christian maturity, making us aware of our limitations and of our need for one another. "Christ, too, in the most tragic hours of His life was alone — abandoned by the very ones He had chosen as...witnesses...and companions...and whom He had loved unto the end" (Priestly Celibacy, n. 59)....

No mature priest, indeed no adult Christian, will suppose that life is or ought to be problem-free. We may reduce conflict by reform and ease tension by understanding, but we shall never eliminate anguish from life. We priests are called to be the first to perceive the true horizon of the human condition, to recognize the essential limitations of creations, to be conscious of the universal effects of sin and of the pilgrim character of human history. Though we labor with all our hearts to heal, we realize that, although he succeeds in eliminating some problems from life, man remains a creature who must always live with contradiction, frustration, even heart-break.

"And if hostility, lack of confidence and the indifference of his fellow-men make his solitude quite painful, (a priest) will thus be able to share, with dramatic charity the very experience of Christ, as an apostle who is not above him, by whom he has been sent..." (Priestly Celibacy, n. 59).

In an age perhaps overly given to introspection, personal problems are intensified by the disposition to concentrate on them. A priest who loses himself in his apostolate, serving God's people, particularly the poor and the neglected, in imitation of his Master will find that much of his loneliness disappears. The loneliness which remains is a small price to pay for a vocation whose sacredness and consolations can hardly be exaggerated. In spite of any problems of the priesthood, there is no greater joy than that which accompanies the work of the dedicated priest, no calling more literally divine than his. In moments of isolation, priests, no matter how great their fears, will recall the words which sustained Christ in His greater loneliness: "I am not alone, for the Father is with me" (Jn. 16:32).

Nothing can be gained by denying that there is a crisis in the modern Catholic priesthood. We read about it daily in our secular and religious newspapers and magazines. There are a number of factors contributing to this upheaval, but we cannot go into them in detail here. The Pope himself is keenly aware of what is going on and wrote recently (June 30, 1968):

Undoubtedly, priests have no special shelter from the repercussions of the crisis of transformation which is upsetting the world today. Like all their brothers in the faith, they, too, experience hours of darkness in their journey toward God. Moreover, they suffer because of the frequently biased way in which certain facts of priestly life are interpreted and unjustly generalized. Therefore, we ask priests to remember that the situation of every Christian, and particularly of every priest, will always be a paradoxical and incomprehensible situation to those who have no faith. Hence, the present state of things urges the priest to deepen his faith, to realize ever more clearly to whom he belongs, with what powers he is invested, with what mission he is charged. Beloved sons and brothers, we ask our Lord to make us able and worthy to give you some light, some consolation.

To all priests, then, we say: Never doubt the nature of your ministerial priesthood, for it is not a commonplace office or service to be exercised for the ecclesial community, but a service which participates in a very special manner, through the sacrament of Orders and with an indelible character, in the power of the priesthood of Christ.

Human frailty

In his encyclical on priestly celibacy, Pope Paul spoke with personal love as well as official concern about those who have tragically abandoned their priestly witness. He saw in their leaving not only individual disasters, the dimensions of which they themselves well know, but a catastrophe for the Church at large. No new appraisal of the sacred and secular, no sympathy born of deeper insights into human frailty or human needs, alters the fact that Christian peoples generally, dedicated religious and seminarians eager to grow in the image of Christ, are scandalized by the derelict priest and threatened in the pursuit of their own sacred destinies.

In their collective pastoral, the U. S. bishops referred to the scandal given by priests abandoning their calling, urged them to a penitential return, and tried to find out where the responsibility lay for the withdrawals. They wrote:

Some priests, whose vocation it remains to mirror Christ, have not only lost their own vision but have sought to shatter the ideals of others and made a public display of their defects. We urge such priests, motivated by their personal need of repentance as well as by a public obligation of example, speedily to reconcile themselves, as priests have done for centuries, with the Christ whose priesthood all unworthily, even in the case of saints, we sinners bear. To the priests of the twentieth century no less than to His contemporary disciples, Christ speaks a language that is diminished in its gravity by no findings of psychology, sociology or theology:

"Anyone who is a scandal to bring down one of these little ones who have faith in me would be better drowned in the depths of the sea with a great millstone round his neck. Alas for the world that there should be such scandals. Scandals indeed there must be but alas for the man who provides them!" (Mt. 18:6-7)

On the other hand, in manner at once impressive and unique, the priest, every priest, is a sign of fidelity to all the People of God; he proclaims God's faithfulness in raising up the priests He promised and he proclaims the Church's faithfulness in serving God and leading men to Him.

Are we and our people to believe that a significant number of priests have lost the vision that gives meaning to their vocation? Even if there are only a few who waver, why has this come about?

To some extent we bishops may be responsible. To some extent the laity may be responsible. It still remains true, however, that, as in any other collapse of ideals or failures of commitment, the individuals involved, in this case priests, have their plain personal responsibility. However, in this sad problem we have no need for accusers or victims. There is too much sorrow, too much guilt among all of us for that.

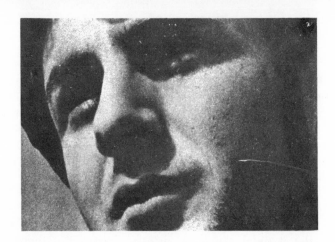

Do you know that His call is for the strong?

(Paul VI)

Undertaking of love

The priesthood has its difficulties, but the priest likewise has many helps in his difficult life. The Vatican II document, *On the Ministry and Life of Priests*, goes into these in detail as follows:

In order that, in all conditions of life, they may be able *to grow in union with Christ, priests,* besides the exercise of their conscious ministry, *enjoy the common and particular means, old and new, which the Spirit never ceases to arouse in the People of God* and which the Church commends, and sometimes commands, for the sanctification of her members. Outstanding among all these spiritual aids are those acts by which the faithful are nourished in the word of God at the double table of the *Sacred Scripture* and the *Eucharist.* The importance of frequent use of these for the sanctification of priests is obvious to all. The ministers of sacramental grace are intimately united to Christ our Savior and Pastor through the fruitful reception of the sacraments, especially sacramental *Penance,* in which, prepared by the daily examination of conscience, the necessary conversion of heart and love for the Father of Mercy is greatly deepened.

Nourished by *spiritual reading,* under the light of faith, they can more diligently seek signs of God's will and impulses of His grace in the various events of life, and so from day to day become more docile in the mission they have assumed in the Holy Spirit. They will always find a wonderful example of such docility in the Blessed Virgin Mary, who was led by the Holy Spirit to dedicate herself totally to the mystery of man's redemption. Let priests love and venerate with filial devotion and veneration this *mother of the Eternal High Priest, Queen of Apostles and Protectress of their own ministry* (n. 18).

Speaking of the place of prayer in a priest's life, Pope John XXIII wrote in the encyclical, *From the Beginning of Our Priesthood:*

"Faithfulness to prayer is for the priest a duty of personal piety, of which the wisdom of the Church has defined precisely several important points, like the *daily meditation,* the *visit to the most Blessed Sacrament,* the *rosary* and the *examination of one's conscience.* And it is also a strict obligation contracted with the Church when it is a question of the *daily recitation of the Divine Office.* Probably because they have neglected some of these regulations, some members of

the clergy have found themselves the victims of an outward instability, of interior impoverishment, and exposed one day without defense to the temptations of life."

There is a crying need for vocations today to care for the People of God. The need is felt everywhere but it is particularly acute in missionary lands, in Latin America, Africa, and the nations of the Far East—India, Japan and China. At the moment, mainland China is closed to the missionary, but this will not always be so, and the time will come when priests and nuns will once more spread the Gospel in that country.

On the World Day of Prayer for Vocations, March 5, 1967, Pope Paul issued a resounding call for more and more vocations.

Why does the Church manifest so much interest in vocations? Precisely because of the extraordinary value each holy vocation carries within itself. How could the Church be indifferent, or negligent—the Church who is mother and teacher of souls—in view of such a spiritual phenomenon, in which the most priceless virtues of a soul manifest themselves and in which the grace of the Holy Spirit is actualized in admirable ways and degrees.

Each vocation toward God's worship and toward service of the Church deserves the most lively attention on the part of those who cultivate, or who watch over the garden of souls. A vocation brings to reality in an eminent degree the flowering of God's kingdom in the world, whether in the Church or in the world as a whole. It is a sign of the presence of Love that comes from above; it is the beginning of a dialogue between the living Christ and the people—the family, the parish, the diocese—from whose bosom the chosen one is called. A judgment of values obliges the Church to concern itself with vocations.

But there is more. A judgment of necessity doubles such an obligation. Vocations are the hope of the Church where its constitutional solidity and its spiritual effectiveness are concerned. The Church, such as Christ wanted it to be, does not live without ministers. Evangelization requires them; the Gospel will be spread in proportion to the number, activity and sanctity of the ministers, called and consecrated to the most sublime, the most indispensable service—that of salvation.

We recall vividly the descriptive words of St. Paul: "For whoever calls upon the name of the Lord, shall be saved. How then are they to call upon him in whom they have not believed? But how are they to believe in him whom they have not heard? And how are they to hear, if no one preaches? And how are men to preach unless they are sent?" (Rom. 10:13-15)

The need for a ministry qualified to irradiate the truth and grace brought by Christ in the world could not be expressed in more positive terms. And here is the drama! The Church does not send forth paid mercenaries; the Church does not organize a network of professional propagandists. The Church sends forth volunteers. She sends forth men who are free and who surely are not paid for what is required by their work in terms of labor, risk and merit.

The Church sends forth special men – poor and generous, free from every compulsion, and bound within by the most sacrosanct of bonds, that of unique, chaste, perennial, consecrated love.

The Church sends forth followers of Christ who give their all to Him. The Church sends forth young men filled with ardent fervor and imagination, who have had an insight into the highest definition of life: an undertaking of divine love.

The Church sends forth humble heroes who believe in the Holy Spirit, and who, like Christ, are ready to give their life for the Church of Christ: "Christ...loved the Church and delivered Himself up for it" (Eph. 5:15); thus are the chosen, those whom the bishop welcomes, tests, instructs and then "ordains," in other words, charges with a sacramental efficacy of power and of tremendous and ineffable gifts, and then sends forth. He sends them forth to God's people; to children, to the poor, to those who suffer, to the weary, to the disciples of the Kingdom, and to the missions, to those far removed, to all! And they go forth. How marvelous!

But where are these chosen ones? Where are the ones who are called? Which are they and how many are they? Ecclesiastical sociology shows, here and there, some statistics which at times are distressing! Where are such vocations which appear to decide the fate of Christianity in our world and in our times? The drama is this: Jesus Himself gave warning of it: "The harvest indeed is great, but the laborers are few" (Mt. 9:37).

But, indeed, there are still vocations in the Church in our century. Our seminaries are rejoicing. Often a singularity of vocations **substitutes for number. There come young men who already have a** conscientious awareness and who are mature men. They know what they are choosing.

At this point, we would like to send to all those who are called to the priesthood and to the religious life: men and women (and what a discourse the women who are "called" would be deserving of!), we would like to send to all of them our affectionate greeting. May all seminarians, may all students with adult vocations, may all novices (men and women) of the religious families know that the Pope stands with them, prays for them, and, with tears of joy and hope, blesses all and each of them in the name of the Christ whom they go to meet.

Nevertheless, our heart still is not free from great anxiety: there are too many empty places in the framework of the services which the Church has need of: the number of vocations is too scanty in proportion to the needs. And we will go further, they are too scanty in proportion to the possibilities for the ministry. At times, this or that community of the faithful appears too indifferent to the problem of recruitment and formation of the clergy for our hearts to be placated.

We wish we could reach the doorways of the homes of many Christian families with a discreet, but frank, word: Do you have any vocations among your children?

We wish we could reach every pastor, every spiritual teacher: Are you watchful to discover the signs of a divine calling among the persons entrusted to your care?

We would like to thank and encourage the superiors and teachers of our seminaries and to tell them of the merit of their great solicitude.

And then, like the messengers of the Gospel word on the roads of the world, we would like to say to youths, among all the rest: Do you know that Christ needs you? Do you know that His call is for the strong; that it is for those who rebel against mediocrity and the cowardice of a comfortable and insignificant life; that it is for those who maintain an understanding of the Gospel and feel the duty to regenerate the ecclesiastical life with their own personal contribution and by bearing the cross?

Would that our cry be heard! But, meanwhile, we ask all, yes, all of you members of the holy Church of God, to welcome our invitation and to do at least one thing: do what Christ Himself commanded: *"Pray...the Lord of the harvest that He send forth laborers into His harvest" (Mt. 9:38).*

Despite the fact that the priesthood is experiencing a severe crisis, the American bishops did not hesitate to sound a clarion call for more vocations. In their collective pastoral, *The Church in Our Day,* they wrote:

It may not be too much to say that countless priests today dwell in the desert of their temptations. Like their Master, they are tempted to become ministers of the temporal city of man, forsaking their consecration as ministers of Redemption and neglecting Scripture's mandate that they "must worship the Lord their God, and serve Him alone" (Mt. 4:10).

No benefits of the affluent society or the age of technology can remove the cross and its redeeming burden from the shoulders of any who bear the name of Christian, especially when they are ordained ministers of Christ as we priests are called to be. Conversely, the joy of the priesthood is and must forever be different from any joy which this world alone or the human condition as such can instill.

This said, let us begin candidly. We need every brother priest who is truly a priest. More: humanity needs him. More still: the Church of Christ needs not merely the priesthood but everyone who qualifies to accept its burdens, dispense its mysteries, achieve its works. Most of all: Christ needs the priest so much that "when he dies (the priest) can say to his Lord: 'I am an unprofitable servant.'

But he can also add: 'You made me a priest, Lord! It was your idea, after all. It was you who pretended that you needed me'" (Abbe Michonneau: *My Father's Business*).

The priest bears within him not only the consecration received through us bishops but the hopes of all the redeemed for the future.

Toward the Gospel ideal

What kind of training is given to students for the priesthood? The Vatican *Decree on Priestly Training* went into details on this matter and the following points, taken from it, are noted:

The spiritual training should be closely connected with the doctrinal and pastoral, and, with the special help of the spiritual director, should be imparted in such a way that the students might learn to live in an intimate and unceasing union with the Father through His Son Jesus Christ in the Holy Spirit....

The students should be taught to seek Christ in the faithful meditation on God's word, in the active participation in the sacred mysteries of the Church, especially in the Eucharist and in the divine office, in the bishop who sends them and in the people to whom they are sent, especially the poor, the children, the sick, the sinners and the unbelievers. They should love and venerate with a filial trust the most blessed Virgin Mary, who was given as mother to the disciple by Christ Jesus as He was dying on the cross.

Those practices of piety that are commended by the long usage of the Church should be zealously cultivated; but care should be taken lest the spiritual formation consist in them alone or lest it develop only a religious affectation. *The students should learn to live according to the Gospel ideal*, to be strengthened in faith, hope and charity, so that, in the exercise of these practices, they may acquire the spirit of prayer, learn to defend and strengthen their vocation, obtain an increase of other virtues and grow in the zeal to gain all men for Christ.

The students should be so saturated with the mystery of the Church, that, bound to the Vicar of Christ in a humble and trusting charity and, once ordained priests, adhering to their own bishop as faithful helpers and engaging in a common effort with their fellow-priests, they bear witness to that unity that attracts men to Christ.

The students are to be made clearly *aware* of the burdens they will be undertaking, and no problem of the priestly life is to be concealed from them. This is to be done, however, not that they should be almost solely concerned with the notion of danger in their future labors, but rather that they might be more readily conformed to a *spiritual life* that more than in any other way is actually strengthened by the very pastoral work they do.

Students ought rightly to acknowledge the duties and dignity of Christian matrimony, which is a sign of the love between Christ and the Church. Let them recognize, however, the surpassing excellence of virginity consecrated to Christ, so that with a maturely deliberate and generous choice they may consecrate themselves to the Lord by a complete gift of body and soul.

They are to be warned of the dangers that threaten their chastity especially in present-day society. Aided by suitable safeguards, both divine and human, let them learn to integrate their renunciation of marriage in such a way that they may suffer in their lives and work not only no harm from celibacy but rather acquire a deeper mastery of soul and body and a fuller maturity, and more perfectly receive the blessedness spoken of in the Gospel.

In the initiation to ecclesiastical studies *the mystery of salvation should be so proposed that the students perceive the meaning, order, and pastoral end of their studies*. At the same time they should be helped to establish and penetrate their own entire lives with faith and be strengthened in embracing their vocation with a personal dedication and a joyful heart....

There should be stirred up in the students a love of rigorously searching for the truth and of maintaining and demonstrating it, together with an honest recognition of the limits of human knowledge. Attention must be carefully drawn to the necessary connection between philosophy and the true problems of life, as well as the questions which preoccupy the minds of the students. Likewise, students should be helped to perceive the links between the subject-matter of philosophy and the mysteries of salvation which are considered in theology under the higher light of faith.

The theological disciplines, in the light of faith and under the guidance of the magisterium of the Church, should be so taught that the students will correctly draw out Catholic doctrine from divine Revelation, profoundly penetrate it, make it the food of their own spiritual lives, and be enabled to proclaim, explain, and protect it in their priestly ministry.

The students are to be formed with particular care in the study of the Bible, which ought to be, as it were, *the soul of all theology*. After a suitable introduction they are to be initiated carefully into the method of exegesis; and they are to see the great themes of divine revelation and to receive from their daily reading of and meditating on the sacred books inspiration and nourishment (nn. 8, 9, 10, 14, 15, 16).

Who will go in my place...

One day a "Kaffir" of South Africa named Paul declared to a missionary: "Father, I have always wanted to become a priest. Please send me to the seminary so that I can study for the priesthood."

"The seminary," the missionary repeated, thinking over his disastrous financial situation. "That means several years of study and costs sixty sterlings. Where will you get them, my son?"

"I already thought of this!" Paul answered quickly. "I am fourteen years old and strong; I will go to Johannesburg and work in the mines. If I save everything possible, in two years I will have the sixty sterlings I need for the seminary."

The life of a miner is not the best suited to cultivate a vocation, but for Paul it represented the great hope of reaching the seminary. So he went to work in the mines of Johannesburg, guarded his vocation and skimped on everything—perhaps too much. After two years he reappeared at the mission.

"Father, I have the sixty sterlings!"

The missionary examined him closely. Paul had grown; his eyes still had their look of goodness, but he had a dry cough which worried the missionary.

"Wonderful!" the priest exclaimed. "But I don't like the sound of that cough. I suggest you see a doctor." The answer given by the hospital was a death sentence: advanced tuberculosis.

After the missionary sadly told this to the young man, the two of them remained silent, without looking at one another. Then with heroic calm, Paul asked: "Father, how much time do I have left?"

"The doctors say two, three years...."

"Two years is enough. I'll return to the mines and earn another sixty sterlings. They can be used for two boys who will go to the seminary in my place...."

The priest embraced the boy with tears in his eyes.

What is a priest?

In the year 1786 a little boy was born in France. As he grew up, he desired to be a priest. He went to the seminary but was so poor in studies that he could not pass his examinations. They were going to send him away, but France badly needed priests, so they ordained him anyway. "God's grace will do the rest," they said. Well, this dunce of a priest loved God and souls to perfection. He never sinned himself, but he prayed, he fasted, he scourged himself to blood for the sins of the world. He spent hours in the confessional forgiving the offenses of others. The devil feared him so much that he tormented him for almost thirty-eight years. This priest, by his prayers and sufferings—not by his brains or his organizational powers!—first converted his parish, practically converted France and if he had lived would have converted all Europe. Lucifer himself cried out in admiration at him: "Three more like you and my kingdom would be destroyed!" This priest died in 1859 and was canonized in 1925. His name? John Baptist Mary Vianney, the Curé of Ars. What is a priest? What is a saint?

Deacons

Recently the diaconate has been revived as a practical functioning order within the Church. Already ordained deacons are at work in various countries throughout the world.

The *Dogmatic Constitution on the Church* had this to say about the diaconate:

At a lower level of the hierarchy are deacons, upon whom hands are imposed "not unto the priesthood, but unto a ministry of service." For strengthened by sacramental grace, in communion with the bishop and his group of priests they serve in the diaconate of the liturgy, of the word, and of charity to the people of God.

It is the duty of the deacon, according as it shall have been assigned to him by competent authority, to administer Baptism solemnly, to be custodian and dispenser of the Eucharist, to assist at and bless marriages in the name of the Church, to bring Viaticum to the dying, to read the Sacred Scripture to the faithful, to instruct and exhort the people, to preside over the worship and prayer of the faithful, to administer sacramentals, to officiate at funeral and burial services.

Dedicated to duties of charity and of administration, let deacons be mindful of the admonition of Blessed Polycarp: "Be merciful, diligent, walking according to the truth of the Lord, who became the servant of all."

Since these duties, so very necessary to the life of the Church, can be fulfilled only with difficulty in many regions in accordance with the discipline of the Latin Church as it exists today, the diaconate can in the future be restored as a proper and permanent rank of the hierarchy. It pertains to the competent territorial bodies of bishops, of one kind or another, with the approval of the Supreme Pontiff, to decide whether and where it is opportune for such deacons to be established for the care of souls.

With the consent of the Roman Pontiff, this diaconate can, in the future, be conferred upon men of more mature age, even upon those living in the married state.

It may also be conferred as a permanent state upon suitable young men, for whom the law of celibacy must remain intact (n. 29).

It is interesting to note that some of the greatest saints in the Church were deacons. St. Stephen, the first martyr in the Church was a deacon. St. Philip was one of the seven deacons chosen by the apostles. St. Lawrence, another martyr, was one of the seven deacons of Rome under Pope St. Sixtus II.

St. Ephrem the Syrian was likewise a deacon and is a Doctor of the Church. The great St. Francis of Assisi was also a deacon.

Religious life

One should not confuse the priesthood or "ecclesiastical state" with the "religious state."

a) The priest receives Holy Orders; the religious, instead, embraces the "religious profession." The religious binds himself to God with the three vows of poverty, chastity and obedience, lived in community life, that is, in union with the other members of an institute or religious order approved by the Church.

b) The religious state can be embraced by women, as well as men, while the ecclesiastical state is reserved for men only.

c) The "calling" to the religious state is open to all and presents itself as the culminating point of Christian perfection, while the calling to the priesthood is reserved to those fortunate ones whom God Himself chooses for such a divine office, not so much for the person's own gain as for the service he will render to Christianity; no man in himself is worthy of such an honor.

d) The founder of the religious state is Jesus, the first and most perfect religious. He offered His whole life as a hymn of praise and a holocaust to His Father. He is the poorest of religious: He was born in a stable; He lived humbly in the little house of Nazareth, earning His bread by the sweat of His brow; He died in utter poverty, nailed to a cross. He is all sanctity and purity: He is the lover of chastity and holy virginity; His Mother, Mary Immaculate, was a virgin, as was His foster father; virgin was His precursor, St. John the Baptist; and He wanted His own apostles to abandon "brothers or sisters, father, or mother, or wife, or children," to be His own disciples and form with Him a new family.

Without obliging anyone, our Lord Himself left us the example of highest religious perfection. He wanted the apostles to renounce everything and live a life in common with Him. And when the rich young man in the Gospel asked Him what he should do, besides observing the commandments, to gain life everlasting, Jesus indicated to him the sublime ideal of religious life: "Go, sell whatever you have, and give to the poor, and you shall have treasure in heaven; and come, follow me" (Mk. 10:21).

Jesus offers the same invitation to many others. Some answer enthusiastically; others do not.

Each religious order or congregation has for its primary purpose the glory of God and the personal sanctification of its members, and as a second aim, the salvation of souls by means of its specific apostolate. To achieve their personal sanctification, religious profess the three vows of poverty, chastity and obedience and live community life. Religious life also entails a rule, silence, recollection, penance and renunciation.

Our Lord says of religious that "they have chosen the best part, and it will not be taken away from them" (Lk. 10:42).

"Religious life," writes St. Mary Magdalene de Pazzi, "is a heaven on earth, where the soul is closely united with God, partaking of the treasures of the Church with greater abundance and enjoying the sweetest peace." The vocation to the religious state is the greatest grace, after Baptism, that the Lord can give to His disciples.

Without doubt, religious life, lovingly and faithfully observed, is the surest way to reach sanctity. As a matter of fact, the majority of canonized saints of the Church belong to religious orders and congregations.

Secular institutes

Secular Institutes are characteristically different from religious communities in that they do not live a common life, in the sense of sharing a common roof and board. While a few of the societies resemble religious congregations, the ideal is for the members to live and develop spiritually in the environment of their own homes while carrying on the work of their particular apostolate.

All those who would like to become members of a Secular Institute must make a complete offering of themselves to God through the vow or oath of chastity. This oath or vow means that these individuals must not only be willing to live celibate lives, that is, freely renounce the rights and privileges of entering the married state, but they also must practice lives of perfect virginity while living in the world.

Some Secular Institutes accept married persons. Since they are married, these same persons do not have full membership in these societies because of their inability to profess the evangelical counsels but they do share in the apostolate of the Institution by becoming associated members.

The vocation to the life of a Secular Institute is a special vocation by which a person through the evangelical counsels of chastity, poverty, and obedience dedicates his life to Almighty God in his everyday work-a-day life.

CHALLENGE

In the world today there are no clearly defined battle lines drawn up, but in this total war against the power of Satan it is all rear guard action with hand to hand fighting. Now Jesus calls for your aid. What must you do?

You are only one person but the good that you do can affect the world and it will live on after you.

Eight hundred years ago St. Francis of Assisi chose to be poor, although he was born rich, and millions have followed his steps. St. Francis Xavier left for the teeming Orient alone and baptized 100,000 souls for Christ. St. Therese, the Little Flower, shows us that one person can remain exactly where he is and still do immeasurable good for Christ. She remained in her convent, dying there when she was in her early twenties, but because she loved the missions she gave invaluable aid to the missionaries and at her canonization the Pope made her patroness of the Catholic Missions.

Do you realize the power you have? Jesus has asked for your help. Your Lord calls for you to live and fight for Him. True, you are just one person. However, you are just the one person that Christ wants.

J.J. D AMATO, *Ready or Not!*

18

MARRIED
LIFE

One day Ignace Paderewski, the great Polish pianist, noticed a woman with a happy face in a group of strangers. "What are you thinking of?" he asked.

"I was marveling at being happier than I had ever dreamed."

"Do you mean that you are happier as an adult than when you were a schoolgirl?"

"Certainly!"

"Madam," concluded the pianist, bowing, "I would be very happy to meet your husband."

In a survey based on the question: "Do you find married life better than you thought it would be?" only 22% answered, "yes." Why?...

Father E. Crippa once wrote:

"At one time it seemed useless for the Church to remind newlyweds to love one another. Then She understood that this admonition was necessary since it is not easy to renew oneself daily in affection, to give without lending; never to ask for a return of the gift already given unless it is to offer it again with more tenderness, a gift made more real from the suffering borne together along the path of life."

There *are* many happy marriages. There are many couples who at sixty are still both teasing and tender, whose marriage still is the "great thing" in their lives, who are still surprising each other with little gifts and treats, who still look for one another at a party if they have been separated for a quarter of an hour.

Husband and wife get out of their marriage what they put into it. If they take the time and make the effort to keep their love alive and growing, to build a home and raise children with sacrifice and loving dedication, the joys they taste are immense — even in hard times.

And through it all they can always count on Christ's help, on the grace of the sacrament with which they began their married life.

Marriage, in the human order, is a legitimate bond between two people—a man and a woman—both of them legally capable of entering into it and conferring upon one another the mutual and perpetual right to actions designed for the generation of children and also for the leading of life together. As a sacrament, marriage is nothing more than the elevation of the human bond to a supernatural level. Both the matter and form of the sacrament consist in the mutual consent given. The ministers of the sacrament of Matrimony are the contracting parties, not the priest, who merely blesses them. However, for validity the presence of an authorized priest and two witnesses is required, except in certain special instances. (At times, for special reasons, the Church makes exceptions to its regulations on the celebration of marriage. Any Catholic who desires further information on these matters may always obtain it from his parish priest.)

The sacrament of Matrimony can be regarded in two ways, the first in the making and then in its permanent state. As St. Robert Bellarmine so aptly puts it:

> For it is a sacrament like to that of the Eucharist, which not only when it is being conferred, but also while it remains, is a sacrament; for as long as the married parties are alive, so long is their union a sacrament of Christ and the Church.

Setting the scene

Getting married is a most important step and calls for much good sense. Particularly is this so today when materialistic secularism weakens the bonds of holy wedlock. Divorce is so common in the United States—a quick look at statistics will convince anyone of this—that one is forced to the conclusion that little if any thought was given to the magnitude of the obligations being undertaken, or the required qualities in either partners. In his encyclical on *Christian Marriage*, Pope Pius XI referred to the important task of preparing for marriage. In regard to the choice of a partner he wrote:

"To the proximate preparation of a good married life belongs very specially the care in choosing a partner; on that depends a great deal whether the forthcoming marriage will be happy or not, since one may be to the other either a great help in leading a Christian life, or, a great danger and hindrance.... They should, in so deliberating, keep before their minds the thought first of God and of the true religion of Christ, then of themselves, of their partner, of the children to come, as also of human and civil society, for which wedlock is a fountainhead. Let them diligently pray for divine help, so that they make their choice in accordance with Christian prudence, not indeed led by the blind and unrestrained impulse of lust, nor by any desire of riches or other base influence, but by a true and noble love and by a sincere affection for the future partner; and then let them strive in their married life for those ends for which the state was constituted by God.

Lastly, let them not omit to ask the prudent advice of their parents with regard to the partner, and let them regard this advice in no light manner, in order that by their mature knowledge and experience of human affairs they may guard against a disastrous choice, and, on the threshold of matrimony, may receive more abundantly the divine blessing of the fourth commandment: 'Honor your father and your mother that it may be well with you and you may be long-lived upon the earth' (Dt. 5:16)."

Speaking of the general preparation for Matrimony, the Pope wrote:

"The religious character of marriage, its sublime signification of grace and the union between Christ and the Church, evidently requires that those about to marry should show a holy reverence towards it, and zealously endeavor to make their marriage approach as nearly as possible to the archetype of Christ and the Church....

"It cannot be denied that the basis of a happy wedlock, and the ruin of an unhappy one, is prepared and set in the souls of boys and girls during the period of childhood and adolescence.

"There is danger that those who before marriage sought in all things what is theirs, who indulged even their impure desires, will be in the married state what they were before, that they will reap that which they have sown.

"Indeed, within the home there will be sadness, lamentation, mutal contempt, strife, estrangements, weariness of common life, and worst of all, such parties will find themselves left alone with their own unconquered passions.

"Let then, those who are about to enter married life, approach that state well disposed and well prepared, so that they will be able, as far as they can, to help each other in sustaining the difficulties of life, and yet more in attending to their eternal salvation and in forming the inner man unto the fullness of the age of Christ."

In most dioceses throughout the United States, the Church provides pre-marriage and marriage counseling, either through the pre-Cana and Cana conferences or their equivalent. Attached to these is a priest, a doctor and very often a practicing psychologist or psychiatrist. Also in attendance are men and women who are themselves married and have wide as well as very practical experience in this field. Enrolling in a movement of this type cannot be too highly recommended. As a matter of fact, one is tempted to say that, given conditions as they are in the modern world, such help is imperative and essential.

Marriage is a holy way of life because it was established by God for two noble purposes: the perpetuation of the human race and the sanctification and mutual comfort of the partners. Not only are husband and wife united to establish a home and rear a family, but they are supposed to help each other by mutual love, encouragement, and good example to reach heaven.

Success in marriage depends upon the practice of virtue. Raising a family demands many sacrifices on the part of any couple. First and foremost in married life comes the practice of purity. Habits of devotedness and self-denial will render everyone peaceful, and happiness will grow with all the members continually practicing kindness, patience, understanding and cooperation toward each other.

Love is based on sacrifice. If we are willing to give up our desires and pleasures for the sake of the other person, then real love is manifested. Usually we find sacrifice irksome; however, if we love truly, sacrifice is easy, and if we love perfectly, sacrifice is a joy. The strength of our love can be measured by how much we are willing to give. Think of Jesus on the cross; you do not have to ask Him if He loves you; you know that He loves you or He would not have given His all — even to the last drop of His precious blood — to save you from hell. "Greater love than this no man has, that a man lay down his life for his friends." Cardinal Newman once said: "I would not give much for the love which is never extravagant," that is, not generous and not willing to sacrifice itself for another.

Although love must be present to make marriage a success, *love alone is not enough for a successful marriage.* Another extremely important factor is sameness of religion. Marriage is a union of two souls, minds, hearts and bodies to form one. Such intimacy requires respect for each other's ideas, mutual agreement on all big issues as well as most lesser ones and a complete sharing. How can the partners possibly be fully intimate with each other and therefore love and understand each other perfectly if they cannot agree on such basic matters as the purpose of life, sin, heaven, and how to get there? Husband and wife are supposed to help each other reach God. What kind of success will they have if they cannot even agree as to who God is and what will please Him? They must walk through life together, yet in the things that really count in life, in their conception of *why* they are living, they are worlds apart. They may agree on where they should live and what they should feed their children, while disagreeing on the far more important matter of how to *bring up* those children. In fact, there are simply very few important issues that such couples can really agree on. They spend most of their lives evading all the big questions "to keep the peace." They are actually lonely in a life that was supposed to mean complete, whole-hearted sharing of joys and sorrows.

Strengthening the bonds

If and when you get married, naturally you will want the union to be as successful as possible. That being so, you will pay particular attention to what follows. First of all you should know the proper meaning of true love. The collective pastoral of the U.S. bishops, *Human Life in Our Day,* issued on November 15, 1968, speaks of this important aspect of marriage in these terms:

"It is of supreme importance to have an exact idea of the characteristic marks and demands of conjugal love.

"This love is first of all fully human, that is to say, of the senses and of the spirit at the same time. It is not, then, a simple transport of instinct and sentiment, but also, and principally, an act of the free will, intended to endure and to grow by means of the joys and sorrows of daily life, in such a way that husband and wife become one only heart and one only soul, and together attain their human perfection.

"Then, *this love is total*, that is to say, it is a very special form of personal friendship, in which husband and wife generously share everything, without undue reservations or selfish calculations. Whoever truly loves his marriage partner loves not only for what he receives, but for the partner's self, rejoicing that he can enrich his partner with the gift of himself. Again, this love is *faithful* and *exclusive* until death. Thus, in fact, do bride and groom conceive it to be on the day when they freely and in full awareness assume the duty of the marriage bond. A fidelity, this, which can sometimes be difficult, but is always possible, always noble and meritorious, as no one can deny. The example of so many married persons down through the centuries shows not only that fidelity is according to the nature of marriage, but also that it is a source of profound and lasting happiness and finally, this love is *fecund* for it is not exhausted by the communion between husband and wife, but is destined to continue, raising up new lives. 'Marriage and conjugal love are by their nature ordained toward the begetting and educating of children. Children are really the supreme gift of marriage and contribute very substantially to the welfare of their parents' (Const. on Church in Modern World, n. 50)."

Both Sts. Peter and Paul counsel husband and wife to love one another, but they also stress the necessity for the wife to obey her husband. Obedience does not stultify personality, nor is it slavery, as many American women are inclined to believe. Neither apostle advocates tyranny on the part of the husband—or indeed of the wife!—but since the husband is the head of the home, he should be obeyed.

St. Peter says:

Let wives be subject to their husbands; so that even if any do not believe the word, they may without word be won through the behavior of their wives, observing reverently your chaste behavior. Let not theirs be the outward adornment of braiding the hair, or of wearing gold, or of putting on robes; but let it be the inner life of the heart, in the imperishableness of a quiet and gentle spirit, which is of a great price in the sight of God. For after this manner in old times the holy women also who hoped in God adorned themselves, while being subject to their husbands. So Sara obeyed Abraham, calling him lord. You are daughters of hers when you do what is right and fear not disturbance.

Husbands, in like manner dwell with your wives considerately, paying honor to the woman as the weaker vessel, and as

Love is sharing, willing, doing the good of another.

It is sacrifice and the forgetting of self.

co-heir of the grace of life, that your prayers be not hindered (1 Pet. 3:1-7).

St. Paul writes:

Be subject to one another in the fear of Christ. Let wives be subject to their husbands as to the Lord; because a husband is head of the wife, just as Christ is head of the Church, being himself savior of the body. But just as the Church is subject to Christ, so also let wives be to their husbands in all things. Husbands, love your wives, just as Christ also loved the Church, and delivered himself up for her, that he might sanctify her, cleansing her in the bath of water by means of the word; in order that he might present to himself the Church in all her glory, not having spot or wrinkle or any such thing, but that she might be holy and without blemish. Even thus ought husbands also to love their wives as their own bodies. He who loves his own wife, loves himself. For no one ever hated his own flesh; on the contrary he nourishes and cherishes it, as Christ also does the Church (because we are members of his body, made from his flesh and from his bones). "For this cause a man shall leave his father and mother, and cleave to his wife; and the two shall become one flesh." This is a great mystery—I mean in reference to Christ and to the Church. However, let each one of you also love his wife just as he loves himself; and let the wife respect her husband (Eph. 5:21-23).

"Staffwork"

Marriage is a full time job, even for people who love one another. Like everything else, it must be worked at, if it is to be successful. Field Marshal Montgomery, one of the most outstanding generals of World War II, once said that marriage requires a lot of "staffwork." This, of course, is everyone's experience, and the numerous proverbs about Matrimony, gathered from all parts of the world, prove the truth of the statement. Just to quote one that almost everyone has heard: "Love is blind, but marriage is an eye-opener." Pope Pius XI spoke of this in his marriage encyclical. He wrote:

"Since it is a law of divine Providence in the supernatural order that men do not reap the full fruit of the sacraments which they receive after acquiring the use of reason unless they cooperate with grace, *the grace of Matrimony will re-*

main for the most part an unused talent hidden in the field
unless the parties exercise these supernatural powers and cul-
tivate and develop the seeds of grace they have received. If,
however, doing all that lies within their power, they cooperate
diligently, they will be able with ease to bear the burdens of
their state and to fulfill their duties. By such a sacrament they
will be strengthened, sanctified and in a manner consecrated."

The Pope continued:

"Let husband and wife resolve: to stand fast to the commandments of God in all things that matrimony demands; always to
render to each other the assistance of mutual love; to preserve
the honor of chastity; not to lay profane hands on the stable
nature of the bond; to use the rights given them by marriage
in a way that will be always Christian and sacred, more especially in the first years of wedlock, so that should there be
need of continency afterwards, custom will have made it
easier for each to preserve it.

"In order that they may make this firm resolution, keep it and
put it into practice, an oft-repeated consideration of their
state of life, and a diligent reflection on the sacrament they
have received, will be of great assistance to them. Let them
constantly keep in mind, that they have been sanctified and
strengthened for the duties and the dignity of their state by
a special sacrament, the efficacious power of which, although
it does not impress a character, is undying."

The Church is very conscious of the fact that the married
state brings its own peculiar problems and during the actual
marriage ceremony, in the Nuptial Mass, prays for both partners, that by the help of grace, they may surmount all difficulties.

As we pointed out already, each sacrament confers a special grace, apart from sanctifying grace. The sacramental grace
of Matrimony consists in this: it confers the grace to beget
and educate children, to control the passions, and to foster
mutual love in a bond of common living. Married people
should remind themselves constantly of this and make use of
this sacramental grace, cooperating with God as much as they
can to smooth over difficulties.

From Christian marriage springs the Christian family, the
basic unit of society. Children must honor and obey their
parents; parents must see to it that their sons and daughters
are properly cared for and given a good Catholic education.

Today in America there can be and is much tension between parents and children. Young people, inexperienced but strongly motivated, are inclined to dismiss their parents as relics of a past age. "Any one over thirty can't be trusted," many of the younger crowd say. On their side, parents may fail to understand the psychology of modern youth, growing up in an atmosphere radically different from that in which their fathers and mothers spent their early years. The result is that a chasm of misunderstanding yawns between old and young, between parents and their children. This must be bridged at all costs and there is but one way — the simple, human way of sitting down together, and through ordinary conversation — call it dialogue if you wish — trying to understand one another.

The *Pastoral Constitution on the Church in the Modern World* refers to parental duties in these wise sentences:

Parents should regard as their proper mission the task of transmitting human life and educating those to whom it has been transmitted. They should realize that they are thereby *cooperators with the love of God the Creator,* and are, so to speak, the interpreters of that love. Thus they will fulfill their task with human and Christian responsibility, and, with docile reverence toward God, will make decisions by common counsel and effort. Let them thoughtfully take into account both their own welfare and that of their children, those already born and those which the future may bring. For this accounting they need to reckon with both the material and the spiritual conditions of the times as well as of their state in life. Finally, they should consult the interests of the family group, of temporal society, and of the Church herself. The parents themselves and no one else should ultimately make this judgment in the sight of God. *But in their manner of acting, spouses should be aware that they cannot proceed as they please, but must always be governed according to a conscience dutifully conformed to the divine law itself, and should be submissive toward the Church's teaching office, which authentically interprets that law in the light of the Gospel.* That divine law reveals and protects the integral meaning of conjugal love, and impels it toward a truly human fulfillment.

Thus, trusting in divine Providence and refining the spirit of sacrifice, married Christians glorify the Creator and strive toward fulfillment in Christ when with a generous human and Christian sense of responsibility they fulfill the duty to procreate. Among the couples who fulfill their God-given task in this way, those merit special mention who with a gallant heart, and with wise and common deliberation, undertake to bring up suitably even a relatively large family (n. 50).

Birth control

On the subject of birth control, the same Vatican II document declared:

God, the Lord of life, has conferred on men the surpassing ministry of safeguarding life in a manner which is worthy of man. Therefore from the moment of its conception life must be guarded with the greatest care. The sexual characteristics of man and the human faculty of reproduction wonderfully exceed the dispositions of lower forms of life. Hence the acts themselves which are proper to conjugal love and which are exercised in accord with genuine human dignity must be honored with great reverence. Hence when there is question of harmonizing conjugal love with the responsible transmission of life, the moral aspect of any procedure does not depend solely on sincere intentions or on an evaluation of motives, but must be determined by objective standards. These, based on the nature of the human person and his acts preserve the full sense of mutual self-giving and human procreation in the context of true love. Such a goal cannot be achieved unless the virtue of conjugal chastity is sincerely practiced. *Relying on these principles, sons of the Church may not undertake methods of birth control which are found blameworthy by the teaching authority of the Church in its unfolding of the divine law.*
All should be persuaded that human life and the task of transmitting it are not realities bound up with this world alone. Hence they cannot be measured or perceived only in terms of it, but always have a bearing on the eternal destiny of men (n. 51).

Before taking final leave of this topic we quote the following from Pope Paul's encyclical, *On Human Life:*

Let married couples, then, face up to the efforts needed, supported by the faith and hope which do not disappoint...because God's love has been poured into our hearts through the Holy Spirit, who has been given to us; let them implore divine assistance by persevering prayer; above all, let them draw from the source of grace and charity in the Eucharist. And if sin should still keep its hold over them, let them not be discouraged, but rather have recourse with humble perseverance to the mercy of God, which is poured forth in the sacrament of Penance (n. 25).

No room for whims

The sacrament of Matrimony is characterized by two qualities — its unity (i.e., the union is between one man and one woman) and its indissolubility (i.e., the bond cannot be broken except by the death of the husband or wife, in which case remarrying is permissible).

Scripture is quoted for both these marks of Christian marriage. Speaking of matrimonial unity, St. Mark says: "From the beginning of creation God made them male and female. 'For this cause a man shall leave his father and mother, and cleave to his wife, and the two shall become one flesh.' Therefore now they are no longer two, but one flesh. What therefore God has joined together, let no man put asunder (10:6-9).

With reference to its indissolubility the same Evangelist writes:

He said to them, "Whoever puts away his wife and marries another commits adultery against her; and if the wife puts away her husband, and marries another, she commits adultery" (10:11-12).

This has been traditional teaching in the Church. Repudiating divorce, St. Augustine once wrote:

"In the sacrament it is provided that the marriage bond should not be broken, and that a husband or wife, if separated, should not be joined to another even for the sake of offspring.

"This is safeguarded in Christ and the Church, which, living with Christ who lives forever, may never be divorced from Him. The observance of this sacrament is such in the City of God...that is, in the Church of Christ, that when for the sake of begetting children, women marry or are taken to wife, it is wrong to leave a wife that is sterile in order to take another by whom children may be had. Anyone doing this is guilty of *adultery*, just as if he married another, guilty not by the law of the day, according to which when one's partner is put away another may be taken, which the Lord allowed in the law of Moses because of the hardness of the hearts of the people of Israel; but by the law of the Gospel."

Pope Leo XIII condemned divorce in these strong words:

"Since the destruction of family life and the loss of national wealth is brought about more by the corruption of morals than by anything else, it is easily seen that *divorce,* which is born of the perverted morals of a people, and leads, as experiment shows, to vicious habits in public and private life, is particularly opposed to the well-being of the family and of the State. The serious nature of these evils will be the more clearly recognized, when we remember that, once divorce has been allowed, there will be no sufficient means of keeping it in check within any definite bounds. Great is the force of example, greater still that of lust; and with such incitements it cannot but happen that divorce and its consequent setting loose of the passions should spread daily and attack the souls of many like a contagious disease or a river bursting its banks and flooding the land.... Unless things change, the human family and State have every reason to fear lest they should suffer ruin."

This position was reasserted by Pope Pius XI in his marriage encyclical. He said:

"Christ Himself lays stress on the indissolubility and firmness of the marriage bond when He says: 'What God has joined together let no man put asunder,' and: 'Everyone who puts away his wife and marries another commits adultery, and he who marries her that is put away from her husband commits adultery.' These words refer to every kind of marriage, even that which is natural and legitimate only; for, that indissolubility, by which the loosening of the bond is once and for all removed from the whim of the parties and from every secular power, is a property of every true marriage."

The Fathers of the Second Vatican Council also re-affirmed this doctrine. We read in the *Decree on the Apostolate of the Laity:*

It has always been the duty of Christian married partners but today it is the greatest part of their apostolate to manifest and prove by their own way of life the indissolubility and sacredness of the marriage bond, strenuously to affirm the right and duty of parents and guardians to educate children in a Christian manner, and to defend the dignity and lawful autonomy of the family. They and the rest of the faithful, therefore, should cooperate with men of good will to ensure the preservation of these rights in civil legislation and to make sure that governments give due attention to the needs of the family regarding housing, the education of children, working conditions, social security, and taxes; and that in policy decisions affecting migrants their right to live together as a family should be safeguarded (n. 11).

CHALLENGE

Every man is lonely. He is an island unto himself. He is separated, anxious, and fearful. He hungers for meaning and communion in his life. To be a man is to spend a lifetime searching for total peace and happiness, searching for God. As St. Augustine put it, "Our hearts are hungry, Lord, and will never be at peace until we are at home with You." Man tries to overcome his aloneness—perhaps by getting lost in the herd, trying to belong by being like everyone else; often by feverish time-consuming activity; sometimes by sinful sexuality, hoping that in these passing encounters he will find union. These methods are foredoomed and man remains alone.

Only in true love does he bridge the gap, does he make contact with the "other" and find union. Love is a sharing, willing, doing the good of another. Love is a sharing and giving of the very self and participating in the personality of another. Love is sacrifice and the forgetting of self.

You have heard that it is better to give than to receive. Why? Not because giving is difficult and because I suffer and accept the sacrifice involved. This is not the deepest reason. But rather, when I love, when I give, it is the highest expression of my power. I know that I am good and have something, be it time, counsel, or patience, that is truly valuable because somebody needs it. Thus, not he who has much is rich but he who gives much.

CANA CONFERENCE OF CHICAGO, *Ready or Not!*

19

AT HOME WITH THE LORD

2 COR. 5:6

We believe in the life eternal.

Look up! There is hardly any need nowadays to give that piece of advice, because everybody's gaze is turned upwards. Instead of "Go West, young man, go West!" young people today are thinking in terms of *"Go space, young man, go space!"*

But "looking up" also means thinking of spiritual values, growing in hope and optimism by thinking of God, of heaven, to which we are all called. Does "thinking space" hinder us from "thinking spiritually"?

Wernher Von Braun, developer of the Saturn rocket and a key figure in the U.S. space program, stated some definite convictions on this subject:

"Our religion, our environment and our outlook have been earthbound," he said. "Astronomy and space explorations are teaching us that the good Lord is a much greater Lord and Master of a greater kingdom."

Dr. Von Braun feels that "manned space flight is an amazing achievement, but it has opened for us thus far only a tiny door for viewing the awesome reaches of space. Our outlook through this peephole at the vast mysteries of the universe only confirms our belief in the certainty of its Creator."

The scientist, director of NASA's Space Flight Center at Hunstville, Alabama, declared:

"I believe the good Lord is full of such tremendous compassion that He will take whatever steps are necessary to bring the truth to His creation."

He sees no reason why God cannot retain the same central position in the world of technology and cyclotrons that He held before the modern scientific world dawned.

Also speaking of the July, 1969, moon landing, Pope Paul VI said much the same thing:

"The Catholic faith not only does not fear a mighty confrontation of its humble teaching with the marvelous riches of modern scientific thought but desires it. It desires it because truth, even if it spreads itself over different spheres and presents itself under various guises, still is in harmony with itself and is one."

What did the renowned physicist have to say about existence after death? On a scientific basis, Von Braun said he felt that spiritual existence continues after death. Science has found that nothing can disappear without a trace. *Nature does not know extinction. All it knows is transformation.*

"Now, if God applies this fundamental principle to the most minute and insignificant parts of His universe, doesn't it make sense to assume that He applies it also to the masterpiece of His creation—the human soul? I think it does."

Transformation! "Life is not lost, just changed." But the *kind* of existence we have after death is of *our* choosing. That is why we have to live *this* life with the next one in mind.

The necessary door

To speak of death is to mention the obvious—and the inevitable. We all know that it will come one day, marking the end of our earthly pilgrimage. "Man's days are like those of grass," say the Scriptures and again: "He is gone and his place knows him no more" (cf. Ps. 102:15, 16). We should often think of death, not in a morbid fashion but as a salutary reminder that in the words of St. Paul "Here we have no permanent city" (Heb. 13:14). In addition, the thought of death is a deterrent to sin. "Remember your last days, and you will never sin" (Sir. 7:36), again say the Scriptures. Our Lord put it very strongly: "For what does it profit a man, if he gain the whole world, but suffer the loss of his own soul? Or what will a man give in exchange for his soul?" (Mt. 16:26-27).

While the fact of death itself is certain, the when, the how, the place and the time of its coming are unknown. Speaking of death our Lord said: "You must be ready, because at an hour that you do not expect, the Son of Man will come," and again: "Two women shall be grinding at the millstone; one will be taken, and one will be left" (cf. Mt. 24:41-44).

In the parable of the foolish rich man, our Lord pointed out the folly of amassing riches just for the sake of riches. The rich owner made up his mind to pull down his barns and build bigger ones. "But God said to him: 'You fool, this night do they demand your soul of you; and the things that you have provided, whose will they be?'" (Lk. 12:16-21).

This parable presents a man who thinks of nothing but this earth. And he is labeled a fool! We must think of death and eternity. A thousand thoughts and cares, a thousand worries and problems occupy man's mind here below. We think about our reputation, about our meals, and about our clothes. Much precaution is taken when it is a matter of the health of the body. But what about the soul? Do we give it thought? And what about death? When the Church places blessed ashes on our foreheads, she tells us: "Remember you are dust!"

Presenting him with a ring, Pope Pius IX once told a man, "Wear it every day. At night, before you retire, read the two words engraved on it: *Memento mori* — Remember, you will die." The man carried out the advice for several nights, but indifferently, almost without thought. One night, however, as he prepared for bed, those words made a deep impression on him. "I am going to die," he thought, "and am I ready? If tonight were my last night on earth, in what state would I find myself as I faced the judgment of God?" The result was that he changed his way of life.

Let us make use of a holy little trick: when we wake up each morning and when we retire in the evening, let us look at the palms of our hands and, seeing the two "M's" traced thereon, think of the Latin phrase *Memento mori* — "Remember you must die." In the morning our thought will be: Today I want to live as if this were the last day of my life. I want to make a perfect act of contrition. In the evening: If death should come tonight, I want to be ready.

If more thought were given to death, how fewer sins there would be! How much more virtue, prayer and merit!

Acting with a view to death means doing now what we will then want to have done, and rejecting or avoiding now what we will then want to have avoided — sin.

"Night is coming, when no one can work" (Jn. 9:4). Let us imagine that our last hour is fast approaching and ask our conscience: what will I wish to have done in my life? the answer will certainly be easy. It will spring from the depths of the heart with devastating conviction.

A farmer who has sown no seed cannot look for a crop to harvest! We reap what we sow. What a pitiful harvest it would be to leave this world with a heart still loaded down with sin. Let us sanctify ourselves now. We still have much time at our disposal. Even a little while is enough!

When Pope John knew that death was near he said: "My bags are packed and I am ready to go!" If we are right with God, we should not have too great a fear of death — a holy fear, yes! — but nothing else. Death itself is painless — have you ever thought of that? It is a passing from one life to another, like going through a door between two rooms. When Mother Catherine McAuley, foundress of the Sisters of Mercy, was dying, she said: "Oh! If I had known that death could be so sweet, I would never have feared it so much!" St. Paul gave us something similar when he wrote:

Always full of courage then, and knowing that while we are in the body we are exiled from the Lord — for we walk by faith and not by sight — we even have the courage to prefer to be exiled from the body and to be at home with the Lord. (2 Cor. 5:6)

Why should we lament about or fear death, when beyond the grave lies the true life — with God, our Lord, the Blessed Virgin, the angels, and the saints — and this for all eternity!

Death teaches us to be patient and wise in surmounting any perplexity in our life. It encourages us to live a good life and it strengthens us in our search for and expectation of future communion with Christ and with our beloved deceased. In other words, it offers us an overall vision of our existence and of the world.

A just trial

After death, Catholic doctrine teaches that there comes the particular judgment. Rev. James Alberione, S.S.P., S.T.D. has given us a vivid account of what this judgment of our whole life will be like. He writes:

In whatever place we die, there shall the judgment-seat be erected, and we shall face it alone, accompanied only by our deeds, good or bad. Christ has no need of witnesses, neither of the devil's accusations nor of the saints' defense of us. He knows all things; He is the all-wise Judge. He sees our mind and the thoughts entertained there. He knows the whole story, in detail, from start to finish. Christ knows every sentiment of our heart, from the lowest to the holiest. He knows these sentiments in all their particulars, in all their fine points, in all their intensity. Christ knows every word uttered, from the first moment of our use of reason down to the last time our lips formed a word. Every word is written in the book of life — empty words, holy words, forgotten words. "The court was convened, and the books were opened" (Dan. 7:10).

Christ knows all our most sublime actions and as well the most common, and the worst. He knows how many letters have flowed from our pen and how much labor we accomplished. He knows every step we have taken, the studies we have pursued, our relationships and correspondence, our daily routine of home life. He is, in short, the all-wise Judge.

Furthermore, our Lord knows how much should have been done, in correspondence to all His graces. He knows the degree of health a person had, the degree of intelligence, keenness of mind, memory, and ability; the graces given in childhood, youth, and adulthood; the inspirations, promptings and occasions received.

A man says to himself: "I did that one night, locked in my room, protected by darkness. It was simply a sentiment of my heart, desire, hatred.... No one ever knew, not even my confessor, for I covered it perfectly." Foolish reasoning! For there is an eye that sees everything, everywhere, always. There is an ear that hears everything, everywhere and always. There is a recording hand that misses nothing. They belong, so to speak, to God.

God sees us! And everything will show up in front of that divine, all-wise Judge. All things are reflected in Him as in a mirror. He keeps a record of everything. It is a characteristic of Divine Wisdom to have all things present at all times; for Him there is no past or future — everything is present.

What tremendous consolation for good souls! What joy for us who now reflect and pray! Christ, the most wise Judge will remember it. Jesus will remember everything — those victories over our passions, those repressions of angry impulses, that diligence at work, those quick ejaculations. Some are so diligent, yet in such a hidden fashion, that no one suspects the worth of those souls. They receive no reward on this earth, but will it always be so? Thanks be to God, it will not, for our God is omniscient, all-knowing. The good done is written on the Heart of Christ, never to be erased! We shall take our good deeds with us, for they are the property of whoever performs them.

If the judgment were to take place now, could we say that we have, for the most part, been faithful to God? A man can say that he is basically faithful if he observes the commandments, loves and serves God, prays and avoids sin. If he should fall at times, he rises again, does penance, and once more goes ahead in faithful service to the Lord. The supreme Judge, therefore, will declare that this soul has done well. "Blessed is that servant whom his master, when he comes, shall find doing his duty" (cf. Mt. 24:46). Instead, if a soul disobeys God, transgresses His laws, pursues selfish goals only, and does his duty only out of fear of what others will say — this

soul will have to admit that he has been unfaithful to God. Everyone does a little good, but we must scrutinize the substance and the
intention behind it. Was it done for God or for ourselves?

Judgment will come. For the sinner, it will be a terrible encounter with an angry Christ! Men have died of fear before facing certain
human courts of justice. Unworthy sons who have brought on the
death of their mother by their crimes cannot bring themselves to
face her on her deathbed.

Judgment will come. And what bliss will flood the faithful
soul when he at last meets Jesus and can contemplate Him in all His
goodness — when he sees the smile on the face of this Savior he has
sought and loved! This will be the meeting of a son with a much-
loved father whom he has yearned to see. It will be the long-awaited
embrace of friend with Friend. It will be a moment of indescribable
joy. What then must it be like to appear before God?

The departure worth missing

Although Pope Paul does not use the word hell explicitly
in his Credo, still he refers to

the fire that is not extinguished.

Hell is abundantly and plainly mentioned in Sacred
Scripture. Thus to give but one example we read in St. Luke:

Jesus passed on through towns and villages, teaching and
making his way toward Jerusalem. But someone said to him,
"Lord, are only a few to be saved?"
But he said to them, "Strive to enter by the narrow gate; for
many, I tell you, will seek to enter and will not be able. But
when the master of the house has entered and shut the door,
you will begin to stand outside and knock at the door, saying,
'Lord, open for us!' And he shall say to you in answer, 'I do
not know where you are from.' Then you shall begin to say,
'We ate and drank in your presence, and you taught in our
streets.' And he shall say to you, 'I do not know where you are
from. Depart from me, all you workers of iniquity.' There will
be the weeping, and the gnashing of teeth, when you shall see
Abraham and Isaac and Jacob and all the prophets in the kingdom of God, but you yourselves cast forth outside. And they
will come from the east and from the west, from the north and
from the south, and will feast in the kingdom of God. And behold, there are those last who will be first, and there are those
first who will be last" (13:22-30).

"In the arms of the darkest desperation, the damned make us hear," says St. Ephrem, "this heart-rending farewell: 'Good-bye Apostles, Prophets, Martyrs, and all the just! Good-bye senate of the Patriarchs! Good-bye army of the anchorites! Good-bye precious and vivifying cross! Good-bye eternal kingdom of heaven, beautiful Jerusalem, mother of the elect, paradise of delights! Good-bye to you, too, our Lady, Mother of God, Mother of Him who has so loved men! Good-bye fathers and mothers, sons and daughters, husbands and wives; good-bye, we shall never see you again, never again'!"

Why does God reward the good and punish the wicked? Because He is infinite justice. The pains with which the damned in hell will be tormented are: 1) the pain of damnation, that is, the perpetual privation of the beatific vision of God; 2) the pain of sense; that is, a real fire which torments without consuming; 3) darkness, remorse and anguish of conscience; furthermore, the company of the devils, of the other damned, and the knowledge that hell will never end.

"Meditate these truths," exclaimed St. Augustine, "and of the fire of hell form a weapon against the flames of temptation which torment you during this life."

In another passage the same saint makes Jesus Christ speak: "O man, I became a child for you, I was placed in a manger, wrapped in swaddling clothes. I bore the sufferings of infancy, the anguish of manhood. I was slapped and spit upon. I was scourged, crowned with thorns, nailed on a cross: see the wounds of the nails, see my side pierced by the sword. Why, then, did you will to lose the merit of that which I suffered for you? Why did you waste and despise the benefits of the Redemption?"

It has become fashionable with some people to ignore the idea of hell and dismiss it with a wave of the hand. They look upon it as a relic of medieval superstition. But hell is a fact—and it is possible for *me!* We must be always on our guard, like the wise virgins in the parable, and have our lamps trimmed, so that when the bridegroom comes, we may be able to go in with him to the wedding feast. Otherwise, like the foolish virgins we will be locked outside (cf. Mt. 25:1-13).

"Watch and pray that you may not enter into temptation," our Lord warned the apostles in the Garden of Gethsemane (Mt. 26:41). These words also contain a warning for us!

Cleansing fire

We believe that the souls of all those who die in the grace of Christ—whether they must still be purified in purgatory, or whether from the moment they leave their bodies Jesus takes them to paradise as He did the Good Thief— are the People of God in the eternity beyond death...

THE CREDO

There is also another state—purgatory—where some souls remain for a while expiating the temporal punishment due to sin. The existence of purgatory is an article of faith defined by both the Second Lateran Council and the Council of Trent. It is also the teaching of both these councils that the souls in purgatory can be aided by our prayers. In the Second Book of Machabees, in the Old Testament, we read (12:43-46), that Judas Machabeus "making a gathering, sent twelve thousand drachmas of silver to Jerusalem for sacrifice to be offered for the sins of the dead, thinking well and religiously concerning the resurrection. (For if he had not hoped that they that were slain should rise again, it would have seemed superfluous and vain to pray for the dead). And because he considered that they who had fallen asleep with godliness had great grace laid up for them, it is therefore a holy and wholesome thought *to pray for the dead, that they may be loosed from their sins."*

Reason itself suggests the existence of an intermediate state between heaven and hell, in other words, purgatory. Let us look at it from this point of view for a moment.

The greater part of mankind is not so wicked or so obstinate in wrongdoing as to deserve hell. Most people sin out of weakness and repent as soon as possible. At least before dying, most have sentiments of sorrow and hope. Will they be condemned to hell? This would be incompatible with the justice of God since only they who die unrepentant in mortal sin are condemned to eternal punishment.

Still the majority of men are not so virtuous and full of love for God that they can enter heaven at once. *These souls who do not deserve hell but who are not yet worthy of heaven go to purgatory, where they stay until purified.* There they finish paying the temporal debt they owe God's justice.

The *Apostolic Constitution on Indulgences* emphasizes the doctrine of purgatory in these words:

That punishment or the vestiges of sin may remain to be expiated or cleansed and that they in fact frequently do, even after the remission of guilt, is clearly demonstrated by the doctrine on purgatory. In purgatory, in fact, the souls of those "who died in the charity of God and truly repentant, but before satisfying with worthy fruits of penance for sins committed and for omissions," are cleansed after death with purgatorial punishments.

God's mercy is thus led to forgiveness, so that sincerely repentant sinners may participate as soon as possible in the full enjoyment of the benefits of the family of God (nn. 3, 5).

The pains of purgatory are of two kinds. First there is the privation of the vision of God. This is the pain of loss. It is temporary and when the period of expiation has ended, souls in purgatory will be rewarded with the beatific vision. There is also another kind of punishment — the pain of sense.

"A man is punished by the very things through which he sins" (Wis. 11:16). The same human faculties which served to commit sin must submit to the torment of purification. The suffering is the same as in hell with the one difference that hell never ceases, whereas purgatory must come to an end; the pains of the former are designed to punish only, but those of purgatory serve to satisfy for sin and to free the soul.

"The fire of purgatory," says St. Augustine, "is more painful than any suffering we can imagine in this life. Oh! Blessed is the soul who will take care to purify herself in this world so as to merit the vision of God immediately after death! It is better to spend an entire lifetime in the purgatory of penance, than to remain even only a single year in the purgatory of the life to come."

We have already pointed out that we the living can aid the souls in purgatory. We are *obliged* in Christ-like charity to do this. In fact, at times this obligation may be a duty of justice, especially when there are souls for whom we are responsible, to whom we gave bad example or who did good to us, materially or spiritually. By praying often for them we hasten the time of their release. This is genuine charity for our deceased, and in return for our help these grateful souls will pray for us from heaven.

We must remember that it is not only the living who deserve our concerned action.

In chapter 8 we referred to the doctrine of indulgences. We can also help the souls in purgatory by gaining indulgences for them. In the *Apostolic Constitution on Indulgences* we read:

The "treasury of the Church," which should not be imagined as the sum total of material goods accumulated in the course of the centuries, *is the infinite and inexhaustible value the expiation and the merits of Christ our Lord have before God,* offered as they were so that all of mankind could be set free from sin and attain communion with the Father. It is Christ the Redeemer Himself in whom the satisfactions and merits of His Redemption exist and find their force. *This treasure also includes the truly immense, unfathomable and ever pristine value before God of the prayers and good works of the Blessed Virgin Mary and all the saints* who, following in the footsteps of Christ the Lord and by His grace, have sanctified their lives and fulfilled the mission entrusted to them by the Father. Thus, while attaining their salvation, they have also cooperated in the salvation of their brothers in the unity of the Mystical Body (n. 5).

Face to face

We believe that the multitude of those gathered around Jesus and Mary in paradise forms the Church of heaven, where in eternal beatitude they see God as He is, and where they also, in different degrees, are associated with the holy angels in the divine rule exercised by Christ in glory, interceding for us and helping our weakness by their brotherly care.

...and we believe that in this communion the merciful love of God and His saints is ever listening to our prayers, as Jesus told us: Ask and you will receive.   THE CREDO

Those who die in the state of grace and do not have to pass through purgatory, as well as those who in due course leave it, having expiated the temporal punishment due to sin, will enjoy the Beatific Vision.

The *Beatific Vision means seeing God face to face, as He is, in a direct manner.* On earth, we do not see God with our bodily eyes. We know Him through reason, through His creatures, and above all through His divine revelation in Scripture. *We know God now by the light of Faith but in heaven we shall know Him by the light of glory.*

We will see in God all natural knowledge—all the wonders of space, of the immense universe, of every external work of His, but more than that, we will behold even supernatural mysteries in a manner proportionate to our finite natures! *Our intelligences* will be in complete possession of the truth and our *wills* will be absolutely satisfied with possession of the God of love, who is Goodness itself.

In heaven, for all eternity, each blessed soul will see, possess, and adore God together with the angels and saints. We read in St. John:

Now we are the children of God, and it has not yet appeared what we shall be. We know that, when he appears, we shall be like to him, for we shall see him just as he is. And everyone who has this hope in him makes himself holy, just as he also is holy (3:2).

St. Paul writes:

We see now through a mirror in an obscure manner, but then face to face. Now I know in part, but then I shall know even as I have been known (1 Cor. 13:12).

Eye has not seen, nor ear heard, nor has it entered into the mind of man what things God has laid in store for those who love him.

We read in the Apocalypse of St. John:

Behold the dwelling of God with men, and he will dwell with them. And they will be his people, and God himself will be with them as their God. And God will wipe away every tear from their eyes. And death shall be no more; neither shall there be mourning, nor crying, nor pain any more, for the former things have passed away (21:3-4).

And there shall be no more any accursed thing; but the throne of God and the Lamb shall be in it, and his servants shall serve him. And they shall see his face and his name shall be on their foreheads. And the night shall be no more, and they shall have no need of lamp, or light of sun, for the Lord God will shed light upon them; and they shall reign forever and ever (Apoc. 22:3-5).

"O God," exclaimed St. Bernard, "You who know—tell us what You keep ready for us. The blessed shall have the goods of Your house in abundance, but which goods? Ah! we are seeking those wonderful marvels which eye has not seen, nor ear heard, nor mind grasped, nor heart tried."

St. Augustine echoes the same thought: "O life which God has prepared for those who love Him, life which is truly life—happy life, certain life, tranquil life, desirable life, pure life, chaste life, holy life, life which does not know death, life without sorrow, without stain, without pain, without concern, without alteration, without change, without worry: life full of beauty, of dignity, the more I meditate you, the more I desire you!" May the thought of heaven be the star of your life: in childhood, youth, manhood, old age, in joy and sorrow, in work and rest. God made us for a very happy and immortal life. We are only on trial while on earth.

All the blessed in heaven see God face to face, but some see Him more perfectly than others. This "inequality" is based on the fact that our merits earned on earth determine the degree of glory that we will attain in heaven.

Of course, there is no envy in heaven: all are completely satisfied and enjoy the glory they prepared for themselves in life.

Grace makes us members of Jesus Christ. Since the members are part of the same body and are one with the head, they share in the joy of the head. For this reason, *the blessed will know the very happiness of Jesus.* And, of course, Jesus, the Son of God, the second Person of the Trinity, enjoys the same glory as His eternal Father.

It will not be another joy that our soul will know when Christ invites us into heaven, saying, "Enter into the joy of your Master." It will be the same happiness as His own though in a different proportion, for we are always creatures.

"O heaven!" exclaimed St. John Chrysostom, "What joy, what glory these words contain: 'Come, you blessed!' and what triumph!" Oh, let us make sure that on that day Jesus can say to us too: "Come, blessed of my Father,...enter into the joy of your Lord." Come from the darkness to the light, from slavery to the freedom of the children of God, from work to eternal rest, from war to peace, from death to life, from struggle to victory, from trial to recompense, from the valley of tears to joy without end, from the earth to the sky, from exile to your homeland.

A link of love

We believe in the communion of all the faithful of Christ, those who are pilgrims on earth, the dead who are attaining their purification, and the blessed in heaven, all together forming one Church...

THE CREDO

The Church founded by Christ is a Church of eternity; in fact, two branches of this mystical vine exist beyond time and space. There is the Church composed of the faithful on earth who struggle against evil and do good in order to earn salvation. This is the *Pilgrim Church*. The Church in purgatory is called the *Church Suffering*, because souls retained there are being purified prior to their entrance into heaven. Finally, there are the number of souls who have been made perfect and who already reign with Christ in His kingdom. They make up the *Church Triumphant*.

These three groups are not isolated from one another. They all truly form the body of Christ, and every member in the state of grace, living and dead, is united with the other members in Christ, the Head. Thus, the saints in heaven, the souls in purgatory and men on earth are united in a spiritual bond.

On this doctrine of the *Communion of Saints* is based the veneration of the blessed in heaven and our firm belief in the value of the reciprocal prayers of each group for the other.

The *Apostolic Constitution on Indulgences* refers to the Communion of Saints in these words:

There certainly exists between the faithful who have already reached their heavenly home, those who are expiating their sins in purgatory and those who are still pilgrims on earth a perennial link of charity and an abundant exchange of all the [spiritual] goods by which, with the expiation of all sins of the entire Mystical Body, divine justice is placated. *This is the very ancient dogma of the communion of saints, whereby the life of each individual son of God in Christ and through Christ is joined by a wonderful link to the life of all his other Christian brothers in the supernatural unity of the Mystical Body of Christ till, as it were, a single mystical person is formed (n. 5).*

Out of the book of life

...and He will come again, this time in glory, to judge the living and the dead: each according to his merits — those who have responded to the love and piety of God going to eternal life, those who have refused them to the end going to the fire that is not extinguished.   THE CREDO

Christ ascended into heaven, but we know from Scripture that He will come again, this time to make a general judgment on all mankind.

"The court was convened, and the books were opened" (Dan. 7:10). The justice of Christ will prevail for He will use the power given Him by His Father to judge the good and the evil. The conscience of each man will be revealed and judgment will be passed. The general judgment will be the public confirmation of the particular judgment.

"And I saw the dead, the great and the small standing before the throne, and scrolls were opened. And another scroll was opened, which is the book of life; and the dead were judged out of those things which were written in the scrolls" (Apoc. 20:12).

Even though each man is judged immediately after death, a public judgment is necessary so that the wisdom, justice and mercy of God will be recognized by all men. Public honor is due the just and public shame to those who rejected God's grace. The universal judgment will mark the triumph of Christ as King.

In the parable of the prudent servant, our Lord warns us, not only of death but of judgment, urging us to be prepared. We read in St. Luke:

The Lord said, "Who do you think is the faithful and prudent steward whom the master will set over his household to give them their ration of grain in due time? Blessed is that servant whom his master, when he comes, shall find so doing. Truly I say to you, he will set him over all his goods. But if that servant says to himself, 'My master delays his coming,' and begins to beat the menservants and the maids, and to eat and drink, and to get drunk, the master of that servant will come on a day he does not expect, and in an hour he does not know, and will cut him asunder and make him share the lot of the unfaithful. But that servant who knew his master's will, and

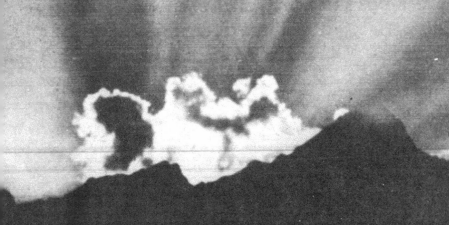

"I will walk in the
presence of the Lord,
in the land of the living."

(Ps. 114)

did not make ready for him and did not act according to his will, will be beaten with many stripes. Whereas he who did not know it, but did things deserving of stripes, will be beaten with few. But of everyone to whom much has been given, much will be required; and of him to whom they have entrusted much, they will demand the more" (12:42-48).

Star differs from star

...beyond death, which will be finally conquered on the day of the resurrection when these souls will be reunited with their bodies.

Thus it is with faith and hope that we look forward to the resurrection of the dead, and the life of the world to come.

THE CREDO

On the day of the general judgment the body of each man will be raised and joined to the soul in heaven or in hell. The "how" of the resurrection of bodies is ultimately explained by the power of God, as St. Paul so clearly teaches. Without a doubt, our bodies will share in the glory or degradation of our souls.

The fact of the resurrection of the body on the last day is clearly attested to in Scripture. We read in St. Luke:

And Jesus said to them, "The children of this world marry and are given in marriage. But those who shall be accounted worthy of that world and of the resurrection from the dead, neither marry nor take wives. For neither shall they be able to die any more, for they are equal to the angels, and are sons of God, being sons of the resurrection. But that the dead rise, even Moses showed in the passage about the bush, when he calls the Lord the God of Abraham, and the God of Isaac, and the God of Jacob. Now he is not the God of the dead, but of the living, for all live to him" (20:27-38).

St. Paul is quite explicit on the doctrine of bodily resurrection.

But someone will say, "How do the dead rise? Or with what kind of body do they come?" Senseless man, what you yourself sow is not brought to life unless it dies. And when you sow you do not sow the body that shall be, but a bare grain, perhaps of wheat or something else. But God gives it a body even as he has willed, and to each of the seeds a body of its own. All flesh is not the same flesh, but there is one flesh of men, another of beasts, another of birds, another of fishes. There are also heavenly bodies and earthly bodies, but of one kind is the glory of the heavenly, of another kind the glory of the earthly. There is one glory of the sun, and another glory of the moon, and another of the stars; for star differs from star in glory. So also with the resurrection of the dead. What is sown in corruption rises in incorruption; what is sown in dishonor rises in glory; what is sown in weakness rises in power; what is sown a natural body rises a spiritual body (1 Cor. 15:35-44).

Again he has this:

Now this I say, brethren, that flesh and blood can obtain no part in the kingdom of God, neither shall corruption have any part in incorruption. Behold, I tell you a mystery; we shall all indeed rise, but we shall not all be changed—in a moment, in the twinkling of an eye, at the last trumpet. For the trumpet shall soon sound, and the dead shall rise incorruptible and we shall be changed.

For this corruptible body must put on immortality. But when this mortal body puts on immortality, then shall come to pass the word that is written, "Death is swallowed up in victory! O death, where is your victory? O death, where is your sting?" (1 Cor. 15:50)

The condition of a glorified body is not exactly stated in revelation. Using St. Paul as a basis, theologians say that a glorified body will have four special spiritual characteristics. These will be: *impassibility:* i.e., freedom from suffering, defect, and change; *clarity or splendor:* i.e., outward beauty coming from the vision of God; *agility:* i.e., ease of motion comparable to the speed of thought; *subtileness:* i.e., power to penetrate material substances. The whole body will have its own beatitude, for all the senses will receive a reward, especially those which were of greater service in knowing, loving and serving God.

It is sad to die, to decompose, to become dust, but the absolute certainty that I will rise from the dead never to die again, is so consoling! Christ will not let our bodies remain in the humiliation of the grave, but will raise them from the dead and make them glorious, incorruptible, resplendent, impassible and beautiful as His.

The kingdom—then and now

And His kingdom will have no end.   THE CREDO

When the general judgment is over, the eternal reign of Christ, Lord of the universe, will begin. As we read in the book of Daniel:

I saw one like a son of man coming on the clouds of heaven; when he reached the Ancient One and was presented before him, he received dominion, glory and kingship; nations and peoples of every language serve him. His dominion is an everlasting dominion that shall not be taken away, his kingship shall not be destroyed (7:12-14).

In the Apocalypse, St. John (21:1-4) also refers to the eternal reign of Christ: "And I saw a new heaven and a new earth. For the first heaven and the first earth passed away, and the sea is no more. And I saw the holy city, New Jerusalem, coming down out of heaven from God, made ready as a bride adorned for her husband.... The former things have passed away." This is a very unique text and biblical exegetes are not agreed as to its precise meaning. In the opinion of some — God will, through His omnipotent power, renew this world on which we now live, so that it will take on a new form, and will contribute in an accidental way to the happiness of the blessed. The *Pastoral Constitution on the Church in the Modern World* declared:

We do not know the time for the consummation of the earth and of humanity, nor do we know how all things will be transformed. As deformed by sin, the shape of this world will pass away; but we are taught that God is preparing a new dwelling place and a new earth where justice will abide, and whose blessedness will answer and surpass all the longings for peace which spring up in the human heart (n. 39).

This concludes our study of the Credo of Pope Paul VI. Your task is now to reduce it to practice, to live it, so as to be witnesses to the truth.

On one occasion a mathematical problem of great difficulty was proposed to the scientists of Europe. No one could solve it. It was given to Isaac Newton, one of the greatest living mathematicians of the day. He solved it after an hour and a half. The problem, with the method of solution, and the answer, was forwarded to Leibnitz, also one of the greatest contemporary mathematicians, who was then living in Germany. Newton was known to Leibnitz through earlier contacts, but this time the name of the solver of the problem was not divulged. Leibnitz studied the problem, checked both method and answer, turned to the person who had brought the letter and said: "The lion is known by his claw!"

There is a great lesson for us in this anecdote. It can be put very simply and very shortly. Let us so live our faith, the faith so clearly expressed by Pope Paul in his "Credo," that when people look at us they will be able to say: "The Catholic is known by the way he practices his religion!"

Says Richard Cardinal Cushing in *Show Us by Your Lives That Christ Lives*:

"Life is a thrilling game in which the winners are always the lovers, the hard workers, the ambitious. Everything has its own particular use. The disappointments, the obstacles, the difficulties, all those things which are generally considered to be of no value in life, can be converted into genuine gems of great worth, if we are ready to act.

"World crises are crises of saints. They all have a solution: they must have. We will find that solution in Christianity and in the Gospels. Stop being pessimistic."

Pope Paul VI, on March 30, 1969, urged a large crowd of young people to put their idealism to work. These are His words:

You have a mission. You have a service to perform in this society of ours which is so exuberant in riches, in energies, in marvels, but also so bewildered with regard to the true and irreplaceable goals to pursue, so proud and so discontented with itself; so cultivated and intelligent and so corroded by doubt and so blind as to the right roads to its happiness; so highly organized and so threatened by its very organization; so filled with expectations and anxieties, and basically so disheartened, skeptical and despairing; so subtle in each of its manifestations, and at the same time so impassioned and corrupt.

You, we say, are children of our present period, highly perceptive with regard to its language, its genius, its spirit. But, you are also pure, free from its contaminations; you are adolescents, mature youths, prodigiously handsome, so determinedly simple, logical and straightforward; you are joyful and lively, free and docile; you are not intolerant, but welcome the wisdom of your families; you grew up in the faith and in prayer; in a word, you are the disciples of Christ.

Yes, yours is the mission to announce to today's world the true Messia, the authentic Christ, the irreplaceable Savior. You must show to the people of our time the luminous countenance of Jesus, luminous because of the profound mystery of His true divinity and because of the evident mystery of His incomparable humanity.

It is the countenance of the Son of God, it is the countenance of the Son of Man. He is the prototype of humanity; He is the Master, the Brother, the leader. He is the Prophet in whom all of us can continue to place our trust; and then, owing to a tragic and very sweet drama, which we cannot evade, He is the man of sorrows. He is the victim of every human iniquity. He is the Redeemer. He is Love that sacrificed itself though innocent. He is Life in its very self. He is death for our sake; and, let us say the final word, He is the One who is risen for our salvation (cf. Rom. 4:25).

But you will say to us: this message is the one intended for apostles, for ministers of the Gospel, for teachers of the Church. Yes, this is their specific office, their ministry. But today, now, this is also your message! This is the novelty of our times; this is the index of the springtime of the present age; this is the act of faith which the Church makes in the Catholic laity, which she makes especially in you young people!

Do you recall the council: "Young persons exert very substantial influence on modern society.... Their heightened influence in society demands of them a proportionately active apostolate.... Children also have their own apostolic work to do" (Decree on the Apostolate of the Laity, n. 12).

And you will still say to us: but how may we carry out a mission so delicate, so difficult, so unpopular?

Yes, you are right in noting the difficulty of the Christian witness in our society. But, hear us further. Do you young people like things that are easy or things that are difficult? Are you inclined to imitate the weak, those who are fearful, the opportunists, the cowardly, or the strong, the courageous, the heroes?

Do you want your Christian vocation today to make you timid, faint-hearted, egotistical, or full of conscious energy, of loving daring?

Was it not perhaps the lack of a certain education which mistook goodness for weakness, piety for human consideration, the Christian faith for private interest?

And furthermore: what is asked of you? Miracles? Extravagant and uproarious actions? No, you are asked to be what you are: young people and Catholics. We will say it with a German author: "Christian, be a Christian!"—but a true, authentic, dynamic Christian, full of ardor, of imagination, of love; in other words, full of that Christian youthfulness, which the Church has been giving rise to, recruiting and blessing.

Furthermore, and We thus conclude, the Christian witness, that of which We speak, is a personal act. It must spring from the free and conscious depth of one's heart. But it is at the same time a joint act. You are not alone. You are united. You are many. Moreover, you are friends, you are agreed. You together make a chorus, a legion. And the Church stands with you, by means of her organizations, her sense of community, her loving assistance.

Whenever you are tempted to think that what you do is unimportant, it will help to remember "the seventh flute."

Let Father Victor Dux convince you of your importance in God's plan in an article called "The Seventh Flute":

"The story of Walter Damrosch and 'the seventh flute' relates more to ordinary life than it does to the world of music, I believe. The renowned orchestra conductor once stopped a rehearsal and demanded, 'Where is the seventh flute? I didn't hear it during that last passage!' Note that it wasn't the first or the fourth flute the great musician called for, it was the *seventh!* For him, the seventh flute player had to play on key and play the proper notes for as many measures as were assigned to him. This was just as important to Damrosch as all the other flutes were. Its absence was noted, at least by his delicate musical ear.

"God may have given you a mission in life that is something like that seventh flute. If you fail your assignment, his delicate ear will detect what is missing. You are important to God's plan — the great Opus of the universe — no matter who or where you are! Sometimes it may be up to the seventh flute, not the first, to carry the melody or to provide the obbligato.

"The greatest forces in the universe are never spectacular. Summer showers are much more effective than hurricanes or tornadoes, but they get no headlines in the newspapers as violent storms do. The world would soon wither but for the fidelity and loyal dedication of those whose names and deeds are unhonored and unsung. It is the humble steady people who give the world security and who work the hardest for peace. These are the ones who are most difficult to replace.

"Just as 'seventh flutes' are necessary to a large orchestra, so are the unsung heroes needed for the progress and fulfillment of the world. God plans it that way; and the great harmony of His creation depends more than we know on the expert and exact rendition of the music that only 'the seventh flutes' can play!

Glamor is not greatness; praise is not fame; noise is not influence. A stone that sparkles is not necessarily a diamond; it may be just a piece of quartz. An American humorist once wrote: 'Some folks seem to get the idea they are worth a lot of money just because they have it.' Having money doesn't make a man successful. Many a wealthy man has left the world poorer for his having lived, simply because he was not a worthy steward of the money he had inherited. Being talented doesn't immediately spell fame. Certainly it is unprofitable to envy a man's genius or other endowments and be unmindful of the *way he uses them.*

Have you heard the expression 'the admirable Crichton'? One of the biographers of James Crichton called him that; and it has since come to mean 'a person who excels at almost anything.' The 'admirable' Crichton was probably the greatest prodigy the world has known. He was born in Scotland in 1560. He received a Bachelor of Arts degree in college at age thirteen, an M.A., at seventeen; and by the time he was nineteen he was going all over Europe challenging all learned men to meet him in open forum. He boasted that he could answer any question in any of ten different languages — he knew all about everything! And he was equally good as a horseman, a dancer, a cardplayer, a painter, a singer — you name it!

"Well, this 'admirable' Crichton was *admired,* but not for long. He was at the height of his fame when he became engaged to tutor a young prince. His usefulness might have begun then, though it is not certain. But in a drunken brawl the young prince killed him. Crichton died at the age of twenty-two. The point which needs stressing here is that at the time of his death he was worse off than an inanimate library when it came to put his vast knowledge to practical use. Crichton accomplished no single useful thing during his short life; and his biographers have their doubts whether a longer life would have made any difference! He invented nothing; he did not enrich the human race in the least, not by so much as one noble or elevating thought that bears his impress. His mind was like the wax on a recording phonograph — it received impressions and reproduced exactly what was recorded, and that was all!

"In the long run, it may be far better to have been a 'seventh flute' than an 'Admirable Crichton'! If handicaps, lack of talent, setbacks, may have prevented you from rising as high as you thought you might go, at least don't let them weigh you down or depress your spirits. There is a definite work for you to do, and nobody else can do the work God has cut out for you. Even for 'the seventh flute' the Divine Maestro writes and directs the music — and he wants to hear it played correctly. So there is no life however humble and unnoticed but has its place in the building of tomorrow's brave world."

378 THE FAITH WE LIVE BY

CHALLENGE

Everyone who walks with Christ understands the words: If you will go with Me, you must go against wind and tide; you must follow Me in My rags as well as in My silver slippers, yes and stand by Me when bound in irons as well as when I walk the streets with applause.

Adversity will lose its power to discourage you when your life has for its purpose the Christ who was crucified. So, too, in the good things you do you are made better by identity with Christ.

RICHARD CARDINAL CUSHING, *The Purpose of Living*

STUDY QUESTIONS

1 For Peace of Mind and Eternal Happiness

1. Does our era need a firm grasp on essential truths? Why?
2. On what basis do we turn to Christ for true and lasting solutions to our problems?
3. Why did Pope Paul VI consider it necessary to proclaim "The Credo of the People of God"? On what is this *Credo* based?

2 God

1. What truth is at the source of all other truths?
2. Explain the various types of atheism.
3. How does Divine Providence aid the sincere non-believer?
4. Summarize the five main philosophical proofs for the existence of God.
5. How are God's attributes described by Scripture, Vatican II and St. Augustine?

3 God, One and Triune

1. At what point in the history of mankind was the innermost life of God revealed?
2. What ancient Creed goes into detail concerning the Blessed Trinity?
3. Explain the analogy which helps to make the mystery of the Trinity a little more understandable to us.
4. In what sense is Jesus Christ the Son of the Eternal Father? In what sense are we also sons of the Father?
5. Why is God the Son called the Word?
6. Why is the Holy Spirit a distinct Personality?
7. Explain what is meant by the "Divine Missions."
8. What can be the effects of God's life in us?

4 "Who Can Probe His Deeds?"

1. Why does God wish to share His bliss with us?
2. How did the angels cooperate in the plan of salvation?
3. What facts convince us of the existence of devils?
4. What does the cosmos tell us about God?
5. What are the two theories about the creation of plants and animals? How does the Church view these theories?

379

6. What truths does Sacred Scripture give us on the creation of man?

7. Could the theory of evolution ever include the *soul?*

8. Summarize the proofs for the spirituality and immortality of the soul of man.

9. On what basis are all men declared to be equal?

10. Why should the salvation of our soul be a major preoccupation?

11. What is the range of God's care for us?

12. Is the presence of evil in the world a reason for denying the loving Providence of God? Explain.

13. Give two examples of confidence in Divine Providence.

5   The Father's Promise

1. What is meant by a preternatural gift?

2. Which gift placed our first parents in a supernatural state?

3. What were the consequences of their act of disobedience? Why was posterity affected?

4. Because of original sin, did human nature become corrupt or only weak? Explain in detail.

5. What advantage would the Father's generous promise of a Savior bring to mankind?

6. What is the central message of the Scriptures? How did the prophets of the Old Testament convey this message?

7. Why do the Gospels have a special pre-eminence?

8. Define *inspiration.* What are its consequences?

9. Explain the interrelation of Sacred Scripture, Sacred Tradition and the teaching authority of the Church.

10. How does knowledge of *literary forms* aid our understanding of what the sacred authors set forth?

11. Why does it belong to the Church to pass the final judgment on the interpretation of Scripture?

12. Name the books of the Old and New Testaments.

6   "Who Shall Declare His Generation?"

1. What forms the core of the historical books called the Gospels?

2. Describe two occasions when Christ *claimed* equality with God the Father. Name one occasion when He *accepted* recognition of His divinity from others.

3. Why can we rely on Christ's testimony of Himself that He is God?

4. What are some of the *miracles* that witness to Christ's divinity? Some of the *prophecies?*

5. Describe one occasion on which Christ claimed, made use of and confirmed with a miracle the divine attribute of forgiving sins.

6. How did God the Father testify to his Son's divinity?

7. Why is Christ our Way?

8. Explain the consequences of the fact of two natures in Jesus Christ.

9. Describe the character of Christ.

10. On what points should we dare to be different?

7   The Encounter with Christ

1. Why is Christ pre-eminently a Teacher?

2. How did Christ explain His law of love? Cite specific examples.

3. Define true love. Why does it possess the quality of heroism?

4. How can Christ's disciples be recognized?

5. How can perfect love of God and neighbor be put into practice?

6. What is the double aspect of personal poverty whereby everyone may imitate the poor Christ? What examples and teachings did He give us on this point?

7. Why is meekness a sign of strength of character?

8. Could suffering ever be *useless?* Why?

9. What does "thirst after justice" signify?

10. How can we imitate the mercy of the Divine Master?

11. What is promised to the pure of heart?

12. How did Christ perfect the Old Law on the point of purity?

13. What practical application can be derived from the biblical warning: "He who loves the danger shall perish in it"?

14. What are our natural and supernatural weapons in our battle against sin? How did the saints react to temptation?

15. How can we lessen occasions of sin by responsible use of TV?

16. Who are the persecuted on whom God's blessing falls?

17. What justifies constant Christian optimism?

18. Why would a daily "probing of the heart" enable us to "carry less" to our judgment?

19. What qualities should we possess in order to witness to our encounter with Christ?

8   His Life for the World

1. What light does medical knowledge shed on the reality and the horror of Christ's agony in the garden?

2. What tortures before Christ's crucifixion were enough to have caused His death?

3. Describe the crucifixion in detail. Refer to Scripture and medical science, proving that Christ *really* died.

4. Whom did Christ visit in Limbo?

5. How did Christ's death affect our outlook on death?

6. Why is man unable to offer fitting reparation for sin? Explain.

7. What did Jesus Christ, the God-Man, merit for mankind? How?

8. How can we realize our responsibility for Christ's sufferings and death? Why does this discovery lead us to gratitude rather than to despair?

9. What concrete advice does St. Paul give us that we may reap the fruits of the Redemption?

10. What is an indulgence?

11. How can we imitate the suffering Christ and sanctify our trials and struggle against evil?

12. What does Christ expect from his faithful followers?

13. How can one put a stop to habitual sin?

9   "I Live and You Shall Live"

1. Why does our faith rest on the resurrection of Christ?

2. Name three occasions when Christ predicted His resurrection.

3. What vital information is given us about Christ's resurrection by the evangelists?

4. Describe one of the apparitions of our risen Lord in detail.

5. Refute some modern objections to the resurrection.

6. What are the effects of Christ's resurrection on our personal lives?

7. What personal message does Christ's ascension into heaven contain for us?

10   Mary—Mother, Teacher and Queen

1. Narrate the biblical account of the Virgin Mary's acceptance of divine maternity.

2. What are some of the unique qualities of Mary's virginity?

3. Explain why Mary was irreconcilably opposed to sin.

4. Why was it fitting that Mary should be raised body and soul to heavenly glory at the end of her earthly life?

5. How does Mary show herself the best of mothers to us? What biblical story illustrates her powerful mediation with her Son?

6. How can we best renew our devotion to Mary, Mother of the Church, in our era?

7. What place does the rosary hold among Christian practices of piety?

8. What practical lessons do the mysteries of the rosary impart to us?

11   This Beloved Church of God

1. How does the heavenly Father continue His quest for men's hearts today?

2. How was the Church foreshadowed in the Old Testament?

3. What image of the Church explains the intimate relationship of members with their Head?

4. In how many ways can we *live* our membership in the Mystical Body of Christ? Give concrete examples.

5. Why did Christ provide a well-ordered structure for His Church?

6. What is the significance of the name which Jesus gave Simon Bar-Jona?

7. What prominent role did Christ give Peter? Show that this role was recognized by the early Christians.

8. Who is Peter's successor today?

9. Why does the Church enter into dialogue with the world?

10. What is the reason for a variety of rites in the Church?

11. What powers did Christ give bishops through the apostles?

12. Explain fully how Christ protects His Church from error.

13. How should we respond to pronouncements of the ordinary magisterium?

14. Why is the Church *catholic?* Why do the missions belong to each of us?

15. Why is the Church *holy?* Is everyone called to sanctity?

16. What does a precise awareness of sin entail?

17. Why is there need for penance?

12   The Issues Today

1. What were some of our Lord's teachings on poverty?

2. Is relief to the poor a matter of charity or of justice? Explain.

3. How does our relationship with our brothers reflect our union with God? And vice versa?

4. How could a technological concept of life complicate our approach to God? On the other hand, how can technology and culture lead to God?

5. What are the reasons for Christian optimism?

6. What is the real cause of war? The true basis of peace?

7. What does the Church offer the world?

13   Prelude to Eternal Friendship

1. What is an encounter? How can we encounter Christ?

2. Which meaning does the word *sacrament* have for us today?

3. Explain the purpose of the sacraments.

4. In addition to the sacraments, how else can we obtain God's gift of grace?

5. What prayer sums up all prayers? Why?

6. What is grace? What are its effects?

14   The New Man

1. Why can we make our baptism a happening here and now?
2. What are the differences between Baptism of water and the baptisms of blood and desire?
3. Why are children baptized?
4. What are the effects of Confirmation?
5. Does Anointing of the Sick prepare us for death or life? Explain your answer.

15   He Loved Me
and Gave Himself for Me

1. What way did Christ find to communicate Himself to us always?
2. Why do we call His Eucharistic presence "real"? Explain in detail.
3. Through the daily Paschal Mystery, how can we offer all honor and glory to God?
4. Are we able gradually to attain a Christlike mentality through the Liturgy of the Word?
5. During the Liturgy of the Eucharist, how can we strengthen the bonds of love with our Lord and with one another?
6. What effect should the Eucharist have on our lives?
7. How can we live our Mass?
8. How can we take advantage of Christ's closeness to us in the Eucharist?

16   Conversion and Progress

1. Why is Penance called "a laborious kind of Baptism"?
2. How can we know our sins?
3. What connection exists between "a change of heart" and true sorrow for sin?
4. Give examples of penance in the Old and New Testaments.
5. Does community penance change the essential structure of the sacrament of Penance?
6. What are the fundamental means of complying with the Lord's precepts of penitence?
7. What main points about penance does the *Constitution on Fast and Abstinence* prescribe?
8. How is Christ's attitude toward sinners brought out in the Gospels?

17   "Set Apart for Me"

1. What is the essential difference between priest and people?
2. In what does priestly dignity consist?

3. How do priests imitate Christ in their observance of celibacy?

4. Can loneliness and other problems lead to human and Christian maturity? How?

5. How is a priest a sign of fidelity for all the People of God?

6. What aids does a priest have in his spiritual life?

7. Why are priestly and religious vocations the hope of the Church?

8. Whom does Christ call to labor in His vineyard?

9. Why does Christ "need" priests?

10. How are seminarians formed for their priestly role?

11. What are the duties of a deacon?

12. What is religious life?

13. What aids does religious life offer its members that they may strive towards the perfection of charity?

14. How do secular institutes differ from religious communities?

18   Married Life

1. What is marriage on the human level? on the supernatural level?

2. Why are prudence, prayer and purity necessary to prepare for a happy marriage?

3. What are the characteristics of marital love?

4. How does the sacramental grace of Matrimony aid the married couple?

5. What mission is proper to parents?

6. The task of transmitting human life has a bearing on the eternal destiny of men. Why?

7. Cite biblical quotes referring to both the unity and indissolubility of marriage.

8. Why is divorce opposed to the well-being of the family and the State?

19   At Home with the Lord

1. What does "transformation" have to do with death?

2. What truths are worth meditating upon if we wish to avoid hell?

3. Why does purgatory exist? How can we help the suffering souls? How can we avoid purgatory ourselves?

4. What is meant by the beatific vision?

5. What kind of life awaits us in heaven?

6. Why is the Church founded by Christ a Church of eternity?

7. Why is a public judgment of all men necessary?

8. What will be the qualities of the glorified body?

9. What is youth's mission today?

10. What is the lesson of the "seventh flute"?

INDEX

Q

R

Daughters of St. Paul

IN MASSACHUSETTS
    50 St. Paul's Avenue, Boston, Mass. 02130
    172 Tremont Street, Boston, Mass. 02111
IN NEW YORK
    78 Fort Place, Staten Island, N.Y. 10301
    625 East 187th Street, Bronx, N.Y. 10458
    525 Main Street, Buffalo, N.Y. 14203
IN CONNECTICUT
    202 Fairfield Avenue, Bridgeport, Conn. 06603
IN OHIO
    2105 Ontario St. (at Prospect Ave.), Cleveland, Ohio 44115
    25 E. Eighth Street, Cincinnati, Ohio, 45202
IN PENNSYLVANIA
    1719 Chestnut St., Philadelphia, Pa. 19103
IN FLORIDA
    2700 Biscayne Blvd., Miami, Florida 33137
IN LOUISIANA
    4403 Veterans Memorial Blvd.,
        Metairie, La. 70002
    86 Bolton Avenue, Alexandria, La. 71301
IN MISSOURI
    1001 Pine St. (at North 10th), St. Louis, Mo. 63101
IN TEXAS
    114 East Main Plaza, San Antonio, Texas 78205
IN CALIFORNIA
    1570 Fifth Avenue, San Diego, Calif. 92101
    278 17th Street, Oakland, Calif. 94612
    46 Geary Street, San Francisco, Calif. 94108
IN HAWAII
    1184 Bishop St., Honolulu, Hi. 96813
IN CANADA
    3022 Dufferin Street, Toronto 395, Ontario, Canada
IN ENGLAND
    57, Kensington Church Street, London W. 8, England
IN AUSTRALIA
    58, Abbotsford Rd., Homebush, N.S.W., Sydney 2140,
    Australia